D0581965

MAO

THE PEOPLE'S EMPEROR

MAO

THE PEOPLE'S EMPEROR

DICK WILSON

HUTCHINSON

TO FRANÇOIS DUCHÊNE

Hutchinson & Co. (Publishers) Ltd
3 Fitzroy Square, London W1P 6JD

London Melbourne Sydney Auckland
Wellington Johannesburg and agencies
throughout the world

First published 1979

Set in VIP Baskerville by Input Typesetting Ltd

Printed in Great Britain by The Anchor Press Ltd
and bound by Wm Brendon & Son Ltd,
both of Tiptree, Essex

ISBN 0 09 134610 X

CONTENTS

LIST OF
ILLUSTRATIONS

THE MAO FAMILY TREE

A reconstruction according to the best or most persuasive evidence.

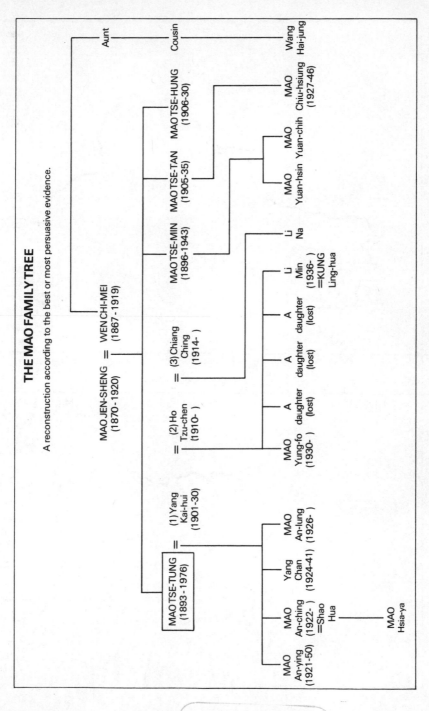

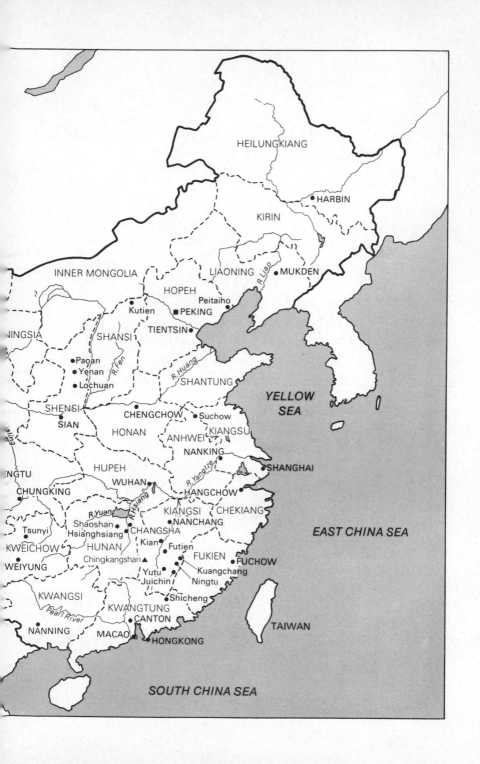

INTRODUCTION

Mao Tse-tung was the last of the great dominating figures of our century. His story is the classic one of the peasant boy who climbed by grim determination, helped by uncanny good luck, to become the ruler of a great nation. There are not many in history of whom it can be said, as was true of Mao, that he governed a quarter of mankind for a quarter of a century.

He invented for China a completely new system of life, economy and government. In the course of devising it he left behind a body of theoretical and expository writing – as well as a small collection of excellent poetry, often composed in the saddle – much of which is quoted or summarized in this book. His self-appointed task was the impossible one of dragging a decayed, corrupt and inefficient imperial order, which had moulded the Chinese people for many centuries, into modernity. By 1920, as a primary school headmaster in a minor provincial city, he became convinced that Communism was the only possible instrument for China to cut cleanly through to social justice and economic advance.

He thus played the role of China's Kemal Ataturk as well as her Lenin – and even, in strict truth, of her Stalin. Whereas Lenin enjoyed only a few short years of creative power after 1917, Mao followed thirty years of struggle to establish a Communist state with almost thirty years of power to build socialism in China. The challenge came less from the anti-Communists than from opponents and rivals within the Communist Party itself. Much of Mao's energy was expended in unnecessary battles with comrades whose basic ideals he shared.

Perhaps this sprang from a certain insecurity in his personality, and several explanations have been offered which derive from his experiences in infancy and childhood. He displayed his independence from a very early age by rebelling against his father in a society where this was considered shocking. As the eldest son in a family of four children his early life was not an easy one, and the independence which he asserted, and which enabled him to pursue single-mindedly a seventy-year quest for personal enlightenment and political power, owes much to those early experiences.

But the price had to be paid in his private life, where not only was he unable to offer his three successive wives any real physical security, but he seemed to avoid emotional commitment as well. To his numerous children he did not offer the normal protectiveness and sustained concern of a traditional father.

It might even be said that he destroyed his own family, in the sense that they had to take second place to his own dangerous career. His two brothers and sister, his cousin and first wife – not to mention numerous close school friends – were killed, often in cruel circumstances, during the civil war between the Communists and their opponents. His eldest son fell in the Korean war. His second wife and second son had mental sickness, while his third wife, two daughters and nephew were disgraced immediately after his own death because of their political activities supposedly on his behalf.

The wonder of it is that Mao himself survived for so long. Luck favoured his life and career. He was saved by inches in 1927 from capture and execution, and a soldier standing next to him was killed in one of the battles of the civil war. Fortunate accident helped him at many stages of the epic Long March in 1935, when he led his army for 6000 miles over snow-capped peaks and vicious swamps, crossing raging torrents and hostile tribal territories to the sanctuary of Yenan.

We will not know for several years what the Chinese themselves really think of Mao. On the one hand he was the standard bearer of equality and social justice, author of the Great Leap Forward and the Cultural Revolution, champion of the underdog in Chinese society. On the other hand, he was also the innovator who could not leave society alone, insisting on a constant and violent turbulence which was exhausting and frightening to many people – especially the artisanate and middle class. Mao himself admitted to the deaths of hundreds of thousands in the course of his introduction of Communism after 1949, though hostile foreign estimates go as high as 50 million. As the father figure of the nation he will not be subjected to detached judgement for some time to come.

Lin Piao, his lifetime disciple who turned against him in the last weeks of his own life, hailed Mao to his face as the 'greatest genius in the world'. But Lin's son, speaking in private for his parents and their intimate circle, called Mao 'the biggest feudal despot in Chinese history'.

Outside China, Mao's reputation is equally ambivalent. For many overseas Chinese he is a hero who stood up for China against foreign pressures, especially from the West and from Russia.

Mao was a Communist who defied Stalin, and Stalin's successors, in order to carry Marxism-Leninism forward to a new modernity and relevance. He was also the first leader beyond the frontier of the white west to face that west with unshakeable confidence and without a sense of inferiority, ready to preach back to their authors corrected and adjusted versions of European theory, suitably mixed with a little native Taoism and Chinese common sense.

Stalin ridiculed Mao as a 'margarine Marxist', and Khrushchev dismissed him as 'a petty-bourgeois'. But Mao did appeal to some European Communists. An East German philosopher declared in the 1950s that 'Khrushchev is just an economic pragmatist, but Mao is a thinker', while another declared: 'We need ideals, and the only place you can get them today is from Mao, ... not from Khrushchev.'

The Chinese context made it difficult for some foreign Communists to appreciate him. Castro denounced him as 'a ridiculous mortal' whom his Party turned into 'a god', while the Chilean poet Pablo Neruda complained: 'Mao Tse-tung has become a living Buddha, separated from the people by a priestly court that interprets in its own manner Marxism and the story of our times.'

But in the less westernized parts of the Third World, in Asia and Africa, Mao was more generally hailed as a heroic figure. When Mao was in the middle of the Cultural Revolution, his last shattering effort to remake the Chinese personality, President Sukarno of Indonesia commented: 'If Mao fails, it will be the end of the era of great revolutions.'

President Bhutto of Pakistan said on Mao's death that 'Men like Mao Tse-tung come once in a century, perhaps once in a millennium. They capture the stage and write the pages of history with divine inspiration.' Mao was 'an Olympian' who had 'made history shrink', and the 'supreme architect of a brilliant new order which had shaken the world'. Even that conservative Englishman, Lord Montgomery, adjudged Mao 'a very great man, a most uncommon man in an age of common men'.

To the end, however, Mao retained his peasant habits. He was frugal to the point of parsimony, wearing patched clothes, sleeping on a wooden board bed without springs or mattress, living in simple quarters and eating simple food.

Mao's tragedy was that he could not in the end bring about in China all the reforms which he wanted: he underestimated the resistance to them. This book presents the story of how he came to form those ideals, how he fought for them – against enemy and friend – and how in the end he failed.

PART ONE
PREPARATION

1
CHILD OF THE SNAKE

Mao Tse-tung was born on 26 December 1893 in the village of Shaoshan in central China, in the nineteenth year of the reign of the Emperor Kuang Hsu. It was also the Year of the Snake in the traditional calendar, so that if his parents had consulted a fortune-teller they would have learned that their first-born would show the qualities of that beast – 'flexibility, cunning and capacity for survival', as a contemporary practitioner described them; 'venomous, striking reaction when protecting its young; dexterity in avoiding and foiling enemies; fondness of the night-time.'

His family were peasants. Mao's father, Mao Jen-sheng (1870-1920), was a man of unusual drive and strong character. By contrast, Mao's grandfather, who survived as a member of the household during Mao's early years, was a weak personality under whose leadership the family had been obliged to sell off some of its land in order to keep going. Mao's father was the one who left home at sixteen in order to earn a wage which could be saved and remitted home. In Mao's later recollection. 'My father was a poor peasant and while still young was obliged to join the army because of heavy debts. He was a soldier for many years. Later on he returned to the village where I was born, and by saving carefully and gathering together a little money through small trading and other enterprises he managed to buy back his land.'

On another occasion Mao recalled that. 'My father used to feel that if a man did not look after himself, he would be damned by heaven and earth. My mother disagreed with him. When my father died, very few people came to his funeral, though many came to my mother's funeral.' When Mao was seventy-five he told some Red Guards quite bluntly: 'My father was bad. If he were alive today, he should be given a "jet-plane ride"' (the painful punishment imposed by the Red Guards during the Cultural Revolution, in which a man had to stoop down with his

head low and his arms held out high behind him). But the man was not entirely ignorant. 'My father had two years of schooling', Mao recalled, 'and he could read enough to keep books.' Mao inherited his tough determination.

Mao's mother, Wen Chi-mei (1867-1919), from the nearby village of Tangchiato, was cast in a quite different mould. She was pretty and plump, with the 'pear-shaped' face so admired in Chinese women. Mao took after her physically more than his father. 'My mother was wholly illiterate', Mao recollected afterwards. But she was respected in the village, in the words of one of Mao's Chinese biographers, 'for her kindness, her modest and friendly demeanour, her fairness, and the pleasure she took in helping others out of their difficulties'. She was a devout Buddhist as well as a strong believer in all the local superstitions.

The tile-roofed family house was divided down the middle and shared with another family, the Chou family. In front of it there was a pond where Mao, it was said, first learnt to swim, and his family also owned a cowshed, a pigsty, a rice barn and a small mill. The village of Shaoshan, loosely strung out along a valley, embraced about three hundred other families, but many of these were also Maos, theirs being the largest clan in the district. The full name of the village, Shaoshanchung, means 'Splendid Peace Silt', and there was a folk song of the area which ran:

> Layer on layer of silt in the Shaoshanchung
> Nine families out of ten are poor,
> Three dangling knives hang above the heads of peasants:
> Heavy debt, heavy rent and heavy interest.
> Three roads are there for the peasants:
> Flight from famine, beggary or prison.

The village lies under mountains verdant with trees, especially bamboo, about thirty miles from the market town of Hsiangtan. But Mao never went to a town until he was a teenager. Shaoshan provided him with an infancy which was quiet, poor and notable only for the localized dramas of his own family and neighbours.

Hunan province, with its 30 million population, used to be regarded in Chinese history as backward and isolated from the main national currents. But in Mao's time it was not only becoming more important and better connected through trade and communications, but was already providing intellectual leadership to China. It had become a natural centre for reform. In the preceding two centuries its scholars, especially Wang Fu-chih, had won fame for their pragmatic re-interpretation of

Confucian teachings, stressing the evolution of human society and political institutions according to the needs of new generations, and the necessity for scientific inquiry into phenomena from which laws could be deduced. Partly under their influence, nineteenth-century Hunan became a pioneer province in introducing modern education and industry and in taking some initiatives towards the liberation of women. This was the intellectual atmosphere of the region into which Mao was born. He himself used to quote the common saying that, 'if China is likened to Germany, then Hunan is its Prussia.'

A quarter of a century later Mao gave this pen-portrait of his native province straddling the Hsiang River:

The masses who live by and around this river are very naive and unsophisticated, knowing very little of the events of the world. They do not possess an organized society; they are dispersed and scattered, each seeing to his own affairs. They know only themselves, and in the very narrowest meaning; they are concerned only with the shortest periods of time. The great majority have never so much as dreamed of a life in common with others or of profound and far-reaching concepts. In their politics there is nothing of conciliation and thorough solutions; they know only private quarrels. . . .

There are some people of talent, who have studied the arts and sciences in the various countries of the world and in various places in China. But these people are never offered the opportunity to exercise their talents; they are blocked with hardly any effort at all, like closing the locks at Tungting Lake.

Mao was born into a country of immense potential.

'Our China [he later lectured his fellow Communists] is one of the largest countries in the world, covering an area larger than the whole of Europe. In this vast territory there are large stretches of fertile land that provide us with food and clothing; there are mountain ranges, plateaux, and plains traversing the length and breadth of the country that provide us with extensive forests and rich mineral deposits; there are many rivers and lakes that provide us with facilities for water transport and irrigation; and there is a long coastline that facilitates communication with other nations beyond the seas. Since ancient times, our Chinese people have laboured, lived and multiplied on this immense territory . . . .

But by Mao's own time, China had come to be stigmatized as 'the sick man of East Asia', a country with a backward economy and a backward culture – 'with no hygiene,' as Mao put it, tongue in cheek, 'poor at ball games and swimming, where the women had bound feet and the men wore pigtails and eunuchs could still be found, and where the moon was inferior and did not shine as brightly as in foreign lands.'

During the decades before and even after Mao's birth, stronger powers outside had humiliated his country.

One of his lectures explained:

After having inflicted military defeats on China, the imperialist countries forcibly took from her a large number of states tributary to China, as well as a part of her own territory. Japan appropriated Korea, Taiwan, the Ryukyu Islands, the Pescadores and Port Arthur; England took Burma, Bhutan, Nepal and Hong Kong; France seized Annam; even a miserable little country like Portugal took Macao from us.

Worst of all, the Chinese found it difficult to organize themselves properly for the various challenges that confronted them. Just after the First World War Mao complained:

Hitherto, our countrymen have only known how each man could manage his own private interests in such a way as to maximize his personal profit, while minimizing social benefit. People in business did not know how to set up a company; people in manual work did not know how to establish a labour union; those engaged in scholarship knew only the old method of working alone in one's study, and not joint research. Large-scale organized enterprise has been quite simply beyond our countrymen. As regards the mismanagement of our political affairs, there's no need to waste words on that.

If there's been any success at all in the postal service and salt administration, it has been thanks to the foreigners. The prohibitions on navigation have been lifted for a long time, and yet we still don't even have one little ship sailing to Europe. The big Chinese shipping companies lose money every year and then invite foreign investment. On all the railways which are foreign-managed, the standard of cleanliness, equipment and service is always better: as soon as a railway comes under the management of our Ministry of Transport, it goes to pot. There is not a single passenger who rides on the Peking-Wuhan, Tientsin-Nanking or Wuhan-Changsha railway who does not snort or gnash his teeth! Moreover, such things as schools are run badly, self-government is run badly, even single families or individual lives are run badly. And everything is like this, all monotonously the same.

Such was the rottenness of Mao's homeland, a rottenness which he was later to dedicate himself to cleansing.

Mao's first three years in Shaoshan village though hardly luxurious, were idyllic in the sense that he had the exclusive attention of a very devoted and affectionate mother. When he was three, however, he was joined by a younger brother, Mao Tsemin (1896-1943). Now began Mao's painful induction into the world of competitors and rivals. He once spoke overtly of this, when he told his colleagues in 1958: 'Worry attends men from their birth. Students are worried about exams and children about their parents' partiality for their brothers or sisters.' The three-year-old Mao would doubtless have been offered 'promotion' in the Chinese family system, in the form of a newly acquired responsibility for minor duties in the house, as compensation for the sudden exclusion from his mother's undivided love and attention. But he was probably too young to appreciate the compensation, and thus the more deeply hurt by the loss.

Meanwhile the family enterprise was paying off. Mao's father was gradually moving up the ladder to become a rich peasant.

As middle peasants then, [Mao later recollected] my family owned 2½ acres of land. On this they could raise 3½ tons of rice a year. The five members of the family consumed 2 tons – about 2½ pounds per day per head, on average – which left an annual surplus of 1½ tons. Using this surplus, my father accumulated a little capital and in time purchased another acre, which gave the family the status of 'rich' peasants. We could then raise 5 tons of rice a year. . . .

Eventually Mao's father became a grain and hog dealer.

At the time my father was a middle peasant he began to deal in grain transport and selling, by which he made a little money. After he became a 'rich' peasant he devoted most of his time to that business. He hired a full-time farm labourer, and put his children to work on the farm as well as his wife. . . . My father had no shop for business, he simply purchased from the poor farmers and then transported it to the city merchants, where he got a higher price. In the winter, when rice was being ground, he hired an extra labourer to do work on the farm, so that at that time there were seven mouths to feed. . . .'

Mao was six years old and the Boxers (unknown to Shaoshan, which lacked newspapers) were besieging legations in Peking, when his father first put him to work on the farm tending cattle and doing odd jobs. Two years later, when he was eight, he started attending the Shaoshan Primary School, where he stayed until he was thirteen. But he was not let off his duties at home. 'In the early morning and at night I worked on the farm. During the day I read the Confucian *Analects* and the Four Classics.'

As soon as Mao had learnt a few characters, his father wanted him to take over the family accounts. 'He was a severe taskmaster' Mao later recollected. 'He hated to see me idle, and if there were not books to be kept he put me to work at farm tasks.'

Mao's mother gave her children religious instruction, 'and we

were all saddened', Mao explained, 'that our father was an unbe-
liever.' When he was only eight, Mao 'seriously discussed with
my mother the problem of my father's lack of piety. We made
many attempts then and later on to convert him, but without
success. He only cursed us. . . . He would have nothing to do
with the gods.' Mao, of course, became progressively more sceptical about religion, so that, 'My mother became concerned
about me, and scolded me for my indifference to the requirements of faith . . .'

Mao took a packed lunch to school, but his mother was surprised to find after a while that he also ate very heavily when he
came back in the evenings.

'Why do you eat so much in the evening?' she asked him. 'Is
the lunch not enough?'

'In our class,' Mao explained, 'there is a new classmate whose
family is poor. Because he does not bring his lunch, I share mine
with him.'

'Why didn't you tell me earlier?' his mother commented, and
thereafter gave him enough lunch for two.

The Chinese classics did not arouse Mao's enthusiasm,
though he proved good at memorizing them. His Chinese
teacher 'belonged to the stern-treatment school. He was harsh
and severe, frequently beating his students. Because of this I ran
away from school when I was ten.'

Afraid to go home to meet his father's wrath, he wandered for
three days before being found by his family. To his surprise he
was received warmly. 'My father was slightly more considerate
and the teacher was more inclined to moderation. The result of
my act of protest impressed me very much. It was a successful
"strike".'

In 1905, when he was twelve, Mao acquired a second brother
called Mao Tse-tan (1905-1935), who was much indulged by his
father. A few months later Mao's parents adopted a girl, who
had originally been his cousin, with the name Tse-chien or Tse-
hung (1906-1930). At about this time the old grandfather died,
and Mao's position in the household thus became one of some
importance. The next year, when he was thirteen, he left the
primary school in order to work full-time for his father on the
accounts and on the land. He planted vegetables, weeded fields,
fed cattle and raised pigs. In the 1950s there was still hanging on
a wall of his house (now maintained as a museum) a metal brush
which he was said to have used for cleaning cows.

But Mao's father continued to be ungrateful for his son's help.

'He was a hot-tempered man,' Mao recalled, 'and frequently beat both me and my brothers. He gave us no money whatever, and the most meagre food. On the fifteenth of every month he made a concession to his labourers and gave them eggs with their rice but never meat. To me he gave neither eggs nor meat.'

By contrast, his mother was a 'kind woman, generous and sympathetic, and ever ready to spare what she had. She pitied the poor and often gave them rice when they came to ask for it during famines. But she could not do so when my father was present. He disapproved of charity. We had many quarrels in my home over this question.'

Indeed, Mao later analysed the situation in his family in political terms. There were two 'parties', he would say. One was his father, the Ruling Power. Mao, his mother, his brother and 'sometimes even the labourers' made up the Opposition. But within the 'United Front' of the Opposition there were differences. Mao's mother in particular did not like direct attack or open shows of emotion, preferring more tactful and subtle pressure.

But even she resisted her son's radicalism. Mao afterwards recollected how some secret society members once burgled their home: 'I thought it was a good thing because they stole articles which they did not have, but my mother could not accept my view.' Presumably they did not take any of Mao's precious books, otherwise he might not have been so charitable.

Mao afterwards explained that he had not learned at his primary school any useful things, such as geography or history or science. What he most enjoyed reading were old novels – especially 'romances of old China and stories of rebellions', such as the fourteenth-century *Water Margin* and *Romance of the Three Kingdoms*. His teacher disliked these 'outlawed' and 'wicked' books, but Mao used to read them in school, 'covering them up with a classic when a teacher walked past. . . . I believe that perhaps I was much influenced by such books, read at an impressionable age.' Mao used to cover his window with a blanket at night so that his father would not see the light of his lamp as he read into the small hours.

A book which had a great effect on him at this time was *Words of Warning to an Affluent Age,* in which a Chinese businessman trained in Japan made a strong plea for greater freedom for private enterprise, in order to promote the modernization of the country by the introduction of Western technology. Indeed, this made such an impression on Mao that he ran away to study with a law student in the area in order to acquire more education. A little later, he studied classics in the village with an old scholar called Mao Lu-chung, a clansman who had won the lowest degree officially conferred on successful exam candidates.

Mao's father was now not only reconciled to the classics, but even eager for Mao to master them, having lost a law suit because his adversary in the court was able to produce an apt classical quotation. Meanwhile the old man continued to grow wealthy, by the standards of the village, no longer buying more land but instead buying mortgages on other people's land, so that his capital grew to $300.*

Mao had two severe clashes with his father when he was about thirteen. One happened at a party where his father invited guests, and then quarrelled with Mao in front of them. 'My father denounced me before the whole group, calling me lazy and useless. This infuriated me. I cursed him and left the house. My mother ran after me and tried to persuade me to return.'

Mao's father also pursued him, cursing and calling him to come back. 'I reached the edge of a pond,' Mao's own recollection went on, 'and threatened to jump in if he came any nearer.' This was enough to make his father pause, and so they agreed on a compromise. 'My father insisted that I apologize and kow-tow as a sign of submission. I agreed to give a one-knee kow-tow if he would promise not to beat me.' According to his best schoolfriend's account, however, Mao kow-towed twice to his father to acknowledge his guilt, once in front of the assembled guests, and then again after they had gone, when his mother brought him once more to his father and told him to kneel down. But Mao would only bend one knee, and so his mother had to press hard on his shoulders with her hands and tell him to kneel on both knees.

'Thus the war ended,' Mao later commented, 'and from it I learned that when I defended my rights by open rebellion my father relented, but when I remained weak and submissive he only cursed and beat me the more ... I learned to hate him ...' This was a remarkable statement for a Chinese to make about his own father, and it was deleted from the Chinese-language editions of the brief autobiography which Mao retailed to Edgar Snow in 1936.

The other incident that year was more personal. Following the

*In those days a Chinese silver dollar or *yuan* was equivalent to an American dollar.

Chinese tradition, Mao's parents 'married' him when he was thirteen to a girl of nineteen, a Miss Yang Tsui-hua. The 'marriage' was arranged, probably with the help of a match-maker, to contribute to the Mao farm economy. Mao's father would be able to use the girl as a worker on the farm without pay, and her presence in the house would ensure that the next generation, with all its potential labour power, would appear on the scene at the earliest opportunity.

But Mao, spurning social tradition, rejected the arrangement. Speaking later about his early life, he referred to this episode in a couple of terse, cold sentences: 'My parents had married me when I was fourteen to a girl of twenty' (he was using the Chinese way of counting years, starting from one at birth instead of nought), 'but I had never lived with her – and never subsequently did. I did not consider her my wife and ... gave little thought to her.' It was said that the girl thus rejected eventually married someone else.

By the time Mao was thirteen years old he had grown as tall and as big as his father, able to bear on a pole over his shoulders two of the heavy baskets of stinking manure which had to be carried out to the fields several times a day. Mao formed the habit of taking a book with him to the fields, and whenever he could he went to sit under a tree behind an old tomb to read about the adventures of the great heroes and bandits of antiquity. But his father complained about his absences and eventually caught him red-handed, book in hand and empty baskets on the ground before him.

'So you have decided to stop work, have you?' he demanded.

'No, father,' Mao replied, 'I'm only having a little rest.'

'But you have not carried any manure at all this whole morning!'

'Oh yes, I have,' Mao protested, 'I have carried several baskets since dawn.'

'How many?' his father asked

'Five or six at least since dawn,' Mao estimated.

'Only five or six in half a day? And do you think that is enough to earn your living?'

'Well,' the boy replied, 'and how many do you think you could carry in half a day?'

'Twenty!' the father replied. 'Or at least fifteen.'

'But from the house to the field is a very long way.'

'I suppose you think I should build the house right to the edge of the field to make your work lighter! Didn't I have to do just the same when I was a boy your age? It seems you no longer care what happens to your family. How do you think we are going to live? There you sit quite calmly as if you had not a care in the world! Have you no sense of gratitude? What good can it possibly do to waste your time reading those stupid books? You are not a child any more and if you want to eat, you must work!'

'Oh hush,' Mao replied, 'that's enough. You are always complaining.'

This was in the morning, and they both went home for their lunch. But at about five in the afternoon Mao again disappeared. His father now knew where to find him. He strode directly to the old tomb and there saw his son just as he had been in the morning, book in hand with the empty baskets before him. The quarrel began again.

'Has your mind been so completely turned by those bad books that you no longer pay any attention to what your father says to you?'

'No, father,' Mao replied, 'I do listen to you. I do everything you tell me to do.'

'You know very well what I want,' his father went on. 'I want you to give your mind to the farm and to work regularly in the fields, and to read no more of these bad books.'

'I will work regularly on the farm,' Mao promised, 'but I want to read my books as well. I promise you I will work first in the fields and then I will read afterwards. When I have finished my work in the fields, I am free, am I not? Then you can't complain and scold. If I do my share of the work in the fields, you have no right to stop me from reading my books when my tasks are finished.'

'But,' the father objected, 'my son, you carry just a few baskets and then you come and hide here to read.'

'Before I came here to read,' Mao insisted, 'I did all that you asked.'

'And what was that?'

'After lunch,' the boy explained, 'I have carried fifteen baskets of manure. If you doubt my word, you may go to the field and count them for yourself. Then you may come back here. But please leave me in peace now. I want to read.'

His father was surprised: fifteen baskets was heavy work for an afternoon, and nobody could complain at that. He went back to the field and counted exactly fifteen baskets. His son had meant what he said. Thereafter the boy continued to read his adventure novels in his favourite hiding place, safe in the knowledge that he had performed the tasks which his father wanted.

Mao's father decided to apprentice Mao to a rice shop in Hsiangtan with which he had some connection. Mao was not against the idea, but he had also heard from his cousin Wen about a new school in his mother's county of Hsianghsiang which taught – and by radical methods – some of the 'new knowledge' of the West, with less emphasis on the classics. Mao had at this time come under the influence of a 'radical' teacher at a local primary school who was opposing Buddhism, urging people to forget the gods and to convert their temples into schools.

He had also read a pamphlet telling the sad story of China's dismemberment. 'I remember even now', he recalled thirty years later, 'that this pamphlet opened with the sentence: "Alas, China will be subjugated!" ' The pamphlet told of Japan's occupation of Korea and Taiwan, the Anglo-French intrusions in Indochina, Burma and elsewhere. 'After I read this I felt depressed about the future of my country and began to realize that it was the duty of all the people to help save it.' Everything led him to seek more modern knowledge.

But he had no money for the school, and at the age of fifteen he would be considered by most people too big and too old for a primary school. When Mao finally decided to raise with his father his desire to go to school again, instead of taking up the apprenticeship in the rice shop, he got a scornful answer.

'What a ridiculous idea!' his father commented. 'How can a full-grown man study with little children? . . . The whole idea is completely mad!'

Mao decided that he would have to make his own way, against his father's opposition, and so he went round to relatives and friends of the family, asking each person to lend him a little money. When he had collected enough, without his father's knowing, he declared at dinner one night:

'I have decided to study in the Tungshan Primary School. I shall leave in three days.'

'Have you been granted a scholarship that you can go to school without paying?' his father scoffed. 'Or perhaps you won a lottery ticket this morning!'

'Don't you worry about the money,' Mao calmly replied. 'I shall not ask you to pay even a penny . . .'

His father left the table to light his pipe, coming back a few minutes afterwards to question:

'Do you have a scholarship? How can you go to the Tungshan

school without my having to pay? I know very well that when someone goes to school, he has to pay for the lessons and also for his board and lodging. All this is very expensive. Little Wang has been wanting to go to school now for several years, but he has never been able to go. Unfortunately, primary schools are not free. They are only for the rich people, not for the poor such as you, I am sorry to say.'

'Don't worry about all that,' Mao said with a disdainful smile. 'You will have nothing to pay. That is all.'

'No,' his father objected, 'that is not all. If you leave home I shall be a labourer short. Who will help me work in the fields when you are gone? You tell me I will have nothing to pay, but you forget I shall have to pay another labourer to take your place. You know, my son, I cannot afford to do that.'

Mao had not thought of this, and had no answer to make. He was outwitted by his father at the last minute. But after a while he went to a distant relative who had a reputation for helping young people to get on in education. He told this man of his ideas and problems and was given a loan.

That night he asked his father:

'How much would a labourer cost?'

'At least a dollar a month,' his father answered. 'That would be twelve dollars a year.'

Mao calmly handed the money over, with the words:

'Here are the twelve dollars. I shall leave for Tungshan tomorrow!'

At daybreak next morning Mao was up packing his things together: a blue mosquito net, two sheets which had turned grey with time and too much laundering, and a few old and faded tunics. These he rolled up together into a bundle which he tied to one end of his carrying pole. At the other end he put his two books, and then slung the pole over his shoulders.

'Are you going to say goodbye to your father?' his mother asked when he was ready.

'No,' Mao replied, 'I am not.'

'Do you need anything more to take with you?'

'No,' he said, 'I have everything I need.'

Without any further word or wave of the hand, Mao strode off down the road and never so much as looked back.

Much later, under a tree at the foot of a mountain, Mao came across a young and smartly dressed boy sitting on the ground with an old peasant. He sat down beside them and talked.

Finding that this boy was attending one of the primary schools in the town of Hsiang hsiang, Mao pumped him for information. His first question was, how many students there were in the school. The second betrayed his own anxieties:

'How big are they? Are any of them bigger than you are?'

Mao then asked how strict the teachers were, and was told that there was one who often hit them and hurt them with a heavy stick.

'And do you put up with that?' Mao asked, 'without doing anything?'

'Of course,' the boy replied, 'what can we do?'

'You shouldn't allow him to punish you like that,' Mao said.

'But we are just children, he is a big man.'

'Yes,' Mao said, 'but there are many of you and he is only one. It would be easy to stop him.'

'Yes, but he is a teacher, and we have to respect a teacher. You just don't understand.'

'When he is cruel to you,' Mao asked, 'do you still respect him?'

'All of us are afraid of him – all of my schoolmates. We dare not say a word against him. Oh no, there is nothing we could do.'

'You boys', Mao said in disgust, 'are just fools.'

'It's all very well for you to laugh at us. If you were in our place, you would do exactly the same.'

'Oh,' Mao replied, 'I would? If I were in your place, I'd kill him.'

When Mao first saw the Tungshan Primary School ahead of him on the road, he stopped and stared, having never seen such a big building before. It was surrounded by a moat, about a hundred feet across, crossed by a big white stone bridge, and around the moat in turn was a solid stone wall about fifteen feet high. The children used to call it 'the Great Wall of China'.

Mao summoned up his courage on that momentous day, walked through the first gate and slowly crossed the white stone bridge. His first encounter was with the janitor who wouldn't let him in because he was too big.

'Why can't I go to school like the other boys?'

One of the boys who had joined the scene yelled, 'You're big enough to go to the university!'

Another one shouted, 'Why do you want to come to school here? We are not labourers.'

Other boys looked at his luggage and discovered the two old and well-thumbed novels there.

'Are these all the books you've brought with you?' one asked.

'Don't you know', said another, 'that we're not allowed to read bad books like these?'

'I beg you', Mao pleaded, 'only to go and tell the Headmaster that I want to speak to him.'

'I dare not go and disturb the Headmaster', the janitor replied, 'with such nonsense. You may be a fool, but I am not! What nonsense!'

'If you will not go and announce me,' Mao cried, 'I'll go myself.'

'Just you dare try,' the janitor shouted back.

The boys also shouted at him, and when Mao picked up his belongings and started to move towards the door, the janitor barred the way, shouting, 'Get away from this door! Tungshan is a school, not a lunatic asylum!'

Meanwhile, one of the boys had run to the Headmaster and told him, 'Oh, sir, a young bandit is trying to get into our school . . . He is attacking the janitor. The janitor is trying to defend himself, and all the boys are trying to help him, but the bandit is big, and strong, and quite savage. You should come and help us. Oh, please come quickly, sir!'

The Headmaster came to find out what was happening.

'What is the matter?' he inquired. 'Why all the noise?'

'Sir,' the janitor said, pointing towards Mao, ' this fool says he wants to enter this school, and he demands to see you. He is nothing but a rogue and a brute! Do you want to see him? Well, there he is!'

Mao went towards the Headmaster and said in humble tones, 'Please, sir, allow me to study here in your school!'

'Bring him into my office,' the Headmaster said to the janitor.

Mao hoisted his luggage on to his shoulders, but again the janitor stopped him: 'Where do you think you are going with that luggage on your shoulders? Leave it here and come with me!'

Mao did not want to leave his belongings behind, in case the boys took anything.

'I want to take my things with me,' he said.

'How can you take such things into the Headmaster's office?' the janitor shouted. 'Leave them here. Who do you think is interested in your precious possessions? This school isn't a mad-house. It's not a school for thieves either, leave your belongings here. I am responsible for them. Yes, I'm responsible for them, I tell you!'

Hesitantly, Mao put his things in a corner of the janitor's room and followed him to the Headmaster's office – whereupon, unknown to him or to the janitor, the boys emptied his luggage on the floor and made away with his precious books.

Once in the Headmaster's office, Mao repeated respectfully, 'Sir, please will you allow me to study in your school?'

The Headmaster stared at him in disbelief, and asked him his name and domicile.

'And how old are you?'

'I am just a little over fifteen years old, sir.'

'You look big enough to be at least seventeen or eighteen.'

'No, sir, I am just fifteen years and some months old.'

'Have you attended your village school?'

'I studied for two years with Mr Wang and I can read novels quite well.'

'What kind of novels do you read, Mao Tse-tung?'

'I have read *Romance of the Three Kingdoms* and *Water Margin* quite a lot.'

'Have you read the primary school books?'

'No, sir, I haven't read them.'

'Are you able to read the second-year school books?'

'Most of them,' Mao replied. 'There are some words that I don't know yet.'

'Have you learned any mathematics?'

'No, sir, I haven't.'

'How much history and geography do you know?'

'I haven't learnt any history or geography yet.'

'I want you to write two lines of classical characters.'

Mao wrote some clumsy ideographs with hands that were big and rough, more used to farmwork than writing.

'No,' the Headmaster declared, 'you cannot come to this school. We have no primary classes for beginners. Besides, you are too big to go to a primary school.'

'Oh, please,' Mao pleaded, 'let me enter your school. I want to study.'

'You could not follow the classes. It's quite hopeless.'

'But I will try,' Mao affirmed, 'please let me stay.'

'No, that's impossible. You could never follow the classes. It would be a waste of your time.'

'But I will try very hard. . . .'

At this moment another master, who had overheard some of the interview, came into the room, impressed by Mao's enthusiasm. He suggested that they allow him to attend classes

for a trial period of five months. The Headmaster agreed to the
experiment, and so Mao entered the Tungshan school.

He paid 1400 coppers for five months' board, lodging and
study materials. His father reluctantly approved, once mutual
friends had put it to him that advanced schooling would enable
the boy to earn more.

Mao was overwhelmed by the other students. 'I had never
before seen so many children together,' he commented later.
Most of them were landlords' children, with expensive clothes.
Some wore gowns and dark jackets over colourful waist bands,
with leather-soled brocade shoes. Very few peasants could afford
to send their children to such a school, and Mao cut a poor
contrast with his peers. 'I owned only one decent suit. . . . Many
of the richer students despised me because I usually wore such a
ragged coat and trousers.'

Mao was also the victim of a complex form of snobbery which
identified him as not a native of Hsianghsiang. He was despised
as an outsider, and afterwards commented: 'I felt spiritually very
depressed.'

Nevertheless, Mao did make friends. One of them was Siao
San, better known as Emi Siao, a delicately boned boy two years
older than Mao with a high forehead and a predilection for
language and poetry, who eventually wrote a book called *Mao
Tse-tung, His Childhood and Youth*.

There were also notable teachers, of whom the one to linger
longest in Mao's memory was a 'returned student' from Japan,
who had cut off his pigtail or queue and therefore, on return to
China, had to wear a false one. 'It was quite easy to tell', Mao
recollected, 'that his queue was false. Everyone laughed at him
and called him the "False Foreign Devil".' This was the period
when one of the acts of defiance against the decadent imperial
rule, on the very eve of its overthrow in the revolution of 1911-12,
was precisely to cut off one's queue, thus disobeying the injunc-
tion by the Manchu Dynasty that all Chinese, whether Manchu
or not, should follow this arbitrary custom out of respect for
the throne.

For all the fun that was made of him, Mao learnt much from
the 'False Foreign Devil', who taught music and English and
talked a great deal about Japan. 'At that time,' Mao recalled, 'I
knew and felt the beauty of Japan, and felt something of her
pride and might,' for example in songs which he learnt about her
victory over Russia in 1905. For the first time one of the despised
Oriental nations defeated a European power in a straight fight,

and Japan's victory over the Tsar inspired young men like Mao not only in China but throughout the rest of Asia.

Mao did well in school, though by his own account he was not well behaved. When a teacher's lectures were dull he used to read novels or doze off – as a punishment, he later explained, for those who would not stimulate their students with questions and dialogue.

'I made good progress at this school,' he recollected. 'The teachers liked me, especially those who taught the classics, because I wrote good essays in the classical manner.' But he admitted that his mind was not on the classics. He was eagerly reading two books given to him by his cousin (who later, to Mao's regret, took the other side in the revolution, opposing the Communists) about the new reform movements in China, especially of those two Cantonese reformers, Liang Chi-chao and Kang Yu-wei. One of the books was the *Journal of the New People*, edited by Liang, while the other was an account of Kang's abortive attempt to introduce political reforms in 1898. 'I read and re-read these,' Mao remembered, 'until I knew them by heart. I worshipped Kang Yu-wei and Liang Chi-chao . . . I was not yet an anti-monarchist. Indeed, I considered the Emperor as well as most officials to be honest, good and clever men. They only needed the help of Kang Yu-wei's reforms.'

After playtime one evening Mao found himself next to Emi Siao in the crowd jostling to go back into the classroom after the bell had sounded. The boy had a book in his hand.

'What do you have there?' Mao asked.

'Heroes and Great Men of the World.'

'May I have a look?'

A few days later Mao returned the book, apologizing for having made it dirty. When Emi Siao opened it he found many passages marked with circles and dots – especially those about Washington, Napoleon, Peter the Great, Catherine the Great, Wellington, Gladstone, Rousseau, Montesquieu and Lincoln.

Mao later commented to Siao: 'We need more great people like these. We ought to study them and find out how to make China rich and strong and so avoid becoming like Annam, Korea and India. . . .'

'I had first heard of America', Mao recalled, 'in an article which told of the American revolution and contained a sentence like this: "After eight years of difficult war, Washington won victory and built up his nation. . . .".'

Meanwhile Mao was responding to some local manifestations

of China's economic and political troubles. He heard about the
popular demonstrations in the provincial capital city of
Changsha during a bad famine, when many of the leaders of the
starving demonstrators were beheaded, their heads being displayed on poles to frighten off any future 'rebels'. This was discussed among Mao's friends and he was deeply resentful of the
way the government had treated the rebels. At about the same
time a local landlord had a dispute with members of a secret
society, the Ko Lao Hui, who broke into his granaries. Their
leader, a blacksmith, was beheaded, to become a hero in the eyes
of Mao and other youngsters in the province.

A year later there was a rice shortage in Shaoshan itself, and
the poor asked the rich farmers to supply free rice to them. 'My
father', Mao explained, 'was a rice merchant and was exporting
much grain to the city from our district, despite the shortage.
One of his consignments was seized by the poor villagers and his
wrath was boundless.' Mao did not sympathize with his father –
'At the same time I thought the villagers' method was also
wrong.'

The boy took his ideals literally. On a visit home for the
Chinese New Year his father sent Mao to collect payment due on
a pig. On the way back, a friend remembered, 'he ran into
several poor people dressed in tattered clothes, whereupon he
distributed among them the money he had collected'.

After five months at the primary school Mao's progress was
such that he was allowed to stay. The boys who had stolen his
two novels became more friendly, and returned them. Indeed,
they came to regard him as an authority on these romantic
stories, and this led to a good deal of argument. *Romance of the
Three Kingdoms* had assumed such significance in Mao's mind
that he would not allow it to be criticized. The history teacher
told him that it was a much romanticized version of the historical
facts, but Mao would not admit this even after heated arguments. He went to the Headmaster for support, but the Headmaster supported the history teacher, so Mao drew up a petition
to the Mayor of the town calling for the replacement of the
Headmaster. None of the other students was willing to sign it.

'You're nothing but a bunch of cowards,' Mao shouted at
them angrily, 'a lot of useless cowards!'

For a while they said nothing, but one of them, who was
particularly friendly with Mao, was brave enough to speak.

'I don't see how you could possibly know more about history',
he said, 'than the Headmaster does. He has a degree and he has

written a lot of books on history. My father's always telling me how much he knows. I don't think you know more than the Headmaster does!'

'You don't believe me?' Mao retorted. 'But surely you've read my books.'

'But, Mao, hasn't the Headmaster told you that's only a romantic novel? It's based on history but it's not a true account.'

'But it is history, I tell you. History! It's just nonsense for you to say that it's not true. Of course it's true!' Mao then accused the boy of being a nephew or stepson of the Headmaster, and the boy replied in similar personal vein. Eventually Mao threw a chair at him, shouting, 'Traitor! Traitor!'

The boy said he would report Mao to the Headmaster.

'I'm not afraid of him,' Mao boasted, 'but if you do go, I warn you, I shall kill you!'

Mao then turned to one of the boys who had been silent and taunted him for cowardice in not backing him up. When this boy said that he agreed with the first boy about the *Three Kingdoms*, Mao burst out:

'You're a traitor, and I shall kill you.'

In this way Mao lost the sympathy which he had initially won from his teachers and schoolmates, and this, according to the account of one of his friends, led him to decide to move on.

2
A STUDENT OF ETHICS

Mao was almost eighteen when he decided to enter secondary school in a big city. He particularly wanted to go to Changsha, the provincial capital about forty miles from his home. After the summer vacation of 1911 he asked one of his teachers at Tungshan to give him an introduction to the Hsianghsiang Middle School in Changsha. Carrying this precious introduction with him, he set off on foot with Emi Siao for the capital, 'exceedingly excited,' in Mao's own words afterwards, 'half-fearing that I would be refused entrance, hardly daring to hope that I could actually become a student in this great school.'

They stopped at the city of Hsiangtan, and then took steerage class accommodation on the river boat to Changsha, which they reached, 'speechless with excitement', in Emi's words, 'on seeing the city bustling with activity and immense crowds thronging the streets.' To Mao's surprise, he was admitted at the Hsianghsiang Middle School without difficulty.

Here he encountered his first newspaper, the *People's Strength,* an organ of the revolutionary movement with stimulating reports of uprisings against the Manchu Dynasty and of Sun Yat-sen's political activities on the eve of the 1911-12 revolution. Sun was the Cantonese peasant boy who went to mission school, became a Christian and went through medical school in Hong Kong before becoming leader of the republican movement. 'I was agitated so much', Mao recalled, 'that I wrote an article, which I posted on the school wall. It was my first expression of a political opinion and it was somewhat muddled.' Still fiercely admiring the political reformers about whom he had read in Tungshan, Mao in his first wall poster advocated the proclamation of a republic with Sun as President, Kang Yu-wei as Premier and Liang Chi-chao as Foreign Minister. As he later admitted, 'I did not clearly understand the differences between them.'

While the imperial regime made desperate efforts to stem the tide of change, anti-Manchu feelings strengthened among the students. A group of patriots at the Hsianghsiang Middle School made a queue-clipping pact, promising to cut off their queues in defiance of the Emperor's order. Mao and one other went through with the plan, but the rest got cold feet at the last minute.

'My friend and I', Mao remembered, 'therefore assaulted them in secret and forcibly removed their queues, a total of more than ten falling victim to our shears.' But Mao did not feel at home in this school. Half a century later he reminisced at a political meeting how, 'When I was a boy, and when I was in middle school, I used to get all steamed up whenever I heard unpleasant things about myself. . . .'

Soon after Mao arrived in Changsha the great republican uprising against the Manchu Emperor burst open in Wuhan. Representatives of the rebels came to speak at Mao's school, inspiring him to join the revolutionary army in its fight. He and some friends decided to go to Wuhan for this purpose. Before going he borrowed some rain-shoes, having heard 'that the streets of Wuhan were very wet'.

But for some reason Mao and his friends were not accepted, so they returned to Changsha. Soon afterwards Mao had a well-remembered conversation with some of the students whom he had met on his way back from Wuhan. One of them, the son of a mandarin, began to talk about the revolution.

'Now', he said, 'our country has become a republic. We no longer have an emperor. We are all equal. The land is ours. We are the masters, and the officials are servants of the state. Even the president of the republic is just a servant! We could all be president. You and I, we could become president. . . .'

One of the other students disputed his right to be president first.

'Can't I be president before you?' he asked. 'I promise you solemnly . . . that you will be my prime minister when I am president of the republic!'

Mao asked the second student not to interrupt the first. 'Let him talk,' he said. 'What he says is all quite true and I am very interested. Let him talk. Tell me,' Mao now addressed the mandarin's son, 'exactly what would you have to do to get elected president of the republic? Would you have to study a lot? Should you learn all about foreign countries after finishing studies at the university? Just what should you do?'

'No,' the first student replied, 'it is not necessary to study to

get into power.' He gave examples – the first Chin Emperor and
Genghis Khan – from Chinese history.

'Well,' Mao pressed him, 'what *do* you do to get political
power?'

'Politicians must fight,' came the answer. 'A politician must
attack fearlessly anyone who attacks or opposes him ... Sometimes it may be necessary to kill. ...'

'But in politics', Mao persisted, 'how do you attack your
adversaries?'

'That is a very important question, Mao,' the boy answered.
'You can't attack them with your two bare hands. It is necessary
for you to have many loyal partisans who march to victory with
you and who are willing to work for you. You have to gather
these partisans together. In a word, you have to organize a political party!'

Meanwhile Mao was able to observe political change at first
hand. On 22 October 1911 he witnessed the republican takeover
of Changsha. The rebels came along the railway line and fought
a big battle outside the city walls, and at the same time there was
an insurrection inside the city. After the gates had been stormed
and taken by Chinese workers, Mao stood on a hill to watch the
fighting.

A new government was installed, but not for long. A few days
later Mao saw the corpses of the new Governor and Vice-
Governor lying in the street, victims of a conservative backlash.
The Emperor had still not abdicated from his throne, and so
Mao decided to join the local republican army in order to help
complete the revolution.

The company which he joined had its headquarters inside the
Court of Justice. Here he carried out regular training, as well as
such extra duties as carrying beds, bedding and clothes baskets
for the officers when they moved to new quarters. Some of the
soldiers also had to go every day to the White Sand Well outside
the city to fetch water for the mess and for the officers' tea. 'My
salary', Mao recollected, 'was seven dollars a month ... and of
this I spent two dollars a month on food. I also had to buy water.
The soldiers had to carry water in from outside the city, but I,
being a student, could not condescend to carrying, and bought it
in from the water-pedlars.' So much for the dignity of labour in
Mao's young eyes.

Mao's main luxury with the rest of his pay was newspapers,
which he read avidly. 'He would read through all the four pages
of an edition,' Emi Siao remembered, 'without skipping a word.

The variety of material contained in the newspapers especially delighted him – news items, commentaries on current affairs, miscellaneous articles and what not. He acquired much useful knowledge through newspaper reading. Most important of all, it led him to apply himself to the study of current affairs and social problems.'

It was in one of these newspapers that Mao read his first article about socialism. It was sketchy and badly written, but it delighted Mao, who promptly started discussing socialism with other soldiers, 'holding it to be the best theory so far advanced for the salvation of the world and mankind', as Emi Siao recalled. Only two of his fellow soldiers won Mao's personal approval, however, a Hunanese miner and an ironsmith. 'The rest were mediocre,' he remembered – 'and one was a rascal.'

After six frustrating and uneventful months as a private soldier Mao decided to quit. There was a truce in the high politics of the republican war, so 'I resigned from the army and decided to return to my books.' It was clear by then that, however successful they might be in toppling the monarchy, there was no way in which the new republican forces could win against the tough and conservative regional warlords of China. Sun Yat-sen was President of the Chinese Republic, but was soon replaced by a general. The revolutionaries in Hunan had already been duped, and their leaders assassinated by Governor Tan Yen-kai representing the landlord bureaucracy.

Mao's military service taught him one good lesson, as one of his teachers later explained: 'Mao's experience of the mercenary soldier in military training camps taught him the futility of depending on such material for revolutionary purposes: it was too difficult to educate them politically. Mao realized that to build up a successful agrarian reform movement . . .it would be necessary to arm the peasants themselves.'

For a year after leaving the army Mao drifted with uncharacteristic aimlessness in the provincial capital. He tried several schools, but was not able to hit on the right one for him. He began by responding to advertisements in the newspapers. Many schools were opening their doors and looking for new students. 'I had no special standard', Mao afterwards explained, 'for judging schools; I did not know exactly what I wanted to do.'

His eye was caught by an advertisement for a police school, so he registered to enter it. But before the examination came, he changed his mind and paid another dollar registration fee for a soap-making school. This enterprising establishment offered full board and a small salary, extolling the great social benefits of soap-making, how it would enrich both the country and the people: 'It was an attractive and inspiring advertisement', Mao found.

Then a law student friend persuaded Mao to join him at his school, for which Mao had read another alluring advertisement promising 'to teach students all about law in three years', and guaranteeing that they would then 'instantly become mandarins'. Mao succumbed to his friend's persuasions and wrote to his family asking them to send tuition money. 'I painted a bright picture for them of my future as a jurist and mandarin.'

But yet another advertisement claimed Mao's attention, this time for a commercial school. Another of his friends argued that the country's real challenge was economic, and what it most needed was economists to build up its strength. Mao was swayed by the argument and spent another precious dollar to register and enrol there.

After he had been accepted, however, he was seduced once again by a new advertisement, this time 'describing the charms of a higher commercial public school'. Mao paid his dollar and entered the school, writing to tell his father, who expressed approval – which meant that the old man was now doing well enough to support his son for a further period of education.

But there was a snag which Mao had not anticipated. 'The trouble with my new school', he discovered, 'was that most of the courses were taught in English, and, in common with other students, I knew little English; indeed scarcely more than the alphabet.' Moreover there was no teacher of English. 'Disgusted with this situation', Mao withdrew at the end of a month and started combing the advertisements again.

His next venture was to register, again for a dollar, for the First Provincial Middle School, where he came top in the entrance examination. This was a big school, specializing in traditional history, and Mao was encouraged by the Principal, who liked his literary composition. But Mao was not happy there. 'Its curriculum was limited,' he decided, 'and its regulations were objectionable,' Having read in his own time outside the classrooms a history book, *Chronicles with Imperial Commentaries*, lent to him by a teacher, he felt that he would be better off reading and studying on his own. After six months he left the school and tried out a new way of life.

During this period, the winter of 1912-13, he went every day to the Hunan Provincial Library at the Tingwang Tower, Liuyang

Gate, to read until closing time. 'At noon I paused only long enough to buy and consume two rice cakes, which were my daily lunch.'

He lodged at the hostel for Hsianghsiang students on Hsinan Lane, off Cheng Street, where the food was cheap. The only trouble was that disbanded and out-of-work soldiers from the Hsianghsiang district also stayed at the hostel, and they were always quarrelling with the students. One night the fight became violent, and the soldiers tried to kill the students. 'I escaped by fleeing to the toilet,' Mao remembered, 'where I hid until the fight was over.'

This was, however, a rich period in Mao's intellectual development. He read the library's translation by Yen Fu, the British-educated Fukienese Darwinist, of many of the leading thinkers of the Western world. 'For the first time' (at eighteen) 'I saw and studied with great interest a map of the world.' Among the books which he read were Charles Darwin's *Origin of Species*, Adam Smith's *The Wealth of Nations*, John Stuart Mill's *System of Logic*, Herbert Spencer's *The Study of Sociology*, Montesquieu's *L'Esprit des Lois*, Jean -Jacques Rousseau's *Le Contrat Social*, and T. H. Huxley's *Evolution and Ethics*.

This last made a particularly strong impact on Mao because it diametrically opposed the received Chinese tradition that the past was better than the present. Besides these major works of philosophy, Mao also read widely: 'I mixed poetry and romances, and the tales of ancient Greece, with serious study of history and geography of Russia, America, England, France and other countries.'

But if Mao revelled in his freedom to absorb all this intellectual stimulation, his father was not so thrilled, eventually putting his foot down and refusing to subsidize Mao any further in his self-study programme. Mao had to leave the hostel and find a new place to live. Meanwhile, he recollected, 'I had been thinking seriously of my "career" and had about decided that I was best suited for teaching.'

Glancing over the advertisements again, he saw one inserted by a teacher's training school or normal school, offering free tuition and board. Two of Mao's friends were also wanting to enter this school, and they asked for Mao's help in preparing their entrance essays. 'I composed essays for my two friends,' Mao recalled, 'and wrote one of my own.' All three were accepted, and so Mao was able to boast that he was accepted three times. 'I did not then think my act of substituting for my

friends an immoral one; it was merely a matter of friendship.'
This was the Mao who was later to demand of the younger
generation of the 1950s that it should put its loyalty to the state
and the state ideology far above any feelings of friendship or
family trust.

Mao was to stay for five tumultuous and formative years in the
Fourth Hunan Normal School, which had been founded in the
wake of the revolution in 1912, only to amalgamate within a few
months with the First Normal School. It stood outside the southern gate of Changsha on Academy Plain, facing the River Hsiang
next to a new industrial area which included a graphite factory,
an electric light company and a mint – as well as the Canton—
Wuhan railway, which after 1917 rattled past the school day and
night.

This was a public school where the students paid no tuition
fee, and its charter was to train primary schoolteachers from
children of poor families unable to go to the university. It was
consciously built on the latest theories of popular education,
incorporating not only traditional subjects but also physical
exercise, social life and moral practice. There was a rich library
and an enlightened faculty. Self-initiative was encouraged, much
to Mao's delight, and patriotism was evident in the use of the
national language as distinct from the provincial dialect and in
the stress laid by the teachers on the need to be conscious of
China's national humiliation.

Mao was already nineteen when he entered the Hunan Normal School in the spring of 1913, and yet one might almost say
that it was here that his education really began. 'For twenty-odd
years,' he later recollected, 'I grew up eating honeydew, being
ignorant about everything.'

Mao calculated that during his time at this school he spent
only $160. 'Of this amount I must have used a third for news-
papers, because regular subscriptions cost me about a dollar a
month, and I often bought books and journals on the news-
stands. My father cursed me for this extravagance. He called it
wasted money on wasted paper. But I had acquired the
newspaper-reading habit, and from 1911 to 1927 . . .I never
stopped reading the daily papers of Peking, Shanghai and
Hunan.' On Sundays, if the students were late for dinner, they
could make up their own meals from the cold rice and vegetables
left in the kitchen. Whereas others would heat up these leavings,
Mao alone would consume them cold, though whether from
frugality, indifference or sheer laziness one is left to speculate.

The school even gave each new entrant a blue woollen uniform. Mao wore his for many years, long after it had faded and holes had appeared in it. In addition Mao often wore a grey cotton scholar's gown, with an old lined jacket inside it during winter, and a pair of baggy white cotton trousers which were to be seen on him all the year round. In summer he almost never wore socks, and his cotton sandals were usually coming apart at the seams. His bedding was a coarse blue cotton wrap-around quilt, with hard old cotton filling inside it.

Mao's daily routine was to get up very early, wash and go to the study room to read. After classes were over he would usually read in the newspaper room or look for books in the library. After everyone else had gone to bed he would stay reading in the tea room, the newspaper room, and even eventually in the corridors where the lights were on all night. He always had a book in his hand, his friends said, and he never played jokes or indulged in idle talk. He also enjoyed going to the hill behind the school to read there by himself, or with his friends. On his rare forays into town he would usually go to Jade Spring Street or Fucheng Street where there were second-hand and new bookshops in which to spend his miserable pocket money.

He studied Chinese literature, ethics, geography and history, and one colleague remembered that he was especially fond of Ssu-ma Kuang's *Comprehensive Mirror for Aid in Government* and Ku Tsu-yu's *The Essentials of Geography for Reading History*, works of the eleventh and seventeenth centuries respectively. It was Mao's habit to compare the foreign names of people and places which he found in newspapers with those in atlases and books, and to search out the original version of quotations. The correct names or quotations he would write down on long strips of paper which he eventually combined into a book, which he could browse in and consult at any time. Whenever he was needed, his friends always knew where to find him: 'In the newspaper room'.

His essays, both in the ancient and modern styles, were good, and his fluency was widely remarked on. He was meticulous in marking his books, circling the characters whose meaning he approved, putting crosses against others and writing comments such as 'absurd' in two or three different ways, one for each time he had read the text. He would even at a second reading add a critique of his earlier remarks on a text.

His Socratic streak was also noticed. He had, as his Chinese biographer put it, 'a particular habit of raising questions, believing that learning and questioning were inseparable'.

But not everything was to Mao's liking. In particular, there were no fewer than thirty-five irritating prohibitions which impinged upon his freedom of action, including those against the conduct of business, political parties, vulgar songs and music, harmful books and unauthorized meetings. Mao also hated the compulsory science courses, since he wished to specialize in social science. 'Natural sciences', he recollected, 'did not especially interest me, and I did not study them, so I got poor marks in most of these courses.' One of his teachers remembered his mathematics as being terrible. At some uncongenial examinations he gave in a blank answer paper.

Most of all, Mao said later, he hated the course in still-life drawing, which he found 'extremely stupid'. His answer was to think of the simplest thing to draw, draw it quickly and then leave. He once drew an oval and called it an egg, which caused him to fail the examination. 'I turned in the paper the fastest because it took only one stroke.'

But Mao's marks in social sciences were very good indeed, offsetting his poor results in science and art. Mao later described his attitude to the classroom as that of a rebel. 'I did not obey the rules,' he confessed, 'my principle was just to avoid getting myself dismissed. As to examinations, my marks hovered between 50 per cent or 60 per cent and 80 per cent, 70 per cent being my average.'

Mao admitted his debt to this school. 'I never formally went to college,' he told a friend, 'and never studied abroad. My knowledge, my learning gained its foundation at First Normal. First Normal was a good school.'

It was here that Mao's aptitude for organization was first noticed. Emi Siao remembered that whenever others talked, Mao would listen, 'with his head slightly inclined, often confining himself to monosyllabic answers like "um" or "yes". Afterwards he would make an orderly analysis, pick out the important points and sum up the problem on hand, all with the minimum of words. His remarks were always to the point and always inspiring. People often came to him with problems. After a brief talk with him, things seemed to clear up and straighten themselves out marvellously.'

Another chronicler of these schooldays noted that Mao 'never spoke recklessly' at meetings, whether as chairman or as a speaker from the floor – and most especially he did not indulge in 'long, digressive and confused speeches', as was the all-too-frequent habit of the leaders of opinion at this time. If the others around him started to argue, even when their altercations became violent, Mao would maintain a quiet composure and listen carefully to all views.

He also affected a puritanical composure in his way of life, heartily agreeing with the view that 'a man isn't worth talking about if he cannot overcome the two crises of money and sex . . .'. His friends said that he was never frivolous, was strict in the demands that he placed upon himself, and was never satisfied with his own behaviour or knowledge.

But all this did not yet add up to a recognized gift for leading others. 'When at school,' one of his teachers, Hsu Te-li, said afterwards, 'Mao showed no special talent for leadership. He had a humble spirit . . . '.

One of Mao's annotated textbooks, together with a book of his own notes, was saved 'from the ashes' when his family burned all his books and papers in the backyard ten years later – when Mao was on the run from his enemies. The notebook contained more than 10 000 words on ninety-four pages, part of them being Mao's handwritten copy of the complete text of two books of fourth-century-BC poetry.

The other part was a classroom record of lectures on ethics and literature, probably taken down in the winter of 1914. The subjects ranged from pre-Chin philosophy, the *Book of Songs*, Han history, Napoleon, Julius Caesar and Fukuzawa Yukichi (the prophet of Japan's Meiji reform and the introducer of European culture to Japan) to natural science.

Several themes emerge from this notebook which are suggestive of Mao's intellectual development at that time. One, developed with boundless egotism, was his own ambition. 'My boundaries must be expanded so that the universe will become one great self.' Mao noted prophetically the existence in ancient times of superior men 'who would see themselves and their families perish and yet would have no regret'. Elaborating this, he noted the saying that when a poisonous snake bites a brave man's hand, he will cut it off at his wrist.

'Benevolent men regard the world and its posterity as their bodies, and regard themselves and their families as their wrists,' was Mao's comment. 'Only because of the sincerity of their care for the world and its posterity do they dare not care for themselves or their families. Although he or his family dies, if the world and its posterity live, then the mind of the benevolent man will be at peace.' Such words in Mao's own handwriting strongly suggest the feelings of social guilt which he had about his own behaviour towards his family, and his consequent need for self-justification at abandoning them – as well as his sense of his own destiny.

A second motif running through his notebook was the importance of hard work and realism. 'The learning that one obtains from behind closed doors', Mao wrote, 'is useless. If one wants to learn from the myriad things of the world, then one must travel widely to the Nine Divisions (of ancient China) and to the Four Canopies of Heaven.' And again, 'If one does not do farming, then one will not understand the difficulty of sowing and reaping. If one does not weave silk, then one will never understand where clothes come from.'

A phenomenon singled out for Mao's severe disapproval in his notebook was laziness. 'Laziness is the source of all evil. ... A lazy nation is marked first by lack of progress, next by retrogression, then by decline and finally by its own downfall. ... A young man must have vitality and vigour otherwise slackness will arise. Therefore laziness is the grave of life.'

Another of Mao's concerns was attention to detail. 'There is one difficult thing in establishing oneself in life; it is being meticulous. ... A person who failed in a great undertaking and through neglect of details and whom we may take as a warning is Caesar.'

The annotated textbook which survived was Friedrich Paulsen's *A System of Ethics*, which was taught by Professor Yang during Mao's last two years at the school, in 1917 and 1918. In a book of 100 000 words, Mao added more than 12 000 words in the margins, as well as making various markings – circles, dots, underlinings, crossings, triangles – in the text itself. Professor Yang once awarded a maximum mark of 100, with the words added 'plus 5', for an essay by Mao on the power of the mind, based on Paulsen. Mao was very proud of this, and, as a friend recalled, 'he never tired of telling people about it'.

Mao was deeply moved by the dilemma of the individual, as the following comment shows: 'Wherever there is repression of the individual, wherever there is a violation of individuality there can be no greater crime. That is why our country's Three Bonds' (the three traditional Confucian social relationships, between prince and minister, father and son, and husband and wife) 'must go, and why they constitute, with religion, capitalists and autocracy, the four evil demons of the world.'

Professor Yang Chang-chi, sometimes known as 'the Confucius of Changsha', was the strongest influence on Mao during his schooldays. 'He was an idealist,' Mao later declared, 'and a man of fine moral character. He believed in his ethics very strongly and tried to imbue his students with the desire to become just, moral, virtuous men, useful in society.'

Yang had studied abroad for ten years – first in Japan, then at the University of London and then at the University of Edinburgh, where he took a degree in philosophy. He studied Kant at a German university before returning to China a confirmed admirer of Samuel Smiles, T. H. Green and Kant. Whereas most of the so-called 'gold-plated' or 'silver-plated' returned students from Europe and Japan respectively became officials, politicians or businessmen in China, Yang dedicated himself to the financially unrewarding task of teaching others so that new talents could be nurtured.

An idealist and evolutionist, Yang had a particular passion for putting ideas into personal practice and seeking out truth through the facts. He believed strongly in the demonstration of mind over matter, and even had a special bathtub made for him in which he took a cold bath every morning, immersing himself in the chilly water regardless of the time of year. 'Every day,' he would explain, 'one must do something difficult to strengthen one's will! Cold water not only strengthens will; it is also good for the health!' He continued, nevertheless, to allow himself to be carried in the three-man sedan chair which was thought proper for his status.

Yang's students adored him, and some of them, including Mao, would go to his house after his lectures on ethics to continue discussion. At such informal sessions in his home he used to urge his pupils to try to make their own life better, leaving fame to those who would come after. 'Anyone who wishes to accomplish great things in society', he added, 'should have far-reaching plans and make no false moves ... ' When Mao paid his first visit to Yang's country home in Pantsang, he 'walked almost forty miles from Changsha,' the teacher's brother recalled, 'in a pair of straw sandals, carrying an umbrella in his hand.'

By contrast Hsu Te-li, the Japan-trained teacher of education from a peasant family, was one of the only two staff members who walked to school, spurning the sedan chair and the rickshaw. Hsu had impressed all of Hunan when he signed a petition to the Emperor seeking the opening of a parliament, and had not only signed in his own blood but had drawn that blood by cutting off his own finger in a 'demonstration of sincerity and determination', as Mao later put it.

Hsu's convictions exerted an important influence on Mao, who said to his old teacher much later when they were both in the thick of the Communist revolution: 'Twenty years ago you were my teacher, you are still my teacher, and in the future you will certainly always remain my teacher.'

The third mentor who figured large in Mao's life in Changsha was Yuan Chi-liu, known as Yuan the Big Beard, who taught Chinese. He 'ridiculed my writing', Mao recalled, 'and called it the work of a journalist. . . . I was obliged to alter my style. . . . Thanks to Yuan Big Beard, therefore, I can today still turn out a passable classical essay if required.' What Yuan did was to reform Mao's writing from the semi-colloquialized style of Liang Chi-chao, on whom Mao had modelled himself but whom Yuan considered a half-literate hack, to the classical ninth-century style of Han Yu.

Mao obeyed him at first, but gradually came to feel that he was too conservative and autocratic. On one occasion he refused to rewrite an essay omitting a phrase of which Yuan disapproved, recopying it unaltered. Yuan tore it up. On yet another occasion, Mao came across Yuan shouting abuse at an office boy. Mao quietly remarked, 'How can a person be so evil to bring on such cursing and screaming?'

In a large staff, there were others who helped Mao. One of them used to give him old copies of the *People's Paper*, another allowed Mao to live in his house during vacations, a third went on to join the Communist Party with Mao. Mao was even more fortunate with his peers, finding two friends in particular who shared not only his interests but his sharpness of intellect. They were Tsai Ho-sen and Hsiao Hsu-tung, better known as Siao Yu – the younger brother of Emi, Mao's old Tungshan friend.

Professor Yang used to say that of the many thousands of pupils whom he had taught in Changsha, the three outstanding were Siao Yu, Tsai and Mao – in that order. The three were not exact contemporaries, but were close enough in age and interests to spend a great deal of time with each other. They came to be known as the *san-ko hao-hsieh* – the three heroes.

Tsai came from Hsianghsiang, and was a cattle-herd before he went to school. He was tall and thin, with two protruding front teeth, stubborn and strong-willed, though he lacked the power of initiative. He told his friends that he wanted to write popular histories about people instead of emperors, and that he wanted to unite the written and spoken languages of China. During the

1920s, until his painful martyrdom in 1931, Tsai was to become Mao's closest collaborator in the Chinese Communist Party.

On the first day of the merger of the First and Fourth Normal schools in the autumn of 1913, Siao Yu, a student at the former institution, gazed with interest at the newcomers from Fourth Normal when they arrived to amalgamate. Unlike the First students, they had no uniforms and looked a pretty ragged bunch.

One of these 'recruits' [Siao Yu recalled afterwards] was a tall, clumsy dirtily dressed young man whose shoes badly needly repairing. This young man was Mao Tse-tung.... His face was rather large, but his eyes were neither large nor penetrating, nor had they the sly cunning look sometimes attributed to them. His nose was flattish and of a typical Chinese shape. His ears were well proportioned; his mouth quite small; his teeth very white and even. These good white teeth helped to make his smile quite charming, so that no one would imagine that he was not genuinely sincere. He walked rather slowly, with his legs somewhat separated, in a way that reminded one of a duck waddling. His movements in sitting or standing were very slow. Also, he spoke slowly and he was by no means a gifted speaker.

They recognized each other from the first day, since their homes were close, but they came together at the school only through the custom of exhibiting prize essays every week. Both Siao's and Mao's essays were selected for this honour in their respective classes on a number of occasions, and they thus read each other's work.

'What impressed me most at the time', Siao afterwards wrote about Mao, 'was his awkward style of handwriting. With his clumsy brush strokes, he never managed to keep quite within the lines of the squared paper, and from a distance his characters often looked like haphazard arrangements of straws.'

Eventually Mao said apologetically to Siao: 'You can write two words in one small square while I need three small squares for two words.'

Siao was then the top student in the school. Mao was also highly placed, although he excelled only in essay-writing, getting no marks for English and only five out of a hundred for arithmetic, and being poor at drawing. Although he was near the bottom of the thirty students in the eighth class in these subjects, essay-writing was considered over-riding. If the essay was good, the student was good, and so Mao was a good student.

He has a retentive memory [Emi Siao later recalled] and if one brings up the name of a place now he can immediately tell in what province and in what county of China it is, or its precise location in a foreign country. . . . In making a special study of geography, he used the same methods with which he studied history – grasping the crux of the matter, collecting extensive data and never flying off on a tangent. . . . This tireless pursuit of knowledge characterized Mao Tse-tung from the very early days, and his painstaking methods of study and research eventually made him a man of immense erudition.

Chinese customs being what they were, it was several months after the amalgamation before Mao found an appropriate occasion actually to talk to Siao. They met by chance in a corridor. Mao stopped in front of his senior and said, in English, 'Mr Siao.' It was the convention in the school for the students to address each other in English.

'Mr Mao,' Siao replied with equal formality.

'What is the number of your study?' Mao asked.

'I am in study number one,' Siao replied.

'This afternoon,' Mao went on, 'after class, I'd like to come to your study to look at your essays, if you don't mind.'

When tuition finished at four o'clock, Mao came to Siao's study and they had a long talk about the school's curriculum, organization and teachers. At the end, Mao took two of his new friend's essays to read, made a formal bow, and left.

On the next day, after classes had finished, Mao suggested that the two of them go for a walk together after dinner. They walked for two hours along the bank of the River Hsiang. Mao complimented his friend on his essays, but he disagreed with one of the arguments which Siao had made on the subject of Yen Kuang, a famous scholar of the first century AD who had enjoyed an intimate friendship with the man who subsequently became emperor. The new ruler invited Yen Kuang to help him govern China, and so the scholar went to the capital at his invitation and slept in the same bed. As proof of their intimacy, it was said that during the night Yen Kuang unconsciously placed his feet on the sacred body of the emperor. The emperor asked Yen Kuang to be his prime minister, but the scholar refused because he considered politics a base profession and did not wish to lead a political life.

Mao argued that Yen Kuang should have accepted the job as prime minister, to which Siao replied that Mao did not understand Yen Kuang's point of view.

'If Yen Kuang could hear your ideas,' Siao said, 'he would say you were despicable.'

Mao was embarrassed, and blushed, so Siao ended the discussion with a joke.

'All right,' he said, 'if you become emperor one day, you will see that you will not invite me to go and sleep with you in the same bed, and put my feet on your body!'

Ironically, when Mao did become a political leader, his only reference to Siao, a quarter of a century later, was to accuse him of responsibility for the theft of national treasures from the Palace museum in Peking, a charge for which the evidence was only circumstantial.

Ho Shu-heng, known as Ho the Moustache, was another of the group of early Communists who were students in this school and friends of Mao. Mao said of Ho that 'he is not a man for learning, but a *doer* ... an ox ... a heap of feeling ...' Others were Chen Chang-fu, Lo Hsueh-tsan, Chang Kun-ti, Kuo Liang and Hsia Hsi – all martyred in the Communist cause, sometimes after torture, in the early 1930s.

While at school in Changsha they jokingly referred to themselves as 'pillars and beams of talent', echoing a phrase from the classics about able ministers of state. But only Mao the unstoppable went on to take the dragon's throne, while Siao Yu pursued his anarchistic road, hating both the Communists and the Kuomintang and living out most of his adult life in exile in Europe and South America.

In all the records about Mao's schoolfriends there is very little reference to his sex life. Mao himself attributed this to the high sense of purpose which they all shared:

It was serious-minded little group of men and they had no time to discuss trivialities. ... They had no time for love or 'romance' and considered the times too critical and the need for knowledge too urgent to discuss women or personal matters. I was not interested in women. ... Quite aside from the discussions of feminine charm, which usually play an important role in the lives of young men of this age, my companions even rejected talk of ordinary matters of daily life.

I remember being in the house of a youth who began to talk to me about buying some meat, and in my presence called in his servant to discuss the matter with him, then ordering him to buy a piece. I was annoyed and did not see this fellow again. My friends and I preferred to talk only of large matters – the nature of man, of human society, of China, the world and the universe.

There were, of course, a few young women who shared the ideals of Mao and his friends, including Tsai Ho-sen's sister Tsai Chang, who went on to become one of the outstanding women leaders of the Communist Party. But shyness and the inhibiting force of social tradition combined to lead Mao in his late teens and early twenties in Changsha to dismiss romantic matters – to be somewhat compensated, perhaps, by the unusually intimate links which boys formed among themselves in the China of the 1910s.

One summer vacation Mao stayed at school to study rather than go home and help his father in the fields. 'His only pair of shoes was very badly worn and cut,' his friend Siao commented. 'Both shoes had holes in the soles; so later he would have to go home at least once to get a new pair made.'

Mao's desk was always in 'complete disorder', Siao recalled, his study invariably untidy and unswept. 'If a great hero', Siao once said to him jokingly, 'does not clean and sweep out his own room, how can he possibly think he is capable of cleaning up the universe?'

'A great hero who thinks about cleaning up the universe', Mao retorted, 'has no time to think about sweeping rooms!'

During the sweltering Hunanese summer, Siao took a bath every day, whereas Mao used to go for several days without a bath, complaining that Siao took too many.

'Jun-chih,' Siao would retaliate, 'you smell awfully sweaty.'

Jun-chih was the (slightly feminine) courtesy school-name taken by Mao, meaning smooth fungus.

This was true, but Mao was not at all sensitive about being sweaty, nor did he mind being told. He did not change what Siao called 'his slovenly habits', and the two other students who were also staying on at school during the vacation and who began by sitting at the same table for meals eventually moved to another table some distance away. Mao did not understand why. But Siao may exaggerate Mao's uncleanliness, for later Mao became famous in the school for his daily bath.

Mao also objected to Siao's brushing his teeth after meals.

'That's typical', he taunted Siao, 'of the son of a rich father! You're quite the gentleman, aren't you!' For Mao, cleanliness implied a bourgeois mentality. In the school they had to wash their own clothes. Mao hated this, whereas Siao quite enjoyed it.

They talked incessantly about the latest news in the papers, particularly about Germany, for which the Chinese had a great respect. Mao, according to Siao, 'adored' Bismarck and Wilhelm II. War had broken out in Europe, a war which would have unexpected consequences for China. Meanwhile China's republican revolution was betrayed by militarist warlords.

3
THE DRAGON IN HIS DEPTHS

Mao's first two years at the Normal School were relatively uneventful, presumably reflecting his concentration on academic
work to catch up with the standards demanded by his teachers –
and demonstrated by his friends. But China's politics called for
his attention after 1915. The new Chinese republic went wrong,
there was unrest in the country and Japan began her series of
imperialist demands on China. Mao plunged into a busy succession of organizational and political activities. Characteristically,
the first of these involved a protest against the school management. The school's principal had decreed that as from the
autumn term every student would have to pay ten *yuan* for miscellaneous expenses.

The students strongly objected, and one of them wrote a
declaration attacking the principal's personal morals. Mao
demurred, saying it was the school management they were
criticizing, not the private life of the principal, and so he was
allowed to write an additional paragraph to the declaration
along these lines. The declaration was duly printed, but was
intercepted on the way back from the printer by the school dean.
He took the matter to the principal, who decided to expel the
seventeen students involved, including Mao. Luckily some of the
teachers interceded and he was reprieved.

One of Mao's most fruitful initiatives at the school was conceived in the middle of the night when he was playing truant
from the dormitory. He and Siao Yu had formed the habit in the
summer of walking along the river bank after supper and sitting
on the grass slopes of the Miaokaofeng hill. Once in 1915 they
stayed out all night on this hill just behind the school working
out their plans to reform China by starting a new association.

Yuan Shih-kai, a former imperial general, had become president of the new republic, and the two boys eagerly discussed the
dramatic events in Peking and how they would alter China's

future. While they were talking, the school trumpet blasted
below them to signal lights out: they were the only two students
not in bed, but they were too engrossed to care.

A new force was required, they agreed. Siao argued that each
individual citizen would have to be reformed.

'We two could do almost anything!' Mao insisted eagerly. But
Siao disagreed: there would have to be many people, all with the
same ideas. 'We two must organize them.'

They considered their schoolmates and agreed to select the
most intelligent and those with the highest ideals. The ten best
could form a nucleus for a new society, the aims of which would
be to encourage good moral conduct among its members, to
exchange knowledge and to form strong bonds of friendship – all
with the ultimate aim of saving the country.

It was agreed that Mao should write a letter to the student
associations in all the schools of Changsha explaining what they
were doing and inviting their interest, signed with the
pseudonym *Erh Shih Pa Hua Sheng* or 'twenty-eight strokes' in
honour of Mao, the three characters of whose name required
twenty-eight brush strokes. While Mao wrote his first draft, Siao
jotted down some rules for the association; then they exchanged
what they had written and suggested corrections. By this time it
was dawn, and suddenly they heard below them the trumpet
again. It was morning, and the students were being told to get
up. They had spent the whole night working on their project.

It was natural that Mao, searching for like minds, should use
his favourite medium, the newspaper advertisement. 'Feeling
expansive,' he recollected, 'and the need for a few intimate companions, I one day inserted an advertisement in a Changsha
paper, inviting young men interested in patriotic work to make a
contact with me. I specified youths who were hardened and
determined, and who were ready to make sacrifices for their
country. To this advertisement I received three and one-half
replies.'

The disappointing outcome was that three of the young men
who replied eventually opposed or betrayed the Communist
Party, and only one – the 'half' – later lived up partially to Mao's
ideals, although even then Mao criticized his stewardship of the
Communist Party leadership. This was 'a non-committal youth
from a local middle school named Li Li-san', who 'listened to all
I had to say, then went away without making any definite proposals himself, and our friendship never developed.'

Mao also, however, widely circulated his famous *Notice in*

Search of Friends by Mr Twenty-Eight Strokes in the autumn of 1915. This open letter was an invitation in similar terms to Mao's advertisement. Its last line was a quotation from the *Book of Songs*: '*Ying* goes the birds' cry in search of their companions' voice.'

Mao personally stencilled and reproduced his letter and sent it out to all the major schools in Changsha with a note on the envelope saying: 'Please post where everyone can see.' But not many people understood this highly unusual overture, and Mao received only half a dozen replies. The provincial Women's Normal School were apparently deeply suspicious of the writer's motives when they first received Mao's letter.

One person who saw the notice on his school board wrote to Mao positively and received the reply that his letter was like 'the sound of footsteps in a deserted valley; at the sound of your feet my face shone with joy.' A meeting was arranged on a Sunday at the Tingwangtai library. No greetings were exchanged, and instead Mao's first words were to inquire what books the young man had been reading. In fact this young man became quite close to him, and he joined the group debates which Mao and his friends sponsored. Later the network of like-minded friends became formalized into the New People's Study Society.

In 1915 Mao was made Secretary of his school's Student Society, and he introduced innovations borrowed from the schools in Japan, such as the organizing of ball games, swimming, hiking and other sports. Mao also organized an Association for Student Self-Government and became a member of the Society for the Study of Wang Fu-chih, the seventeenth-century Hunanese anti-Manchu thinker. This was founded in 1915 as a forum for patriotic Hunanese who were distressed by China's national degradation, and Mao urged his classmates to attend its weekly meetings.

In September 1915 Chen Tu-hsiu in Peking began to publish the magazine *New Youth*, which heralded the literary renaissance of the new republican China, with articles by such writers as Li Ta-chao and Lu Hsun, mostly in the vernacular language and with a strong concern for democracy and science. Professor Yang ordered several copies of *New Youth* for his students, one of them earmarked for Mao. *New Youth* carried the seminal articles by Li Ta-chao which did more than anything else to inspire the younger generation to smash the old China and remake it anew, calling on them to 'break through the old historical net'. Mao was thrilled by the language and content of these articles.

Mao now began to conduct correspondence with several progressive scholars in different parts of China, using Professor Yang's introduction, on such subjects as national affairs, methods of study, physical culture, philosophy and world affairs. He warned one of them, who was said to be about to join the service of that over-ambitious warlord, President Yuan Shih-kai: 'Today evil forces are gaining with every passing day and justice is buried over. At this time of great crisis, scholars should be hidden from view, like the dragon in his depths. They must wait for a time to act and not be impatient to advance.' This was in November 1915, and within a few days Yuan, in an ill-fated move, announced that he would take the title of emperor – arousing such opposition that he never recovered, and died the following summer.

In March 1917 Mao made his first direct approach to a foreigner. He and Emi Siao wrote a letter to the famous Japanese nationalist intellectual Miyazaki Toten, who had come to China to attend the funeral of a friend. 'We have long admired your towering integrity,' they wrote, 'but fate has not bestowed upon us the fortune of making your acquaintance. Even from afar, the sound of your name inspires men ... Your lofty friendship pierces the sun and the moon; your sincerity of heart moves gods and spirits. This is something rarely heard across the whole earth ... '

The letter then came down to brass tacks: 'Emi and Tse-tung are students in Hunan who have done some reading in the classics and who have to some extent disciplined their wills. Now we long to have the opportunity to gaze upon your noble countenance and to listen to your broad and profound teachings. If, sir, you do actually grant us a meeting, our happiness will know no bounds ...' We do not know whether the meeting ever materialized.

Mao was indeed disciplining his will. 'I myself', he explained, 'was afflicted with a weak body.' So he and his friends became ardent physical culturalists.

In the winter holidays [Mao recalled] we tramped through the fields, up and down mountains, along city walls, and along streams and rivers. If it rained we took off our shirts and called it a rain-bath. When the sun was hot we also doffed shirts and called it a sun-bath. In the spring winds we shouted that this was a new sport called 'wind-bathing'. We slept in the open when frost was already falling and even in November swam in the cold rivers. Perhaps it helped much to build the physique which I was to need so badly later on in many marches back and forth across China.

Mao's first published article, 'A Study of Physical Culture', printed in *New Youth* in April 1917, urged that physical education was, just as important as moral or intellectual. Students who neglected it developed 'white and slender hands' (a phrase from a famous Han poem), but 'when they climb a hill they are short of breath, and when they walk in the water they get cramps in their feet.'

Mao's favourite piece of physical training was now a cold bath every day, which he never missed, even in winter. During his last two years at the school, according to his official biographer,

he organized more than twenty students to go to the well at early morning, haul up water in the bucket, take off their clothes, dowse each other with bucketfuls of water and scrub their whole bodies.

During the rain, snow and bitter piercing cold winds of winter and autumn they would often go to the hill behind the school and, wearing nothing above the waist, run around rubbing their bodies. ... Once, during a school athletics contest, there was suddenly a gigantic downpour. Everyone fought to get back inside the building. Only Mao was not a bit put out. He waited until everyone had gone before he returned to the classroom, dripping wet from head to toe.

Another favourite exercise was swimming. With Tsai Ho-sen and other friends Mao used to swim in the Hsiang River every day after classes had ended. During the summer holiday when they were staying at the Yaolu Mountain they would swim at sunset in a narrow shoal of the Hsiang River: afterwards, in the official record, 'they either sat or slept on the beach, or raced on foot, talking all the time about life and politics. Their bodies had bathed in the clear currents beneath the evening rays of the sun, but their minds had vaulted to the battlefields of human life and the universe.'

Mao was thoroughly familiar with the saying of Mencius: 'When heaven is about to confer a great office on any man, it first exercises his mind with suffering, and his sinews and bones with toil. It exposes his body to hunger and subjects him to extreme poverty. It confounds his undertakings. By all these methods it stimulates his mind, hardens his nature and supplies his incompetencies.' It was as if he knew the trials he would encounter on his way to the top.

Mao's qualities were beginning to be recognized. In June 1917 he was voted 'Student of the Year', in a complicated school election in which 400 students cast votes for different candidates. Mao won the highest rating for moral and intellectual education, with particularly good scores for respectability, self-control, literature, articulation, aptitude and courage.

Just before the summer vacation that year Mao went round to his friend Siao Yu, who had now graduated and was teaching at a school in Changsha that year. He wanted to know how his friend would be spending the holiday.

'I have a new plan', Siao explained, 'for this summer. I have decided that I'm going to try being a beggar.'

Mao was incredulous and inquisitive. A few years ago, Siao elaborated, he had spent two or three days living as a beggar and had found it exhilarating and releasing. He wanted to try it again, this time for a longer period, drawn by the challenge of overcoming the difficulties of living in the society of others without money.

'It sounds very interesting,' Mao said. 'May I go with you?'

Actually, Mao had already read an article in the *People's Paper* about the adventures of two Chinese students who had travelled right across China as far as Tibet. 'This inspired me very much,' he later recalled. 'I wanted to follow their example; but I had no money, and thought I should first try out travelling in Hunan.' Mao makes it sound as if this novel holiday adventure were his own idea, whereas Siao claims it as his own.

It was agreed that they would beg together. Mao came after his term had finished, wearing his old worn white shorts and tunic, and with his head shaved like a soldier. He carried an old umbrella and a bundle containing a change of clothes, a towel, a notebook, a writing brush and an inkbox. Neither of them took a single cent on the journey.

They left Changsha with Siao in front and Mao behind him: Siao later made a drawing of the scene. Soon they came to the River Hsiang. They did not wish to get their belongings wet; they had no money for the row-boat service and they didn't want to take the easy way out of walking up-river to the free ferry. In the end they crossed in a row-boat but did not tell the boatman that they could not pay until they were already half-way over, judging that he would not turn back since he had several other passengers on board. On the other side of the river, after an acrimonious argument with the boatman, they changed from their heavy-soled cloth shoes into straw sandals.

In the afternoon, when they were hungry, they inquired whether any family of intellectuals lived nearby, and wrote a poem for the doctor of arts and retired prefect, previously unknown to them, whose house was not far off. They were received and given money, which enabled them to survive for the next day or two.

Next they went to the house of Ho Shu-heng – their old schoolmate Ho the Moustache.

'We are making an experiment,' Mao explained to the surprised Ho. 'We are trying to travel as far as we can without money. We are living like beggars.'

Ho was shocked. Siao explained that they wanted to see if they were equal to solving difficulties.

'What strange fellows you are,' Ho sighed. 'What strange things you do!'

The two young men continued on their way, but the next house at which they begged would not give them food, so they sat down in the doorway and refused to go until the old man inside would tell them why. Eventually the niggardly householder offered them some uncooked rice if they would go away.

'Only', Mao irritatingly insisted, 'if you promise to treat other beggars who come to your house well.'

The old man finally agreed.

During their wanderings Mao and Siao talked of politics and society. They argued about the character of the third-century-BC emperor Liu Pang, whom Mao considered a great hero because he was the first commoner to become an emperor. Siao, on the contrary, despised him as a cruel tyrant.

'You can't really call him cruel,' Mao objected, 'if you take into account the age in which he lived and compare him with other emperors of his time.'

'He was treacherous,' Siao insisted, 'and absolutely devoid of human sentiment. Remember the friends and generals who risked their lives fighting for him? When his armies were successful, these men became famous leaders and he became afraid that one or other of them might try to usurp his throne; so he had them all killed. Some of them, you remember, were literally cut to pieces, and he had whole families and near relatives of others exterminated! He bore a knife in his breast in the place where his heart should have been ... '

'But if he hadn't killed them,' Mao argued, 'his throne would have been insecure and he probably wouldn't have lasted long as emperor.'

'So in order to be successful in politics, one must kill one's friends?' was Siao's retort, and he concluded his argument: 'From the most ancient times in China, those who have worshipped power have been mean in spirit. The two things seem to go hand in hand. To struggle for a high position by the use of force indicates meanness of spirit.'

But he didn't pursue the argument, knowing that Mao identified himself with Liu Pang in his ambitions.

On another occasion they discussed the institution of the family.

'I think', Mao suggested, 'it is because the idea of family is so strong in China that the people are so lacking in nationalistic sentiment.'

Siao agreed that it was wrong for a son to be regarded as belonging exclusively to the family and bound to support his parents in their old age – 'but neither does he belong to the state! An exaggerated nationalistic idea is just as bad as an exaggerated family system.'

'Your ideas of children', Mao said, 'are new and strange even to me. . . . I believe that the state comes before everything else. . . . In the ideal state of the future, children will be taken from their parents and they will be brought up and educated at public expense. . . . The first and foremost need is for a strong and powerful government!'

Siao objected that if the government became too strong the people's freedom would be curtailed: they would be like a flock of sheep, with the government as shepherd. It should be the other way round, the people being the master and the government their servant.

'But I do regard the people', Mao insisted, 'as a flock of sheep, and it is obvious that the government must play the part of the shepherd. If there is no shepherd, who will guide the sheep?'

Siao said that the people who would become masters would be those sheep of the worst kind, the ones who schemed for power and were the bandits of the flock.

'If you don't want sheep to form the government,' Mao persisted, 'who will be the shepherd?'

A little further along the road, Mao said:

'When people are starving to death, they are not going to meditate on their moral development.'

At an inn they met a young woman who claimed the art of reading faces and palms, so Mao asked her to read theirs. She agreed, provided they promised not to be angry at what she said.

'Your physiognomy', she told Mao, 'indicates that you can become a great officer, a prime minister or a great bandit chief. . . . You are very audacious and have great ambition, but you have no sentiment at all! You could kill ten thousand or even a hundred thousand people without turning a single hair! But you are very patient. If you have not been killed by your enemies when you are thirty-five, you can consider yourself safe by the time you reach fifty, and you will be lucky day by day. Around fifty-five you will be even more fortunate. You will have at least six wives but not many children. I see that you and your family do not get along well together. You will never live in your home town, and I see that you will have no fixed home.'

Mao was amused by this surprisingly accurate reading.

A month after they had set out, they returned to Changsha, having walked 300 miles, and parted ways. Siao told Mao that he would be going home to see his parents. 'What will you do?' he asked.

'I also shall go back home,' Mao replied. 'They were making two pairs of shoes for me and they will be waiting for me.'

Mao's own summary of the journey was: 'We walked through five counties without using a single copper. The peasants fed us and gave us a place to sleep; wherever we went we were kindly treated and welcomed.' In his own mind he compared the journey he had made with that of the second-century historian Ssu-ma Chien, who had at a similar age travelled the Chinese empire of his day and written about the people living in it.

One year during his time at the First Normal School, Mao shared a pavilion with his friends Tsai Ho-sen and Chang Kun-ti, on the top of the Yaolu Mountain on the other side of the river from the city. They took neither breakfast nor supper, and when they did eat it was mainly fresh broad beans. Early every morning they would climb to the top of the hill in order to meditate, and then come down for a cold swim in the river or a pond. Another of their hobbies was 'voice training'. They would go to the hills, Emi Siao recalled, 'and shout, or recite the poets of the Tang Dynasty, or climb up the city walls and there inflate their lungs and yell to the roaring wind.'

While they were living in the pavilion the three boys had little more than a towel, an umbrella and a minimum of clothes each. Mao usually wore a long, grey gown at that time which set him apart from the others. Even when they eventually returned to the school, the three slept out on the playground until winter arrived.

Other friends later joined the trio, and it grew into a kind of summer commune in which these friends worried about their country's future and learnt to undergo hardship as a training for their coming struggles to reform their state and society. This was the young Mao whose earliest known poem read:

To fight with Heaven is infinite pleasure!
To fight with earth is infinite pleasure!
To fight with men is infinite pleasure!

In the autumn of 1917, at the time of the moon cake festival, they discussed whether politics or teaching provided the better avenue for saving China. Mao insisted that it was necessary to fight.

Something of the flavour of these stirring days of physical and intellectual adventure is conveyed in the diary of one of Mao's friends, Chang Kun-ti:

16 September 1917. Today it is Sunday and I walked for an hour or two with Tsai Ho-sen and Mao Jun-chih. After breakfast the three of us took a walk along the railroad tracks. The weather was scorching, but luckily there was a big breeze. . . . After we had walked three miles we rested at a teahouse located on the side of the tracks and drank some tea to quench our thirst. After sitting for a short while we resumed our journey. In another three miles or so we passed the village of Tatopu and two more brought us to a restaurant where we rested and ate lunch. Every large bowl of rice cost fifty *wen* and every bowl of vegetables twenty *wen*. The three of us ate altogether five large bowls of rice. After we ate we rested a bit and thought about bathing in the pool behind the restaurant, but because the water was shallow and didn't even reach our thighs we didn't pursue the idea. And so we went to the restaurant, picked up our travelling things and were off.

Less than a mile away we found a deep and clear creek-dam and the three of us went bathing. Because I was not much of a swimmer I was very cautious. After bathing we went four miles and reached our destination just when the sun was about to set. We ascended the mountain from the rear by the stone steps. There was the blue of the Hsiang River at the foot, and the soaring grace of the mountain peak at the top. It was called Chaoshan (Splendour Mountain). There was a temple there called Splendour Mountain Temple. There were three or four Buddhist monks in the temple, and at first the monks were unwilling to let us stay, and we were of a mind to spend the night in the open air in a grove of trees. Then the monks let us in, and we temporarily gave up our plans for sleeping outside.

After dinner the three of us went down the front slope of the mountain and bathed in the Hsiang River. After bathing we sat on the sand and talked. A cool breeze broke the heat and the sound of the waves punctuated our talks. Our joy knew no bounds. After some time we ascended by the original path, now walking, now talking. We could no longer see the mountain's reflection in the river, because the sun had set. The monks were waiting at the front gate. The starlight shone down from above and suddenly, from amidst the deep green of the trees, there arose an indistinct mist. We soon entered the temple, and the monks led us to a guest house, indicated an empty bedstead as a place for us to sleep, and lent us a small quilt. Outside the house there were a tower and a hut. We went to the small tower to take in the cool air. A strong southern breeze blew recklessly, and the three of us chatted pleasantly for hours. We talked for a long time and enjoyed it immensely.

In another entry a few weeks earlier Chang had described how he had stayed the night at Tsai's house where Mao also spent many happy times: 'The bed consisted of two long benches with one door plank and was set up along the side of the verandah. Tsai said that ever since he had moved to this place to live he had never gone inside to sleep overnight.'

Mao by this time was full of the ambition to change China and create a new society in his ancient land. His friends used to say of him: 'Not a penny in his pocket, a concern for all the world.'

And yet the circumstances of China, especially of Hunan province itself, were steadily deteriorating. The post-imperial political forces had polarized, with a feudally minded warlord government in Peking, to the north, and a rival republican one under Sun in Canton, in the south. The Chinese warlords fighting against each other had 'pulled the wolf into the house', by colluding with one or other of the imperialist powers only too anxious to get a foothold in China. In the Hsiang River in full view of Changsha city were warships flying the 'sun flag' of Japan, the 'checkered flag' of the USA and the 'rice-character flag' of Britain, while on the river bank itself stood the warehouses of Butterfield and Swire, Jardine Matheson and other foreign companies.

Natural disasters added to the damage inflicted by the soldiers. In 1915 four rivers, including the Hsiang, overflowed to cause widespread destruction and death. In these conditions bandits were freely plundering and burning towns and villages, raping women and holding prisoners for ransom. The province had not seen as bad times for several hundred years, and no ray of hope appeared on the horizon. The view was widespread that China was about to collapse and that things were utterly hopeless.

Mao and his friends were exceptions, retaining a confidence and a sense of responsibility about the future of their country. They were particularly inspired in the second half of 1917 by Tolstoy, 'the great spirit of Russia', and his dreams of universal love and peace. In Chang Kun-ti's diary for 23 September he quoted Mao as saying after their swim: 'Our people's thought is

narrow. How can China have a great revolutionary in philosophy and ethics like Russia's Tolstoy who would develop new
thought by washing away all the old thought?' Mao also called
for 'a revolution of the family-system and of the relations between teacher and student'. What he meant by revolution was
'not a confrontation of arms, but the elimination of the old and
the establishment of the new.'

Mao elaborated some of these thoughts in a commentary written in his Paulsen textbook:

> I was worried that our China would soon perish, but now I know this
> is not so. I have no doubt about setting up a new form of government,
> changing the national character, or improving society. But how to effect
> this change is the problem. My idea is that we must reconstruct, so that
> new things will come into being through destruction and will have a
> new existence just as a baby is born from its mother's womb. It is so
> with the nation, with the people, and with mankind. Throughout the
> centuries people have raised great revolutions, constantly cleansing the
> old and renewing it.

In a letter to two scholars in Peking in August 1917, Mao
asserted the need to refashion the philosophy of China. It was
not simply a question of substituting Western ideology, because
the bourgeois democracy of the West had also shown itself
incapable of solving the problems of mankind. Ideas from both
East and West should be used: 'I agree that the East is backward, but the Western ideology should also be remoulded at the
same time.'

Once at a football game between the First Normal School and
Yale-in-China (the preparatory school favoured by Westernized
Chinese), Mao suddenly stood up in the crowd of spectators to
yell for his team to, 'Beat the slaves of foreigners!'

In 1917, having been the secretary of the school's Student
Society for two years, Mao became its general affairs officer and
head of educational research. He decided that the
Society should pay attention to both scholarly study and physical training, and it established fifteen departments devoted to
various aspects of these, including handicrafts, military arts,
swordsmanship and gymnastics. He even wanted it to start a
commercial department which would become a sort of co-
operative, but the school would not agree to it.

Mao was also instrumental in ensuring that the department
heads in the Society were senior students rather than teachers, as
had been the case in the past. He argued that fourth- and fifth-
year students on the eve of graduation should develop their

capacity for initiative and administration. Among the resolutions passed by the Society at Mao's suggestion were plans to publish student marks and set up a grades exhibition centre, found a library and put together a budget.

What it amounted to was that the boys at the school were to stay on after class in the evenings to do various kinds of academic or athletic work to develop further their personalities and skills. Such a large self-governing student body was unprecedented in Hunan, and it was apparently mostly Mao's doing. The Student Society held open debates, scholarly research meetings and public lectures and organized athletic meetings and outings. To provide activity on rainy days, Mao set up ping-pong tables in the school.

Mao would usually take the chair at Student Society meetings, and his semi-official Chinese biographer makes this comment:

When everyone was in the midst of vehement argument he would not rashly express his own opinion, but would wait until everyone had finished making his own ideas known; then he would get up and present a summation. His summaries always included the good points and excluded the poor ones. ... He was able to make a penetrating analysis of every problem and every argument, and for this reason everyone was always in hearty agreement with him. Many arguments found a solution because of his incisive and uncomplicated analysis.

Mao had by now made contact with many scholars and students in other cities, largely through correspondence. 'Gradually,' he later recalled, 'I began to realize the necessity for a more closely-knit organization. In 1917, with some other friends, I helped to found the New People's Study Society.' There were a number of similar groups being formed at this time in the big cities of China, such as the Awareness Society which Chou En-lai helped to start in Tientsin. All were more or less influenced by the periodical *New Youth*.

The New People's Study Society which Mao founded, following his night-time brain-wave on the hillside with Siao Yu in 1915, was formally launched on 18 April 1918 by a meeting held at the home of Tsai Ho-sen. Among the thirteen founder members present that Sunday, apart from Mao and Tsai, were Ho Shu-heng, Chen Chang, Chang Kun-ti and Lo Hsueh-tsan. All the others wanted Mao to be the general secretary, but he declined the office and was eventually made vice-secretary. A year later, the membership had grown to more than seventy, most of them outstanding students and progressive teachers.

There were even a few women members, including Tsai Chang, Ho-sen's sister, which at that time was highly unusual. The problem of women's status was a concern of the Society from the start. The Society met every week or every fortnight to discuss under Mao's chairmanship issues of scholarship or politics. Sometimes, according to one account, 'the discussion of a problem would last for as long as a week.'

Mao drafted the Society's Manifesto, setting as the aim 'to reform China and the world', while opposing prostitution, gambling, concubinage and similar low behaviour. Among the dozens of candidates whom Mao recruited into his New People's Study Society in 1918 were some who later constituted the nucleus of the Maoist faction in the Chinese Communist Party. They included Liu Shao-chi, Jen Pi-shih and Wang Jo-fei.

As if all this were not enough, Mao also took charge of running a night school. This had been done by the Normal School teachers before 1917, but when they were unable to continue it, the Student Society took it over. Mao saw this enterprise as an opportunity for the school to make an impact beyond its gates, and also to create in the night school some of the things which were depressingly lacking in the First Normal itself, where Mao was often bored. He said to a friend one morning: 'Last night I almost quit school. I went up to the Principal's office three times prepared to make a request to leave.'

The night school aimed at the industrial workers in the immediate neighbourhood. It advertised for students in *paihua*, i.e. the vernacular as distinct from the literary language, and this was quite a novelty for those days.

Copies of the invitation were distributed through the police department, but only nine persons responded, so Mao and his fellow students took 600 copies of the announcement on a house-to-house distribution, as a result of which more than 120 people registered in the first three days, and others applied later, even though limited space prevented them from being accepted. 'It was like the wailing of a baby waiting to be fed,' Mao wrote in the *Night School Record*.

The announcement was composed by Mao. 'My friends,' it began,

come listen to me say a few words in vernacular: Do you know what is the greatest disadvantage with which you are all faced? It is precisely that, to use a common expression, "you can't write down what is spoken; you can't read what is written; and you can't do figures." Under these circumstances, isn't a man just like stick or stone? Therefore you should all gain a little knowledge. ... Our First Normal School has set up a night school especially for you workers. Classes are held for two hours every evening, from Monday to Friday. We teach you how to write letters, how to work out bills. ... We provide the instruction completely free of charge. Classes are held at night, so they do not interfere with your work.'

During the 1910s Hunan had become a cockpit for the struggle between northern and southern warlords of no particular political persuasion, and almost every year armies entered the main cities from one side or the other to recruit soldiers, buy horses, burn and loot. Mao observed this at first hand on a number of occasions, first in 1913 and again in 1917 and 1918. The visiting armies often took over the schools as quarters, so that education was constantly interrupted. The First Normal School in Changsha had a large and capacious dormitory and was next to the railway, which made it especially attractive for visiting armies. It was occupied three times during Mao's career there.

In 1913 the students and faculty were incensed because the temporary military authorities censored articles opposing their policies. Mao, under the name of the Student Society, reprinted some earlier articles by leading intellectuals and made them into a small pamphlet which set out arguments against the disliked policies, and all the students praised him, saying: 'All we knew was how to criticize surreptitiously. We couldn't think how to take it any further.' The military sent police to the school to search the students' books and baggage, but Mao had prepared for this beforehand, and they found nothing.

When soldiers approached again in November 1917, Mao led the school's student volunteer army, equipped with wooden practice rifles. But when the troops actually threatened to enter the city he acquired a few real guns from the local police station and held the area behind the school. In the words of one account:

Timid students and faculty all hid in the courtyard of the dormitory, in the rear, not daring to make a move. The school's working personnel now all took their orders from Mao Tse-tung. He waited until Wang's defeated troops were not far away and then ordered the police to sound their rifles at the top of the hill. The rest of the students who were holding the wooden rifles shot off a great number of firecrackers, yelling in unison, 'Fu Liang-tso has fled and the Kui Army has already entered the city. If you hand over your weapons there will be no trouble!'

As a result of this stratagem the straggling troops handed over their rifles and dispersed after being given money by the local chamber of commerce. Mao again led his fellow students in organizing a 'garrison force' the following year, when the city was invaded a third time. It joined with other schools to organize a student public safety corps to patrol the centre of the city and stop the looting. It also organized a team to go out on the streets and help women and children who had fallen victim to the fighting. 'Well,' Mao commented, 'this is the first time I have taken military command.' It was, as he sensed, not going to be the last.

'Finally,' Mao later recollected in self-deprecatory mood, 'I actually got my degree', in May 1918. At the end of that month he handed over the Student Society to his successors. He remembered his life at the First Normal School as eventful: 'During this period my political ideas began to take shape. Here also I acquired my first experience in social action.'

He was still, of course, unfamiliar with the work of Karl Marx. At the time he left school in 1918, 'my mind was a curious mixture of ideas of liberalism, democratic reformism and Utopian Socialism. I had somewhat vague passions about "nineteenth-century democracy", utopianism and old-fashioned liberalism, and I was definitely anti-militarist and anti-imperialist.'

About the actual content of his education in the classrooms of Changsha, Mao remained scathing to the end. Nearly fifty years later he summed up what he felt he had learned in school:

I myself studied in the Green Forest University, the school of hard knocks, where I managed to learn something. I read Confucius, the Four Books and the Five Classics, and, after reading them for six years, I could recite them even though I couldn't understand them. I believed then in Confucius and even wrote some articles. Later I attended bourgeois schools for seven years. Six years plus seven years make a total of thirteen years. I studied the whole bag of bourgeois natural sciences and social sciences. I also studied education. I spent five years in normal school and two years in middle school, including my time in the library. . . . What I learned in thirteen years was useless for making revolution. I could use only the tool – language. Writing articles is a tool.

All the same, it was comparatively easy to identify the social problems of the nation from the classrooms, corridors and hillside fields of Changsha. After his graduation Mao now had to face the immensely more difficult challenge of finding a way to implement the ideals so firmly lodged in his mind.

4
CONVERSION

Mao was twenty-four years old and his student career was over, but the initial weeks of his new life as a free and employable adult were spent in a romantic prolongation of the life he had come to love. With his select circle of friends he continued to live on Yaolu Mountain in the modest 'commune' which had by then acquired the grand title of 'Hunan University Preparatory Office'. Here they lived on their accustomed diet of boiled rice and beans, striding up the mountain barefoot or in straw sandals to fetch firewood and walking the long distance to the nearest water. As always, they devoted the rest of their time to studying books and discussing their plans for the future, occasionally going to sight-see at the Aiwan Pavilion, the Yunlu Palace or the gravestone of the Emperor Yu.

During that summer of 1918 Mao made another tour of Hunan on foot, this time with Tsai Ho-sen, carrying a towel wrapped around an umbrella, a pair of sandals and little else. The two friends, soon to become close collaborators in the Communist Party, spent two months investigating the manners and customs of different villages, the lives of the peasants, the conditions of the rent, the relations between landlords and tenants and the dire poverty of the landless, often living out in the open on hill haws and berries.

Meanwhile the members of the New People's Study Society met to discuss their future and raised the idea of going abroad to study. 'First,' Mao told the meeting, 'we must decide on the country, and then on how to get there. We must have everything well organized. I think it is best if our colleagues study abroad in different countries. The chief ones should be America, England, France and Japan.'

Professor Yang Chang-chi had gone to take up a post at Peking University, and had written to Mao telling him about the new movement for young Chinese to go to France. 'Many students from Hunan', Mao recollected, 'were planning trips to

France, to study under the "work and learn" scheme which France used to recruit young Chinese to her cause during the World War. Before leaving China these students planned to study French in Peking.'

Mao vigorously supported the idea of people joining this movement and getting to understand the real facts of the revolutions in Russia and Europe, and so he and Tsai began to organize for this among the progressive students of their own province. Tsai went to Peking at the end of June to get further details and make the necessary connections. In the letters that he sent back, Tsai urged Mao to join him in Peking in order to take up the leadership of the work-study programme for France, adding that Professor Yang also looked forward to Mao's coming to study at Peking University.

In September Mao responded to the appeal, taking with him to Peking more than twenty comrades volunteering for the programme. The Yellow River had overflowed its banks that year and cut the railway line, so that the trains were blocked near Chengchow in Honan. Mao took advantage of the delay to visit villages in the vicinity and investigate the living conditions of the peasants.

When Mao did reach Peking there were altogether over forty young men who had come from Hunan for the programme, more than from any other province. Even Mao's old teacher, Hsu Te-li, left his professorship in Hunan to go to France when he was already over forty.

Mao paid particular attention to encouraging his young women friends to take advantage of the programme. In Changsha he had already organized a Girls' Society for Work and Study in France. Years later, when Mao was famous, there were rumours that at this time he had taken a more than intellectual interest in Tsai Chang, the sister of his best friend (who in fact went on to marry the Communist Vice-Premier, Li Fu-chun) and one or two other women members of the New People's Study Society. For what it is worth, Tsai Chang herself recalled that she and her brother as well as Mao had all at that time expressed themselves against marriage, declaring 'that they would never marry'.

When a group of Hunanese girls, including Tsai Chang and her brother's future wife, were about to embark for France, Mao said earnestly to the latter: 'I hope that you will be able to lead a large group of female comrades abroad, for each one you take with you is one you save.'

Along with Siao Yu and two other friends, Mao was invited to live in Peking with his former teacher, Professor Yang, in his new house at Toufuchih Hutung. But they soon moved to a two-roomed house at 7 Chian East Lane, Sanyenching (Three Eyes Well) Street near the university. This was a typical Peking house with a courtyard overlooked by rooms on three sides. No fewer than eight enthusiasts from the New People's Study Society of Changsha squeezed themselves into this accommodation, using one room as a study and the other as a bedroom.

The bed was a *kang*, the North-Chinese-style stove bed made of bricks and heated by a fire underneath. But the eight Hunanese students could not afford to heat the fire, and so they had to huddle together on the *kang* to keep themselves warm in the icy cold of the Peking winter. 'When we were all packed fast on the *kang*,' Mao recollected, 'there was scarcely room enough for any of us to breathe. I used to have to warn people each side of me when I wanted to turn over.' They cooked their meals on a small stove and shared all the work and expenses. There was only one coat between the eight of them, so they had to take it in turns to go out during the coldest spells. By the end of the year the one coat had increased to three, but Mao himself never did manage to buy one.

The house was excellently placed, however, for the work and intellectual interests of Mao and his friends. They could go freely to Peking University and attend lectures. Lo Hsueh-tsan, one of the eight, wrote about them in a letter home, that they were 'all of excellent character and hard-studying men, and I have great admiration for them. I am with them morning and night and am constantly benefited.'

Despite all his exercise, Mao's health was not good. According to one of his friends in Peking at that time he was spitting blood, presumably with tuberculosis, and therefore insisted on having separate chopsticks from the others. He also suffered from an infection on the sole of his foot, for which he was treated in hospital for about a month.

But if the conditions were tough, 'the beauty of the old capital was a vivid and living compensation', as Mao afterwards remembered. He admired the early northern spring in Peking's parks and old palace grounds. 'I saw the white plum blossoms flower while the ice still held solid over the Peihai Lake. I saw the willows over Peihai with the ice crystals hanging from them and remembered the description of the scene by a Tang poet who wrote about Peihai's winter-jewel trees looking like "ten thousand peach-trees blossoming". The innumerable trees of Peking aroused my wonder and admiration.'

In the end, although Mao was invited to go to France, he chose to stay behind. This was an interesting decision on his part, the first time for him to turn down a major opportunity for advancement. He explained afterwards: 'I did not want to go to Europe. I felt that I did not know enough about my own country, and that my time would be more profitably spent in China.'

To his old teacher, Hsu Te-li, Mao explained his reasons in a slightly different way.

Mao made a special study of the failure of the 1911 revolution [Hsu said afterwards] and concluded that it was caused by the isolation of the Chinese intelligentsia from the common people. It was imperative that the intellectual leaders of any successful revolution must be in close touch with the peasant masses of the country. It was for this reason that Mao refused to come with me when I invited him to go to France just after the last war was ended. He preferred instead to increase his knowledge of China.

Mao gave his student friends four reasons for staying behind. One was the obvious financial problem. He had no money at all, and although the fare required was greatly reduced, 200 *yuan* still represented a huge sum for him and he knew no one who might lend it him. Secondly, he was no linguist, and at school had not even been able to manage the simplest English pronunciation – let alone French. Thirdly, he felt that in Peking he could not only continue his studies but also recruit new members for the Study Society and act as a reliable contact in Peking for those going to France. Finally, he realized that he was a man of action whose future lay in political organization rather than in scholarship, so that he was not really interested in going abroad for the sake of study. Study for Mao was a means to an end.

To those whom he did not know so well Mao stressed, first of all, his greater age, being twenty-five at this time (the others had an average age of about nineteen), and secondly his poor aptitude for languages. But the real reason was perhaps never clearly expressed, though it came out in a passage in a social analysis of classes in China written by Mao seven years later, where he noted that students from small landlord families who studied abroad in capitalist cities had 'obviously, alongside their being half-Chinese, become half-foreign'. Mao feared that the French experience would render him an internationalist in culture, and therefore lose him the possibility of gaining genuine support as a leader from the ordinary men and women of his own country. He also sensed that he would not shine among his peers in a foreign environment.

The others agreed that Mao should remain behind, and Siao Yu and Tsai Ho-sen had several discussions about how he could support himself in the capital. They were recruiting members for the Society at the university, and so the best place for him to work would be there. 'We thought', Siao later recollected, 'of a classroom-cleaner job because he could listen to the lectures, even as he carried out his simple tasks.' The university used to employ someone to clean the blackboards and sweep the class-rooms after each lecture, and the person who did this light work was inevitably put in frequent contact with the professors and students. But how could Mao obtain such a job?

They went to the Rector, who had been taking a close interest in the work-study in France movement, and he gave them a note to the Director of the University Library, Li Ta-chao: 'Mao Tse-tung requires employment in the university in pursuance of a work-study programme. Please find a job for him in the library . . . ' Li dutifully assigned Mao to the task of cleaning the lib-rary and keeping the books and newspapers tidy.

'This', Siao remembered, 'was all accomplished through an intermediary, since Li was a very highly placed person and had no direct contacts with hiring menial workers.' Years later Li remembered the incident with embarrassment. 'When I gave Mao that job of cleaning the library,' he told Siao, 'I was merely obeying the Rector's orders. Naturally I did not know your good friend and I hope you will forgive me.'

Li Ta-chao was the man whose articles in *New Youth* had so inspired Mao in the past and who was to become the effective introducer of Marxism into China, and now Mao found himself in the adjoining room. He was paid, he recalled, 'the generous sum of eight dollars a month'. Five or six dollars was enough, in those days, to live for a month, but Mao continued to be extremely frugal, eating only in the evening, and then only sweet potatoes and peanuts, never meat or green vegetables. He is said to have invented a novel method of cooking Peking cabbage stalks, thrown away by most people, by boiling them with salt.

If Mao had hoped through this employment to meet the intel-lectual giants of the day, he was disappointed. 'My office', he complained, 'was so low that people avoided me. One of my tasks was to register the names of people who came to read newspapers, but to most of them I didn't exist as a human being.' Among the people who came to use the library Mao recognized famous literary and intellectual names, people in whom he was intensely interested. 'I tried to begin conversations with them on political and cultural subjects, but they were very busy men. They had no time to listen to an assistant librarian speaking southern dialect.'

Hu Shih, doyen of the Chinese intellectual renaissance at this period, recalled afterwards that Mao asked to listen to his lectures. 'As a prose writer', Hu commented, 'he was superb.' But there is another story that when Mao tried to ask Hu a question after one of his lectures, Hu rebuffed him because he was not a registered student.

Neither Chen Tu-hsiu, the dean of literature and editor of *New Youth*, nor Li Ta-chao, the librarian and essayist, who were the two radical leaders in the university and indisputable pioneers of Marxism in China, paid any attention to Mao during this first ignominious visit to the Chinese capital. He had no way of making any claim on their attentions. Once again, as before, Mao was given the cold shoulder by those who superficially were his superiors. It was the story of his life: the more he was spurned as a rude and unpolished provincial, the more he determined to force his claims on society through the hard road of radical organized politics.

His time in Peking was not entirely wasted. He joined the Philosophy Society and the Journalism Society, which enabled him to attend university classes. In these circles he met such people as Chang Kuo-tao, later his rival for the Communist Party leadership.

But his best friends in the capital were anarchists, including three of his Hunanese room-mates, as well as another student. None of these four became Communists, although all of them advocated mass action and revolution. They introduced Mao to the books of Kropotkin, Bakunin and Tolstoy.

He was in Peking at a time when the impact of the October Revolution in Russia was being digested in China. Thirty years later he declared that: 'Before the October Revolution, the Chinese were not only ignorant of Lenin and Stalin, they did not even know of Marx and Engels. The salvoes of the October Revolution helped the progressives in China ... to adopt the proletarian world outlook as the instrument for studying a nation's destiny and considering anew their own problem. Follow the path of the Russians – that was their conclusion.'

In October 1918 Mao joined the Marxist Study Group of Li

Ta-chao, as well as a similar but broader fellowship, the Young People's China Study Group, of which Li was also an organizer. Mao's own reading at this time was traditionalist in bent. He told his friends that he was reading a lot of history, especially the classic work of Ssu-ma Kuang.

But it was Marxism which appealed to Mao's sense of injustice. He liked its rational and materialist premises, its doctrinal certitude and its assertion of human equality and dignity, but even more he admired the example of its successful use as a revolutionary doctrine in Russia. The same went for many others of Mao's generation in China.

The following February, just before Mao left Peking, Li Ta-chao's article entitled 'Youth and the Villages' was published. Some of its phrases must have struck home to Mao, especially this one: 'Our China is a rural nation and the majority of the labouring class is composed of these peasants. If they are not liberated then our whole nation will not be liberated.'

It was also here in Peking that Mao, according to his own acknowledgement, had his first affair of the heart. 'Here ... ', he recalled, 'I met and fell in love with Yang Kai-hui. She was the daughter of my ... ethics teacher, Yang Chang-chi, who had made a great impression on me in my youth, and who afterwards was a genuine friend in Peking.' But they were not to be married until the following year.

Early in 1919 Mao accompanied the students bound for France on their journey to Shanghai, where they were to take ship. 'I had a ticket only to Tientsin', he remembered, 'and I did not know how I was to get any farther.' With his usual luck, however, he was able to borrow $20 from another student which enabled him to go on to Nanking. During these travels in northern China, Mao was able to see many of the great sights of his country.

'I walked on the ice', he proudly recalled, 'of the Gulf of Peihai,' and circled the historic walls of Paoting, Suchow and Nanking. 'I stopped at Chufu and visited Confucius' grave. I saw the little stream where Confucius' disciples bathed their feet and the little town where the sage lived as a child.' Mao saw the famous tree which Confucius is supposed to have planted, and the birthplace of Mencius. He climbed Taishan, the celebrated mountain of Shantung and one of China's five most famous peaks.

Most Chinese intellectuals were desperately concerned at this time about the domestic upheavals of the country as well as its international fate in the peace conference at Versailles. Japan openly bought over part of the Chinese delegation to consent to a Japanese presence in China, and the other victorious nations were no more willing to give up their extraterritorial "rights' in China however hard Woodrow Wilson preached self-determination. The May Fourth movement of 1919 was a spontaneous student protest in Peking against all this. Mao, however, was busy visiting the holy places of his own land – and visibly drawing nourishment from them.

From Nanking onwards, 'I was again without a copper, and without a ticket.' This time none of his group could lend him any money, and he did not know how he was going to proceed. 'But the worst of the tragedy happened when a thief stole my only pair of shoes!' Good luck came to his rescue as usual, in the form of an old friend from Hunan whom he ran into outside the railway station. This man lent him enough to buy some shoes and a ticket to Shanghai, where he found that enough funds had been raised not only to send the students to France but also to get Mao back to Changsha.

The students sailed late in March on a Japanese ship. Mao saw his friends off and then returned to Changsha, where he took up lodgings on the side of the river opposite the city and resumed his old Spartan life of one meal a day of beans and rice.

One of his duties back on his home ground was to maintain the cohesion of his New People's Study Society, many of whose members were now in different parts of Europe. He organized a monthly correspondence system, printing and sending out for further study the letters sent to him by members in France as well as their questions: three volumes of this correspondence were eventually published under his editing.

Inevitably, however, the harmony of this young group could not be perpetuated. Most of them were revolutionaries, like Mao, who repudiated the status quo, but there also emerged a reform faction ready to work from the status quo, as well as a group in the middle which could not make up its mind one way or the other. Later, when the Communist Party was formally started in Hunan, the society broke up and most – but not all – of its members joined the new party.

Mao now began to put his learning to practical use, by teaching history at the Hsiuyeh Primary School. As a bachelor he lived at the school with his usual collection of simple belongings – 'one old blue mosquito net made of Chinese linen,' according to the official record, 'an old sleeping mat, a few books for a pillow and a long gown of glazed cotton which he wore regularly and which had been washed so much that it was quite faded, somewhere between blue and white.' At long last, at the age of twenty-five, Mao was a wage-earner.

Life in a primary school was hardly, however, luxurious. Within a few weeks of taking up his classroom duties, Mao gave, in the course of a long article, this picture of a teacher's lot:

My friends! We are primary school teachers. .... All day long we eat chalk dust, yet there is no place where we can relax and clear our throats of it. .... There are so many classes which we must go to teach, right on the hour with no deviation permitted; we don't have the time left over, we don't have strength left over to carry out our own studies – our spirits just aren't up to it! Thus we have been turned into gramophones, all day long repeating nothing but authentic versions of the lectures handed down to us by our professors of by-gone days.

Our bellies are empty. Our monthly salaries amount to eight or ten *yuan*, and even from this they still make deductions. Some of our honourable headmasters, moreover, . . . take the money sent by the government to line their own pockets. . . .

Then personal tragedy struck. One of the reasons for Mao's hasty return from Shanghai was the news that his mother was ill, and in October of 1919 she died of acute tonsillitis. Mao wrote an ode for the occasion:

My mother had many excellent virtues. The first was her universal love.
This love extended to relatives and friends, both near and far.
Her compassion and kindness moved the hearts of everyone.
Wherever her love went, it came from true sincerity.
She never lied or used deception.
In reason and judgement her mind was clear and true.
Everything she did was done with care and consideration.
When we were sick she held our hands, her heart full of sorrow;
Yet she admonished us, saying, 'You should strive to be good.'

Despite his teaching commitment, Mao threw himself into organizational work in Changsha. Within the space of five weeks, in June and July 1919, he helped to launch three associations, all concerned with reforms of one kind or another.

But his distinctive contribution to the Hunan political scene was through journalism. On 14 July there appeared the first issue of a new magazine, the organ of the United Students' Association, called the *Hsiang River Review*, with Mao as editor. It consisted of one sheet of newsprint cut into quarters. The first issue was quickly sold out, and the print order for subsequent issues was 5000. In this *Review* Mao explained to the progressive readers of Hunan the trade union and strike activities in the West and the moves made by the Western powers to divide the spoils of war at the Versailles peace conference. He denounced Lloyd George and Woodrow Wilson as 'a gang of robbers'.

On the night before the *Review* went to press, it often proved impossible, in the delicate words of Mao's Chinese biographer, 'to gather together all the manuscripts that had been promised'. Mao would then write more articles to fill the gaps. Despite the sweltering weather and the mosquitoes, he 'often wrote until after midnight. In the morning, as soon as he had got out of bed, and with no time to wash or eat, he would immediately go to the classroom and teach.' He was responsible for writing the whole of the first issue, two-thirds of the second and half of the third and fourth issues of the *Review* – and his responsibility did not end with writing and editing, but extended to setting type and proofreading. Mao even sold his product on the streets.

In the second issue of the *Hsiang River Review* appeared the opening instalment of Mao's first major article, entitled 'The Great Union of the Popular Masses'. It was here that Mao set out his earliest strategic concept of the need to establish a popular revolutionary united front, urging his countrymen to follow Marx and form peasants' and workers' organizations.

The decadence of the state [the article declared] the sufferings of humanity and the darkness of society have all reached an extreme. . . . The common people have long been entombed in the fields and the factories which pour forth the money, looking with envy at the ease and comfort of the capitalists, and they want to dip their own fingers in the gravy . . .

We are awakened! The world is ours, the nation is ours, society is ours. . . . Our Chinese people possesses great inherent capacities! . . . One day, the reform of the Chinese people will be more profound than that of any other people, and the society of the Chinese people will be more radiant than that of any other people. The great union of the Chinese people will be achieved earlier than that of any other place or people.

Gentlemen! Gentlemen! We must all exert ourselves! . . . Our golden age, our age of glory and splendour, lies before us!

The *Hsiang River Review* upset the government in Changsha, and after the fifth issue it was banned. Mao immediately took over the editorship of another journal, *New Hunan*, a weekly publication of the local student association, but that in turn was closed by the government.

By this time Governor Chang Ching-yao was getting angry with the students, and in September he called a meeting of their representatives to rebuke them for interfering in politics, and in particular for disrupting the government's policy towards Japan. 'If you don't listen to me,' he told them, 'I'll cut off your heads.' Faced by this kind of threat, one of the girl students began to cry, but Mao, who was standing near her, told her to pay no more attention to Chang than to a dog barking.

Mao had become most eloquent in his journalism about the status of women, especially the double standard applied regarding chastity – the loss of which was a frequent cause of suicide among women, whereas the sexual adventures of men did not usually carry any disgrace. He wrote about this in a magazine called *Women's Bell*, and his long article on the 'The Great Union of the Popular Masses' included this passage:

> My friends! We are women. .... We too are human beings; why then are we not allowed to take part in government? We too are human beings; why then are we not allowed social intercourse? ...
> Shameless, villainous men make us their playthings and force us to prostitute ourselves to them indefinitely. Devils, who destroy the freedom of love! Devils, who destroy the sanctity of love! They keep us surrounded all day long, but this 'chastity' is confined to us women! Everywhere there are shrines to virtuous women, but where are the shrines for chaste boys?

On 14 November 1919 something happened in Changsha which became a sensation in the province and stirred Mao to the core. A young woman called Chao was engaged by her father, an optician, through a match-maker in the usual tradition, to marry the son of a rich antique dealer in the neighbourhood. She formed a strong dislike for the boy on the few occasions when she was allowed to see him before the wedding, and yet her protests went unheard. When the day of the wedding came, as the unfortunate Miss Chao was being installed in the bridal chair to be delivered to the home of her bridegroom, she drew out a dagger and cut her throat.

The suicide became a *cause célèbre*. A local newspaper commentary described the poor woman as 'a sacrifice to the reform of the marriage system'. Within forty-eight hours Mao published the first of nine articles on the tragedy in the *Ta Kung Pao*, the Changsha newspaper, ending the series only two weeks later. They were influenced by Ibsen, to whom an entire issue of *New Youth* had recently been devoted.

Mao called the bridal sedan chair a 'prisoner's cart'. He went further than other critics in saying that it was not merely the bride's and groom's families which should bear the guilt for Miss Chao's death, but also society itself. Young people, he declared, should have the courage to stand up for themselves and resist demands which the older generations made of them. Mao satirized:

As soon as a person drops out of his mother's belly, it is said that his marriage has been settled. When he grows up and it is necessary for him to marry, he himself would never dare raise the issue of marriage. He merely calls upon his parents and match-maker to arrange it. ... We must ... destroy all superstitions regarding marriage, of which the most important is the destruction of belief in 'predestined marriage'.

Once this belief has been abolished, all support for the policy of parental arrangement will be undermined and the notion of incompatibility between husband and wife will immediately appear in society. Once a man and wife demonstrate incompatibility, the army of the family revolution will arise *en masse* and a great wave of freedom of marriage and freedom of love will break over China.

As for the girl's suicide, Mao rejected it. 'Man's goal is to seek life, and he should not go against the grain of his natural tendency and seek death. ... Although suicide results from the fact that society deprives people of all hope ... , we should struggle against society in order to regain the hope that we have lost. ... We should die fighting .... '

Was the passion which Mao exhibited in the cause of Miss Chao's suicide a sign of lingering guilt over abandoning the marriage which his own parents had arranged?

The campaign against the hated Governor Chang came to a head on 2 December, when the United Students' Association, flouting his orders, held a public demonstration to burn Japanese goods. Students who had been investigating breaches of the boycott against Japanese products brought in loads of Japanese cloth to be burnt in one of the central squares. But the Governor's brother broke up the rally with a battalion of mounted troops who insulted the student leaders.

That night Mao summoned all the members of the New People's Study Society and the leaders of the United Students' Association, and told them that the people's anger against Governor Chang had reached boiling-point. Chang was opposed by other warlords in central China and was thus isolated. It was a good time to move against him.

The students organized a general strike of classes to begin two or three days later, and formed an Expel Chang Delegation to carry out propaganda and diplomatic work against the governor in various centres of China including Peking. At the beginning of 1920 Mao took charge of the group which was to go to Peking, subsidized by the Changsha Chamber of Commerce, for this purpose.

But his motives may not have been wholly political. On 17 January his revered Professor Yang Chang-chi died in Peking. Mao's friend Siao Yu argued that the Spartan habit of taking cold baths in the icy winter of Peking might have contributed to the Professor's death. The funeral notice which was signed by Mao as well as other students of the late teacher read: 'Mr Yang was pure in action, earnest in ambition and fond of study. ... Our country's learning is not prospering, and scholars of merit are as few as morning stars. Certainly he was fond of study to the end of his days, but because Heaven did not grant him a longer life, he did not achieve even one of the many ambitions he had when alive.'

Even in death, one could say that Mao was ready to chide his best teacher for weak political judgement. Undoubtedly Mao used the opportunity of being in Peking to help in the settlement of the Professor's affairs, including the question of the future of his daughter, of whom more will be heard.

But Mao did not travel directly to Peking. He and his group stopped in Wuhan, where he drafted a proclamation calling for the expulsion of Governor Chang and sent it to the local newspapers. He also pulled off a propaganda coup by photographing at a bus station there more than twenty sacks of opium seed which were being sent to Governor Chang in Changsha by a member of his family. When this was published in the papers, the Governor's reputation fell even further. Mao also held a mass meeting with the Hunanese students and others to report on the 'Campaign to Expel Chang'.

On this second visit to Peking Mao stayed at the Lama Temple at 97 Peichang Street. He busily tried to spread the anti-Chang message, and took part in an appeal to the Premier's office on 4 February, though without result. He was made head of the news agency to promote the fight not only against Chang but against militarism in general, and he also joined the Young China Association, a patriotic group organized by Li Ta-chao and others to oppose Japanese imperialism.

Mao wrote a continuous stream of letters to his comrades in

Changsha, reporting on the situation in Peking and giving his own recommendations about their activities in Hunan. He suggested that they should organize a Russia Travel Team to go and study the experience of the Russian revolution, and he repeatedly urged that the New People's Study Society become a militant organization with a unified ideology, carefully carrying out a well-formulated two-year or three-year plan for its activities in Changsha.

Inevitably, Mao also found time for a great deal of reading, notably the new translations of Communist works which were just then appearing in Peking. 'Three books', he afterwards remembered, 'especially deeply carved my mind, and built up in me a faith in Marxism from which, once I had accepted it as the correct interpretation of history, I did not afterwards waver.' These books were the *Communist Manifesto* (of which it was said by a friend of the translator, who had taken it from a Japanese text, that he had not really understood it at all), Kautsky's *Class Struggle* and Kirkupp's *History of Socialism*.

If Mao had indeed come to Peking in order to pay respects to his dead professor, he suffered there another loss which most Chinese would find heavy but which Mao probably affected to dismiss. In March his father died of typhoid. Forty years later, revisiting his birthplace and remembering his parents, Mao observed: 'They would not have to die if they were attacked by those diseases today. Their diseases are now easy to cure.' But even if Mao felt nothing for his father, he was bound to feel responsible for making the best possible arrangements for the rest of his family after the loss of their chief breadwinner.

Far from going directly home, however, he chose to linger on the way, first at Shanghai and then at Hengyang. He had to sell his only warm winter coat in order to buy his railway ticket to Shanghai, where he met his living expenses by working as a laundryman. He wrote to friends in Changsha saying that washing clothes was not hard, but because he had to use a bus to collect the clothes and deliver them again, much of the income from his work was wasted.

He went to the docks in his pale blue gown to see off another group of Hunanese students sailing down the Huangpu River towards Europe, but had so much other business in Shanghai that he did not wait to see the boat drift over the horizon.

He discussed with Chen Tu-hsiu, the editor of *New Youth* and the man who was to become the first leader of the Communist Party, the plans of his friends for the reconstruction of Hunan, as well as the Marxist books he had just read. Mao said of Chen at this time that, 'he had influenced me perhaps more than anyone else,' and that 'Chen's own assertions of belief had deeply impressed me at what was probably a critical period in my life.' Mao then went to Hengyang where he talked to one of his former teachers in the Hunan Normal School, who had now become a senior figure in the Kuomintang, the party of Sun Yat-sen leading China's non-Marxist republican-cum-nationalist movement.

While Mao was away from home, Governor Chang was forced out of Changsha by rival warlords. His overthrow delighted the people of Hunan, and there was a flurry of debate about the best use to make of the opportunity it presented. Other warlords to north and south were ready to grasp the province if they could, and so the spirit of the times dictated a certain provincialism, a determination to establish Hunan autonomy and have Hunanese manage the province's affairs. There were also calls for democracy and people's rule, in the afterglow of the Russian revolution. The new strongman, Governor Tan, professed to support these sentiments.

Mao was still outside the province, but he followed Hunanese developments attentively and helped his colleagues to prepare a document discussing the various ways ahead for the province, arguing for the abolition of warlord rule, for the villages and towns to have their own autonomous status, for banks and factories to be run by the people, with trade unions and guaranteed freedom of speech and assembly. He met and collaborated with various Hunanese exiles sharing some of these ideas.

Before joining in these events in Changsha, Mao went home to Shaoshan to 'rest in the quiet of my native place for three weeks'. He doubtless discussed with his family how the farm was to be run – he had become a landlord! – and how his brothers and sister would pursue their education. Mao was now the head of the family, and all three of the others left in his care eventually joined him in his commitment to the Communist revolution.

By the time he did return to Changsha, he had turned a crucial corner in his intellectual and political development. 'By the summer of 1920', he later recalled, 'I had become, in theory and to some extent in action, a Marxist, and from this time on I considered myself a Marxist.'

He brought back from Peking to Changsha a number of Communist books which he set about distributing in a new venture which he formed in July called the Cultural Book Society. Professor Yang's widow, at their daughter's suggestion, handed

over to Mao the money which the university had given her on
her husband's death, in order to help him start it. Mao's intro-
ductory announcement explained that, 'at present the Hunan
people are starving in their minds, which is actually worse than
starving in their stomachs.' Mao helped to raise funds and gain
patrons from various circles in Changsha society, and even persuaded the new governor to write the characters for its name-
plate.

On 2 August the Society used a room in the primary school
where Mao worked for its inaugural meeting, at which Mao
became one of the twenty-seven investing shareholders who put
up a total of 519 *yuan*, as well as one of the three directors. He
became the Society's 'special negotiator', and ensured its early
success through having a network of reliable progressive representatives across the province. Since it was in business, the Society was able to borrow money, and could thus be depended on
to help Mao and his comrades in their political activities
whenever they needed it. But Mao was very insistent that the
Book Society should keep its accounts properly and in good time.
It took premises in a building owned by Yale-in-China.

One of Mao's close collaborators in organizing the Book Society was the late Professor Yang's most brilliant girl student,
Miss Tao Szu-yung, whom their mutual friend Siao Yu
described as 'a very superior person'. Siao also said that Mao fell
in love with this brilliant colleague, but that they differed in their
political ideas and so after a while separated on friendly terms.

For all the Marxism which Mao may have brought back to
Hunan, the agenda for the comrades in Hunan was a highly
localized one. The programme of the New People's Study Society
was, Mao recalled, 'for the independence of Hunan – meaning,
really, autonomy.' Disgusted with warlord-militarist government in the north and 'believing that Hunan could modernize
more rapidly if free from connections with Peking, our group
agitated for separation. I was then', Mao added, 'a strong supporter of America's Monroe Doctrine and the Open Door.'

Mao quickly found himself in the thick of all the activities
which Governor Chang's repression had interrupted. The
United Students' Association resumed its public activities and
new radical bodies appeared. Mao and his friends organized an
Association for the Promotion of Hunan Reconstruction, and
they published in July a declaration of their goals:

The reason why things in Hunan are rotten to the core is that most
people are incapable of self-awareness; they cannot stand up and give

their opinions. If they have something to say, they don't say it; if they have an idea, they don't let it out. The militarists of the north and south have successfully taken advantage of the situation to persecute us, occupy Hunan as their own territory, and tie up the people's wealth in their own sack. ... What we advocate as Hunanese self-determinationism does not at all mean tribalism; neither is it localism. It is simply that the people of Hunan should take responsibility themselves for the creation of their own development. They dare not, and cannot, decline this responsibility. The people of Hunan should freely develop their own nature and create their own civilization – this is what we mean by Hunanese self-determinationism.

In the midst of all this Mao won a promotion. From being a humble junior member of staff of one primary school he became the director of another. This good fortune was owed to the former teacher whom he had met a few weeks before in Hengyang, and who now returned to Changsha to become director of the Normal School. He appointed Mao director of the Normal School's attached Primary School, thus giving Mao his first full status of headmaster and his first decent salary. He took up this job in the autumn, teaching Chinese as well as administering the school.

In letters to his colleagues in Peking Mao stressed that the autonomy movement in Hunan was a temporary expedient rather than a fundamental proposal, defending it on the grounds that if it enabled reformists to bring out improved conditions in the area, then this would be helpful for the future.

But Mao's enthusiasm for Wilsonian self-determination was quite transparent. 'The experience', he wrote on 16 September, 'of great wars and confusion during nine years of our false republic has forced people to wake up to know ... that the best thing is ... to go about planning separately for the diverse development of the various provinces. ... Hunanese have but one possibility ... to build, on the territory of Hunan, a Hunan Republic.'

On the following day Mao penned a long account of how Hunan had suffered in its subjugation to China in previous centuries and dynasties. Hunan should now 'build on the banks of Tungting Lake a new heaven and earth, and become the leader of twenty-seven small Chinas.' From the self-determination of the Hunanese, the Cantonese and the Szechuanese would come the self-determination of other Chinese provinces.

The argument between the Hunanese reformers and the new Governor of Changsha, who resisted their ideas, came to a head in October when Mao found himself at the front of a crowd said to number almost 10,000, marching through pouring rain to demonstrate for a democratic government. Governor Tan diplomatically received leaders of the march and pretended to agree with their views. But the flag of the old discredited Provincial Assembly was still flying, so someone (a rumour said it was Mao himself) climbed up and tore it down. This gave the new Governor the excuse he was looking for to clamp down.

'From this time on,' Mao remembered, 'I became more and more convinced that only mass political power, secured through mass action, could guarantee the realization of dynamic reforms.' In the weeks that followed, 'I organized workers politically, for the first time, and began to be guided in this by the influence of Marxist theory and the history of the Russian Revolution.' It was in the course of his labour-organizing activity that Mao made another important transformation, overcoming his earlier exaggerated notion of the indignity of labour. He later described this in a passage from a famous speech in 1942:

I began as a student and acquired the habits of a student, surrounded by students who could neither fetch nor carry for themselves. I used to consider it undignified to do any manual labour, such as shouldering my own luggage. At that time it seemed to me that the intellectuals were the only clean persons in the world; next to them, the workers and the peasants seemed rather dirty. I would put on the clothes of other intellectuals, because I thought they were clean, but I would not put on clothes belonging to a worker or peasant, because I felt they were dirty. Having become a revolutionary I found myself in the ranks of the workers, peasants, and soldiers of the revolutionary army, and gradually I became familiar with them, and they with me. It was then and only then that a fundamental change occurred in the bourgeois and petty-bourgeois feelings implanted in me by the bourgeois schools. I came to feel that it was those unreconstructed intellectuals who were unclean as compared with workers and peasants, while the workers and peasants are after all the cleanest persons, cleaner than both the bourgeois and the petty bourgeois, even though their hands are soiled and their feet smeared with cow dung. This is what is meant by having one's feelings transformed, changed from those of one class into those of another.

Mao's inchoate ideas about Marxism gradually began to take shape in actual organization. In the summer of 1920 Mao was bombarded by letters from his old friend Tsai Ho-sen, then studying at the College de Montargis, near Paris. In August he wrote urging Mao to organize a Communist Party in China. Fourteen of the Chinese comrades in France had already held a five-day meeting and found themselves split into a revolutionary faction led by Tsai and another reformist or gradualist faction. Both sides wrote long letters to Mao pleading for his endorsement. It was easy to guess which way Mao would go.

He was already sponsoring a Russian Affairs Study Group in Changsha, as well as a work-study scheme for going to the Soviet Union. In September or October he formed the first Communist cell in Changsha, after receiving memoranda from his Marxist colleagues in Peking and Shanghai. A few weeks later, he formed a branch of the Socialist Youth League, another precursor of the Communist Party.

The dilemma of the Hunanese reformers was brought to a head in a most unlikely manner by the visit to Changsha of a young British aristocrat, Bertrand Russell. The British philosopher was spending a year teaching in China, and he came to Changsha in October as part of a tour of provincial cities: he first met the famous American educationalist John Dewey there at a banquet given by the very Governor against whom Mao was struggling (Dewey had come to speak out for federalism in Changsha).

Mao listened to Russell's lecture and told his friends in Paris afterwards that Russell had taken 'a position in favour of Communism but against the dictatorship of the workers and peasants. He said that one should employ the method of education to change the consciousness of the propertied classes, and that in this way it would not be necessary to limit freedom or to have recourse to war or bloody revolution.'

This might be all very well in theory, Mao went on sternly, but was quite impracticable. 'Education requires (1) money, (2) people and (3) instruments. In today's world money is entirely in the hands of the capitalists. Those who have charge of education are all either capitalists or slaves of capitalists. In today's world, the schools and the press, the two most important instruments of education, are entirely under capitalist control. In short, education in today's world is capitalist education.'

In the midst of all this intellectual turmoil Mao married his late professor's daughter Yang Kai-hui. The exact date is not known, and it is likely that it was undertaken as a private understanding between autonomous revolutionaries. Edgar Snow commented in 1936 that 'it seems to have begun as a trial marriage', and that it was celebrated as an 'ideal romance' among the radical younger generation in Hunan. Miss Yang was certainly a brilliant girl and a good student.

She was described as 'rather small in stature and round-faced', with 'deep-set, smallish eyes' and white skin, unlike her swarthy father. She was said to resemble Mao's mother in looks. Already in 1919 and 1920 she was working for the Hunan Students' Association, and in her own school, the Fuchiang Girls' Middle School, she was a blue-stocking. This outraged conservatives, although her bobbed hair added to her natural attraction. Because of her radical reputation many schools would not admit her, and in the end she had to go to a Christian school.

It might have been supposed that Mao had first come to know Miss Yang from his visits to her father's house in Changsha. This is not fully confirmed by the description which their mutual friend Siao Yu gave of those visits, which took place usually on Sundays, for a discussion with the Professor followed by lunch. At the lunch-table they were joined by Mr Yang's wife and daughter.

When they entered, [Siao Yu later recalled] we merely bowed our heads politely in greeting but none of us ever spoke. Every week for two whole years we ate our meal rapidly and in silence, not one of us ever uttering a single word. ... Sometimes our lines of vision crossed, especially if two of us started to help ourselves from the same dish at the same time. We communicated only by means of our eyes and eyebrows, but we never smiled at each other. ... Mr Yang himself never spoke a word and we all respected his silence. ... The atmosphere reminded one of people praying in a church. Mr Yang paid a great deal of attention to matters of hygiene but apparently he did not realize that it is better for one's health to talk and laugh normally during meals, that a happy atmosphere aids digestion.

Later, however, the Professor invited his daughter to join the discussions.

Mao was not Miss Yang's first choice. Eight years earlier, before Mao even knew him, Professor Yang had approached an intermediary with a view to marrying his daughter to Siao Yu, only to learn that the boy was at that time already married. It seems that marrying Siao was the girl's wish, though she was not even a teenager at that time, and so it is legitimate to infer that Mao was, at best, her second choice.

It is possible that Miss Yang was not Mao's first choice, either. His name had already been linked with two Hunanese girl students, Miss Tsai (now in France) and Miss Tao, of the Cultural Book Society. It is just possible that the marriage was influenced by the imminent birth of the boy who was to become their first son, Mao An-ying. The boy's birth-date is uncertain, but some reports place it actually in 1920, in which case he would have been conceived in Peking.

At this point there is the first of what were to become a number of gaps in the busy calendar of Mao's life. For the whole of the first half of 1921 there is very little specific activity recorded by Mao, and it is tempting to believe that he went to ground for a while with his new wife (and possibly his new son) before resuming politics again.

In March Siao Yu returned from Paris and Peking. That spring Mao and his old friend held numerous discussions in which it became evident that they had come to an intellectual divide. Mao's interest had turned from the Study Society to Communism. 'If we want to bring about reforms,' he told Siao, 'we must have a revolution. If we want the revolution to be successful, the best thing we can do is to learn from Russia! Russian communism is the most suitable system for us and the easiest to follow. There is only one road to walk and I hope that you will walk this road with us.'

But Siao harped on the need for freedom, and could not go along with a blind imitation of Soviet revolution. They often talked all night, and sometimes ended in tears because they could not agree.

Humanity, Siao argued, was like a rickshaw running on two wheels – freedom and Communism. He was against capitalism and for Communism, but without freedom the vehicle would require superhuman pressure to maintain equilibrium.

'Pressure', Mao agreed, 'is the very essence of politics. If you are successful in keeping up the pressure, that means that your politics are good. In the final analysis political influence is quite simply the constant maintenance of pressure.'

Siao put the classic objections of the liberal anarchist against well-meaning authoritarianism.

'If the leaders have no power,' Mao retorted, 'it is impossible to carry out plans, to obtain prompt action. The more power the leader has, the easier it is to get things done. In order to reform a country one must be hard with oneself and it is necessary to victimize a part of the people.'

Siao would rather do without victimizing for the hypothetical good of future generations, but Mao replied that if one became sentimental about such matters the ideals of the social revolution would not be attained in a thousand years. Siao said he could wait that long.

'I admire your patience', Mao said, 'in being willing to wait a hundred or a thousand years. I cannot wait even ten years. I want us to achieve our aims tomorrow! . . . I like to see things happen before my very eyes.'

The argument went on, with neither side making any concession, until the eve of the meeting in Shanghai in July 1921 to form the Chinese Communist Party, at which Mao was to be a delegate.

'That last night', Siao remembered, 'we slept together in the same bed, talking till dawn, and Mao still begged me to attend the meeting at which the fateful decision was to be made.'

'If we work hard,' he explained, 'in about thirty to forty years' time the Communist Party may be able to rule China' (a remarkably accurate prediction).

That day, under a black sky covered with rain clouds, the two friends, together with the other Communist delegate, Ho Shu-heng, left Changsha by the West Gate on the river boat that sailed through the central lakes of China to Wuhan and Shanghai. The two Communists had not allowed their other friends to see them off. Mao and Siao shared a cabin, with Mao in the lower berth. When Siao went up on deck the following morning, he found Mao with a book called *An Outline of the Capitalist System*.

5
WE MASONS

Leaving Siao behind in Wuhan, where he had business to do, Mao went on to Shanghai to a secret address in the French concession of the city. Chinese radicals trying to form political associations were usually hounded out by local government or warlord police: Shanghai was safer than other cities because it was ruled by Western powers and the repressive Chinese writs did not apply, but even so the foreign policemen had to be avoided. The First National Congress of the Chinese Communist Party was held in the living room of one of the Marxist pioneers in Shanghai, a room only just big enough to seat the fifteen people present. Most of the delegates were put up in the adjoining Girls' School, which was empty except for the cook-watchman who prepared dinner for them every day. They began their meetings at eight o'clock in the evening.

For three nights they discussed the foundation and constitution of their new party. But on the fourth evening, assembling after supper as usual, they were startled by a stranger in a long coat who pretended to be in the wrong house. Maring, the European Comintern representative, said: 'Must be a detective. We must disperse immediately and change the place of the conference.' They all scattered, just in time to a miss a team of fifteen French detectives and armed policemen who searched the house but found nothing.

Mao went back to his lodgings to find that his friend Siao had arrived, having finished his affairs in Wuhan. He told Siao that they had decided to continue their conference on a boat in the tourist South Lake outside Shanghai, throwing the police off the scent on the way. Siao agreed to go along.   Mao had been elected as one of the two rapporteurs, but that was not a mark of great distinction, and he played little part in the formulation of the theses of the Congress. Mao had, after all, at this time almost certainly still not read any major work of Lenin, and the leader of the new Party, Chen Tu-hsiu, probably regarded him a provincial nationalist concerned primarily with Hunan. The cell which he had recruited in Changsha for the Communist Party and the Youth Corps came almost exclusively from his fellow students, his own pupils, his former teachers, his intimate friends and members of his own family. He had not yet made any genuine contact with the Hunanese proletariat or peasantry. Yet from these personal resources came the nucleus of his faction, which was one day to rule the whole of China.

Some of the other delegates to this inaugural Congress recorded their impression of Mao. Chang Kuo-tao, later to be his political rival, described him as 'a pale-faced scholar, a youth of rather lively temperament, who in his long gown of native cloth looked rather like a Taoist priest out of some village.' Mao had a great fund of general knowledge, but little understanding of Marxism. He loved an argument and 'delighted in laying verbal traps into which his opponents would unwittingly fall by seeming to contradict themselves. Then, obviously happy, he would burst into laughter.'

Another early fellow Communist wrote:

He left me with a strange impression. I saw in him the plain and sincere quality of a rural youth – he wore torn cloth shoes and a gown of coarse fabric. It was rare to encounter such a person in a place like Shanghai. But I also detected from his appearance an air of the dilapidated scholar class. His hair was as long as that of an old warrior ... and his face looked as though it had never been washed, or at least never been washed clean: you could have scraped away at least a pound of dirt from his neck and body. ... Everybody ... as good as took him for a lunatic – and the nickname, Lunatic Mao, first came about at that time.

He was inconsistently happy and angry, and spoke at sixes and sevens, challenging everybody at meetings almost to the point of coming to blows. When he was carried away with anger, his mouth dribbled. ... Everyone excused his straightforwardness, and even liked him for it. It was only later on that I realized that behind his "straightforwardness" lay hidden a kind of real cunning. This was probably one of the major sources of his authority in the future.

The delegates hired a big boat on the lake, bought food and wine, and completed the work of the inaugural Congress under the guise of a group outing on the water, thus successfully dodging the police. They went on until eleven o'clock at night, undeterred either by the press of holiday-makers earlier in the evening or a fall of rain later. Afterwards Mao returned to his lake-side lodging, where he found Siao already asleep behind the mosquito net.

'We were able to talk quite freely in the boat,' Mao said eagerly, waking up his friend, 'at long last! It's too bad you didn't go.'

'You see, you appreciated the "freedom"!' Siao replied. 'How is it that you like your freedom so much yet you deliberately decide to destroy the freedom of your fellow countrymen, to make China a second Russia?'

But they could not agree, and Mao joined him in the bed.

'What a smell', Siao afterwards recalled, 'of hot, sweaty, unwashed flesh!' He suggested to Mao that he might like to have a bath, but his friend said he was too lazy. Even so they talked almost until dawn.

They never saw each other again. After this Mao and Siao had to pursue their friendship by correspondence, and from the standpoint of conflicting political views.

Siao later made the following summary of Mao's abilities as he knew them in 1921:

'I do know, first, that Mao is a person who takes great pains to plan very carefully whatever he undertakes and that he is a great schemer and organizer. Second, he can estimate quite accurately the power of his enemies. Third, he can hypnotize his audience. He's got a really terrific power of persuasion and there are very few people who are not carried away by his words. If you agree with what he says you are his friend; if not, you are his enemy.'*

A fellow delegate to the First Congress had drinks with Mao at a Shanghai restaurant one evening. Somewhat intoxicated, Mao inquired of his colleague whether there had been in Chinese history any cases of men who by their own efforts, with nothing to help them, became great. His companion could think of only two, the first Han emperor and Sun Yat-sen.

'Right!' Mao struck the table with his fist, upsetting the Shaohsing wine, and making the fried shrimps jump from their plate. Unruffled, he lifted his right hand and wiped the spilt wine and food off the table with his coat sleeve.

---

*Siao went on to become a museum director and Vice-Minister of Agriculture in the Kuomintang government. Later he went back to France to teach at the Sorbonne and became active in UNESCO and the World Federation of United Nations Associations. In the 1950s he went to direct an important international Chinese library in Montevideo, Uruguay, where he died.

'I, Mao Tse-tung,' he continued with great self-confidence, 'will be the third.'

Mao spent the next two years with his wife and son in Changsha, concentrating on organizing industrial labour unions and strikes. He also had his two brothers with him, the youngest, Tse-tan, completing his education. 'When I was young,' Mao later confessed, 'I showed bad temper towards Mao Tse-tan, and threatened him with a stick because he said that the Communist Party was not the ancestral temple of the Mao family.'

In September 1921 Mao went with two anarchist labour leaders to visit the Anyuan coal mine, a hundred miles to the east. Calling themselves 'observers', the three went down the mine shafts and saw the railway machine shop and other factories, both Chinese and foreign-owned. The mines supplied fuel for a nearby iron mine and iron works, using its own railway, all part of the same enterprise, recently taken over by Japanese ownership.

There were foreigners among the management personnel, including Germans who carried hardwood sticks with which to beat the workers. The 12,000 miners had endless complaints: 'squeeze' had to be paid to the foremen, hours of work were between twelve and fifteen a day, wages were low and paid in arrears, while accommodation, food, clothing, safety equipment and medical treatment were all inadequate.

Mao's first response was to start schools for workers' children, followed by a night school for the workers themselves, both supervised by Li Li-san, the young man who had responded half-heartedly to Mao's student advertisement. He was now just back from France, destined to become yet another of Mao's rivals for the Communist leadership.

Mao moved house in 1921, from the Wang Fu-chih Study Society premises to an elegant house, originally built for a pawnbroker, at Chingshuitang, outside the Hsiaowu Gate. The address also served as the headquarters of the Communist Party's Provincial Committee, of which Mao was made first secretary at the inauguration on 10 October.

After the local Communist Party had been formed, it utilized the cash flow of the Book Society. At one point Mao floated shares and set up a cotton mill in order to provide the Party with some income, but because the mill could not compete with foreign cotton it had to be sold after one year. Mao's mother-in-law also subsidized the Party.

In the new year Mao opened a protracted campaign against

Changsha's latest tyrant, the new Governor Chao, who had just had two anarchist leaders beheaded in the snow. Mao organized a strike campaign in protest. In the summer he went to Shanghai to get more support for the struggle against Governor Chao and also to take part in the Second Congress of the Communist Party at Hangchow.

'I intended to attend,' Mao said afterwards. 'However, I forgot the name of the place where it was to be held, could not find any comrades, and missed it.' Even given the high secrecy necessary for the Communists to survive, this is a strange episode. There is a report that Mao did in fact meet Maring, the Comintern delegate, and it is inconceivable that he would not have learnt from him where the Congress was to be held. One guess is that Mao's colleagues in the Party, heavily beleaguered by problems on other fronts, may have decided beforehand not to give their full backing to the anti-Chao campaign in Hunan. They may have barred him from the Congress, or he may have boycotted it out of pique.

Mao did, however, go along with the Communist Party's United Front with the Kuomintang which was formed later in 1922. The Kuomintang was impressed by the Russians for giving up their extra-territorial privileges in China (unlike the Western powers), and Sun Yat-sen was disillusioned with the Anglo-Saxons. Mao joined the Kuomintang and began to reorganize it in Hunan as a disciplined underground party. It still had the potential of a radical party, and it had many more members than the Communists.

At the beginning of September Mao went again to the coal mines at Anyuan and, according to his Communist biographer, judged the time ripe for a strike. Liu Shao-chi, his fellow Hunanese and contemporary who had recently returned from training in Russia and was to become his Party colleague and later rival, was put in command. It must have been from Liu that Mao gained his first detailed impressions about life in the Soviet Union. They had many meetings at his home in Chingshuitang.

After some false starts and wavering, the miners struck in mid-September. Mao wrote their manifesto: 'Formerly we were beasts of burden; now we want to lead the life of human beings ... ' On the fifth day the management caved in and met their demands in full. The men then organized themselves formally into a workers' club, which in turn organized a co-operative managed by Mao. Years later, when Mao had left the urban centres and taken to guerrilla fighting in the countryside, it was the Anyuan coal miners who provided many of his fighters, and their organization which transmitted his documents and enabled him to keep in touch with the Provincial and National Committees of the Communist Party.

Two workers later remembered Mao during the strike, with a straw hat and trousers tied up around his knees 'as if he had just returned from labour work'. He was often seen, they added, 'wearing a ragged uniform with a large T-shaped patch on his back and, like other workers, he ate his meals squatting, plunging his chopsticks into the vegetable dishes on the ground.' Another miner commented that although the labour movement was then at a low ebb, Mao 'had the attitude of "sitting solidly on a fishing boat regardless of the rise of winds and waves." He was completely at ease as if he had already had everything planned within himself' – a comment that many others were to make on Mao's comportment during a crisis.

Another labour victory which Mao helped to win was the strike of the Canton-Wuhan railway workers in September. The issue was the usual one of low wages, irregularly paid, complicated by the unpopularity of two overseers who were constantly cheating and abusing the men under their charge. Because of good preparation, the strike was fully supported, so that the locomotives, in the phrase of a Chinese account, 'lay motionless on the tracks like dead snakes'.

After a while the government brought troops and blackleg workers to beat the strike, and in one incident these troops were confronted by workers and their families who lay down on the tracks to prevent the wagons moving. More than seventy people were wounded in this incident, of whom six later died: 'some heads were split open, and some arms and legs were hacked off; some people had all their limbs hacked off.' The massacre steeled the determination of railway workers in other areas and Mao arranged for telegrams to be sent throughout the country saying: 'Even Japan's treatment of Korea and England's treatment of India were not as cruel as this .... ' In the end the government had to capitulate.

Meanwhile in Changsha itself Mao personally led more than 4000 masons and carpenters in a strike for higher wages and freedom to do business. It went on for almost three weeks, and became the first strike victory ever won by the workers of the city. After helping these unorganized and self-employed craftsmen to form a union and state their case through the press, Mao was among them when they marched to the city hall in the pouring rain to press their demands on the government.

'We masons and carpenters', he cried from the top of a raised flower bed in the middle of the lawn outside the city hall, 'can't live from day to day because our wages are so low. It was only when this point was reached that we asked the government to increase our wages ... ' He blew a whistle every now and then as a signal for the men to shout slogans. When the officials realized that he was the leader, they came to apprehend him, but he slipped through the trees and was swallowed up again in the ranks of the workers.

The city administration agreed to hold a conference to discuss the claim, and Mao presented the masons' case.

'What is the gentleman's name?' asked one of the officials, surprised by the quality of the presentation. 'Is he a worker?'

'You, sir,' Mao replied, 'have asked about my credentials. I reply that I am a representative of the workers. If you want to make an investigation of my background, it would be better to talk about it another time. Today, in my capacity as a representative of the masons and carpenters, I am demanding that the government settle the wage problem.' Again the government gave in.

Other groups helped by Mao in industrial action around this time were the type-setters and rickshaw-pullers. For a time Mao served as secretary of the Type-machinists' and Type-setters' Union, and he taught at the rickshaw workers' night school.

At the same time Mao lost his job as head of the First Normal School's Primary School in Changsha. It sounds as if he was not able to spend much time at the school anyway in view of his labour organizing, but there were also political reasons. Anti-Communist activity was afoot and the new Governor was less liberal than his predecessor. He did not lose his interest, however, in education. He had already in the previous year helped to form a Self-Study University in Changsha (and was to put his younger brother into it), and at the end of 1922 he helped to form the American-backed Mass Education Movement, in which the YMCA also had a stake. Mao's mother-in-law helped him financially after he lost his salary.

In November 1922 the by now numerous trades unions in Hunan met to form a provincial federation. Mao was elected its General Secretary. It was in this capacity that he found himself in a face-to-face confrontation with the hated Governor Chao. After the rash of strikes in Changsha, Chao began to spread the word that they were the work of a small group of extremists hired by people outside Hunan to make trouble, and made it clear that he would henceforward take strong repressive action against the workers.

This caused some of the workers and their representatives to waver, and Mao decided to seek a meeting with the Governor. In a discussion about the right of people to have freedom of assembly, Mao cited legal articles from England and France in order to support his contention that: 'Unless the people directly violate the law in their actions, there really should be no intervention' by the government.

Asked later why he did not kill Mao at this time, when he had him in his power, Chao answered: 'I didn't know he was going to turn out to be so formidable.'

But the Governor did not forget Mao, and in April 1923 he issued a warrant for his arrest. Mao spent two weeks underground briefing his successors in the various organizations he was concerned with and winding up his affairs in the city, before leaving for Shanghai, where he began to work at the Communist Party Centre. Mao's wife was with him in his exile, and it was about this time that their second son, An-ching, the boy who was later described as being mentally unstable, was born.

Almost immediately Mao and his wife went down to Canton for the Third Congress of the Communist Party held at the end of June 1923. The comrades were dismayed by the massacre of striking workers which the northern and central warlords had perpetrated earlier that year, and Chen Tu-hsiu, the Party leader, under Comintern pressure, drew the conclusion that the Communists could not ride to victory on the backs of the infant proletariat but would need strong allies – and the Kuomintang of Dr Sun Yat-sen was the obvious candidate.

Chen moved that the Communists join the Kuomintang and lead the workers and peasants into its ranks in order to become a powerful left wing within it. Mao opposed the idea, however, and said that as far as Hunan was concerned, the number of industrial workers was very small, and the ranks of Kuomintang or Communist Party members was even smaller, whereas the mountains and valleys were 'filled with peasants'. If the peasants could be organized as the coal miners had been in Hunan, and if the Communists cultivated the peasants as hard as the Kuomintang had done, then they could hope for success. But Maring and Chen did not share Mao's enthusiasm for the peasants, and Mao was probably left feeling that the Kuomintang had a better understanding of the peasant question than his fellow Communists.

Chen's motion to enter the Kuomintang was also opposed by Chang Kuo-tao, who had been organizing the trade union side of the Party's work. He moved an amendment declaring the workers' movement and unions independent to make their own decisions about collaborating with the Kuomintang.

The vote was tied on this amendment, eight votes to eight, so Chen as chairman was able to reject it. Those who had opposed Chen were now invited to state their position, and Chang Kuo-tao recollected that 'Mao Tse-tung declared in an easy tone that he would accept the decision of the Congress majority' – making it clear that he felt Mao had let him down. In fact it looks as if Mao were merely following the normal committee convention. Mao was then elected to the Central Committee, which ran the affairs of the Party in between congresses and gave instructions to the various provincial committees. Later in the year he replaced Chang Kuo-tao as head of its Organization Bureau. It is probably from this period that the personal rivalry between Mao and Chang can be dated. Whatever the ins and outs of the protocol surrounding Mao's voting at the Third Congress, there is no doubt that he took up with enthusiasm the implementation of what he called 'the historic decision . . . to enter the Kuomintang, co-operate with it, and create a United Front against the northern militarists.'

Back in Shanghai again in July and August, Mao published a series of vivid articles attacking the abject submission of the northern warlords – who controlled the so-called central government in Peking – to Western and Japanese economic demands. 'America is actually the most murderous of hangmen,' he wrote in one article, and on the question of the cigarette tax, his comment was:

The Council of Ministers of the Chinese Government is really both accommodating and agreeable. If one of our foreign masters farts, it is a lovely perfume. If our foreign masters want to export cotton, the Council of Ministers thereupon abolishes the prohibition of the export of cotton; if our foreign masters want to bring in cigarettes, the Council of Ministers thereupon 'instructs the various provinces by telegram to stop levying taxes on cigarettes'. Again, I ask my 400 million brethren to ponder a little: Isn't it true that the Chinese Government is the counting-house of our foreign masters?

Mao directed his anger particularly against England: 'Do the Chinese people only know how to hate Japan, and don't they know how to hate England? Don't they know that the aggression of the English imperialists against China is even more atrocious than that of the Japanese imperialists?'

In the autumn of 1923 there is another three-month 'gap' in which no public activity of Mao is recorded. But at the end of the year he sailed again for Canton, this time to attend the first congress of the Kuomintang in January 1924. Mao and Li Li-san were the two senior Communists at the congress, and Chang Kuo-tao said afterwards that whereas Li had criticized the Kuomintang in his speeches, Mao took 'a completely different stand; he always borrowed the manner of speaking of Dr Sun . . . . '

Mao clearly remembered listening to Sun's speeches and talking with him in Canton. 'He was an orator', he recalled, 'and an instigator, speaking very eloquently and earning huge applause. . . . He would not allow others to argue with him or to present their own views. In fact his words were full of water, but had very little oil, and he was rather undemocratic.' And in the same conversation forty years later Mao recalled with amusement the nickname which one of his fellow Hunanese had given to the Cantonese leader, namely Big-Cannon Sun or Loud-mouth Sun.

One of the Kuomintang delegates remembered how a man with a Hunanese accent shouted from the back for the chairman to give him the floor, saying, 'I demand that this discussion should now be ended, and the question be put to the vote at once.' It was 'a medium-sized man, pale-faced, arrogant and stubborn, in a long cotton-padded gown. He looked like a country cousin in town – a man without manners and culture. After some enquiries, I learned his name was Mao . . . . '

At Canton Mao was elected to senior posts in the Kuomintang organization, so that afterwards in Shanghai he, in his own words, 'combined my work in the executive bureau of the Communist Party with membership in the executive bureau of the Kuomintang'. In the latter work he collaborated with Wang Ching-wei (who was later to become Premier) and Hu Han-min, two leftward-inclined Kuomintang leaders. Li Li-san ridiculed Mao by calling him Hu's 'secretary', and most of his fellow Communists felt that Mao was collaborating too enthusiastically with the Kuomintang.

In the middle of Mao's liaison work with the Kuomintang, an important meeting of the Communist Central Committee was held in May 1924 which decided, in the absence of both himself and Li Ta-chao, to re-assert the Communists' independent role in the labour movement and loosen their ties with the Kuomintang. But Mao persisted in seeing the United Front as the best available policy for the Communists. 'That summer', he recalled, 'the Whampoa Military Academy' (in which the Communists collaborated with the Kuomintang in training military cadres) 'was set up. Galen became its adviser, other Soviet advisers arrived from Russia and the Kuomintang-Communist Party *entente* began to assume the proportions of a nation-wide revolutionary movement.' He exaggerated.

The strain of serving two masters proved too much. For the rest of 1924 Mao was again comparatively inactive, and he himself claimed that he had 'become ill in Shanghai' and so 'returned to Hunan for a rest'. He was no doubt hardened to the criticisms which the Kuomintang leaders were making of him, but he may have found it more difficult to swallow the insults of his Communist peers, especially without the backing of the one among them who was sympathetic, namely Li Ta-chao, now away in Moscow on a Comintern assignment. The pressure may have become unbearable after October, when Chang Kuo-tao, his most scornful critic within the Communist Central Committee, was released from detention and re-entered the political fray. Mao continued during this period to stress the importance of uniting the peasants, and probably consulted Borodin, the latest of the Russian 'experts' to arrive in Shanghai to advise the Chinese comrades, on this question before returning home.

His depression or illness took him back to his childhood village of Shaoshan, where he spent his thirty-first birthday as a patriarchal figure surrounded by his younger brothers and sister, his wife and his two sons, pondering the political dead-end which he appeared to have reached.

6
THREE POTATO RICE

There is no reason to doubt the illness that brought Mao back to the village where he first saw light. But there was more significance to the event than mere recuperation. His withdrawal from active politics for the whole of the winter of 1924-5 and most of the following spring must be connected with his disappointment at not being admitted to the magic circle of inner leadership in either of the two parties, the Communist Party or the Kuomintang. In spite of being, at thirty-one, on the Central Committees of both parties, he was not fully accepted, and he had dismally failed to convince any of the national leaders of the importance of the peasant factor in China's revolutionary equation.

Mao had no university degree, no books to his name, no academic achievement or social status. His standing fell below that of the established leaders, and the fact that he more than made up for all that in energy, imagination and personality had not yet made any real difference. Despite his occasional journalistic success, the political journals were largely monopolized by writers with an acknowledged reputation or by students who had returned with an overseas qualification. Beside the work of such men, Mao's literary offerings seemed parochial.

He had not even lived or worked in a big industrial city, and could not therefore match the experience of colleagues like Li Li-san, Chang Kuo-tao or Liu Shao-chi. While he was in the Hunanese countryside in the early part of 1925, for example, there was a nation-wide campaign against foreign imperialism in the cities of China which never touched Mao, and in which he played no part whatsoever. What he had to do, therefore, was somehow to prove the authenticity of the peasant weapon in the Chinese revolution, and there was no more appropriate place to ponder such a challenge than Shaoshan.

By retreating there, Mao missed a number of important

events, including the Fourth Congress of the Communist Party in Shanghai in January and the death in March of Sun Yat-sen, which placed in jeopardy the future of the Communist-Kuomintang alliance. But even the Hunanese peasant organizations were affected by the killing of Chinese workers by British police in Shanghai on 30 May.

'I had not fully realized', Mao explained, 'the degree of class struggle among the peasantry, but after the 30 May incident, and during the great wave of political activity which followed it, the Hunanese peasantry became very militant. I left home, where I had been resting, and began a rural organizational campaign. In a few months we had formed more than twenty peasant unions, and had aroused the wrath of the landlords, who demanded my arrest.' Tsai Ho-sen was back from France to help Mao in this crisis, while Mao's wife was instrumental in setting up the Shaoshan branch of the Communist Party.

Years later Mao re-evoked his experiences of those days in conducting rural investigations. You could not, he recalled, merely go to the villages and hope to understand their structure and sociology just like that.

It took more than ten years before I was able to understand them. I went to tea houses and gambling parlours to meet everyone and investigate them. ... I sought out poor peasants in my native village for investigation. They had no rice to eat, and their lives were dismal.

There was a peasant whom I invited to play Chinese dominoes. ... Afterwards I invited him to dinner. Before, during and after the meal, I talked with him and learnt how violent class struggle was in the rural villages. He was willing to talk to me because, first, I treated him like a person: secondly, I invited him to eat; and thirdly, he could win some money from me. I would lose to him, paying out one or two silver dollars, and he was quite satisfied. There was a time when he was so desperate that he came to me to borrow one dollar. I gave him three dollars without expecting any repayment. It was impossible in those days to get any assistance which did not require repayment.

The slogans during this campaign were, 'Down with the militarists' and 'Down with the rich foreigners'. It was not altogether surprising that Governor Chao, at the insistence of the landlords, eventually put out an order for Mao's arrest, and sent troops in October to get him. Mao fled to Canton, but not before composing, in a nostalgic mood, his first published classical poem, about the city he loved, Changsha:

Alone I stand in the autumn cold
On the tip of Orange Island,

The Hsiang flowing northward;
I see a thousand hills crimsoned through
By their serried woods deep-dyed,
And a hundred barges vying
Over crystal blue waters.
Eagles cleave the air,
Fish glide in the limpid deep;
Under freezing skies a million creatures contend in freedom.
Brooding over this immensity,
I ask, on this boundless land
Who rules over man's destiny?
I was here with a throng of companions,
Vivid yet those crowded months and years.
Young we were, schoolmates,
At life's full flowering;
Filled with student enthusiasm,
Boldly we cast all restraints aside.
Pointing to our mountains and rivers,
Setting people afire with our words,
We counted the mighty no more than muck.
Remember still
How, venturing midstream, we struck the waters
And waves stayed the speeding boats?

Mao arrived in the semi-tropical city of Canton, the Kuomintang capital, in the autumn of 1925 to find a certain amount of optimism in the air, with Wang Ching-wei, his former boss, as the new chairman of the Kuomintang government after Sun's death. Chiang Kai-shek, his colours still ambiguous, had become commander of the First Army. The fifth session of the Peasant Movement Training Institute had just opened, with more than a hundred students of whom two-fifths were from Hunan, including Mao's brother, Tse-min. Mao took over responsibility for the propaganda department of the Kuomintang under Wang Ching-wei, and was appointed editor of the Kuomintang journal, *Political Weekly*. In this capacity he came to know the left Kuomintang scholar-poet, Liu Ya-tzu, with whom he afterwards maintained a famous literary friendship. It seemed that he was quickly welcomed back into the Kuomintang fold. But then the Kuomintang itself split, into a right-wing group (ultimately led by Chiang) opposed to working with the Communists, and a left-wing group (under Wang) which Mao continued to support.

In December Mao published a number of articles in the *Political Weekly* condemning the Kuomintang rightists. One of them contained his first published reference to Hong Kong, which he had never seen but now called 'that waste-land of an island'. It was in this series that he for the first time identified himself with the language of the street about foreigners, by asking what would it matter if the workers of Shanghai were to imprison 'all the red-haired chaps'.

On Christmas Day of 1925 Mao learnt from labour organizers fleeing from Hunan that Governor Chao had brutally suppressed another miners' strike at Anyuan by sending in an armed regiment. The director of the union, a Communist, had been shot, several miners had been killed and the union was smashed. Storming with anger, Mao went to Shanghai to organize a campaign by the Communist Party against Governor Chao, but to his intense frustration and disappointment Chen Tu-hsiu refused to support him. The Central Committee, following the Comintern line, had just voted to keep the Kuomintang confined to Kwangtung province, and a campaign of the sort which Mao envisaged in Hunan would be seen as open encouragement for Chiang Kai-shek's plan to march north against the warlords. Mao's need to avenge his friends had to bow to Stalin's whims in Moscow.

Smarting from the rejection of his political ideas in Shanghai, Mao now published an important analytical article delving into class relations in China, which eventually became the first text in the canon of his *Selected Works* of the 1950s. Entitled 'Analysis of the Different Classes of Chinese Society', it proved highly controversial.

Out of a Chinese population of 400 million at that time, Mao in this article estimated the 'big' bourgeoisie at 1 million and the middle bourgeoisie at 4 million. These were the only two groups whose attitude could be called counter-revolutionary, and even the left-wing of the middle bourgeoisie was capable of joining the revolution – although it would compromise with the enemy and was therefore to be regarded as untrustworthy.

All other sections of the Chinese population were in some way or another ready to support the revolution. Of the 150 million petty-bourgeoisie, the 15 million who were well off were normally close to the semi-counter-revolutionary thinking of the middle bourgeoisie, but in time of war would go along with the revolution. The 75 million who were self-sufficient would be neutral in normal times but would also support the revolution in time of war, while the 60 million who were not self-sufficient welcomed the revolution.

Of the 200 million members of the semi-proletariat, all would more or less actively join the revolution, including the 50 million semi-owner peasants, the 60 million half-share tenants, the 60 million poor peasants (who would be 'brave fighters'), the 24 million handicraftsmen, the 5 million shop assistants and the 1 million pedlars.

As for the 45 million proletariat, the 2 million industrial proletariat were, of course, the 'main force' of the revolution, the 3 million urban coolies were a main force second only to the industrial workers, the 20 million agricultural proletariat were, like the poor peasants, 'brave fighters' and the 20 million lumpenproletariat could be led to become a revolutionary force. Mao's conclusion from this arithmetic was a piece of obvious morale-boosting:

How many are our true friends? There are 395 million of them. How many are our true enemies? There are a million of them. How many are there of these people in the middle, who may be either our friends or our enemies? There are four million of them. Even if we consider these four million as enemies, this only adds up to a bloc of barely five million, and a sneeze from 395 million would certainly suffice to blow them down. Three hundred and ninety-five millions, unite!

The final sub-category in Mao's list, the lumpenproletariat or *éléments déclassés*, was something of a novelty in Marxist analysis and was to become a hobbyhorse for Mao. Here is his description of them:

The *éléments déclassés* consist of peasants who have lost their land, handicraftsmen who have lost all opportunity of employment as a result of oppression and exploitation ... or as a result of floods and droughts. They can be divided into soldiers, bandits, robbers, beggars, and prostitutes.

These five categories of people have different names, and they enjoy a somewhat different status in society. But they are all human beings, and they all have five senses and four limbs, and are therefore one. They each have a different way of making a living: the soldier fights, the bandit robs, the thief steals, the beggar begs, and the prostitute seduces.

But to the extent that they must all earn their livelihood and cook rice to eat, they are one. They lead the most precarious existence of any human being.

They have secret organizations in various places. ... These serve as their mutual-aid societies in the political and economic struggle. To find a place for this group of people is the greatest and the most difficult problem faced by China. ... The number of *éléments déclassés* in China is fearfully large; it is roughly more than twenty million. These people are capable of fighting very bravely, and, if properly led, can become a revolutionary force.

The earliest version of this article, Mao's first essay in a new genre, was produced in January 1926 and sent to the Communist leadership. 'Chen Tu-hsiu', Mao recollected, 'opposed the opinions expressed ... which advocated a radical land policy and vigorous organization of the peasantry under the Communist Party, and he refused it publication in the Communist central organ.' It perhaps fell between two stools, being for the most part not truly original in terms of what had been published by other Chinese Marxists in the preceding three or four years, but being, in those areas where it was original, somewhat unorthodox in terms of Marxism.

Mao reworked his article into a second version in February, but Chen still would not publish it and so Mao placed it in *The Chinese Peasant* in Canton. Mao's disenchantment with Chen Tu-hsui began with this episode: 'I began to disagree with Chen's Right opportunist policy about this time, and we gradually drew further apart ...' That Mao himself was not happy with some of the expressions in his article was evident when it came to be included in the *Selected Works* in the 1950s, where numerous changes were made.

A typical passage to be omitted was: 'The attitude of the various classes in China towards the national revolution is more or less identical with the attitude of the various classes of Western Europe towards the social revolution,' a sweeping analogy which had echoes of Trotsky rather than of Stalin. And in the 1950s the romantic list of the five constituents of the lumpen-proletariat – soldiers, bandits, robbers, beggars and prostitutes – was omitted.

The upshot of his article was to divide Chinese society into various strata on the basis of wealth and property, identifying the large landlords with the urban bourgeoisie as people against whom the rest of the population would revolt, but thereby confusing the feudal and capitalist stages of historical development which, in the Marxist view, are quite distinct. The peasants emerged as a major and 'semi-proletarian' revolutionary force.

Despite his appeals to the Communists, the thrust of Mao's effort in the coming months was to be with the Kuomintang, whose Second Congress was held in Canton in January 1926. Its policy towards the Communists remained unchanged, and Mao was re-elected as an alternate member of the Central Executive

Committee. This was one of the few occasions when he competed with Chiang Kai-shek. Chiang, along with the other top-ranking Kuomintang leaders, received the maximum of 248 votes. Mao did rather well to get 173 votes.

He spoke at the Congress as an advocate of maintaining and widening the United Front for national liberation, even to this end backing the re-integration of the Kuomintang rightists. On 8 January he delivered a Report on Propaganda – proudly remarking, *inter alia,* that, 'in the last two years anti-Christian organizations and propaganda have spread all over the country and have taught the masses of the people to understand the religious aggression of the imperialists.'

In March, Mao was appointed by the Kuomintang Principal of the Peasant Movement Training Institute. He presided over its sixth training session in Canton from May to October, himself lecturing for thirty-three hours on the peasant question in China, and for nine hours on methods of rural education.

During these lectures he was able to introduce images and illustrations familiar to his pupils. He talked about the Ox Prince Temple and three potato rice – referring to the landlord courts and the mixture of three parts sweet potato and one part unhulled rice which the farmers of the Tungchiang region near Canton used to eat. But Mao wanted information in return, namely 'the conditions in the villages under which everyone lived, the conditions of the inhabitants and the land, the mode of life, and people's origins, how so-and-so got rich, how so-and-so became poor, how much official or public land there was in the village, who managed it, who worked it, the rent ...' Mao would use this information in texts to discuss with his students, as well as for his own analysis.

Mao even taught a little geography, and in September he took all the students on a fortnight's trip to Haifeng, where the famed Communist leader Peng Pai explained his peasant government system. The sessions were held in a Confucian temple, and when Mao saw one of the students making fun of the ancestral tablet of Confucius he locked him out of the lectures for several days. Mao would not countenance such impolitic mockery.

Some Communists may have believed that Mao was doing too much for the Kuomintang, but he told his intimates that he was preparing cadres at his Institute who would rally to the Communist cause in the coming guerrilla war. The Communists were at this time influential in the higher ranks of the Kuomintang organization. But their dream of coming to power on the

Kuomintang's coat-tails was severely shattered on 20 March 1926 when Chiang Kai-shek advertised his take-over of the Kuomintang by expelling Communists from some posts and arresting many leading Russian advisers and Chinese Communist leaders. Mao lost his position in the Propaganda Department of the Kuomintang Central Executive Committee, but continued to direct the Peasant Movement Training Institute.

This may have been because Chiang did not wish to upset the important Hunan branch of the Kuomintang, which was leftist and sympathetic toward the Communists, because their help would be needed in prosecuting Chiang's forthcoming Northern Expedition against the warlords of central and north China. Mao's rival, Chang Kuo-tao, later accused Mao of not attending the Communist Party meetings to decide how to react to Chiang's coup, and of remaining detached from the recriminations: instead he 'stood with his hands folded and just looked on'. Actually there was very little the Communists could do, although a Russian report says that Mao did urge the Soviet Union to take immediate action against Chiang.

Within days of this abrupt divorce between the two Chinese parties, Mao put a resolution to the Kuomintang Peasant Movement Committee calling for the movement to be developed in those provinces which would be crossed by the Northern Expedition. He thus linked peasant development with Chiang's pet military project, and secured the maximum help from the Kuomintang for the rural work which was eventually to provide the Communists with their grass roots support. In this he flew in the face of Stalin, who opposed the Northern Expedition.

The 'poet laureate' of Communist China, Kuo Mo-jo, met Mao during this period, and left a suggestive pen portrait. He recalled one of the remarkable descriptions of a famous man in the Chinese classics which described the writer as imagining his hero with a magnificent and imposing appearance – 'but when I saw a portrait of him, he had the face and figure of a . . . pretty woman'. The Communist poet then went on:

> To me, this could also be said of Mao Tse-tung. Short hair, parted in the middle and swept over to both sides, a modest, restrained and profound glance, a pale and delicate skin, and in conversation a low but mild and persuasive voice. At that time, however, I had not yet discovered that he certainly would be 'magnificent and imposing'. Among Chinese, especially among members of the revolutionary party, it was a kind of miracle if there was anyone who spoke with a soft voice. And Mao really spoke softly, so that, coupled with the fact that I have

always been hard of hearing, I didn't catch as much as a third of what he was saying.

Mao single-mindedly pursued his organization of the peasants, using the facilities of the Kuomintang in the absence of anything better offered by his Communist colleagues. He was made head of the Communist Party's new Peasant Department in the summer, and went to Shanghai to discuss its programme. But he found no peasants there and was probably unable to work with Chen Tu-hsiu, and so he returned to his Institute in Canton. In September he wrote a foreword for a series of Kuomintang books on the peasant movement, where he stated his position squarely: 'The peasant question is the central problem of the national revolution. If the peasants do not revolt, if they do not join in or support the national revolution, then it will fail.' He went on, in another article, to spell out why the peasant revolution was different from the urban:

At present, the political objectives of the urban working class are merely to seek complete freedom of assembly and of association; this class does not yet seek to destroy immediately the political position of the bourgeoisie. As for the peasants in the countryside, on the other hand, as soon as they arise they run into the political power of these village bullies, bad gentry, and landlords who have been crushing the peasants for several thousand years ... and if they do not overthrow this political power which is crushing them, there can be no status for the peasants. This is a very important peculiarity of the peasant movement in China today.

The Communist leadership, acting on a telegram from Stalin, decided in spite of Chiang's arrests to go on working for unity against the nothern warlords, and, in the interest of that unity, to refrain from discussing the land problem or arming the peasant associations in the villages. Mao was now back in his Changsha base. One of his aides who went to work at his house there about this time, and who spent the next four years there with him and his wife, remembered that Mao 'always went out to work, and sometimes did not return home for several days.' Chen appointed Mao inspector of the Hunan peasant movement, presumably in the hope that he would prevent the peasants from causing any trouble as the Northern Expedition went through the province.

But Mao had no intention of damping down the ardour of the peasants in Hunan. In a closing speech to a conference of peasant and worker delegates in Changsha in December he called for a struggle against the landlords. Under his leadership the peasant associations immediately began to confiscate land and redistribute it, taking over missionary stations for their administrative headquarters.

The provincial peasants' union took over five houses belonging to the YMCA and the Theological Institute in Changsha. In Hsianghsiang, the home of Mao's mother and of his old friend Tsai Ho-sen, and one of the most radical districts in the province, missionaries were actually ordered out of their homes and twenty people were executed by the peasant association under the banner of 'people's power'. The peasant association also commandeered rice hoarded before the spring harvest and distributed it as 'people's food' at low prices to poor peasants.

All this may have been very admirable, but the Communist Party leadership under Chen feared that if the peasants went on pressing their demands so hard, the all-class front against imperialism would collapse and the conservatives in the Kuomintang armies would turn their guns against the workers and peasants. These fears proved justified.

Mao's reaction to these conflicting pressures was, as usual, to go to ground, but this time in order to undertake a detailed investigation which was finally to make his name. It led to his *Report on an Investigation on the Peasant Movement in Hunan*, the text in which he committed himself most fervently and with most skill to the idea of a non-proletarian revolution which was to amaze Marxists in China as well as in Europe. Published in *The Weekly Guide* in March 1927, it was immediately translated into Russian and English. The Comintern translation was offered as 'the most revealing report on conditions in the Chinese villages yet published in English', and Bukharin, the Comintern leader, called it 'an excellent and interesting description'.

The inspection in January covered five counties including the one where Mao was born, the one where his mother was born and where he went to primary school, and the one where he went to secondary school. During the course of the investigation he called at the home of the late Professor Yang, his father-in-law, at Pantsang, where his brother-in-law remembered him conducting a forum with 'three poor peasants, one handicraftsman, one shop assistant and two primary school teachers . . . after supper . . . until midnight.' His wife, Yang Kai-hui, helped to organize the materials and copy the documents. What the report most clearly revealed was the energy which the peasants in his homeland were exhibiting in the business of revolution, and this both surprised and invigorated him.

In a very short time, in China's central, southern and northern provinces, several hundred million peasants will rise like a mighty storm, like a hurricane, a force so swift and violent that no power, however great, will be able to hold it back. They will smash all the trammels that bind them and rush forward along the road to liberation. They will sweep all the imperialists, warlords, corrupt officials, local tyrants and evil gentry into their graves.

Every revolutionary party and every revolutionary comrade will be put to the test, to be accepted or rejected as they decide. There are three possibilities. To march at their head and lead them? To trail behind them, gesticulating and criticizing? Or to stand in their way and oppose them? Every Chinese is free to choose, but events will force you to make the choice quickly.

'Almost half the peasants in Hunan are now organized,' Mao concluded. In many areas the peasant associations had become 'the sole organs of authority', settling quarrels between husband and wife as well as economic disputes, so that almost nothing could be done without the presence of one of their officers: 'even the mere fart of the man from the peasant association carries weight'.

To give credit where credit is due, if we were to assign to the achievement of completing the national revolution a total of ten points, then only three points would go to the accomplishments of the townspeople and the military, and seven points would go to the accomplishments of the peasants in the course of the revolution in the countryside. . . . Countless thousands of the enslaved – the peasants – are striking down the enemies who batten on their flesh. What the peasants are doing is absolutely right; what they are doing is fine!

It was idle for some people to say that the peasants were 'going too far'; they were merely reacting against the age-old tyranny of local gentry and landlords. 'The peasants are clear-sighted. Who is bad and who is not, who is the worst and who is not quite so vicious, who deserves severe punishment and who deserves to be let off lightly – the peasant keeps clear accounts, and very seldom has the punishment exceeded the crime.'

In any case, Mao continued, rebutting the Kuomintang theme that peasant revolt should be subordinated to the national goals of the United Front, 'a revolution is not a dinner-party, or writing an essay, or painting a picture, or doing embroidery; it cannot be so refined, so leisurely and gentle, so "temperate, kind, courteous, restrained and magnanimous" ' (the epithets traditionally attached to Confucius' criteria for gaining influence). 'A revolution is an insurrection, an act of violence by which one class overthrows another.'

During this phase of revolutionary upsurge it was necessary to establish 'the absolute authority of the peasants' and 'to overthrow the whole authority of the gentry. . . . To put it bluntly, it is necessary to create terror for a while in every rural area, or otherwise it would be impossible to suppress the activities of the counter-revolutionaries in the countryside or overthrow the authority of the gentry. Proper limits have to be exceeded in order to right a wrong, or else the wrong cannot be righted.'

Mao explained in his *Report* that there were 'three kinds of peasants, the rich, the middle and the poor. The three live in different circumstances and so have different views about the revolution.' The rich peasants remained inactive during this revolutionary upsurge. The middle peasants were vacillating:

. . . they think that the revolution will not bring them much good. They have rice cooking in their pots and no creditors knocking on their doors at midnight.'

'The only group in the countryside that has always put up the bitterest fight is the poor peasants. Throughout the period of underground organization and that of open organization, it was they who fought, who organized, and who did the revolutionary work. They alone are the deadliest enemies of the local bullies and evil gentry and attack their strongholds without the slightest hesitation; they alone are able to carry out the work of destruction. . . .'

These were the people whom the rich peasants mocked as having 'neither a tile over your heads nor a speck of land under your feet'. But they were the majority: the survey of Changsha county showed the poor peasants as comprising 70 per cent of the population, the middle peasants only 20 per cent, and the landlords and rich peasants 10 per cent. Almost all the chairmen and committee members of the peasant associations at the lowest level were poor peasants, and Mao would not allow that they should be criticized for this.

Without the poor peasants there would be no revolution. To deny their role is to deny the revolution. To attack them is to attack the revolution. They have never been wrong on the general direction of the revolution.

Mao described some of the actions that the peasants were taking against the landlords.

This sort of thing is very common. A tall paper hat is stuck on the head of one of the local tyrants or evil gentry, bearing the words 'Local

Tyrant So-and-so' or 'So-and-so of the Evil Gentry'. He is led by a rope and escorted with big crowds in front and behind. Sometimes brass gongs are beaten and flags waved to attract people's attention. This form of punishment more than any other makes the local tyrants and evil gentry tremble. Anyone who has once been crowned with a tall paper hat loses face altogether and can never again hold up his head.

But execution, Mao reported, was confined to the worst local tyrants. He named several examples:

When the local tyrants and evil gentry were at the height of their power, they literally slaughtered peasants without batting an eyelid. Ho Mai-chuan, for ten years head of the defence corps in the town of Hsinkang, Changsha County, was personally responsible for killing almost a thousand poverty-stricken peasants, which he euphemistically described as 'executing bandits'. In my native county of Hsiangtan, Tang Chun-yen and La Shu-lin, who headed the defence corps in the town of Yintien, have killed more than fifty people and buried four alive in the fourteen years since 1913. Of the more than fifty they murdered, the first two were perfectly innocent beggars.

Tang Chun-yen said, 'Let me make a start by killing a couple of beggars!' and so these two lives were snuffed out. Such was the cruelty of the local tyrants and evil gentry in former days, such was the White terror they created in the countryside, and now that the peasants have risen and shot a few and created just a litttle terror in suppressing the counter-revolution, is there any reason for saying they should not do so?

Mao then set out the traditional sociology of his homeland by explaining that 'a man in China is usually subjected to the domination of three systems of authority', namely the political authority of the state, the social authority of the clan system and the religious authority of supernatural beliefs.

Besides this, women were also dominated by men, and these were the 'four thick ropes binding the Chinese people, particularly the peasants.' (Peasant women, however, ' . . . also enjoy considerable sexual freedom. Among the poor peasantry, triangular and multilateral relationships are almost universal.') But now, in the rural revolution in Hunan, these authorities were being overthrown. The old rule, for instance, banning women and poor people from banquets in the ancestral temples had been broken.

'The women of Paikuo in Hengshan county gathered in force and swarmed into their ancestral temple, firmly planted their backsides on the seats and joined in the eating and drinking, while the venerable clan bigwigs had willy-nilly to let them do as they pleased.'

But Mao also warned his readers against an artificial accelera-
tion of these acts of rebellion. 'It is the peasants who made the
idols, and when the time comes they will cast the idols aside with
their own hands; there is no need for anyone else to do it for them
prematurely.' Mao quoted in his *Report* a propaganda speech
which he had made to some of the villagers against superstition
which made them 'roar with laughter'.

If you believe in the Eight Characters [a system of fortune telling by
birth date] you hope for good luck; if you believe in geomancy, you
hope to benefit from the location of your ancestral graves. This year,
within the space of a few months the local tyrants and evil gentry and
corrupt officials have all toppled from their pedestals. Is it possible that
until a few months ago they all had good luck and enjoyed the benefit of
well-sited ancestral graves, while suddenly in the last few months their
luck has turned and their ancestral graves have ceased to exert a beneficial influence?

The Gods? Worship them by all means. But if you only had Lord
Kuan [a second-century warrior worshipped as the god of loyalty and
war] and the Goddess of Mercy and no peasant association, could you
have overthrown the local tyrants and evil gentry? The gods and god-
desses are indeed miserable objects. You have worshipped them for
centuries, and they have not overthrown a single one of the local tyrants
or evil gentry for you! Now you want to have your rent reduced. Let me
ask, how will you go about it? Will you believe in the gods or in the
peasant association?

The new rural revolt threw up new taboos. Mah-jong,
dominoes and card games were completely forbidden wherever
the peasants' associations were powerful, and one of them had
burned two basketfuls of Mah-jong sets. Opium pipes were being
surrendered. 'Vulgar performances' of the flower drum dance
were forbidden in many places. In some counties sedan-chairs
had been smashed, or else the peasants had considerably
increased the fares charged for being carried in them, in order to
penalize the rich. Luxury at feasts was forbidden. In Shaoshan,
Mao's own village, 'it has been decided that guests are to be
served with only three kinds of animal food, namely chicken, fish
and pork. It is also forbidden to serve bamboo shoots, kelp and
lentil noodles.'

The peasants were setting up their own evening classes
according to their own ideas, and were not following the example
of the 'foreign-style school' which had previously been regarded
as the most up-to-date. Mao conceded in this connection that he
once had wrong ideas about schools:

In my student days, when I went back to the village and saw that the peasants were against the 'foreign-style school', I, too, used to identify myself with the general run of 'foreign-style students and teachers' and stand up for it, feeling that the peasants were somehow wrong. It was not until 1925, when I lived in the countryside for six months and was already a Communist and had acquired a Marxist viewpoint, that I realized I had been wrong and the peasants right.

And finally Mao had a word for Chiang Kai-shek and 'other such gentlemen' who were upset and dismayed by the peasants' initiative, comparing them to the famous Lord Sheh, a figure from the distant Chinese past who was so fond of dragons that his whole palace was filled with drawings and carvings of them. But when a real dragon heard about his infatuation and paid a visit, he was frightened out of his wits. 'To talk about "arousing the masses of the people" day in and day out and then to be scared to death when the masses do rise – what difference is there between this and Lord Sheh's love of dragons?'

This incidentally was Mao's first public condemnation of the man – Chiang Kai-shek – with whom he was later to struggle over fourteen years for the leadership of China. Yet Mao's first act after writing this report was to go to Wuhan for a conference of the Left Kuomintang, where he defended the violent action of the peasants against the landlords and argued for a land reform policy even more radical than that of the Comintern. He wrote a short poem there called 'Yellow Crane Tower':

> Wide, wide flow the nine streams through the land,
> Dark, dark threads the line from south to north.
> Blurred in the thick haze of the misty rain
> Tortoise and Snake hold the great river locked.
>
> The yellow crane is gone, who knows whither?
> Only this tower remains a haunt for visitors.
> I pledge my wine to the surging torrent,
> The tide of my heart swells with the waves.

In April the Kuomintang established a special committee to deal with its land policy problem, where Mao went on arguing for forcible expropriation not only of landlords but also of rich peasants – which even Stalin jibbed at – with retroactive legalization. At the final meeting Mao presented a resolution attempting to accommodate the conflicting points of view, only to be lambasted from both left and right for either going too far or not going far enough. Right in the middle of the discussions came news from Shanghai of Chiang Kai-shek's bloody masssacre of workers and Communist leaders, using the Green and Red Gangs of semi-criminal secret societies which were his allies. His troops had only just, with the secret societies' help, taken the city and brought it under Kuomintang rule. The rightists in the Kuomintang were now out in the open and dominant, with a charismatic leader in Chiang.

Mao put his radical solution of the land problem to the inaugural congress in April of the All-China Peasant Association, and was supported by those peasant leaders with a genuine experience of local organization, as well as by two Russian Comintern advisers. The conference backed him, and he was made chairman of the new association.

But when the Communists held their Fifth Congress, at Wuhan a few days later, they would not hear of these ideas.

I think today [Mao recollected ten years later] that if the peasant movement had been more thoroughly organized and armed for a class struggle against the landlords, the Communist base areas would have had an earlier and far more powerful development throughout the whole country. But Chen Tu-hsiu violently disagreed. He did not understand the role of the peasantry in the revolution and greatly underestimated its possibilities at this time. Consequently, the Fifth Congress ... failed to pass an adequate land programme. My opinions, which called for rapid intensification of the agrarian struggle, were not even discussed, for the Central Committee, also dominated by Chen Tu-hsiu, refused to bring them up for consideration.

On the second day of the Congress Li Ta-chao, the man who had introduced Mao to Marxism, was captured in a raid on the Russian Legation in Peking and garrotted by northern warlord forces. The shocked comrades in conference in Wuhan were perhaps strengthened in their resolve to hang on to their alliance with the Kuomintang, in spite of the killings in Shanghai and in spite of the personal misgivings which most of them now had about Chiang Kai-shek himself. Mao's land programme did not fit in with their views, and his radical theses were rejected. He was sacked from directing the Peasant Section, and had the humiliation of being elected only as an alternate and not a full member of the Central Committee.

After a few days Mao stopped attending the meetings, feigning illness. He went back to Changsha and acquired his first and not very glorious experience of leading armed peasant rebellion against the landlords and their military backers, who prevailed on the new militarist Governor of Hunan, General Tang, to issue a secret order for Mao's arrest.

But Mao's luck held. His colleagues got wind of the order and in May he fled to Liuyang, near the Kiangsi border, with a handful of friends. But the peasants continued to confiscate land even in the shadow of the city of Changsha, and the garrison commander there retaliated by destroying the offices of the peasant unions and the Cultural Book Society and declaring allegiance to Chiang Kai-shek. One of Mao's close friends was killed in this so-called Horse Day incident in Changsha. As a result of the shootings, most of the leaders of the Provincial Committee of the Hunanese Communists joined Mao in Liuyang in order to organize a new rebellion.

According to one account, they began to mobilize about 300,000 peasants for an attack on the provincial capital on 30 May, but a senior Communist official sent from Wuhan at the last minute told them to cancel the plan. He argued that the only result of its success would be to provoke Governor Tang, who was personally not ill-disposed to the Communists, to march on Wuhan and overthrow the Communist-supported government there. Reluctantly the provincial committee agreed with this 'shameful' decision, as Mao's supporters regarded it – but too late to prevent several thousand peasants from exposing themselves to the fire of the Changsha commander's troops and being mercilessly slaughtered. Mao returned to Wuhan to answer to Chen and the Party leaders. He was openly following a policy line at this time far to the left of the Central Committee and the Comintern.

The post-mortems were extended and agonized, before both the Left Kuomintang government and the Communist Party leaders. According to Kuomintang reports, Mao was critical of the excesses of the peasant movement which had led up to the Horse Day incident in Changsha, saying that the peasant associations were controlled by local gangs equally ignorant about the Kuomintang or the Communist Party: all that they knew were manslaughter and arson.

On 13 June Mao wrote *The Latest Directives of the National Peasant Association,* a sour and bruised admission of defeat. The peasant movement had developed quickly, but the 'ferocious counter-attacks of the local bullies and evil gentry' had been greater than expected and 'direction by the upper levels has, inadvertently, not always been too close' (a veiled criticism of the Communist and Left Kuomintang leaders). Recording that thousands of Communists and peasants had lost their lives in the struggles of the preceding months, Mao lamely called on peasant associations to 'request' the national government to protect them and guarantee their freedom to carry out the revolution and 'the campaign to punish Chiang Kai-shek'.

'Because the authority of the local tyrants and evil gentry has not been crushed, it has proven impossible to establish village self-rule and set up a democratic government; still less has it been possible to realize economic construction and thus there has been no way to consolidate the base of the national government.' It had been a costly lesson in the need to prepare revolutions more thoroughly.

In these circumstances Mao now separated from his wife and children because the political situation made it too dangerous for them to live together. He was never to see his wife again, and it would be seventeen years before he would see the two boys. There was now a baby too, a third boy called Mao An-lung, but he completely disappeared in the turmoil of the years that followed. All four were now sent to Mao's brother-in-law's house in Changsha for safety.

The Communist break with the Left Kuomintang finally came in July. Instead of playing along any more with inadequate allies, the Communists decided on a series of risings to coincide with the autumn harvest, and meetings were held to plan them in July. Mao was to play a big role in the new violent phase in the Communist Party's struggle for power which now began.

PART TWO
STRUGGLE

7

A MOUNTAIN KINGDOM

At the beginning of August 1927 Mao and his fellow Communists conferred anxiously at Kiukang to consider their future after their abrupt dismissal by the Left Kuomintang. Chen Tu-hsiu, diplomatically absent from the conference, was dismissed from office and made the scapegoat for the failings of the Party and its Russian advisers (or, as some would say, masters). Chu Chiu-pai – a Russian-trained journalist – took his place as General Secretary. Mao, restored to the Central Committee, told his colleagues that armed struggle was necessary, and they agreed. The Autumn Harvest Uprising had already been launched at Nanchang by Chou En-lai, Ho Lung and Chu Teh, on what was afterwards celebrated as the official founding day of the Red Army.

Mao was promptly sent to Changsha, travelling secretly on a freight train, to organize an Autumn Harvest Uprising in Hunan province. He was to sever the provincial Communist Party from the Kuomintang, and create a peasant-worker revolutionary army there. At the first meeting of the re-organized Provincial Communist Party Committee a self-confident Mao set out his radical plans for the revolt, going much further than the Central Committee by speaking of the creation of rural bases and expropriating landlords' property.

Mao wrote to the Central Committee advocating the establishment of base areas of workers and peasants under the Communist flag. 'I have come to understand'. he wrote, 'that the Hunanese peasants definitely want a complete solution of the land question.' He proposed the confiscation of all land, 'including that of small landowners and peasant proprietors', to be distributed fairly to all the peasants on a collective basis. The Central Committee admonished Mao for these heresies, but he refused to toe the line, and put his ideas to work in the Autumn Harvest Uprising.

The uprising began on 9 September, with four 'regiments' assembled by Mao made up of Anyuan coal miners, local peasant forces and dissident soldiers who had crossed over from the Kuomintang. But Mao himself was not able to command the operation. While organizing his four regiments he was captured by Kuomintang guards and taken to their headquarters to be shot, along with other suspected Communists. He afterwards recalled:

Borrowing several tens of dollars from a comrade, however, I attempted to bribe the escort to free me. The ordinary soldiers were mercenaries, with no special interest in seeing me killed, and they agreed to release me, but the subaltern in charge refused to permit it. I therefore decided to attempt to escape, but had no opportunity to do so until I was within about two hundred yards of the guards' headquarters. At that point I broke loose and ran into the fields.

He reached a high place, above a pond, surrounded by tall grass, and hid there until sunset. The soldiers pursued him, making some peasants help them search.

Many times they came very near, once or twice so close I could almost have touched them, but somehow I escaped discovery, although half a dozen times I gave up hope, feeling certain I would be recaptured.

At last, when it was dusk, they abandoned the search. At once I set off across the mountains, travelling all night. I had no shoes and my feet were badly bruised. On the road I met a peasant who befriended me, gave me shelter and later guided me to the next district. I had seven dollars with me, and used this to buy some shoes, an umbrella and food. When at last I reached the peasant guards safely, I had only two coppers in my pocket.

In the Kuomintang version of the story the bribe worked.

The uprising went well for the first few days, with many important towns falling to the rebels. The workers of Changsha did not, however, rise up in support of the peasants as Mao had expected. The tiny rebel army then faced an internal disaster when the two groups of Kuomintang deserters decided to have a pitched battle between themselves, whereupon the Anyuan miners were almost annihilated and Mao's peasant regiment ambushed.

Within a week of the start, Mao had to call the entire operation off as hopeless. As he admitted, 'discipline was poor, political training was at a low level and many wavering elements were among the men and officers. There were many desertions'. During the uprising, the Communists killed and burnt the houses of many Kuomintang people whom they had called comrades during the United Front period, hence the bitter song which became popular in Hunan at that time:

> Cut, cut, cut! Comrades cut off the heads of comrades!
> Burn, burn, burn! Comrades burn down the houses of comrades!

Mao assembled the remnants of his rebels at Wenchiashih, in Liuyang county, and after a meeting of the Front Committee led them towards Chingkangshan on 20 September – taking the opportunity along the road of releasing Communist prisoners, opening public granaries and distributing grain to the peasants.

His men were ambushed at Luhsi, but at the end of September Mao was able to regroup them and re-invigorate them at Sanwan in Yunghsin county. That evening Mao re-organized these 400 men into one regiment, promising them democracy, Party control over the officers, no beatings and free speech, and this was, in another sense, the beginning of the Red Army.

In October, having marched more than 300 miles from Wenchiashih, Mao and his precious regiment reached the place which was to serve him not only as a mountain base off and on for the next several years but also as a source of inspiration for the rest of his career – the Chingkang Mountains, or Chingkangshan, on the borders of Hunan and Kiangsi.

Afterwards Mao put the blame for the disasters of 1927 squarely on Chen (the Chinese) and on the two Comintern advisers – Roy (the Indian) and Borodin (the Russian). Chen Tu-hsiu's 'wavering opportunism' was most responsible, but Borodin 'was ready to do everything to please the bourgeoisie, even to the disarming of the workers, which he finally ordered', while M. N. Roy, the Indian delegate of the Comintern, 'stood a little to the left of both Chen and Borodin, but he only stood'. Roy was a talker and a fool, Borodin a blunderer and Chen an unconscious traitor. For his part Roy dismissed Mao as 'completely unstable, one of those who persistently and deliberately sabotaged all our revolutionary plans'.

Mao's judgements come awkwardly from the man who himself made such a volte-face in his view of the revolutionary prospects during the four weeks of late August and early September. In August Mao had expressed the conviction that China was about to see her October Revolution, but after the failure to take Changsha by force he came to believe that 'from the point of view of the cities the movement appeared lost'. He had misjudged his chances.

There is no doubt that he had grossly exaggerated the real
potential for peasant uprising. As one of the comrades of the time
put it afterwards, 'Mao promised Chu Chiu-pai 100,000 Hunanese peasants, Chu telegrammed Moscow a figure of 200,000, and
in the end only 5,000 turned out'.

The Communist Politburo meeting on 14 November put the
blame on Mao for the disaster in Changsha: 'Comrade Mao
should shoulder the most serious responsibility for the mistakes
made by the Hunan Provincial Committee. He should be dismissed from his position as alternate member of the Provisional
Politburo of the Central Committee . . .' He was accused of military opportunism, inadequate peasant mobilization, collaboration with bandits and failure to obey Central Committee directives.

Mao's explanation of his disgrace was somewhat tongue-in-
cheek: Chu Chiu-pai's people 'came across a pamphlet of mine
in Hunan which contained my remark "Political power comes
from the barrel of a gun". This infuriated them. How could
political power possibly come from the barrel of a gun? So they
stripped me of my position . . .' He was unrepentant: 'We
nevertheless held our army together at Chingkangshan, feeling
certain that we were following the correct line. . . .'

Actually Mao and the Central Committee were not far apart
in the essentials. They both agreed that the goal was to surround
the cities from the countryside by using the organized revolutionary energy of the peasantry (which was the main force), co-
ordinating it with military and urban insurrection (the auxiliary
forces).

But Mao, unlike the Central Committee, had little faith in the
impact of scattered risings over broad areas of terrain. Moreover
the forces which he was using in Hunan had become mixed up
with regular army troops, so it was not surprising that they
should be treated as 'another guest army passing through'. The
Central Committee's criticism of Mao, that he had contacted
only 'bandits and rag-tag troops without getting the broad peasant masses to rise', had some truth in it.

The highland base where Mao now found sanctuary free from
Kuomintang and warlord pursuers was a desolate and sparsely
inhabited circle of mountains about thirty miles across and 180
miles around. Only half a dozen narrow winding trails lead
through the forests of pine, spruce and bamboo with their great
flowering creepers into the heart of Chingkangshan, whose
towering volcanic peaks are usually shrouded in fog. Mao gave

this description of it in his first report to the Communist leaders:

In the mountains there are paddy-fields and villages. . . . All these places used to be infested by bandits and deserters but have now been turned into our base area. Its population is under two thousand, and the yield of unhusked rice is less than 600 tons, and so the entire grain for the army has to be supplied from Ningkang, Yunghsin and Suichuan Counties. All the strategic passes in the mountains are fortified. Our hospitals, bedding and clothing workshops, ordnance department and regimental rear offices are all here. At the present moment grain is being transported to the mountains from Ningkang. Provided we have adequate supplies the enemy can never break in.

It was no rest home for Mao's 'regiment'. Many of the soldiers had only thin cotton clothes to protect them from the snow and frost of the winter, and the only foodstuff in generous supply was pumpkin.

As they came to Chingkangshan, Mao's men encountered two secret society bandit leaders, from the Society of Elders or Ko Lao Hui, who had 600 men and 120 rifles. Obviously Mao's small force had no hope of overcoming these men, and so Mao struck up an alliance with them instead, regarding them as socially transformable under Communist leadership.

'While I remained on Chingkangshan,' he afterwards claimed, 'they were faithful Communists, and carried out the orders of the Party. Later on, when they were left alone on Chingkangshan, they returned to their bandit habits. Subsequently they were killed by the peasants, by then organized and sovietized and able to defend themselves'.

Mao's critics in the Party subsequently rebuked him for taking as allies such demonstrably un-progressive people. But Mao had already made clear his views on the so-called *éléments déclassés*, and in any case it was a question at Chingkangshan of sheer survival.

One of his critics claimed that Mao told him later, at the end of the 1930s, that he had had the two bandit generals murdered at a dinner a year after entering Chingkangshan, by which time he was safe in the company of the various Communist forces which had come to join him. He was then able to disarm the bandit ranks.

If this was his new kingdom, Mao also acquired, in the absence of Yang Kai-hui, left behind in Changsha, a new queen. During 1928 he began to live with Ho Tzu-chen, 'a small, delicate woman with a pretty face and a shy, modest manner', who was barely half his age – eighteen to his thirty-five. A landlord's daughter, she had studied at the Hunan Normal School, become a teacher and joined the Communist Party in 1927. She had led a regiment of women in the Nanchang Uprising, and was in all these respects a natural partner for Mao in his exile.

The only criticism made of her was that, because of her family's high living standards, she never got used to manual work and was unwilling to undertake the chores of domestic life. On the other hand she was regarded by the other Communist women as a 'domestic' type who preferred to look after Mao personally rather than delegate the job to others.

The common attitude towards liaisons such as this was well put by Mao's later comrade-in-arms at Chingkangshan, General Chu Teh, who explained his own marriage while in the field in this way:

It was not a conventional marriage. I had a wife in Szechwan whom I had not seen since 1922. We had sometimes corresponded, but she had long since known that my life belonged to the revolution and that I would never return home. Both Wu Yu-lan and her family knew all this, but they were not bound by conventional forms. Of course Wu Yu-lan, like other women, kept her own name, had her own work in the political department, and spent the major part of her time out in the villages.

Mao's case was not identical: his beloved Yang Kai-hui was fully committed to the revolution, and he doubtless hoped to return to her. For him Ho provided a companionship which he needed, but without at this stage any commitment to a long-term relationship. Mao admitted in discussion with comrades that the sight of a pretty girl would arouse his 'voluptuous feelings'.

From this virtually impregnable base, a kind of Chinese Sherwood Forest, Mao sought to extend his influence, and gradually his 400 men swelled in numbers and came to control more territory. He had to go down to the surrounding farmlands in order to get food and other supplies. But instead of merely raiding, he set up his first independent government, of what the Chinese Communists were to call a soviet, with its capital at Chaling. A People's Council was the executive, while representatives of the workers, peasants and soldiers formed a legislature. The land policies in Chaling were moderate, and Mao, learning from the consequences of his earlier enthusiasm, neither confiscated nor redistributed land. He did lead guerrilla uprisings against the land-owning gentry in the district in order to get food and weapons. But he got no co-operation from the local peasants, who still treated him with the same reserve as other 'guest armies'.

He was soon harried by other Communist officials whose responsibility extended to this remote border area, notably the Southern Hunan Special Party Committee and the regular Hunan Provincial Party Committee which was the official agent of the Politburo. Five months after Mao's arrival in Chingkangshan an emissary came from the Southern Hunan Committee depriving Mao of his power and reorganizing his local government, leaving him as merely a troop commander. Mao was regarded now as being too soft towards landlords: a year or two earlier it was he who had been the extremist, but now he had learnt to be more subtle in accelerating social changes among the peasants.

As a result of all this the Chingkangshan base was temporarily lost, but Mao joined forces in southern Hunan with the great hero of the Nanchang Uprising, Chu Teh. Chu had arrived at Kueitung, in the south of Hunan, with a motley band of survivors from the Uprisings – men from numerous armies and peasant forces who had been defeated during the previous autumn. Chu Teh had drawn up his own plans for peasant uprisings in southern Hunan, and Mao sent his brother, Tse-tan, to liaise with him. Chu was not successful, however, and was forced to retreat yet again from the southern Hunanese cities eastwards into Chingkangshan. The two men met at Linghsien in May.

'Chu Teh', his biographer wrote, 'had seen Mao Tse-tung once, but only across a dim hall during a secret meeting, and they had never really met'. It was the most significant encounter in Mao's life, since he was able to establish with this bluff and indomitable soldier a rapport which ensured the most puissant alliance in the Chinese Communist ranks. It may be a slight exaggeration to say, as one historian of the Communist Party does, that 'Mao would have become a bandit for the rest of his life, were it not for Chu Teh ...' But it is legitimate to suppose that if this union had not come off, Mao would have remained at best a discredited provincial leader.

Chu's story was even more colourful than Mao's. Seven years older, he came from a Szechuanese peasant family and had joined not only the predecessor organization to the Kuomintang but also the Ko Lao Hui, the secret society (he had to drink a blood oath). He lost two brothers in action, and his wife and son were murdered by warlords. In the early 1920s he became an opium addict, but was cured and sailed to Europe for further studies at Göttingen. He was a straightforward and much-loved man of great resourcefulness: he once saved his life after being captured by shouting, 'Don't shoot me, I'm only the cook.'

The two leaders and their men, augmented by 8000 peasant soldiers recruited by Mao during his expedition to southern Hunan, now retreated to Maoping in Kiangsi, under the shadow of Chingkangshan. They were immediately joined by Lin Piao, who was then only nineteen but who went on to become in the 1970s Mao's last great rival for power. Lin was a Hupeh peasant boy who followed his elder brothers and cousins into revolutionary activity, training at the Whampoa Military Academy before serving on Chiang Kai-shek's Northern Expedition as a platoon commander. He led first a company and then a battalion in the Nanchang Uprising. At Chingkangshan he merged his men with the Fourth Red Army and served initially as a battalion commander to help defend the base from Kuomintang troops. Mao said of him: 'Lin Piao is not only a man of ability, but also a general of talent. A person like him is capable of keeping the whole situation in mind, and our armed forces will need such a person to lead them in the future.'

A comrade who visited Mao's base at this time remembered his conversation over dinner:

During dinner, Mao smiled often. When he talked about the good prospects of the future, he laughed heartily. But his expression changed to a worried and sad look when he talked about current economic and food problems. He became extremely angry when he mentioned how he was given several warnings by the Party Centre. . . . He was called a 'deserter abandoning the masses' when he retreated to Chingkangshan. Mao clenched his fist and railed at the responsible Central leaders for their knowing only empty talk without heeding real situations. His manner suggested that he would not be satisfied until he had his vengeance. I feel that Mao had a talent for acting. In a short time he displayed all the sentiments of joy, anger, sadness and happiness.

On 20 May 1928 the Communist leaders on Chingkangshan endorsed, at a conference in Maoping, a platform containing all the essential features of what was to become in the ensuing years the Maoist policy line. In military policy this included the famous quatrain:

> The enemy advances, we retreat.
> The enemy halts and encamps, we harass.
> The enemy seeks to avoid battle, we attack.
> The enemy retreats, we pursue.

It also embraced the famous 'three rules of discipline' and the 'eight points for attention' which had been devised to govern the conduct of the Communist troops and help them gain the trust and support of the people. The three rules of discipline were: (1) Obey orders in all your actions; (2) Don't take a single needle or piece of thread from the people; and (3) Turn in everything which you capture. The original six points for attention set out a few months later were: (1) Put back the doors which you have taken down for bed-boards; (2) Put back the straw which you use for bedding; (3) Speak politely; (4) Pay fairly for what you consume; (5) Return everything you borrow; and (6) Pay for everything you damage. A year or so later two more points were added: (7) Don't bathe within sight of women, and (8) Don't search the pockets of captives.

Instead of working through political directors, the Red Army in Chingkangshan established soldiers' soviets, which were more democratic and educational. 'When the political departments existed,' Mao commented, 'the soldiers believed that political work was to be done only by the few persons in the political departments. All others had only the duty of fighting. After the political departments were abolished everyone both fought and did political work. This broke the precedent of simple military-mindedness.'

The Chingkangshan area should, the Maoping conference agreed, be consolidated as a revolutionary base and then gradually extended by a series of waves. Land would be confiscated without compensation and distributed to the peasants, who would be armed and organized to defend that land. But moderate policies would be followed towards small merchants and middle and rich peasants.

This platform was based on five theses which Mao put to his colleagues at Maoping. Firstly, he told them, China was a semi-colonial country, uneven in political development, with few industrial workers but many peasants. Secondly, it was a huge country with abundant resources for revolution. Thirdly, however, the counter-revolutionary forces were strong, and controlled China through the political organization of the Kuomintang helped by international recognition from the imperialist powers. Fourthly, the revolutionary forces were weak, with Red Armies established only in poor backward areas. Finally, the peasants stood ready to revolt and redistribute land if they had the opportunity.

All these propositions made sense to Chu Teh and the others, although they knew that Mao was not in good standing with the official leadership of the Party.

But in the summer these cosy arrangements were upset when Mao's seniors in the Communist leadership managed to get through to him in Chingkangshan. They first ordered him to send most of his men into southern Hunan, leaving only a token force to defend the Chingkangshan base itself. Mao's comrades decided to disobey this extraordinary order, but one regiment was convinced by direct intervention from one of the Party emissaries – and when it had gone, General Chu decided he had better send more men to back it up. One of the emissaries sent by the Party had papers of his own appointment in Mao's place, and so Mao was obliged to stand on the sidelines for most of that summer while half his army was destroyed in these misguided manoeuvres.

According to von Braun, the German Comintern adviser, Mao was angry with his new partner, General Chu Teh, for his passive acceptance of these outside orders which led to such a military fiasco, accusing him of 'opportunist deviations' and 'theoretical ignorance' – while General Chu was in turn critical of the idea of using Chingkangshan all the time as their main base.

When the two men were reconciled in 1929, Mao systematically undermined Chu's authority as army leader, according to von Braun, winning over some of Chu's senior lieutenants, including Chen Yi, his political commissar, and Lin Piao, then one of his battalion commanders, to his side. Chu apparently resigned himself to this loss of authority, remaining as formal commander. Much of what Braun claimed would have been the natural consequence of putting the army under political control, a principle on which Mao and Chu had agreed. But Lin Piao's later allegations against Chu supported the idea that General Chu was not the strong pillar which some accounts portrayed him as. He had obvious military qualities, but lacked political judgement and tended to waver when conflicting orders came from different political headquarters. His loyalty could be depended upon only as long as Mao was by his side.

There was one unexpected result of the interregnum in leadership. Many of the recently recruited Communists in Chingkangshan became turncoats, and when Mao took over again in September after the return of the defeated Red Army, he instituted a drastic purge of the local Party involving the re-registration of membership. This, together with a new parallel security organization which he created at the same time, allowed Mao to preside over a much more loyal and disciplined organization than before.

Within a few weeks Mao and Chu had recovered most of the territory they had lost during the year, and their base was once more a viable concern. Mao celebrated this in an upbeat poem entitled 'Chingkangshan'.

> Below the hills fly our flags and banners,
> Above the hilltops sound our bugles and drums.
> The foe encircles us thousands strong,
> Steadfastly we stand our ground.
>
> Already our defence is iron-clad,
> Now our wills unite like a fortress.
> From Huangyangchieh roars the thunder of guns,
> Word comes the enemy has fled into the night.

In October Mao analysed the nature of institutions like the Chingkangshan base in an article with the title, 'Why is it that Red Political Power can Exist in China?' 'The long-term survival', he boasted, 'inside a country of one or more small areas under Red political power completely encircled by a White Regime is a phenomenon which has never occurred anywhere else in the world.'

But the economic stranglehold which their enemies were putting on them was stifling. 'Because of the tight enemy blockade,' he wrote, 'necessities such as salt, cloth and medicines have been very scarce and dear all through the past year . . .' The Red Army 'even lacks funds to pay the daily food allowance of five cents per person which is provided in addition to grain: soldiers are undernourished and many are ill, and the wounded in the hospitals are worse off.'

Mao acquired one piece of property towards the end of 1928 which greatly satisfied him. The Red Army captured a dun-coloured horse at Changting from a Kuomintang general who commanded his men from a sedan-chair. It was allocated to Mao and became his favourite mount, which he was to ride for years.

8
MUTINY

In November 1928 Mao sent his Central Committee a long and agonized plea for help, in a report called *The Struggle in the Ching-kang Mountains*. Casualties were mounting, both among the soldiers and among the Party officials. In the context of military casualties Mao justified his use of bandit recruits. 'The contingent of *éléments déclassés*', he conceded, 'should be replaced by peasants and workers, but these are not available now.' Besides, they were 'especially good fighters', so the only course was to retain them but also to 'intensify political training, so as to effect a qualitative change in these elements.'

But more Party members were needed in the base, and Mao hoped that 'at least thirty' would be assigned from the outside. Soldiers were ill from 'malnutrition, exposure to cold or other causes', and the hospitals had more than 800 patients to treat without enough doctors or medicine. Mao urged the Central Committee to 'send a few doctors with Western training, and some iodine.'

He explained why the difficulties had not stopped the Communists in their tracks. 'The reason why the Red Army has been able to carry on ... is its practice of democracy. The officers do not beat the men, officers and men receive equal treatment, soldiers are free to hold meetings and to speak out, trivial formalities have been done away with, and the accounts are open for all to inspect.

The soldiers handle the mess arrangements, and, out of the daily five cents for cooking oil, salt, firewood and vegetables, they can even save a little for pocket money, amounting to roughly six or seven coppers per person per day, which is called 'mess savings'. All this gives great satisfaction to the soldiers. The newly captured soldiers in particular feel that our army and the Kuomintang army are worlds apart. They feel spiritually liberated, even though material conditions ... are not equal to those in the White Army.

But spreading revolution outside the base was depressingly difficult.

As the feudal family system prevails in every county, and as all the families in a village or group of villages belong to a single clan, it will be quite a time before people become conscious of their class, and clan sentiment is overcome in the villages.

Having extolled the democracy that prevailed in the army, Mao admitted the weakness of the democratic idea at large. 'The evil feudal practice of arbitrary dictation is so deeply rooted in the minds of the people and even of the ordinary Party members that it cannot be swept away at once; when anything crops up they choose the easy way and have no liking for the bothersome democratic system.'

For all these reasons the progress of the revolution was slow. 'Wherever the Red Army goes, the masses are cold and aloof, and only after our propaganda do they slowly move into action.' There followed one of the most moving and painful sentences to come from his brush at this stage of his career. 'We have an acute sense of our isolation which we keep hoping will end.'

Reinforcement did in fact come a few days after writing this report, but not from the Central Committee. Another military unit came to join Mao in Chingkangshan led by General Peng Teh-huai, a Hunanese ex-Kuomintang officer who had mutinied in the summer and led one of the Autumn Harvest Uprisings which had failed. His men brought the Mao-Chu numbers up to almost 4000, ten times as many as Mao's original force.

Peng was a remarkable character, described as 'open, forthright and undeviating' and also as 'a man who spoke with machine-gun rapidity'. As a young boy he had actually been sentenced to death by his own parents, at the insistence of his grandmother, merely because in a fit of temper he had kicked over her opium stove. Only the intervention of a brave uncle had ensured his survival. He was now to become one of the main pillars of the Red Army leadership loyal to Mao, along with Chu Teh and Lin Piao.

Early in 1929 Mao and Chu swept down from their Chingkangshan lair, where the tight stranglehold of encircling Kuomintang troops had created a shortage of food. They marched to the granaries of southern Kiangsi and western Fukien in search of land to add to their base area and make it more viable, capturing Juichin and Tingchou.

Here Mao received a letter from the Central Committee under

its new leader – Li Li-san, the one who had answered Mao's student advertisement in Changsha and with whom Mao had collaborated in organizing the Anyuan coal miners. Instead of offering help, however, Li ordered Mao to dissolve the Red Army and come to Shanghai to help lead the proletarian revolution which he claimed was about to break out, leaving rural risings until the urban strength of the Communists was rebuilt.

Mao refused, and replied with a rebuke. 'To dread the development of the strength of the peasants, to believe that it would harm the revolution if the strength of the peasants were to surpass the leadership of the workers – we consider this false.' Instead Mao stayed in Kiangsi to consolidate the newly enlarged base area centred on Juichin, implementing a mild land reform which took land only from landlords but not from rich or middle peasants. Mao wanted the interests of the merchants to be protected, so as not to drive these men caught in the middle to the other side.

Mao's rebellion against Party authority was wholesale. He rejected Li Li-san's orders on three matters – postponing the land reform, splitting up the Red Army into small autonomous guerrilla units, and dismantling the rural bases – as well as differing from his assessment of the revolutionary tide in the countryside. Mao was clear in his own mind that he was right and the more theoretical leaders were wrong, and he was confident that a large number of people with practical experience in the field agreed with him.

During the next two years Mao reorganized the Red Armies in order to consolidate his own power base. He now had, including new recruits and smaller partisan units in the area, about 100,000 men at his disposal.

In September 1929 Mao was struck down by malaria, and convalesced in the market town of Kutien in the mountains of Fukien. Here he commented on Chiang Kai-shek's fight with the Kwangsi warlords:

> Sudden veer of wind and rain
> Showering misery through the land,
> The warlords are clashing anew –
> Yet another Golden Millet Dream.

> Red banners leap over the Ting River
> Straight to Lungyen and Shanghang.
> We have reclaimed part of the golden bowl
> And land is being shared out with a will.

He also composed a poem on the local autumn festival:

> Man ages all too easily, not Nature:
> Year by year the Double Ninth returns.
> On this Double Ninth,
> The yellow blooms on the battlefield smell sweeter.
>
> Each year the autumn wind blows fierce,
> Unlike spring's splendour,
> Yet surpassing spring's splendour,
> See the endless expanse of frosty sky and water.

Mao used his enforced idleness to write a tract inveighing against various kinds of wrong thinking among his followers. Some of them were obvious, like individualism, or an excessively military viewpoint. Others were more complex, such as ultra-democracy, the source of which Mao identified in 'the petty bourgeoisie's individualistic aversion to discipline'.

Democracy, he warned, should be under centralized guidance. Party leaders had to give the correct line, but should 'be familiar with the life of the masses' as well as with the circumstances of their juniors in order to have an objective basis for giving guidance correctly. Decisions should never be made casually, but once made should be promptly transmitted. 'The minority should submit to the majority', but criticism within the Party would strengthen it, as long as members understood that its purpose was 'to increase the Party's fighting capacity ... and that it should not be used as a means of personal attack.'

Another extreme, that of absolute egalitarianism, was to be avoided. 'When officers rode on horseback, it was regarded not as something necessary for performing their duties, but as a sign of inequality.' Some people demanded uniformly equal rations and loads: 'The headquarters would be abused for occupying larger rooms.' This absolute egalitarianism, 'like ultra-democracy in political matters, is the product of a handicraft and small peasant economy.' Mao explained that 'even under socialism there can be no absolute equality.'

When the Fourth Red Army leaders met in conference at Kutien on New Year's Day 1930, Mao agreed to reinstate the Political Commissariat at the expense of the powers of the soldiers' soviets. Now that he had reorganized the troops and their commands in such a way as to consolidate his own leadership, democratic institutions like soviets would only give an opening to his opponents.

He also proposed a stiffening up of the Party presence in the army, with Party cells in which officers and men would be mixed together. Those who had 'mistaken political attitudes', wanted only to 'eat well and live high', smoked opium, gambled, tried to get rich on foreign gold or frequently committed crimes and would not reform should be expelled from the Party.

As for the Red Army itself, Mao proposed that the military command and Political Commissariat should participate 'jointly and equally' in decision-making. He spelt out a new and strict disciplinary code requiring both soldiers and officers to work through the Party's political organs.

In all this he went a little too far for his comrades. Lin Piao supported him, but Peng Teh-huai did not. After two years of marching in and out of Chingkangshan, Mao's field commanders were apparently disappointed with the abandoned villages of Kiangsi as a base to support the Red Army. The superficially more appealing line of Li Li-san, of building up the revolution in the urban areas, now sounded more attractive than Mao's. The commanders looked forward to being quartered for once in a city. Mao had in any case upset a number of senior officers by organizing and shuffling their commands.

Mao celebrated New Year's Day with a short poem evoking the rural setting of his life in the base area:

> Ninghua, Chingliu, Kueihua –
> What narrow paths, deep woods and slippery moss!
> Whither are we bound today?
> Straight to the foot of Wuyi Mountain.
> To the mountain, the foot of the mountain,
> Red flags stream in the wind in a blaze of glory.

Lin Piao supported Mao at Kutien, but perhaps his faith needed buttressing, so Mao wrote him a letter on 5 January under the title 'A Single Spark can Start a Prairie Fire'. Here Mao gave reasons for his optimism. 'All China', he wrote, 'is littered with dry faggots which will soon be aflame.' The goal of creating an independent popular regime in the three provinces of Kiangsi, western Fukien and western Chekiang within a year could be attained. Only the time limit was perhaps mistaken, conveying 'a flavour of impetuosity', but Mao held nevertheless to the view that 'there will soon be a high tide of revolution.' How should that word 'soon' be interpreted? Mao answered his own question in ringing prose.

Marxists are not fortune-tellers. They should, and indeed can, only indicate the general direction of future developments and changes; they should not and cannot fix the day and the hour in a mechanistic way. But when I say that there will soon be a high tide of revolution, I am emphatically not speaking of something which in the words of some people 'is possibly coming', something illusory, unattainable and devoid of significance for action.

It is like a ship far out at sea whose masthead can already be seen from the shore; it is like the morning sun in the East whose shimmering rays are visible from a high mountain top; it is like a child about to be born moving restlessly in its mother's womb.

The Red Army was now doing fairly well, in spite of Li Li-san's scorn for Mao's 'old-fashioned ideas of evasive dispersion'. Mao commemorated the high morale of his men in a poem on the eve of their first capture of Kian, the Kiangsi town which they took no fewer than nine times that year.

> The whole wide world is white,
> Through the snow eagerly we press on.
> Crags loom above our heads,
> We cross the great pass, red flags waving in the wind.
>
> Where are we bound?
> To the snow-swept River Kan.
> Yesterday the order was given,
> One hundred thousand workers and peasants march on Kian.

At the end of March Mao acquired a new orderly. The lad well remembered his first sight of 'Commissar Mao', as he was then called.

'I looked at him curiously,' the young man later recollected. 'His grey uniform was the same as ours. The only difference was that the pockets on his coat seemed to be especially large. His black hair contrasted sharply with his fair complexion. Maybe he was a bit too thin.'

Mao turned to welcome his new helper, who had until that morning been a bugler at the Fourth Army Headquarters.

'What's your surname?' he asked.

'Chen,' the soldier replied.

'What are you called?'

'Chang-feng.'

'How old are you?'

'Sixteen.'

'Why did you join the Red Army?'

'The Red Army is good. It fights the local despots!'

At this point Mao made the young man sit down and asked

him with interest, 'Are there local despots in your home village?'

'Yes, I was driven away by them myself.'

Chen blurted out his story.

'Well,' said Mao, 'now you'll have to work and study hard. Can you write your name?'

Chen stood up and twisted the edge of his jacket in embarrassment.

'I've never been to school. I don't know how to write.'

'Then you'll have to learn . . .'

Some time later Mao wrote a letter to his orderly's father for him to send in the post.

Mao's possessions at this time consisted of two cotton-and-wool-mixture blankets, a cotton sheet, two ordinary grey uniform jackets and trousers, a grey woollen sweater, a worn overcoat, a patched umbrella, an enamel mug and a grey brief-case with nine compartments filled with maps, documents and books – one of them being his boyhood favourite, *Water Margin*.

When he was on the march he used to carry his briefcase and the umbrella, while his orderly made a roll of the other things. When they made camp, the orderly used to find two wooden boards, put them together and spread the blanket and sheet on them, folding up Mao's uniforms to make a pillow. This would be Mao's bed.

After the evening meal Mao would invariably light his lamp, open up his briefcase and take out his maps, documents, books, papers and writing brush and sometimes work until dawn.

Chen remembered:

I used to sit by him. I was very young and could never keep awake. I would drop off to sleep and slide down to the floor. He would often wake me up about midnight, saying, 'Let's have some cold water.' I used to fetch cold water in a little bucket so that he could freshen up. We had no basin, and he dipped his towel in the water.

He would feel hungry after that, and I would give him 'three-level food' in his mug – that is, rice in first, then whatever vegetable was going, and then more rice. The food consisted of reheated leftovers from the afternoon meal. If he could not finish his three-level food he would cover it up with a piece of paper and eat it another time. He would never waste food.

Once Chen threw away the rice Mao had left, and on the next day Mao asked:

'Chen Chang-feng, where is the rice I left yesterday?'

Chen told him what he had done, and Mao protested.

'There is a struggle for every grain of rice that the people grow. In future you mustn't throw away what I leave. Keep it for the next meal.'

In April Li Li-san launched a campaign which became the Communist Party's most dismal failure. Criticizing Mao's conservatism and ordering him to attend a conference of soviet region representatives in Shanghai, Li ordered a grand offensive by the Red Armies to try to seize power in central China. He 'over-estimated', Mao later recalled, 'both the military strength of the Red Army at that time and the revolutionary factors in the national political scene. He believed that the revolution was nearing success and would shortly have power over the entire country.' Li felt that Chiang Kai-shek and the warlords would knock each other out in the chaotic political situation of China, leaving the country open for the Communists, whereas Mao was less sanguine: their two enemies might collaborate against them.

Mao ignored the order to go to Shanghai. It was about this time that *Inprecor*, the Comintern magazine in Europe, published his obituary. There were to be several such premature announcements.

In May 1930 Mao found time for a pedagogic essay entitled 'Oppose Bookism' which began:

If you have not made an investigation of a particular problem, your right to speak on it is suspended. Is this too drastic? Not at all. If you have not made an investigation of the actual and historical conditions of the particular problem you are discussing, if you do not know its background, you will inevitably be talking through your hat. . . . Many inspectors, guerrilla leaders and newly-assigned work cadres like to declare their political opinion the moment they arrive on the scene. After seeing some superficialities, some side issues, they gesticulate and criticize, pointing out mistakes and errors. Such subjective, irresponsible talk is most reprehensible. One who talks this way will inevitably ruin the matter and lose mass support.

Mao's advice to leaders was to 'stretch your legs, take a walk around your work area and learn the Confucian way, "inquiring into everything".' Investigation was the 'ten-month gestation', while the solution of a problem was the 'one-day delivery'.

Li Li-san's offensive quickly petered out. General Peng Teh-huai captured Changsha briefly, only to be forced out again – with dire results for Mao's family. Unaware of the personal price he was about to pay, Mao hailed these events in an exultant mood.

In June Heaven's armies chastise the corrupt and evil,
Seeking to bind roc and whale with a league-long cord.
Red glows the far side of the Kan,
Thanks to our wing under Huang Kung-lueh.
A million workers and peasants rise up,
Sweeping Kiangsi straight towards Hunan and Hupeh.
To the *Internationale*'s stirring strains
A wild whirlwind swoops from the sky.

Shortly afterwards Mao and Chu marched on Nanchang, but were unable to breach its defences. They had to turn back to Changsha, combining with Peng's forces to carry out Li's latest instruction to try once again to capture the provincial capital.

There was a long and bitter fight in the first half of September which involved the Red Army in huge losses. Shaken by these, Mao at last persuaded his comrades to defy the Central Committee, call it a day and retreat to southern Kiangsi in order to salvage what they had left of their armies. Regrouping at Pingkiang, this combined force then assaulted Kian, which yielded in October.

But meanwhile Yang Kai-hui and her son, Mao An-ying, together with Mao's sister and other relations, were arrested in Changsha, 'by some sixty gangsters of the reactionary Kuomintang clique', according to one account, 'following a tip-off by a secret agent'. A few days later, on 24 October, Mao's wife was executed in public outside the Liuyuan Gate in Changsha. It was said that the police had offered to spare her life if she would openly break with her husband and his Party and give them the names of all the Party members in Changsha. Yang refused, and was tortured – but even so, she maintained silence until the end.

Mao allowed himself, in public at least, no tears for the tragedy. He was tersely factual when he described these events six years later, even mentioning the loss of his property before the slaying of his family:

My land ... was confiscated by the Kuomintang. My wife and sister, as well as the wives of my two brothers ... and my own son, were all arrested.... My wife and younger sister were executed. The others were later released.

The prestige of the Red Army even extended to my own village ... for I heard the tale that the local peasants believed that I would soon be returning to my native home. When one day an aeroplane passed overhead, they decided it was I. They warned the man who was then tilling my land that I had come back to look over my old farm, to see whether or not any trees had been cut. If so, I would surely demand compensation from Chiang Kai-shek, they said.

Above: Mao's home in Shaoshan

Below, left to right: Mao's younger brother Mao Tse-tan, his father, his uncle, Mao

雨華行囊背一肩　歌無冠戴手二言　幾支省沿山千萬里

呂伯糧頓休空拳

一九一七年暑假余作乞丐周
遊　毛澤東惜行者黃
今在日泥上題詩此首春人
一九五六年書再與慕黃田
悵遲兩

　　　　青蕭瑜並識

近百人多莫沿東心
圓春初日忘瘊大者不去
其病不在小諸未可畫行之不用畫適也

孝隱夫人高忌弟子邱題

Mao and Siao Yu as beggars

Opposite: Mao as student in Changsha (third from left)

Early pictures of Mao

Opposite above: Chingkangshan

Opposite below: Yenan

Top left: On the Long March

Top right: Mao and US ambassador Hurley

Above: Chou En-lai, Mao, Lin Piao in Yenan, 1939

Opposite above: From Yenan to Chungking, 1946

Opposite below: Mao's bedroom in the Yenan caves

Above: Mao's white horse

Above right: Mao reviews troops entering Peking

Right: Proclamation of the People's Republic 1949

Many years afterwards Mao wrote a poem to the widow of a comrade who had fallen in these Red Army campaigns in the early 1930s, playing on the meaning of names: his wife's name Yang meant 'poplar', and his dead comrade's name meant 'willow'.

> I lost my proud Poplar and you your Willow,
> Poplar and Willow soar to the ninth Heaven.
> Wu Kang, asked what he can give,
> Serves them a laurel brew.
>
> The lonely moon goddess spreads her ample sleeves
> To dance for these loyal souls in infinite space.
> Earth suddenly reports the tiger subdued,
> Tears of joy pour forth falling as mighty rain.

An old friend later asked Mao what he meant by using the adjective 'proud' to portray his wife.

'A woman', Mao explained, 'got her head cut off for the revolution. Isn't that something to be proud of?'

Some time after Yang's execution, Mao legitimized his union with Ho Tzu-chen by marrying her. He also sent instructions to the Yang family in Changsha for them to send his three boys (the eldest had been released from captivity) to Shanghai to attend the Tatung kindergarten which was operated by the underground Communist network there. By all accounts they had a very thin time in Shanghai over the next few years, living in alleys and picking garbage under false names.

At the beginning of October the Red Army captured Kian again. Mao's orderly found a thermos flask 'in the house of a local despot who had run away'. He was delighted at the prospect of always having hot water ready for Commissar Mao. But he knew that if Mao found out about it he would probably tell him to give it back, or pay for it, and therefore he found someone else to carry it on the march so that Mao would not know.

More important, General Chu found in the Kuomintang police files in the town some materials about local members of the notorious Anti-Bolshevik Corps of the Kuomintang, which had been infiltrating into the Communist Party – including a receipt for money signed by a local landlord whose son was one of Mao's critics within the Communist Party.

Mao's response was to infiltrate his own secret agents into the Anti-Bolshevik Corps, and in the end he was prepared to say that some of his opponents were actually Kuomintang agents. But there were differences of policy also between him and his critics among the Kiangsi Communists, and they were once arguing about land reform policy at a conference in Kian in the middle of November when they had to disperse in a hurry because of the approach of Kuomintang troops.

This business of taking, losing and constantly retaking Kian sent some big ripples around the Communist pond. Chou En-lai told the Politburo in November that Mao had completely ignored the Comintern's instructions to 'consolidate defence positions before advancing further', while the Party's General Secretary complained that Mao's loss of Kian so soon after capturing it had caused 'a hopeless situation.'

At the end of November Mao moved against suspected Kuomintang agents, arresting more than 4000 officers and men of the Red Army. Some of those who were arrested gave evidence which implicated senior Communists in opposition to Mao. It then seems that Mao, through one of his secret agents, incited a Red Army officer to revolt, to make some demonstration of disloyalty which would enable Mao to take action against others. What this officer did, however, was far beyond anything Mao might have expected. Early in December he led 400 of his men in a mutiny.

They arrested their commander, made a forced march to Futien, attacked the prison, released some of Mao's prisoners there, brought down the local Red government and arrested some of its members. About a hundred of Mao's supporters at Futien were killed and many more captured, along with their relatives. General Chu Teh's wife may have been among them.

It was often said that Mao used brutal methods to quell the mutiny at Futien. A hostile source claimed that a witness revealed the use of torture.

Burning kerosene lamp wicks along with grilling were employed to extract confessions during interrogations. Fingernails of the comrades were pulled out and their bodies scorched as they groaned. Their wives (such as comrade Pai Kang's) were also detained. Their clothing was stripped off with their hands bound behind their backs, their hands were beaten with hard instruments, their breasts were cut off, their genitals burned and some comrades were executed without trial.

The persecution spread from Kiangsi to the Red areas of western Fukien, where Mao sent his young brother to take charge. According to this hostile source, 4000 officers and cadres were liquidated in this incident.

After his escape from prison in Futien, the leader of Mao's

critics called for his overthrow, attacking him as 'a Party emperor' who subverted the instructions of the Central Committee. He organized a rival Red government from a neighbouring town. Mao's enemies in the Party sent a letter late in December to General Chu and General Peng listing the crimes of 'Mao Tse-tung the traitor', including a controversial alleged letter from Mao to one of his agents. This ordered an attack on various units during which their leaders should be made to confess that Chu and Peng were the 'arch-criminals' acting for the Kuomintang – 'these confessions should be forwarded to us so that we can immediately arrest and kill them...' The slogan which Mao's opponents raised was, 'Down with Mao Tse-tung and up with Chu Teh...'

The most revealing incident which arose out of this violent eruption of factional struggle was that of a certain comrade Lo who was 'exposed' by the investigations of Mao's opponents as a Kuomintang agent, only for them to discover that he had in fact been put in by Mao as a secret counter-spy. In other words, both Mao and his rivals in the Party had been penetrating the Anti-Bolshevik Corps without informing each other. They had begun to uncover a part of each other's underground network in the belief that they were ferreting out genuine Kuomintang agents.

Distrust between Mao and Chu was certainly one facet of the complicated manoeuvring at Futien. It was said that General Chu was angry with Mao for sending 5000 Red soldiers to their death in counter-reaction drives. A comrade visiting Chu not long afterwards found him bewailing the execution of two of their mutual companions by 'you know who' – meaning Mao. One of Mao's victims was said to be an officer and relative of Ho Lung, another legendary Red general.

In the post-mortem held by the Central Party authorities Mao was insistent that the mutiny had been instigated by the Kuomintang. But Generals Chu and Peng introduced an element of doubt about that, and the Central authorities gave even less credence to Mao's explanation of a Kuomintang plot. In the end Mao had to shift his position to say somewhat lamely that some of the men arrested had not in fact been Kuomintang agents, but had been guilty of implementing the wrong land reform policy and had in that way played into Kuomintang hands. In the end the senior comrades unanimously condemned Mao for his part in the Futien mutiny.

Mao's doggedness paid off, initially at least. He and his supporters were able to gain control of the new Party Bureau for the

Soviet Areas at the beginning of 1931. One of the first decisions
by the new Central Bureau was to expel from the Party those
who had challenged Mao in Kiangsi. 'No doubt', Mao rational-
ized, 'the Futien incident was in fact an act directed against the
Party and the revolution. Though it has not yet been proved that
they are organizationally all members of the Anti-Bolshevik
Corps ... their action against the Party and against the revolution has objectively been in agreement with the reactionary
behaviour' of the Corps.

But then the ground was taken away from under Mao's feet.
Just as he was consolidating his position in the Red base areas,
there was a palace revolution in the Central Committee. In 1930
a group of Chinese Communists trained in Moscow during the
1920s had returned to China. Their distinction was that while in
Russia they had consistently sided with the Stalinists against
Trotsky, and had therefore won Stalin's trust. They were
immediately christened the Returned Students, and when their
principal leader, Wang Ming, wrote a pamphlet on 'Bolsheviz-
ing the Party', they acquired the further nickname of the
Twenty-Eight Bolsheviks, other members including Po Ku and
Lo Fu.

At the beginning of 1931 they captured control of the Chinese
Communist Party, and for the next three or four years the battle
was to rage between Mao's 'real power faction' and the internationalist Twenty-Eight Bolsheviks under Wang Ming.

9
IN DISGRACE

By now Chiang Kai-shek was thoroughly aroused to the revolutionary potential of the Communist base area in Kiangsi. He launched at the end of 1930 what was to become the first of five consecutive 'campaigns of encirclement and annihilation'. He sent 100,000 soldiers to surround the Red areas, but by skilful manoeuvring Mao and General Chu Teh were able to repel them. Mao explained afterwards:

Following out the tactics of swift concentration and swift dispersal, we attacked each unit separately, using our main forces. Admitting the enemy troops deeply into our territory, we staged sudden concentrated attacks, in superior numbers, on isolated units of the Kuomintang troops, achieving positions of manoeuvre, in which, momentarily, we could encircle them, thus reversing the general strategic advantage enjoyed by a numerically greatly superior enemy.

But Mao afterwards blamed the internal disunity of the Communists for their failure to follow up with a counter-offensive.

Mao celebrated the repulse of the first encirclement campaign – and capture of the enemy general – with a poem:

Forests blaze red beneath the frosty sky,
The wrath of Heaven's armies soars to the clouds.
Mist veils Lungkang, its thousand peaks blurred.
All cry out in unison:
Our van has taken Chang Hui-tsan!

The enemy returns to Kiangsi two hundred thousand strong,
Fumes billowing in the wind in mid-sky.
Workers and peasants are wakened in the millions
To fight as one man,
Under the riot of red flags round the foot of Puchou!

After the Twenty-Eight Bolsheviks had gained control of the Party in January 1931, a new Central Bureau for all the various Red bases was established under Hsiang Ying. Mao was a member, but not in command of it, and his influence in Kiangsi began to wane. 'During the four years from 1931 to 1934', he afterwards lamented, 'I had no voice at all in the Centre.' His role was increasingly limited to such civilian matters as the new marriage law which he wrote, and which was promulgated on 28 January 1931:

Free choice must be the basic principle of every marriage. The whole feudal system of marriage, including the power of parents to arrange marriages for their children, to exercise compulsion, and all purchase and sale in marriage contracts shall henceforth be abolished.

Although women have obtained freedom from the feudal yoke, they are still labouring under tremendous physical handicaps (for example, the binding of the feet) and have not obtained complete economic independence. Therefore on questions concerning divorce, it becomes necessary to protect the interests of women and place the greater part of the obligations and responsibilities entailed by divorce upon men.

Children are the masters of the new society. Under the old system little attention was paid to children. Consequently special regulations have been established concerning the protection of children.

In the spring, after a respite of only four months, Chiang launched his second encirclement campaign, doubling the men put in to smash the Red base. But the Communists were able to use their old tactics with success, and Mao composed another poem commemorating the defeat of the second encirclement campaign:

> The very clouds foam atop White Cloud Mountain,
> At its base the roar of battle quickens.
> Withered trees and rotten stumps join in the fray.
> A forest of rifles presses,
> As the Flying General descends from the skies.
>
> In fifteen days we have marched 250 miles
> Crossing misty Kan waters and green Fukien hills,
> Rolling back the enemy as we would a mat.
> A voice is heard wailing;
> His 'Bastion at every step' avails him nought!

This time there was only a month's respite until the third encirclement campaign, led personally by Chiang Kai-shek, with an army of 300,000 – almost ten times bigger than Mao's. But by marching fast into the heart of the Red base area he supplied the Communists with perfect conditions for guerrilla tactics. By October Chiang had to retreat, and Mao afterwards quoted the comment of one of the enemy generals, that 'Our stout men have worn themselves thin, and our thin men have worn themselves to death.'

During the summer fighting the Central Committee of the Communist Party left Shanghai, where Chiang had made it no longer safe for them, for various parts of the interior. Chou En-lai was the first to arrive at Juichin, the capital of the Kiangsi base area, disguised as a bearded Catholic priest. Once he was established, it was inevitable that Mao, his Party junior, should become little more than a figurehead chairman of the Red republic in Kiangsi.

Chou was a totally different character from Mao. Five years younger, he came from a Mandarin family, and his graceful manners made him stand out from his fellow Communists and perhaps even contributed to his deferential sense of inferiority to them. He organized the Chinese Communist group in France in 1920-1, and from the beginning he excelled in diplomacy and in the composition of political statements.

Mao's actions and policies now came under criticism with increasing frequency. A Chou directive to the government of the base area of 1 September 1931 opposed Mao's positions on strategy, army administration and land reform, and Mao had to sign a proclamation in which his own ideas about the treatment of rich peasants were rebutted. The lessons he had learned in the field about the inappropriateness of theoretical radicalism would have to be learned all over again by the new Party leaders.

In between his own ups and downs Mao had to steel himself to the horrible fates of his friends and loved ones. Following the earlier execution of his wife and sister, he now learned in 1931 that the school friend and Party comrade to whom he had been most genuinely close and in whose home he had stayed innumerable times, Tsai Ho-sen, had been arrested in Hong Kong and extradited by the British to Canton, where counter-revolutionary hangmen had, according to one account, 'spread out his limbs, nailed him to the wall, beat him to death in cold blood, and cut his chest and stomach to pieces.'

In September the Japanese, who had already advertised their ambitions to control events in China, seized Manchuria by force, thus consolidating the various privileges they had insisted on in northernmost China. It was obvious that unless it was resolutely resisted, Japanese imperialism would soon spread over the whole of China.

Mao drafted and signed an open letter from the Red Army to the Kuomintang army calling on them to rebel: 'Soldiers, our brothers! You must think of another way out. There is a way out for you – revolution! You now have guns and cannons in your hands. First kill your reactionary superior officers; then unite with the workers, peasants, and all the toiling masses of your area to overthrow the fucking Kuomintang government!'

Mao argued fiercely with the new Politburo on these larger national political issues. After the Japanese attacked Shanghai in January 1932, for example, he pleaded for a coalition government and a united army made up of everyone willing to fight the Japanese – a policy quite unacceptable to the Moscow-influenced Chinese Politburo. In April 1932 the Kiangsi government declared war on Japan, at Mao's initiative, but again the Politburo withheld its backing.

At the beginning of November 1931 a Party Conference was held in Juichin to prepare the line of the new Politburo, dominated by the Twenty-Eight Bolsheviks, to be put at the forthcoming First All-China Soviet Congress. It adopted a political resolution which savagely attacked the Maoist policies, accusing the Communist leaders in the Kiangsi base area of backing down from a strong 'class and mass line', rebuking them for not having linked up with other base areas, attacking the guerrilla tactics of Mao's Fourth Red Army and condemning his 7 February Land Law on the grounds that equal distribution was a surrender to the rich peasants.

Mao himself was found guilty of narrow empiricism, opportunistic pragmatism and 'general ideological poverty'. The new national leaders of the Party reasserted the premise that the agrarian revolution should be led by the proletariat. The Red Army should occupy urban areas, adopt regular forms of warfare and jettison the old-fashioned idea of guerrillaism.

The First All-China Soviet Congress assembled a few days later, but the newly arrived Twenty-Eight Bolsheviks did not quite have enough support in the base areas to rout the Maoists. Mao was elected Chairman of the Central Executive Committee of the All-China Soviet Government, and kept his post as chief political commissar of the First Front Army. Moreover, a number of Mao's supporters, like Chu Teh, Teng Tzu-hui and Ho Shu-heng, were elected commissars for various departments in the government. This produced a deadlock: Mao had control of the government and the army, but his new rivals controlled the Party.

Furthermore, because of the strong pressure which the Politburo, able to claim Comintern backing, could exert, the delegates to the Congress adopted most of the substantive proposals of the Twenty-Eight Bolsheviks – the base area constitution, land law and Red Army directives – with minor modifications bowing modestly to the Maoist point of view.

A few weeks later, at the beginning of 1932, Mao and Chou En-lai came to loggerheads over military policies and the handling of the Red Army. Mao was still advocating mobile guerrilla tactics, including the device of luring the enemy deep into the base area. But Chou's strategy was to hold the base tightly, to fight positional warfare and carry it into enemy territory instead of allowing the enemy behind the Red lines.

The two leaders collaborated in planning an assault on Kanchow in January, but with disastrous consequences. Because of their disagreements over tactics the Communists failed to capture the city, which controlled the whole of southern Kiangsi.

By August Chou had had enough. He expelled Mao from the Military Committee of the Central Bureau, forcing Mao to confine himself to civilian government work.

Under Chou's leadership the Central Bureau began to denounce Mao, particularly for his use of terrorist methods in the Futien rebellion – although one report also says that Chou was successful at this time in conciliating Mao with the friends of those he had killed at Futien.

So far Mao's demotion in the Party had been primarily in the political field, and his position as a leader of the Red Armies was not in question. But in August 1932 Chou En-lai, having consolidated his grasp over the political structure in Kiangsi, went on, at a Party conference in Ningtu, to take control of the Red Army. Chou's advocacy of offensive positional warfare to meet future Kuomintang attacks won more support that Mao's guerrilla line. Even Chu Teh, Peng Teh-huai and Chen Yi (but not, probably, Lin Piao) deserted Mao in favour of the new line.

General Liu Po-cheng, the 'one-eyed dragon' of earlier campaigns, backed Chou's views of military strategy in a Red Army publication, and was particularly scathing about Mao's attitude to modern weapons. 'The sword', he wrote, 'may be useful to men who don't even have rifles, but it is pedantic to insist on substituting a mediaeval copper water-clock for a modern timepiece.' Obviously the generals preferred the prospect of more men, better trained and better equipped, to fighting over the constantly changing ground of a guerrilla campaign.

Mao later alleged that 'during the Ningtu conference, Lo Fu wanted to expel me, but Chou and Chu did not agree.' Lin Piao

may have first advertised his almost life-long loyalty to Mao at
this point because Mao had just appointed him commander of
the First Army Corps, so that he became at twenty-one the
'youngest general'.

In the winter of 1932-3 the senior leaders of the Twenty-Eight
Bolsheviks – Po Ku and Lo Fu – arrived in Juichin from Shanghai, along with the German Comintern adviser, Otto von Braun,
who had been given the Chinese name of Li Teh. Mao became
even more outnumbered.

The fourth encirclement campaign preoccupied the Red
Armies during the winter of 1932-3, but in the middle of it the
battle of wills between Mao and Chou En-lai, the latter now
backed by the Twenty-Eight Bolsheviks, escalated. Chou chose
to take issue with what was called the Lo Ming line. Lo Ming
was a veteran commander in Fukien who refused to follow the
new Chou En-lai 'forward and offensive line' of February 1933 of
expanding his forces, incorporating local militia and mobilizing
all possible economic resources. Instead he continued to follow
the guerrilla tactics of the Chu-Mao line from Chingkangshan.

Lo Ming was backed in his disobedience by such leading
Maoists as Mao's brother, Mao Tse-tan, Teng Hsiao-ping, Tan
Chen-lin and some of those who had most helped Mao in suppressing the Futien mutineers. From February until July Chou
pressed his campaign against the so-called Lo Ming liners, dismissing many of Mao's supporters, including Teng Hsiao-ping.

In May Chou replaced Mao as the political commissar of the
First Front Army, and became the supreme authority within the
Red Army structure. Meanwhile Chou's supporters attacked
Mao within the base area government structure for his 'rightist'
deviations on land policy.

In spite of all this harassment, Mao devoted himself to legisla-
tion on economic and social matters, showing a fine sense of
detail. He spoke in August at an economic construction conference under the title 'Pay Attention to Economic Work',
emphasizing the need for the almost three million citizens governed by the Communist regime to pay their own way and make
their own living. He condemned those comrades who believed
that economic construction was impossible in the midst of a
revolutionary war and would have to wait until the peaceful
conditions after the final victory. He was quite specific about
what needed to be done. 'We must restore the output of such
local products as wolfram, timber, camphor, paper, tobacco,
linen, dried mushrooms and peppermint oil to former levels, and

market them in the White areas in quantities.'

He also kept up with international affairs, expressing his scorn for the pretensions of the Lytton Report on Sino-Japanese differences in a telegram: 'The League of Nations is a league of robbers by which the various imperialisms are dismembering China.'

The fourth encirclement ended in a stalemate, and Mao composed a wry little poem for it:

> Red, orange, yellow, green, blue, indigo, violet –
> Who is dancing, waving this coloured ribbon against the sky?
> The sun returns slanting after the rain
> And hill and pass grow a deeper blue.
>
> A furious battle once raged here,
> The village walls, bullet-scarred,
> Now adorn hill and pass
> And make them doubly fair.

In November the Communists had a stroke of luck. The Nineteenth Route Army of the Kuomintang mutinied in Fukien province and tried to set up a popular regime in opposition to Chiang Kai-shek. Its leaders had made contact with Communists in Shanghai before the revolt, but the cautious Communists were uncertain how to respond. The Red Army and its base government – i.e. Mao and Chu – signed an alliance with these non-Communist rebels, but the Politburo regarded the Fukien mutineers as sham democrats who were not worth supporting. Mao and Chu hoped that the Fukien rebels would give freedom to the people of that province and form a sincere alliance with the Communists.

While they were arguing about it, the revolt was put down by loyal Kuomintang troops. Once the opportunity for fruitful collaboration with the mutineers had gone, Mao joined the Politburo in denouncing them. If action had been taken more promptly, the Fukien soldiers might have been reinforced by the Red Armies, thus enabling their mutiny to succeed and denying considerable territory and resources to the enemy – although the military strategists in Juichin had to consider whether forces could be spared from the Red base without jeopardizing its own security. Mao afterwards blamed his Party rivals for mishandling the Fukien rebellion.

In January, just after Mao's fortieth birthday, the Central Committee held a plenary session where all of Mao's policies were attacked right down the line. Anticipating what would happen, he told his colleagues that he could not take part in the conference because of bad health. But the German adviser, Otto von Braun, recalled that, 'Po Ku remarked sarcastically that Mao was once again suffering from a "diplomatic illness", because he was annoyed that Lo Fu was to give the report "On the Chinese Soviet Movement and its Tasks" instead of himself, and that his attempt to join the Standing Committee of the Politburo would not succeed.'

Mao was indeed thrown off the Politburo on this occasion and replaced by Lo Fu, one of the Twenty-Eight Bolsheviks. He never stopped resenting this, and complained to a Communist audience thirty years later about Lo Fu having been elected to the Politburo 'when he was not even a member of the Central Committee. If we now investigate whether or not Lo Fu was a Party member when he entered the Party, or who introduced him, we will not be able to find the answers. None the less he was elected to the Politburo, while I, a member of the Politburo, was not allowed to participate in the congress.'

Of all the leading Chinese comrades in Juichin at this critical point of their revolution, von Braun found that

Mao was unquestionably the most streamlined figure. A slim, almost delicate forty-year-old, my first impression of him was more of a thinker and poet than of a politician and soldier. On the rare occasions when we met informally at festivities, he preserved a dignified discretion, but provoked the others to drinking, telling stories and singing. He himself usually contributed to the conversation only aphorisms, which sounded harmless enough, but always had a pointed meaning and sometimes held a malicious insinuation. . . .

When for the first time the question was put of whether our main forces should break a way through the blockade . . . he replied uncivilly with a phrase which I think comes from Lao Tse: 'A bad butcher cuts through the bones with a sharp axe, a good butcher separates them with a blunt knife'. . . . Such sayings, comparisons and images . . . betray his pragmatic, utilitarian way of thinking, but they did not fail to get a reaction. . . . Mao not only used them in personal conversation or in a narrow circle, he also put them in his speeches and made up impressive slogans with revolutionary pathos. I myself was often a witness to how he brought the peasants and soldiers who listened to him under his spell and swept them along.

His knowledge of Marxism was only superficial. . . . Mao had never lived in another country and spoke no foreign languages. But in China there was a lack of Marxist literature. What was to hand was at least second-hand, and one could count the original works on the fingers of one hand. [Braun himself, innocent of Chinese, could hardly, however, be the last word on that.]

What was worse was that Mao gave new interpretations in an eclectic way to Marxist concepts and filled them with new content. So he would frequently speak of the proletariat, understanding thereby not at all only the industrial workers but all layers of the poorest population – rural workers, tenant farmers, artisans, small merchants, coolies and even beggars . . .

But neither Po Ku and his friends nor the Comintern wanted to break with Mao, knowing that he had built up a wide mass support across the base areas.

In January 1934 the Second All-China Soviet Congress convened in Juichin. In spite of all the mud that had been poured over the Maoist faction in the previous three years, Mao was re-elected as Chairman of the Soviet Government.

But this time he was only a figurehead. The Twenty-Eight Bolsheviks had a majority on the Praesidium within the Central Executive Committee which elected a chairman from its own ranks. They could thus afford to elect Mao, and could always dismiss him if he did not co-operate with them. Mao's post was honorary and essentially powerless, whereas Lo Fu became in effect the Premier of the government with almost limitless power.

Two passages from one of Mao's speeches to the Congress show what a force he still represented.

The Kuomintang is now pursuing a policy of blockhouse warfare, feverishly constructing their 'tortoise-shells' as though they were iron bastions. Comrades! Are they really iron bastions? Not in the least! Think of the palaces of the feudal emperors over thousands of years, were they not powerful with their walls and moats? Yet they crumbled one after another the moment the masses arose. The Tsar of Russia was one of the world's most ferocious rulers, yet when the proletariat and the peasantry rose in revolution, was there anything left of him? No, nothing. His bastions of iron? They all crumbled. Comrades! What is a true bastion of iron? It is the masses, the millions upon millions of people who genuinely and sincerely support the revolution. That is the real iron bastion which no force can smash, no force whatsoever . . .

I earnestly suggest to this congress that we pay close attention to the well-being of the masses, from the problems of land and labour to those of fuel, rice, cooking oil and salt. The women want to learn ploughing and harrowing. Whom can we get to teach them? The children want to go to school. Have we set up primary schools? The wooden bridge over there is too narrow and people may fall off. Should we not repair it? Many people suffer from boils and other ailments. What are we going to do about it? All such problems concerning the well-being of the

masses should be placed on our agenda. We should discuss them, adopt
and carry out decisions and check up on the results. We should convince the masses that we represent their interests, that our lives are
intimately bound up with theirs. We should help them to proceed from
these things to an understanding of the higher tasks which we have put
forward, the tasks of the revolutionary war, so that they will support the
revolution and spread it throughout the country, respond to our political appeals and fight to the end for victory in the revolution.

But Mao's political humiliation went on. In February he lost
his presidency of the Council of People's Commissars, and thus
forfeited a further position of influence. (In the same month his
orderly found an enamel lunch-box for him, so he no longer had
to eat his 'rice-sandwiches' out of his drinking mug.) In March
Lo Fu issued a decree from that same Council criticizing Mao's
handling of land reform.

Meanwhile, Chiang Kai-shek had unfurled his fifth and last
encirclement campaign, having, in Mao's own words, mobilized
'nearly one million men and adopted new tactics and strategies.
Already, in the fourth campaign, Chiang had, on the recommen-
dation of his German advisers, begun the use of the blockhouse
and fortifications system. In the fifth campaign he placed his
entire reliance upon it.'

The Communists attempted to meet the vastly superior forces
of the enemy in positional warfare, and this was disastrous. After
a damaging defeat at Kuangchang in April 1934, the arguments
about military policy became divisive within the Communist
camp. Mao described the battle of Kuangchang as a 'catastrophe', and he laid it at the door of what he called 'the military
troika' of Po Ku, Chou En-lai and von Braun.

He accused them of passive defence, war by fortification, dis-
sipating forces and going into battle without the certainty of
victory. 'He repeated these accusations . . .', von Braun remembered, 'at every opportunity in order to degrade us three in the
eyes of the troop commanders, and also did not hesitate to use
personal insults. He did this less in official sessions than in private conversations with his supporters.'

Mao understandably chose von Braun as the main butt of his
attacks, and von Braun complained that he did not hesitate to
play on the national pride and xenophobia of his compatriots in
order to spread the idea that no foreigner could ever understand
the peculiar conditions of the Chinese revolution.

In early May the Central Committee held an emergency meeting following the defeat at Kuangchang. Po Ku presided and a

bewildering variety of plans was put forward. Mao proposed a four-pronged counter-offensive which would divide the Red Army into four sections, each advancing in different directions in order to draw away the Kuomintang forces. But he won no support for this, and in the end Chou En-lai's compromise proposal was accepted for a strong defence line to the north of Shihcheng, for a detachment of the Red Army to harass the enemy behind its lines in Futien and Chingkiang, and for secret arrangements to evacuate the Central Soviet Area.

If Mao had any forebodings about the future in the light of all this dissension over military policy, he did not show it in a poem written in the summer of 1934:

> Soon dawn will break in the east.
> Do not say 'You start too early';
> Crossing these blue hills adds nothing to one's years,
> The landscape here is beyond compare.
>
> Straight from the walls of Huichang lofty peaks,
> Range after range, extend to the eastern seas.
> Our soldiers point southward to Kwangtung
> Looming lusher and greener in the distance.

He did, however, hold out grounds for justifying a withdrawal from the Kiangsi base in the context of the coming war against Japan, whose expansionism in northern China was growing. The Japanese had now crossed the Great Wall and defeated a Chinese army there, and had installed the one-time boy-emperor Pu Yi as their puppet ruler of the new 'republic' of Manchukuo.

But as the fifth encirclement bore relentlessly into the Red areas, Mao was suddenly rebuked by the Central Committee for serious agrarian and military errors, excluded from all Party meetings and sent into disgrace. He probably went into hiding with Liu Shao-chi, his fellow Hunanese who had also been sniped at by the Twenty-Eight Bolsheviks, at the village of Shachoupa, a few miles outside Juichin.

Mao's fall from grace was partly the result of the accusations of the Twenty-Eight Bolsheviks now appearing most authoritatively as an appendix to a new edition of Wang Ming's book *The Two Lines* which had been published in Moscow in 1932 with the imprimatur of the Comintern. There was also probably an order from Moscow resulting from Mao's actions during the Fukien rebellion, while Chou and Po Ku could not forget the Lo Ming line episode.

By August Mao was under house arrest at Yutu, a town sixty miles west of Juichin, and he was expelled from the Central Committee for the third time. Thanks to the combined efforts of Wang Ming in Moscow and Po Ku in Juichin, Mao now faced the prospect of permanent expulsion from the mainstream of the Chinese Communist leadership. He responded by going down with malaria and had to be nursed by the Christian doctor, Dr Nelson Fu Lien-chang, with a blazing temperature.

Hearing about his detention, Kung Chu, an old colleague who was later to desert the Party, brought him some wine and a chicken to eat one day, and they reminisced about their first meeting years before on Chingkangshan. They went on sipping wine long after the sun had set, and when his friend was about to leave, Mao sighed and said, 'Alas, this is no longer the world of the comrades of Chingkangshan.'

But the towns and villages went on falling to the enemy, and at the beginning of October Mao, in his modest and limited capacity as political commissar of the First Front Army, took part in a highly charged meeting with Chou En-lai, Po Ku, von Braun and other leaders where the decision was made to evacuate the Kiangsi base. Two weeks later the Long March began.

10
THE LONG MARCH

'Mao and about twenty others', his orderly recalled, 'left Yutu by the north gate, and then turned to the left towards the river which was all yellow, roaring and foaming, as though calling on the armies to advance. Soon the sun set and gusts of bitter wind chilled us. The Chairman wore a grey cloth uniform and an eight-cornered military cap, with no overcoat. He walked with enormous strides along the riverbanks.' It was five o'clock on an October evening and the 6000-mile epic which came to be known as the Long March had begun.

But most of the time Mao, described as 'thin and emaciated' after his fever, 'had to ride because he was sick,' his orderly explained. The horse was still Mao's favourite dun-coloured steed which had been captured six years before. In addition to Chen, the orderly, Mao's party included his second wife, Ho Tzu-chen, in spite of her being several months pregnant; the male nurse, Chung Fu-chang, who had been assigned to Mao during his malaria; and a secretary, Huang Yu-fang.

But his two children by Ho Tzu-chen were too young to go and had to be left with peasant families in Kiangsi. They were never heard of again, though Mao had the army search the area when it came back fifteen years later. His youngest brother Tse-tan was also left behind in the rearguard with his new wife (Ho Tzu-chen's sister). They were never to be seen alive by Mao again, but the middle brother Tse-min came on the Long March as treasurer in charge of the base area government's money, bullion and machinery.

The Long March was, Mao later declared, 'our worst period . . ., blocked in front and pursued from behind.' He compared the loss of the Kiangsi base with the failure of the 1905 revolution in Russia. On another occasion he asserted that the Long March had been 'entirely unnecessary', since better generalship could have defeated the fifth encirclement.

The Red Armies did not really know where they were heading. When Mao was asked later about their goals when the March began, he replied: 'If you mean, did we have any exact plans, the answer is that we had none. We intended to break out of the encirclement and join up with the other base areas. Beyond that, there was only a very deliberate desire to put ourselves in a position where we could fight the Japanese.'

It had not been at all certain that Mao would go on the Long March. If his malaria had not cleared up he might well have been left behind in the rearguard along with other sick leaders like Chu Chiu-pai (and, like them, captured by the Kuomintang). Even given his recovery, the feeling against him and his faction was running so strong within the leadership group that it is by no means impossible that they might have decided to dump him in Kiangsi. As it was a number of his close comrades and supporters were left behind, including Chen Yi, Tan Chen-lin, Hsiao Hua and Teng Tzu-hui. Clearly the men in control of the party hoped to avoid on their journey the kind of squabbling which had so lowered their morale in the months before the break-out. But Mao, being just well enough, had to go with the armies as the political commissar for the Fourth Army. According to one account, some of the Twenty-Eight Bolsheviks had wanted to leave Mao behind, but Lin Piao and other generals insisted that he should come.

The first improvement in Mao's fortunes came after the Red Army had broken out of the Kuomintang encirclement, at the cost of almost half its numbers, only to find its path to the nearest Communist base area, that of Ho Lung 250 miles to the north, blocked by Chiang Kai-shek. Mao came forward with a plan to give up the attempt to join Ho Lung and to wheel instead toward Kweichow, where the enemy was weak. By following a long arc through Kweichow and over the Yangtze River, the Red Army would have a chance of reaching the Szechuan base of Chang Kuo-tao, Mao's old – and future – rival, without meeting Kuomintang forces. Mao's idea was accepted at a time when the military commanders were becoming doubtful about the generalship of von Braun and Chou En-lai.

The Red Army halted at Liping during the difficult crossing of Kweichow province, defended by troops of the Kweichow warlords, and a Politburo conference was held where the disagreements about military leadership came out into the open: Mao regained a *de facto* seat on the Central Committee. It was decided to continue to Tsunyi. During this stage of the Long March,

Mao's wife, Ho Tzu-chen, was wounded in an attack by low-flying bombers. It was said that twenty pieces of shrapnel lodged in her body, and yet she lived on to give birth to another baby and complete the March. Mao wrote three short poems during this early part of the Long March, all celebrating the forces of nature.

> Mountains!
> I whip my swift horse, glued to my saddle.
> I turn my head startled,
> The sky is three foot above me!
>
> Mountains!
> Like great waves surging in a crashing sea,
> Like a thousand stallions
> In full gallop in the heat of battle.
>
> Mountains!
> Piercing the blue of heaven, your barbs unblunted!
> The skies would fall
> But for your strength supporting.

At Tsunyi, temporarily secure from attack, they were able to spend twelve days resting, recruiting new soldiers and arguing about their disagreements. An enlarged meeting of the Politburo was convened, in which the regular members were supplemented by a number of senior Central Committee members and by generals or political commissars.

Mao went into the attack at the beginning of the conference, arguing that the Politburo under Po Ku and the Military Commission had been defeatist in the face of the fifth encirclement. In the words of his resolution which was ultimately adopted:

At the present stage of the Chinese civil war, when we do not yet have the support of urban proletarian uprisings and mutinies of army units pitted against us; when our Red Army is still very small; when our bases constitute only a tiny portion of China; when we do not yet have aeroplanes, artillery and other sophisticated weapons; when we are still fighting on interior lines; and when the enemy are still attacking and surrounding us; our strategic line has to be one of decisive battles for defence.... We must not engage the enemy in a decisive battle in which we have no confidence to win....

We must check the enemy with mobile warfare while our main forces should retreat to a suitable distance or transfer themselves to the enemy's flank or rear. They should be secretly assembled, awaiting a favourable opportunity to strike.... Fighting on interior lines, the Red Army's retreat and hiding can tire the enemy out....

We should wait until he has advanced to a suitable distance before surrounding and annihilating him, this is to lure the enemy to penetrate deeply into our territory. For victory, we must not refuse to give up some parts of our territory and even to withdraw temporarily our main forces out of our base area.

Po Ku was condemned by Mao for not correcting Chou En-lai's 'mistaken way of conducting the war', and for failing to respond to criticism. The thing to do now, Mao told his comrades at Tsunyi, was to correct all these mistakes, and then to go on to 'find a new base area in the vast territories of Yunnan, Kweichow and Szechwan, to recover our lost bases' and eventually triumph across the whole country. Chou, sensing that things were going in Mao's direction, admitted the errors of which he had been acccused and proposed that Mao take over his post as Chairman of the Revolutionary Military Council. This effectively pre-empted the matter, so that Po Ku and others among the Twenty-Eight Bolsheviks had no practical alternative but to accept Chou's suggestion.

This is turn meant that Mao now became a member of the Politburo Standing Committee, since it had been the Party's habit for some years, in view of the importance of the armed struggle, to give the Chairman of the Revolutionary Military Council a seat on the Politburo Standing Committee. After his two years of demotion from the higher councils of the Party, this secured for Mao a position in the inner core of the Party leadership which he never again relinquished, and from which he was able to drive his way to the top ten years later. He was now indisputably one of the top five or six men in the Party.

In the normal event there were probably only two of the twenty or so participants in the Tsunyi conference who would have accepted the description of being Mao's supporters: Lin Piao and Nieh Jung-chen. But Mao was able to exploit the growing resentment against the leadership of the Twenty-Eight Bolsheviks. Teng Fa, Director of the Political Security Bureau, was probably disenchanted because the leadership had accused him of excessive cruelty and carnage in suppressing counter-revolutionaries. Generals Peng Teh-huai and Liu Po-cheng were very angry with the military decisions which had been made. The cadres were demoralized, the decision to carry with them all the civilian equipment had weighed the army down, the loss of the Kiangsi base had caused consternation and there was a general air of not knowing where to go next.

Mao was able to profit from this mood of disillusion because of his distinctive and down-to-earth military policies, and also because, like Churchill, he was able to offer at a time of near desperation a clear voice of patriotic certitude. Like Churchill, he knew how to appeal to the deepest instinct of his countrymen and arouse their will to fight, to resist, to endure against all the odds.

But it was Lo Fu who perhaps must be credited with the decisive role in working out a compromise at Tsunyi, by upholding the old leadership's 'correct' political line, and thus calming the fears of the Twenty-Eight Bolsheviks, yet at the same time renouncing its 'erroneous' military line, thus placating the discontent among the generals. As Mao later remarked of Lo Fu: 'During the Tsunyi conference he played a useful role, and at that time one couldn't have got by without him.'

Lo Fu thus replaced Po Ku as the senior Party leader in the General Secretary's chair, while Mao sneaked into the Politburo through the back door, so to speak, by virtue of his new Chairmanship of the Military Council. From this day he acquired his perennial title of Mao *Chuhsi* – 'Chairman Mao'. Lo Fu climbed to what had until then been the plum job in the Party, while Mao secured his first step on the ladder to ultimate power.

It is possible that Mao came to some understanding with Chou before the Politburo decisions of 8 January 1935, because from this time onwards Chou never again attempted to lay down the law on military or ideological matters, and remained for the next forty years Mao's loyal lieutenant, never challenging him for the top job.

There were, of course, practical reasons why some of the voters at Tsunyi thought it wise to turn to Mao for the particular period that lay ahead. They were now operating deep within the Chinese hinterland, where the foreign training and city expertise of the earlier leadership was irrelevant. They would be better off with a man of the people, a genuine peasant leader, at least until they won through to the stage of capturing cities again.

The talking over, Mao now concentrated on the military challenge ahead, relying heavily on Chou for organizational support and Liu Po-cheng for military planning. His forces had fallen to only 30,000 when they took Tsunyi, but 20,000 new soldiers were recruited in the city to bring the Red Army up to about 50,000. The problem was how to cross the heavily defended Yangtze River to Chang Kuo-tao's base in northern Szechuan. The first attempt took five weeks, but was unsuccessful, and Mao's men found themselves in Tsunyi again at the end of February. At least, however, they won a major victory against their opponents here, and Mao celebrated the recapture of the Loushan Pass in a poem:

> Fierce the west wind,
> Wild geese cry under the frosty morning moon.
> Under the frosty morning moon
> Horses' hooves clattering,
> Bugles sobbing low.
>
> Idle boast the strong pass is a wall of iron,
> With firm strides we are crossing its summit.
> We are crossing its summit,
> The rolling hills sea-blue,
> The dying sun blood-red.

But then Mao heard on the Red Army's primitive radio that Chang Kuo-tao had been obliged, under enemy pressure, to abandon his Szechuan base and head west to a point where he could no longer help Mao's campaign to cross the Yangtze. In March Mao began a series of complex manoeuvres to get across on his own. He sent men to cross the Chihshui River for the third time, in order to mislead the Kuomintang into moving its forces to that stretch of the Yangtze's northern bank. But the Communists quickly turned about, recrossed the Chihshui and made a forced march south towards Kweiyang, capital of Kweichow province. It was concerning these back-tracking operations that recriminations surfaced forty years later about the alleged unwillingness of Generals Lin Piao and Peng Teh-huai to follow Mao's orders.

By an intricate series of feints, forced marches and ruses, the Red Army eventually crossed the River Yangtze at Chiaochia, where the river is locally called the Chinsha River – River of Golden Sand – with fierce currents and treacherous navigation. The Communists succeeded in capturing half a dozen boats from the other side and were then able to ferry themselves across in small lots over nine successive days and nights.

Mao's orderly described the river as 'in spate, with angry dragon-headed waves confronting us'. He crossed with Mao just before dawn, and afterwards Mao became angry with him for setting up his makeshift bed and boiling his water before having found him a surface to work on.

'I couldn't find anything to use as a desk,' Chen explained. 'Why don't you have a bit of a rest and a drop of water first?'

'The work's the all-important thing at a moment like this,' Mao replied. 'Rest, or food and drink are trifles. Twenty to thirty thousand of our comrades are still waiting to cross the river there. Thirty thousand lives in peril! Go on, find me a board or something to use as a desk before you do anything else.'

Chen ran off and hunted high and low, eventually finding a small board. Mao helped to set it up, wedging it underneath to make it steady, and spread out his maps and documents with relief.

The crossing of the River of Golden Sand was owed to a combination of daring and good luck. But it is also likely that the local warlord was far from being a whole-hearted supporter of the Kuomintang, since he eventually rebelled against Chiang and was given honoured positions under the People's Republic after 1949: this was one of the provinces which the Kuomintang's forces could not enter under its complex political arrangements with various regional warlords.

Mao now came to a part of China totally unfamiliar to most Chinese. 'When we came to the south and crossed the Yangtze', he recollected afterwards, 'we ran into snakes, mosquitoes, scorching weather and a shortage of food.' But he was elated by his success so far, and convened a Politburo meeting at Huili where Lo Fu gave his seal of approval to the military leadership.

But Mao made a diatribe against Lin Piao, who had not shown enough faith in his orders. Lin had telephoned General Peng Teh-huai to say that, 'The present leadership is no good. You come out and take command.' Lin also wrote to Mao complaining about what he regarded as the unnecessary weakening of the army by all these diversions.

'You are a boy,' Mao told him, 'and know nothing. At this time we cannot put ourselves in direct confrontation with the enemy. It is necessary ... to take a circuitous route and advance in a roundabout way.'

The next hazard was to cross the Tatu River, a mountain torrent which provided the most difficult obstacle in the whole of the Long March. The Red Army attempted to cross it at Anshunchang, where the Taiping rebels of the nineteenth century had been defeated and where many heroes of *Romance of The Three Kingdoms* had fallen in battle.

By an incredible chance the enemy commander was on the south bank to feast with his wife's relatives, thinking that the Communists would take many more days to cover the ground from their previous known position. A Red detachment was able to capture him and his boat, and then cross and secure the other boats. The Red Army then began to cross, using the three ferry boats day and night for three days. But the onset of the spring waters (it was late May) made it increasingly difficult, taking more and more time on each crossing, and meanwhile Chiang's bombers were harassing them and enemy forces were racing in from at least two directions. They decided to march to the Luting bridge, further north, which would be their last chance to cross over into north China. In those despairing days Mao even discussed with von Braun the possibility of crossing Sikang and Chinghai to join with the Russians in Sinkiang: the German dissuaded him.

The capture of the Luting bridge was another feat of heroism. This was a string of thirteen iron chains, across nine of which there were normally planks for walking – the other four protecting the crosser at the sides. When the Communists arrived, the enemy had cleared away more than half of the planks, assuming that no one would be so foolhardy as to try to cross on the chains alone.

They found an enemy directive which said: 'Chu Teh and Mao Tse-tung are going to become the second Shih Ta-kai (leader of the Taiping rebels). Ahead of them is the Tatu River, behind is the Golden Sand River. They're caught like fish in a bottle. Now is the time to annihilate the Red bandits.'

So Mao's soldiers did what was not expected of them. They crossed the chains dangling hand over hand, and although the men in front were inevitably shot, to fall into the wild torrent below, enough of them reached the north bridgehead to take it. By then the enemy had set fire to the planks left on their side, but even so the Communists were not stopped. Meanwhile, from behind, the Red Army engineers were laying tree trunks on the chains from the southern side as a new floor.

Mao watched the crossing with his heart in his mouth. One stick of dynamite at the moorings would have ended his career and his movement.

'After crossing the Tatu River,' Mao later recollected, 'where should we go? We racked our brains to make a decision.' In fact there was little choice: they had to continue northwards, skirting the edge of civilized China to reach the Shensi Red base. But the physical obstacles were formidable. The first of these was the Great Snow Mountain.

On the way they were suddenly dive-bombed by three enemy planes while crossing an open valley. The bodyguard standing next to Mao was hit, and lay silently, clutching his abdomen, while Mao bent over him.

'You'll be all right, comrade Hu Chang-pao,' Mao said, 'just keep quiet, and we'll carry you to Shuitseti, where we can get a doctor who will see to you.'

But the man's head fell over and his eyes closed. Mao slid out his arm from under him, where he had been cradling his head, and stood up. He laid a quilt over the body, and then they buried it. Mao had been inches from death.

The Red Army had to climb 16,000 feet in order to cross the Great Snow Mountain, and many of the men came to grief. Mao himself succumbed to malaria again and had to be carried on a stretcher for part of the way. He wrote a poem which brilliantly fused the immediate environment with its geopolitical context:

> Far above the earth, into the blue,
> You, wild Kunlun, have seen
> All that was fairest in the world of men.
> Your three million white jade dragons in flight
> Freeze the sky with piercing cold.
> In summer days your melting torrents
> Flood the streams and rivers,
> Turning men into fish and turtles.
> Who has passed judgment on the good and ill
> You have wrought these thousand autumns?
>
> To Kunlun now I say,
> Neither all your height
> Nor all your snow is needed.
> Could I but draw my sword o'ertopping heaven,
> I'd cleave you in three:
> One piece for Europe,
> One for America,
> One to keep in the East.
> Peace would then reign over the world,
> The same warmth and cold throughout the globe.

On another peak, Mao remembered, 'one army corps lost two-thirds of its transport animals. Hundreds fell down and never got up.' During this next phase of the Long March Mao felt that he was entering some mysterious wonderland.

There are territories near Sikang [he recollected] where there are so few fishermen that the fish just aren't afraid of people. . . . We killed our oxen and horses for meat, and carried them on our few remaining baggage animals, and then in the end we ate the baggage animals and carried the meat ourselves.

It was desperately hard, and the best fighters we ever had to face were the aboriginal tribes – the Miaos, the Fans, the Mis and the Huans. We learnt more from them than we learnt from anyone else. . . . We have to thank the Generalissimo for driving us into all those strange places – we would never have seen them if it had not been for the Generalissimo.

But then Mao had his confrontation, in the unlikely foothills of Tibet, with his rival Chang Kuo-tao, leader of another Communist base area and Mao's equal in Party service, and the commanders of the Fourth Front Army. They had retreated to the western regions two years earlier. The reunion took place on 20 July in the village of Lianghokou, in the pouring rain.

That night General Chu Teh walked back with Chang to his quarters, and talked with him until dawn, explaining that the Tsunyi decisions had been taken at a time of pressing difficulty when Mao had offered an initiative at a moment of crisis and was elected to assume responsibility in the Party to resolve the dispute within its leadership. Chu urged Chang to stick to the military agenda for the immediate future and not to bring up political questions.

But Chang could hardly fail to take heart from the comparison between his army and Mao's. They may have been about equal in numbers, possibly as much as 45,000 each, but the Fourth, not having had to fight with Chiang Kai-shek's crack troops, and having had a good rest, was in far better shape, better fed, better clothed and better equipped. One of the Long Marchers commented of the Chang force: 'They acted like rich men meeting poor relatives.' After the feasting and public speeches, the leaders went into stormy private debate at a Politburo conference. Chang's idea of retreating further west towards Sinkiang, where Russian support would be available, was rejected. He made the mistake of defying both the Twenty-Eight Bolsheviks and the Maoists at the same time, as well as pressing his claims to be the Party's General Secretary.

Mao, knowing that Lin Piao and other generals were not fully satisfied with his own leadership, confessed afterwards that this confrontation with Chang Kuo-tao was 'the darkest moment of his life', when the break-up of the Party and even civil war amongst its leaders 'hung in the balance'. But a majority of his own First Army colleagues and the Politburo members who had been with him on the Long March from Kiangsi accepted his own plan to continue moving north towards Mongolia.

The two armies now joined, but divided again into two columns of mixed units, one under Mao and the other under Chang. This may have been a compromise suggested by General Chu Teh. Chu also proposed that Chang be made Chief Political Commissar of the combined armies, serving alongside Chu himself as Commander-in-Chief. Chang claimed afterwards that he had accepted this new position, but that Mao sabotaged it by continuing, as Chairman of the Military Council, to see all the documents, take all the decisions and transmit them to GHQ for execution instead of leaving the day-to-day running of the army to GHQ.

What is difficult to tell is Chu's motive in all this. Was he bored with playing second fiddle to Mao in military affairs? Did he hope to gain more scope for manoeuvre by bringing Chang more closely into the centre of military decision-making? Did he even toy with playing off the two rivals against one another? Did he merely prefer Chang's ideas at this point, either because he yearned to stay in his native south-west or because of the appalling dangers of the terrain that lay ahead? The fact that the southerners, used to rice, were unable to digest the millet which was the staple food of these areas, was merely one physical manifestation of the dislike which all southern Chinese have for living in the north.

On the other hand, most of Chang's soldiers were recruited in Szechuan, and it is possible that Chu, as the most acclaimed Szechuanese Red General in the field, would be able to appeal above Chang's head to the native Szechuanese who formed most of his army. Chu was the one person who might plausibly bring the two rival forces together, and if this was in his mind then he may have taken Mao into his confidence all along.

The two columns moved off at the beginning of August by different routes towards the north, but were suddenly separated by a river which swelled up into a raging torrent and defied passage. Chang declared that the river could not be crossed and that his column must therefore return to Sikang; Generals Chu Teh and Liu Po-cheng, together with the only radio generator in the army, would have to go with him. Chu and Liu refused, upon which Chang took General Chu prisoner and ordered him to denounce Mao and cut off relations with him.

'You can no more cut me off from Mao', Chu is supposed to have replied, 'than you can cut a man in half.'

To this Chang said that if General Chu refused to obey him, he would be shot.

'That is within your power,' Chu replied, 'I cannot prevent

you. I will not obey your orders!'

But Chang did not carry out his threat, perhaps because the troops loyal to Chu would have risen against his own army. Rather than see this dreadful spectacle of two Communist armies at each other's throats, General Chu reluctantly agreed to turn back with Chang.

Chang's story is that he radioed Mao's column ordering him to halt, but Mao took his column on rather than go back to consult or help his comrades. Kuomintang reinforcements then came in to prevent Chang from following along Mao's route, so he swung south. In the end he was to keep his men for a whole year in the south-west before rejoining Mao and the others in Shensi.

Mao's column now spent six days crossing the Grasslands of Chinghai. This is a high plateau about 8000 feet above the sea where it rains for most of the year (especially in August) and the drainage is poor. It has therefore become a vast swamp stretching for hundreds of miles without trees or shrubs, birds or insects, without even stones.

'If we turn south,' Mao briefed his officers, 'it means running away, and the end of the revolution. We have no choice but to go forward. Our enemies have assumed that we will move into eastern Szechuan rather than attempt the Grasslands road into Shensi and Kansu. But the enemy does not understand us at all. We purposely choose the path which he least expects us to take.'

The Red Army had to acquire food before going into the Grasslands, and took considerable amounts of wheat, sheep, cattle and turnips (each one big enough to 'feed fifteen men', according to Mao) from the tribesmen of this area.

'This is our only foreign debt,' Mao said humorously after reaching the Shensi base, 'and some day we must repay the Mantzu and the Tibetans for the provisions we were obliged to take from them.'

Mao's orderly recalled of the swamp itself: 'The sodden earth squelched monotonously, *pu-chih, pu-chih*, as we laboured over it. A careless step could send you to a fearful death in its muddy depths, trap your feet in a morass. Once caught it was difficult to pull your legs out of the quagmire without the help of your comrades.'

The last mountain range to be crossed was Liupan, where Mao's faithful orderly almost died of malaria. Mao wrote a poem about its capture:

The sky is high, the clouds are pale,
We watch the wild geese vanish southward.
If we fail to reach the Great Wall we are not men,
We who have already measured six thousand miles.

High on the crest of Mount Liupan
Red banners wave freely in the west wind.
Today we hold the long cord in our hands,
When shall we bind fast the Grey Dragon?

At the end of October 1935 Mao and his Long Marchers came at long last to the town of Wuchichen in the Shensi soviet area. They stayed for the first time in caves cut in the side of the hills, mostly dismayed to find that even among friends there was no rice, only golden millet. Mao's cook served a leg of mutton ungarnished because he knew no way of cooking millet. 'Learn to do it,' said Mao when he heard of this, 'it isn't difficult. We've got to learn new ways of living when we come to a new place, otherwise we'll starve to death.'

Mao quickly led a party through falling snowflakes to Hsiashihwan, the headquarters of this Red base area, to meet its leaders.

'In his worn overcoat,' his orderly recalled, 'which he had brought along from Kiangsi, and his old cap, the Chairman nodded and waved at the crowd again and again. Then the people cleared a way for a score of leading comrades to come and shake hands with the Chairman.' They included Liu Chih-tan and Hsu Hai-tung, Commander of the 25th Red Army.

'Is this comrade Hai-tung?' Mao asked, like Stanley. 'Thank you for taking so much trouble to come here to meet us.' Of the 100,000 who had left Kiangsi almost exactly a year before, only about 5000 survived the full journey and emerged in Shensi foot-sore, bedraggled, starved and exhausted. They had eaten tree-bark and drunk their own urine; they had fought the sun and the rocks and the snow. They had crossed the morass and survived. Now the ordeal was over.

Mao's military leadership was vindicated; it remained for him to assert his claim to the political leadership. His own immediate assessment came in a famous poem called, simply, *The Long March*:

The Red Army fears not the trials of the Long March,
Holding light ten thousand crags and torrents.

The Five Ridges wind like gentle ripples
And the majestic Wumeng roll by, globules of clay.
Warm the steep cliffs lapped by the waters of Golden Sand,
Cold the iron chains spanning the Tatu River.
Minshan's 300 miles of snow joyously crossed,
The three Armies march on, each face glowing.

The outside world was astonished, and the supporters of the
Communists delighted at the survival of Mao's band to fight
another day. Lu Hsun and Mao Tun, the leading progressive
writers of China, sent a telegram of congratulations to Mao declaring that: 'The future of China and mankind lies with you.'

Mao's more considered reflection on the incredible 6000-mile
saga came in a report which he gave to his colleagues a few weeks
afterwards:

For twelve months we were under daily reconnaissance and bombing
from the skies by scores of planes, while on land we were encircled and
pursued, obstructed and intercepted by a huge force of several hundred
thousand men, and we encountered untold difficulties and dangers on
the way; yet by using our two legs we swept across a distance of more
than six thousand miles through the length and breadth of eleven provinces. Let us ask, has history ever known a long march to equal ours?
No, never. The Long March ... has proclaimed to the world that the
Red Army is an army of heroes.

A Churchillian hyperbole, perhaps, but in the circumstances
justified.

11
YENAN

For the first time since his student days, Mao was now able to lead a reasonably settled life. He stayed in the Shensi Red base for more than eleven years, the first of them in the old walled town of Paoan, which had once been a fortified imperial stronghold against Mongols and other invading nomads, and the rest in Yenan, the city which he was to make famous and which gave its name to his distinctive brand of Communism. For those eleven years, basking in the glory of the Long March, he lived in the security of a large and well-defended base area, within which his own ideas about reform and revolution could be implemented and from which he could speak not only to the rest of China but to the outside world. The Yenan years were afterwards to be recalled with nostalgia and affection.

In Paoan Mao had a two-roomed cave-house whose chief luxuries were a mosquito net and maps for wallpaper. After years of leadership of his Party, after hundreds of confiscations of property from landowners and officials, his personal possessions would not have filled a suitcase, and although he was a commander of the Red Army he wore on his collar only the two red bars that were the insignia of any Red private.

Mao ate the same food as the others, except that as a Hunanese he had the so-called *aila* or 'love of pepper'. He even had pepper cooked into his bread, but apart from this passion he scarcely seemed to notice what he was eating. At dinner one night a visitor heard him expound his theory about pepper-loving people being revolutionaries.

'He first submitted his own province, Hunan, famous for the revolutionaries it has produced. Then he listed Spain, Mexico, Russia and France to support his contention, but laughingly had to admit defeat when somebody mentioned the well-known Italian love of red pepper and garlic, in refutation of his theory.' He was very fond of a facetious song called 'The Red Hot Pepper', in which the pepper lamented its pointless vegetable existence, waiting to be eaten, and sang its scorn of the placid contentment of the cabbages, spinach and beans with their invertebrate careers: the pepper ended 'by leading a vegetable revolution'.

The settled life of the north-west did not, however, suit Mao's digestion, and his constipation was a matter of general knowledge in Paoan, so much so that Edgar Snow reported that 'Mao's once-a-week bowel movement was an event for congratulations.' When asked once which life he preferred, the sedentary life of a head of government or the roving life of the field, Mao replied with down-to-earth candour: 'I prefer the military life. My bowels never worked better than during the battle of Changsha.'

But he was otherwise fit. A Chinese medical student just returned from Europe gave him a thorough physical examination and pronounced him in excellent health. Peter Fleming, among other writers, was spreading a story that Mao had had tuberculosis or some other 'incurable disease', but this was not true. 'His lungs are completely sound,' according to a witness of the medical inspection, 'although, unlike most Red commanders, he is an inordinate cigarette smoker.'

Cigarettes had been one of Mao's worst deprivations on the Long March, and he had experimented along the way with all sorts of vegetable substitutes. His teeth were blackened, and when a pretty German dentist came to inspect them in Yenan a few years later she had to pay ten visits to complete the fillings.

Mao's simplicity of behaviour extended, unusually for a Chinese in his position, to the foreigners whom he began to meet for the first time in Shensi. An American visitor, while talking with Mao, once saw him 'absent-mindedly turn down the belt of his trousers and search for some guests' – in other words, fleas. On another occasion, when the American was interviewing Lin Piao in a small room with Mao present, it became very hot.

'Rape it, it's hot!' Mao said at last, pulling off his trousers and sitting down again as naturally as Gandhi in his loin-cloth. During this time, the visitor reported, Mao was working 'thirteen or fourteen hours a day, often until very late at night, frequently retiring at two or three. He seems to have an iron constitution.'

That resilience was to stand him in good stead in the political struggle which lay ahead.

Although Mao had, through a combination of good luck and good judgement, passed his test of leadership on the march since Tsunyi, his pre-eminence was not yet generally accepted in political terms. He led, after all, a force which by the end of the Long March had lost almost everything – territory, the hardware and symbols of government, even its best arms and clothing. Mao had already gone through the humiliation of being visibly inferior in these matters to Chang Kuo-tao when they had met in Szechuan. He now faced an almost similar situation in Shensi, where the local Red leaders had been not only holding but even extending their ground during the time that Mao's group was being squeezed out of Kiangsi. When the bedraggled Long Marchers came to the end of their road in 1935 they were much in the debt of the Shensi Communists, without whose success they would have had no haven.

From Mao's personal point of view it was lucky that the Red leadership in Shensi happened to be divided, and along lines strikingly parallel with the divisions in Kiangsi and along the Long March. Two 'native' partisan leaders, Liu Chih-tan and Kao Kang, were at odds with more theoretical and Russian-oriented leaders sent in by the Party headquarters from outside Shensi. Mao was in a position to mediate, and he naturally backed Liu and Kao, whose stance corresponded with his own. This put them in Mao's debt.

Even so, their personalities and following made them formidable candidates for national Party leadership. Liu was killed in the field soon after Mao arrived in Shensi, but Kao went on to become a major figure in the Yenan hierarchy, going to Moscow for a short period of training but coming back to become the Red boss of the strategic north-east, the industrial region on the Russian border.

While he was in Yenan Mao was always careful to praise Kao 'who, following the right policy, had created a base for the Red Army and the revolution in northern Shensi.' Mao deferred to Kao on certain local issues. But Kao's challenge to Mao was not to come until the 1950s. In Yenan his chief preoccupation was the attempt of Po Ku and the other Twenty-Eight Bolsheviks, claiming support from Russia, to return to the leadership now that the weary travels of the Party and the Red Army were over.

The first clash came on Christmas Day of 1935 at a Politburo meeting in Wayaopao. Japan was again encroaching on China's territory, and patriotic non-Communist Chinese were indignant. Why not join them against Japan and hope to influence them to become more sympathetic towards Communist aims in China? This was Mao's argument, but the Bolsheviks were aghast.

Mao damned his critics as advocates of 'closed-door tactics', and he parodied them. 'Was there ever a cat that did not love fish, or a warlord who was not a counter-revolutionary? Intellectuals are three-day revolutionaries whom it is dangerous to recruit. It follows therefore that closed-doorism in the sole wonder-working magic, while the United Front is an opportunistic tactic.'

Later in his speech he emphasized how the party should no longer regard itself as dependent on outside leadership from Moscow; 'the Communists are no longer political infants and are able to take care of themselves and to handle relations with their allies.'

'The question is', Mao declared, 'whether ... the national bourgeoisie can change. We believe it can. ...' And he went on to elaborate what, for a Marxist party, was an extremely important point of doctrinal judgement:

There is ... a clash of interest between the working class and the national bourgeoisie.... But if the national bourgeoisie joins the united front against imperialism, then the working class and the national bourgeoisie will have interests in common. The people's republic will not, in the era of the bourgeois-democratic revolution, abolish non-imperialist and non-feudal private property, but will encourage the development of industrial and commercial enterprises of the national bourgeoisie rather than confiscate them. We shall protect any national bourgeois so long as he does not support the imperialists and traitors. In the stage of democratic revolution, a limit is set to the struggle between labour and capital.

Mao tried to make the anti-Japanese national alliance a reality for his comrades by leading a military expedition across the Yellow River in the hope of engaging with the Japanese troops who were now occupying Hopei and even controlling Peking itself as part of their gradual assimilation of China. But Kuomintang units frustrated this Red expedition, which had to return to Shensi. This was when Mao wrote his most famous poem, 'Snow', in which his presentiment of his own destiny, unconsciously compared with that of China's great emperors in the past, became most transparent:

> North country scene:
> A hundred leagues locked in ice,
> A thousand leagues of whirling snow.
> Both sides of the Great Wall
> One single white immensity.

The Yellow River's swift current
Is stilled from end to end.
The mountains dance like silver snakes
And the highlands charge like wax-hued elephants,
Vying with heaven in stature.
On a fine day, the land,
Clad in white, adorned in red,
Grows more enchanting.

This land so rich in beauty
Has made countless heroes bow in homage.
But alas! Chin Shih-huang and Han Wu-ti
Were lacking in literary grace,
And Tang Tai-tsung and Sung Tai-tsu
Had little poetry in their souls;
And Genghis Khan,
Proud Son of Heaven for a day,
Knew only shooting eagles, bow outstretched.
All are past and gone!
For truly great men
Look to this age alone.

Kuomintang aircraft were at this moment dropping leaflets addressed to any one of Mao's soldiers, with the words: 'Kill Mao Tse-tung ... and we will give you $100,000 when you join our army.' Later the tag was raised to a quarter of a million dollars.

Having decided on his basic tactic for the political situation which the Communists then faced in China, Mao, in his capacity as Chairman of the Central Chinese Soviet Government, bustled with activity. In May 1936 he cabled to the Kuomintang government urging it to collaborate with the Communist Party in a united front against Japan. He offered the Muslims of China autonomy if they would support such a united front, and he proposed a conference of all patriotic anti-Japanese forces. He even made a vivid appeal for the support of the Ko Lao Hui, the famous secret society, in which such eminent Communists as Chu Teh and Ho Lung were leaders.

Mao had been criticized in the past by his own Politburo for associating with bandits and triad leaders, but now he offered these men respectability in resisting the Japanese threat to China. 'You support striking at the rich and helping the poor; we support striking at the local bullies and dividing the land. You despise wealth and defend justice, and you gather together all the heroes and brave fellows in the world; we do not spare ourselves to save China and the world . . . .' The world of *Water Margin* was becoming real.

But a personal letter sent by Mao and other Communist leaders to Chiang Kai-shek, urging a truce between them against Japan, met with disdain.

In July of 1936 an eager Missouri-born American journalist called Edgar Snow arrived, the first Western writer to reach Mao's headquarters in Shensi. He had been reporting from China for the *New York Herald Tribune* and other journals for several years. Snow found Mao

a gaunt, rather Lincolnesque figure, above average height for a Chinese, somewhat stooped, with a head of thick black hair, and with large, searching eyes, a high-bridged nose and prominent cheek bones. My fleeting impression was of an intellectual face of great shrewdness . . . .

He had the simplicity and naturalness of the Chinese peasant, with a lively sense of humour and a love of rustic laughter. His laughter was even active on the subject of himself and the shortcomings of the soviets – a boyish sort of laughter which never in the least shook his inner faith in his purpose. He is plain-speaking and plain-living, and some people might think him rather coarse and vulgar. Yet he combines curious qualities of naivety with the most incisive wit and worldly sophistication.

Snow went on to describe Mao as 'an accomplished scholar of classical Chinese, an omnivorous reader, a deep student of philosophy and history, a good speaker, a man with an unusual memory and extraordinary powers of concentration, an able writer, careless in his personal habits and appearance but astonishingly meticulous about details of duty, a man of tireless energy, and a military and political strategist of considerable genius.' Mao had a 'deep sense of personal dignity, and something about him suggests a power of ruthless decision when he deems it necessary.'

Snow found Mao well informed on current world politics. 'He was very interested in the Labour Party of England, and questioned me intensely about its present politics, soon exhausting all my information.'

Mao could not understand why there was still no workers' government in a country where the workers had the vote. 'He expressed profound contempt for Ramsay Macdonald, whom he designated as a *Han-chien* – an arch-traitor of the British people.' On the other hand he regarded Roosevelt as anti-fascist, and thought China could co-operate with him. He pressed on Snow questions about India, offering the opinion that Indian independence would not be realized until there were an agrarian revolution, and about US minority groups.

Mao agreed to answer Snow's questions, and Snow described the scene:

On July 16, 1936, I sat on a square backless stool inside Mao Tse-tung's residence. It was after nine at night. 'Taps' had been sounded and nearly all lights were out. The walls and ceiling of Mao's home were of solid rock; beneath was a flooring of bricks. Cotton gauze extended half-way up windows also hollowed from stone, and candles spluttered on the square, unpainted table before us, spread with a clean red felt cloth. Mrs Mao was in an adjoining room making compote from wild peaches purchased that day from a fruit merchant. Mao sat with his legs crossed, in a deep shelf hewn from the solid rock, and smoking a Chien Men cigarette.

At the end of one of the several interviews that Mao gave to Snow, when it was gone two o'clock in the morning and Snow was exhausted, there came a distraction:

Mao suddenly bent over and gave an exclamation of delight at a moth that had languished beside the candle. It was a really lovely thing, with wings shaded a delicate apple-green and fringed in a soft rainbow of saffron and rose. Mao opened a book and pressed this gossamer of colour between its leaves.

Asked about a most sensitive issue, namely his relations with Russia, Mao explained that:

... although the Communist Party of China is a member of the Comintern, still this in no sense means that soviet China is ruled by Moscow.... We are certainly not fighting for an emancipated China in order to turn the country over to Moscow!...

When soviet governments have been established in many countries, the problem of an international union of soviets may arise, and it will be interesting to see how it will be solved. But today I cannot suggest the formula – it is a problem which has not been and cannot be solved in advance. In the world today, with increasingly close economic and cultural intimacies between different states and peoples, such a union would seem to be highly desirable, if achieved on a voluntary basis.

Actually Mao was somewhat scathing about the Russians when he spoke to Snow in private: 'In his interviews with me Mao called the Soviet Union his "loyal ally". Over compote he referred rather satirically to the "Russian aid which never arrived".'

'For a people being deprived of its national freedom,' Mao told Snow at another point in his interviewing, 'the revolutionary

task is not immediate Socialism, but the struggle for independence. We cannot even discuss Communism if we are robbed of a
country in which to practise it.'

After the political questions, Mao reluctantly turned to Snow's
personal questions. The American urged him to correct the dis-
torted and false reports which were spreading about him.

'Suppose,' Mao said at last, 'that I just disregard your questions, and instead give you a general sketch of my life? . . .'

'But that's exactly what I want!'

And so, for the next four nights, they met 'like conspirators
. . . huddled in that cave over that red-covered table, with splut-
tering candles between us.' Snow wrote until he was ready to
drop, while the interpreter sat next to him rendering Mao's soft
southern dialect 'in which a chicken, instead of being a good
substantial Northern *chi*, became a romatic *ghii,* and Hunan
became Funan, and a bowl of *cha* turned into *tsa*, and many
much stranger variations occurred. Mao related everything from
memory, and I put it down as he talked.'

There followed, in an early section of Snow's *Red Star Over
China*, the only autobiography which Mao Tse-tung was ever to
give the world. It covered fifty-four pages in the original Left
Book Club edition. The story was as interesting to Mao's own
colleagues as it was to the Western visitor. Snow observed:

During Mao's recollection of his past, I noticed that an auditor at least
as interested as myself was . . . his wife. Many of the facts he told
about himself and the Communist movement she had evidently never
heard before, and this was true of most of Mao's comrades in Paoan.

Later on, when I gathered biographical notes from other Red leaders, their colleagues often crowded round interestedly to listen to the
stories for the first time. Although they had all fought together for
years, very often they knew nothing of each other's pre-Communist
days, which they had tended to regard as a kind of Dark Ages period,
one's real life beginning only when one became a Communist.

In the autumn of 1936, Chang Kuo-tao and General Chu Teh
returned in disarray from Szechuan to join Mao in the Shensi
base. Not only did Chang have to concede that he had been
wrong to turn south at the critical point of the Long March, he
also made the mistake of sending the best units of his Fourth
Front Army on a disastrous wild-goose chase in the western
interior just before reaching Shensi. He hoped thereby to bring
territory of his own to add to the Shensi base, but instead he had
ignominiously to ask Mao for help in rescuing the force. Mao
refused to take the risk, in case there were attacks from other

quarters, and he rebuked Chang for losing valuable men to no purpose. This affair made it easier for Mao to dispose of Chang as a serious rival to his leadership in the months that followed.

General Chu Teh, Mao's old partner, doubtless made his own peace with Mao, and the concentration of Communist leadership in Shensi was completed when Ho Lung, the Red 'bandit', brought his men into the base from the south soon afterwards. All was now set for Communism to strike out decisively into China from this north-western base area.

'In the morning of 12 December 1936 an unusually lively bustle broke out in Paoan,' von Braun later recalled. 'The field telephone which linked Mao's headquarters with the other Party, government and army leaders was ringing the alarm. Mao Tse-tung himself, who normally worked at night and liked to sleep till midday, was already out and about. Chou En-lai came to him, then a little later Lo Fu, Po Ku and some others. What had happened?' It was the most dramatic episode in the twenty-two-year-long contest between Mao and Chiang Kai-shek for the control of China. One of the leading northern warlords – 'neutral' between the Kuomintang and the Communists – had taken Chiang prisoner while the Generalissimo was visiting him in Sian.

News of the so-called Sian Incident flashed round the world, causing apprehension in many capitals. Mao excitedly demanded that Chiang Kai-shek be brought to Paoan for trial and punishment for his heavy debts to the Chinese people. But Stalin judged differently. He cabled that Chiang Kai-shek was the only possible leader of a Chinese united front against Japan, and so Mao should try to get him released.

Mao sent Chou En-lai to Sian in order to influence events in the Communists' favour, and on 19 December, to placate Stalin, he cabled to Chiang Kai-shek urging him to convene an all-party conference to discuss how policies to resist Japan could be co-ordinated. 'We didn't sleep for a week...', Chou En-lai later confessed. 'It was the most difficult decision of our whole lives.'

At last the warlord released Chiang on Christmas Day after the Generalissimo had promised to patch up a truce with the Communists, resist Japan more firmly and run China more democratically. Mao had not been able to pin down a divided Politburo as to how Chiang should have been treated, but the Kuomintang leader was now at least more publicly committed to goals shared with the Communists.

The Red Army was meanwhile extending its domain. It captured the city of Yenan, and the capital of the Chinese People's Soviet Republic was moved to this larger and more convenient site. Yenan is an old town in the angle of a river, completely surrounded by hills of yellowish clay, out of which cave dwellings have been hollowed. It is a market town with historical relics, including a pagoda dating back to the Sung Dynasty.

Mao moved into a three-roomed cottage in Yenan, with a 'victory garden' in which he grew vegetables and tobacco. Later, when the Japanese began to bomb Yenan, he moved further out into a large cave in the cliffs of Yangchiapiang which was completely bomb-proof, although he continued to use the house for meetings. 'Life was quite cosy in the caves,' von Braun remembered. 'They offered protection from the cold in winter and from the heat in summer, and to a degree from the Japanese bombs. Only the sand fleas and rats gave us trouble until we got used to them.'

But all was not well in Mao's personal life. His wife, Ho Tzu-chen, never fully recovered from her frightful experiences on the Long March, when she was badly wounded in an air raid at about the time when she gave birth to her fourth child by Mao. She arrived in Shensi in a state of physical and mental collapse, having gone most of those 6000 miles on a stretcher, and never properly settled in Mao's new headquarters. She was once described as a stubborn woman who 'never came to understand the political world of Chairman Mao'. Their fifth daughter was conceived in Shensi and was born during Edgar Snow's visit in the summer of 1936. Mao was very fond of this girl, who grew up to become Li Min, and rose to fame during the Cultural Revolution.

If his home life was less than ideal, Mao was able to find in Shensi an active social life in an unusual moral climate. This was, after all, a community of Communists endeavouring to base their lives to some extent on reason. Large numbers of students and young intellectuals and artists were now pouring into the base from Shanghai and other parts of China with all kinds of ideals, and for the soldiers who lived through the privations of the Long March it could become intoxicating.

One group of students was arrested for forming a 'Free Love Club', and von Braun noted how 'the strong discipline and unqualified puritan way of life that had been the hallmark of the Red Army ... loosened with time in Yenan.' He and the other foreign resident, Dr George Hatem (a Lebanese American), used to entertain artists of all kinds at the weekends: 'we conversed about everything possible, mostly art and politics, played ping-pong and even danced sometimes, which had hitherto been taboo as a bad foreign habit.'

As the years went on, the social climate became more relaxed, and the Saturday night dances at the Pear Garden were looked forward to by everyone. The music came from scratched old records, or from a band whose instruments ranged from old-fashioned Chinese fiddles and a Cantonese zither to a pedal-organ (left behind by missionaries), mouth organs and Western violins. Traditional Chinese tunes were played along with Western foxtrots and waltzes, but what was most remarkable was that the women demonstrated their emancipation by choosing their own dance partners, contrary to Chinese tradition. Mao himself was not immune to these new modes and manners. A female comrade was entitled to turn to him and ask respectfully: 'Please dance with me.'

The foreign visitors revelled in these Saturday night occasions. One of them described how 'you might see bushy-haired shirt-sleeved Mao Tse-tung ... having a grand time dancing a fast one-step with a cute co-ed' from Yenan University. Mao was also able to spend time with the Chinese women Communists, and was particularly drawn to the Bohemian writer Ting Ling, a fellow Hunanese and old schoolfriend of Yang Kai-hui.

Ting was one of the most liberated personalities in the movement, who had, for example, participated in a *ménage à trois* and had written with untraditional candour, in literary form, about her own emotional experiences. Mao used to spend many hours talking to Ting Ling in his cave, and some of his colleagues regarded it as an infatuation. One comrade wrote of him a few years later, that, 'Although he is now almost fifty, his enthusiasm for women has not diminished in thirty years.'

Mao also enjoyed his first opportunity to hobnob with Western women. Two American journalists, the flamboyant Agnes Smedley, who wrote for the *Frankfurter Zeitung* and the *Manchester Guardian*, and Helen Foster Snow, Edgar Snow's wife, who wrote under the pseudonym of Nym Wales, were both early visitors to Yenan. They did not take to each other, and became rivals in gaining the confidence of the Chinese Communist leaders, but they both saw a good deal of Mao and he liked their company.

Then there was Anna Wang, a German blonde who had married one of the young Chinese Communists in Europe. A few days after she had arrived, she was taking coffee with Agnes

Smedley in her courtyard when Mao sauntered in to join them.
When he learned that she had a son, he immediately asked:

'Does he have blond hair or black hair? And are his eyes blue
like yours, or dark?'

Slightly surprised, Anna Wang explained that the boy had
black hair and dark eyes. Mao then wanted to know more about
his skin, whether it was pale or like that of a Chinese.

'More like that of a Chinese.'

'Isn't it strange,' Mao drew the jocular moral. 'Your compat-
riot von Braun has a Chinese wife and their child has the black
hair, dark eyes and the pigmentation of a Chinese as well. You
see, you Germans are always boasting of how powerful you are,
but it seems that you're inferior to us Chinese. So we are the
stronger race after all!'

It was through Smedley, though indirectly, that Mao got into
trouble. On her first day in Yenan in the spring of 1937, she
called on Mao at midnight. She wrote afterwards:

I pushed back a padded cotton drape across a door in a mountain
cave, and stepped into a dark cavern. Directly in the centre of this
darkness stood a tall candle on a rough-hewn table. Its glow fell on piles
of books and papers and touched the low earthen ceiling above. A
man's figure was standing with one hand on the table; his face, turned
towards the door, was in shadow. I saw a mass of dark clothing covered
by a loose padded greatcoat. . . . The tall, forbidding figure lumbered
towards us and a high-pitched voice greeted us.

Then two hands grasped mine; they were as long and sensitive as a
woman's. Without speaking we stared at each other. His dark, inscrutable face was long, the forehead broad and high, the mouth feminine.
Whatever else he might be, he was an aesthete. I was in fact repelled by
the feminine in him and by the gloom of the setting. An instinctive
hostility sprang up inside me . . .

Later Smedley found that . . .

the sinister quality I had at first felt so strongly in him proved to be a
spiritual isolation. As Chu Teh was loved, Mao Tse-tung was
respected. The few who came to know him best had affection for him,
but his spirit dwelt within itself, isolating him. . . . In him was none of
the humility of Chu. Despite that feminine quality in him, he was as
stubborn as a mule, and a steel rod of pride and determination ran
through his nature. I had the impression that he would wait and watch
for years, but eventually have his way.

After that first meeting Mao often went to Smedley's cave,
which she shared with Lily Wu – the girl whom Smedley had
chosen as her interpreter, described as the 'only girl in Yenan

with a permanent wave', and as a girl of dazzling grace and talent who came to 'fascinate Mao'.

'The three of us', Smedley recollected, 'would have a simple dinner and spend hours in conversation. Since he had never been out of China, he asked me a thousand questions. We spoke of India; of literature; and once he asked me if I had loved any man, and why, and what love meant to me. Sometimes he quoted from old Chinese poets or recited some of his own poems.'

According to Nym Wales, on 31 May 1937 she was talking to Smedley and Lily Wu in their cave, roasting potatoes and preparing dinner, when Mao called in high spirits. He sat and talked with them, and after a while Lily walked over to sit beside him on the bench, putting her hand on his knee rather timidly and announcing that she had had too much wine. 'Mao also appeared startled,' Wales recollected, 'but he would have been something of a cad to push her away rudely, and he was obviously amused. He also announced that he had had too much wine. Lily then ventured to take hold of Mao's hand, which she repeated from time to time during the evening.' Von Braun alleged that Smedley proceeded to arrange meetings between Mao and Lily Wu in George Hatem's cave.

Inevitably Ho found out about the affair, and was very angry: von Braun was a witness to one 'fierce argument' at the end of 1937. One of the Red wives described Ho as having 'the temper of a Hunanese donkey'. Von Braun alleged that Mao then arranged for Lily Wu to go to von Braun's cave while the German was there, and to be discovered with the German by a third party so that the world could conclude that Lily Wu's assignations were with von Braun rather than with Mao himself, but this story sounds less plausible. Ho formally charged Lily Wu with alienating her husband's affections, but Mao denied her allegations.

Meanwhile Mao was consolidating his leadership in the Party. In early April 1937 he held a conference for the condemnation of Chang Kuo-tao, whose men were accused of raping, torturing and punishing women prisoners by 'playing with their vaginas'. But there was a backlash from cadres in Chang's Fourth Front Army, loyal to their old commander. A hundred of them (including Hsu Shih-yu, the officer who went on to become in the 1970s military commander of the Canton region, protector of Teng Hsiao-ping and an explicit critic of Mao) planned to break out of the Shensi base and start a new one of their own under the slogan: 'Down with Mao Tse-tung, Up with Chairman Chang Kuo-tao.'

But they were betrayed by one of their members who at the eleventh hour could not bear to leave his mistress, the wife of the legless Hsu Meng-chiu (who had suffered frostbite on the Great Snow Mountain during the Long March and had to have both his legs amputated). The men were eventually pardoned.

In many respects Mao's personality did not lend itself to the leadership of a mass organization. Edgar Snow was perceptive about this on his visit:

> Where subordination of the individual to the mass will amounted to a cult, Mao was distinctly an individualist. Smoking was among the Communists considered an indication of lack of personal discipline and was discouraged; Mao was an incessant cigarette smoker. Most of Paoan was up at daybreak; Mao worked at night and could seldom be roused before noon . . . .
>
> Most of Mao's followers had Prussian haircuts. Mao hated to have his hair cut and wore it very long. . . . In contrast to the neat, alert and military bearing of Chou En-lai and others, Mao slouched when he walked, his shoulders bent, a peasant in his gait. When I took some photographs of him and Lin Piao reviewing cadets Mao gave the feeblest imitation of a salute I ever saw. Chou En-lai looked you straight in the eye; whatever he was saying, he always seemed anxious that you believe him. Mao had a way of gazing sidelong at you, waiting for the effect of his words and their logic to be understood, and challenged. Seemingly relaxed to the point of carelessness, he masked an ever-alert and imaginative mind.

But Snow also correctly observed the positive ingredients in Mao's appeal as a party leader:

> Mao had an extraordinarily good memory. He was able to recall dates, names, exact conversations and details of incidents over many years. His method of bossing the party was not overt but indirect and subtle. He spent hours conferring with various committee members, sounding out their views and reconciling them with his own. After he had talked to each of them individually, and was sure of a consensus, he then stated his own opinion as a synthesis.
>
> He certainly believed in his own star and destiny to rule. But he was relaxed, natural and unaffected in his personal relationships. He built confidence and trust by his loyalty to those who were loyal to him. He was also magnanimous to those who disagreed with him. Those who fought against him and his ideas would in time lose influence but they were not purged or physically destroyed on the scale of Stalin's personal rivals.

Mao began to deal more often with foreign affairs, reflecting his new Party pre-eminence. 'Were it not that we are face to face with the Japanese enemy,' he wrote to the Spanish people on 15 May 1937, 'we would join you and take our place in your front ranks.' A few weeks later he was writing to the American Communist leader Earl Browder – 'the good friend of the Chinese people'.

A succession of foreign visitors came to see him, seeking his views on the international issues of the day. In addition to Snow and Smedley, he received in the early part of his Shensi period Owen Lattimore, T. A. Bisson, James Bertram and Violet Cressy-Marcks. Miss Cressy-Marcks was not well informed about Chinese politics, and her opening exchanges with Mao were a little tense.

'What have you heard about me?' Mao asked.

'Only, of course, propaganda for and against,' the British lady explorer replied.

'What in favour of me?'

'That you are wonderfully good, that you are improving the lives of thousands in China and that you can do no wrong.'

'And what', Mao asked, 'have you heard against me?'

'That you have killed, in some towns, all the inhabitants over forty and under eight, that you are a robber and a rogue.'

At this point, Cressy-Marcks remembered, everyone in the room remained very still, although the guard standing behind her chair with a large naked sword trembled slightly as her words were translated. Mao did not move a muscle while she had been speaking, keeping his eyes on her.

'No,' he said with a sudden smile, 'I don't eat babies for *tiffin*,' and the ice was broken.

12
BLUE APPLE

Besides women and politics, Mao was able, in the settled conditions of Paoan and Yenan, to indulge in his third consuming passion, namely books and ideas. He spent much of his time coming to grips with the philosophical basis of his own thought and of Marxism. Understandably, in view of his having to compete with other leaders who were better trained in the theoretical side of Marxism, he read and digested during his first two years in Shensi – at leisure and for the first time in proper sequence – a large number of Russian philosophical works in Chinese translation. Little of this had been possible while he had been on the run in guerrilla conditions.

Snow recalled a night when he was interviewing Mao during the summer of 1936. A visitor arrived with a parcel of new books on philosophy. 'Mao asked me to postpone our engagements. He consumed these books in three or four nights of intensive reading, during which he seemed to be oblivious to anything else.'

One of Mao's early actions in Shensi had been to found a new academy for cadres to acquire military and academic learning, where he himself gave lectures in both military strategy and philosophy. From these lectures he developed his major writings. The first was his full-length study of military strategy, *Problems of Strategy in China's Revolutionary War*, where he crystallized the costly experience acquired in Kiangsi and on the Long March, now to be utilized against Japan's creeping aggression.

Mao conceded that his advocacy of guerrilla warfare was a temporary one. 'In the future this guerrilla character will definitely become something to be ashamed of and to be discarded, but today it is invaluable and we must stick to it.'

Mao did not let slip the opportunity to tilt at his Soviet-trained rivals. 'Although we must value Soviet experience, and even value it somewhat more than experiences in other countries throughout history, because it is the most recent experience of revolutionary war, we must value even more the experience of China's revolutionary war, because there are a great number of conditions special to the Chinese revolution and the Chinese Red Army...'

This military manual closed with a characteristically brilliant piece of bravado. 'Our basic policy is to rely on the war industries of the imperialist countries and of our domestic enemy. We have a claim on the output of the arsenals of London as well as of Hanyang, and, what is more, it is delivered to us by the enemy's transport corps. This is the sober truth, it is not a jest.'

Mao's philosophical writings, derived from the reading and ratiocination of these years in Shensi, by way of his lectures at the Red Army College, were to become controversial. He had not yet, after all, been able to read and digest the whole of the Marxist-Leninist canon – if only because it had not all been translated into Chinese. His *On Dialectical Materialism*, for example, was found by a Western scholar to be largely plagiarized from Chinese translations of Soviet philosophical works, and it has been calculated that on this particular aspect of Marxism Mao had been able to read only about a third of what Engels and Marx had written, and only about four-fifths of what Lenin had contributed. Mao later denied his authorship of *On Dialectical Materialism*, but not all Western scholars were convinced.

The two best known of Mao's published theoretical writings are *On Practice* and *On Contradiction*, both published in the summer of 1937. But the verdict of Western critics was that, on the showing of these two essays, described as 'mediocre' and 'dull', Mao had little talent as an abstract thinker. One Politburo member found them 'full of errors', and there is a suggestion that Chou En-lai was also less than enthusiastic. Later these works were polished by Chen Po-ta, a Communist intellectual who was released from gaol by the Kuomintang later in 1937 and came to Yenan to become Mao's personal secretary.

In *On Practice* Mao crystallized his arguments against the so-called dogmatists (the Twenty-Eight Bolsheviks) who tried to persuade the Chinese comrades to follow the Soviet textbook to the letter regardless of the ways in which Chinese revolutionary experience was different. He elaborated the concept that in order to know about something you must actually have contact with it, and indeed change it.

'If you want to know the taste of a pear, you must change the pear by eating it yourself.' He quoted the old Chinese saying, 'How can you catch tiger cubs without entering the tiger's lair?'

This process of changing the world through practice. . . .

has already reached a historic moment in the world and in China, a great moment unprecedented in human history, that is, the moment for completely banishing darkness from the world and from China and for changing the world into a world of light such as never previously existed . . . .

'The objective world which is to be changed also includes all the opponents of change, who, in order to be changed, must go through a stage of compulsion before they can enter the stage of voluntary, conscious change. The epoch of world communism will be reached when all mankind voluntarily and consciously changes itself and the world.

This was a high point in Mao's voluntaristic super-optimism.

On Contradiction elaborated the importance of studying the interconnection between forces and events, and of analysing the contradictions that arise between them. In a specific sense Mao sought to supply the answer to the debate in Moscow over the so-called Deborin School of philosophy, which denied that there were any contradictions between the kulaks and the peasants in the Soviet Union of that time.

Mao explained: 'The question is one of different kinds of contradiction, not of the presence or absence of contradiction. Contradiction is universal and absolute, it is present in the process of development of all things and permeates every process from beginning to end.' The contradiction between Soviet kulaks and peasants was a non-antagonistic one, which 'will not become intensified into antagonism or assume the form of class struggle.'

While he was writing these essays, the Japanese army attacked at the Marco Polo bridge just outside Peking, escalating the tension into formal hostilities after years of cumulative Japanese persecution and useless Chinese appeasement. On 7 July 1937 the Sino-Japanese war opened. General Chu Teh rushed to the front, and Agnes Smedley asked Mao's advice about whether she should stay in Yenan to finish her biography of General Chu or go to the front and write about the war. Mao counselled the latter course: 'This war is more important than past history.'

He was right. This was to be the factor which prevented a much stronger and more numerous Kuomintang from destroying the Communist Party in China. Afterwards, in the 1960s, when a leading Japanese figure expressed regret to Mao for the invasion, Mao replied:

'There is no need to apologize. If the Japanese had not occupied half of China, it would have been impossible for the entire Chinese population to rise and fight the Japanese invader.

And that resulted in our army strengthening itself by a million men, and in the liberated bases the population increased to 100 millions.'

Mao then paused and smiled, and said: 'Should I thank you?'

The Japanese launched a major attack on Shanghai in August, and all at once the Kuomintang became serious about a united front with the Communists, responding to Mao's cables. By September their agreement to fight the Japanese together was formalized, and it became permissible in Yenan to wear either the Central Government's uniform or the Red Army uniform. Mao personified the United Front in a very direct way, by putting his National Revolutionary Army cap on to receive visitors from outside Yenan, but donning his old Red Army cap with its five-pointed star for Communist meetings. The Reds also, by an irony which they thoroughly enjoyed, were paid salaries by the Central Government to run the Eighth Route Army: Mao now received $5 a month from the Generalissimo.

The Politburo met in Lochuan at the end of August to decide its tactics in this new situation. It was here that Chang Kuo-tao was finally condemned for his 'rightism' and had to deliver a (perfunctory) confession of his mistakes. The following spring he fled Yenan and defected to the Kuomintang. The big issue, however, was the degree of independence on which the Communists should insist while fighting under unified Central Government command. Mao took the view that the Communists should not take any orders from the Kuomintang but should enlarge their own forces instead. Chou En-lai and Chu Teh, more timid, disagreed.

The Lochuan meeting was important in an unexpectedly personal way, because it was there that Mao first met someone who was to influence his future most profoundly. During the four-day conference a group of young people from artistic circles in Shanghai arrived on their way to Yenan to join the Communists in the wake of the Japanese aggression. Among them was the twenty-three-year-old film actress who became known to posterity as Chiang Ching, but who was then better known as Lan Ping, the Blue Apple.

She had arrived in Lochuan on an army truck which was carrying rice to the Red headquarters. Along with the others from Shanghai, she met Mao and his Politburo colleagues. The looks which were exchanged on that day were to lead to marriage and a stormy political partnership during the Cultural Revolution of the 1960s. When Mao drove back to Yenan, Chiang

Ching rode in the back of the truck just behind him.

Chiang Ching was born in 1914 in Shantung province, the daughter of a poor wheel-maker. All her brothers and sisters were much older, and she had a lonely childhood, suffering also from her father's fits of blind rage. She never had new clothes and always had to make do with a brother's hand-me-downs.

She was selected as one of the few token girls from working-class families admitted to a gentry school 'for show'. When her family moved to Tsinan, Chiang Ching joined the city's Experimental Art Theatre where she was able for the first time to study drama and music, including the piano, without charge.

So keen was she on acting that she joined a touring theatrical group which went to Peking. 'I left without telling my mother,' she confessed, 'only mailing her a letter at the railway station just before the train pulled out.' She was then sixteen.

Her main impression of Peking was the cold of its winter. She had no underclothes, and the family's best quilt which she had taken with her was worn thin by age. She quickly moved on to Tsingtao where the man who had taught her in Tsinan had become Dean of the University. He arranged for her to be admitted, and the gossip was that she became his mistress.

In Tsingtao she developed a love of novels and poetry, and read her first Marxist book, Lenin's *State and Revolution*. She had already joined various left-wing associations and soon met Li Ta-chang, the organizer of the local Communists. She claimed that by 1933 she had won her Party card, revealing, however, that she had to pay a price in cash for it.

The story spread that she married in Tsingtao a Communist called David Yu, a brother-in-law of the her ex-lover, the university dean, and highly connected in Kuomintang government circles.

Sooner or later every young artist in China was drawn to Shanghai, the 'Paris of the East', where the spirit of Western civilization flowed in openly from abroad, and Chiang Ching was no exception. In Shanghai the Communist writer Chou Yang arranged for her to work with a proletarian drama troupe. Later she joined a Young Women's Christian Association night-school programme for working women.

By now the Kuomintang suspected her politics, and she was kidnapped and kept in prison for eight months. Ironically it was only when a foreigner (an American?) from the YWCA came to protest and guarantee her innocence that she was released.

In 1935 she played the role of Nora in *A Doll's House* ('I threw

myself completely into the part'), as well as other leading Ibsen
and Gogol roles. Realizing that her seniors in the company were
contemptuous of her acting ability, she made desperate efforts to
improve her skills.

In 1936 she entered the world of the cinema, under the name
Lan Ping. The two characters which she had chosen meant Blue
Peace, but, to her annoyance, her sponsor changed the second
character to a much more exciting one meaning Apple. She
made several films in Shanghai, the most famous being *Wang
Lao-wu*, an explicit treatment of social exploitation and patriotic
resistance to Japan set in an urban slum.

The rumours flew even more wildly in Shanghai. One was that
she had married the actor and film critic Tang Na, but had then
left him in a state of such grief that he was driven to the edge of
suicide. It was also said that she was jilted by another film
director Tsang Min in 1937, and that when she left Shanghai
later that year to go to Yenan, her escort was none other than her
ex-husband, David Yu. Such were the titillating rumours surrounding this beautiful woman of five foot five on her arrival in
Mao's domain in the far north-west.

Chiang Ching's biographer, Roxane Witke, wrote that Mao
'had his eye on her as soon as she arrived in Yenan'. The lady's
own story has it that Mao looked her out personally soon after
her arrival and offered her a ticket to a lecture which he was to
give at the Marxist-Leninist institute. She sat in the front row
and made herself conspicuous by asking questions afterwards.

One of the Communists present at that time commented: 'Lan
Ping is very pretty and she can act. When she arrived at Yenan
old Mao was ecstatic. He applauded her performances so loudly
that Ho Tzu-chen became jealous. The two of them often fought
about this, with terrible results.'

For her new Communist career Lan Ping gave herself the
name of Chiang Ching. It means literally Azure River. She
denied that Mao chose it for her.

Several of the other Communist leaders were appalled at
Mao's recklessness. No doubt his political critics were glad to
find any stick to beat him with, but even his friends had reservations. Ho Tzu-chen had proved herself a loyal and brave comrade in the field, whereas Chiang Ching's commitment to Communism was felt to be unproved. Po Ku spoke disapprovingly of
her 'colourful' past, meaning her illicit relationships, and also of
her unclear relations with senior Kuomintang personalities as
well as her 'vague' attitude to the Party. Von Braun said that she

was generally considered on her arrival in Yenan as a non-Party person, although later it was put about that Kang Sheng had accepted her into the Party in the early 1930s, confirming her own account.

Chiang Ching made her own motivations fairly clear in her later observation about those years in Yenan, that 'sex is engaging in the first rounds but what sustains interest in the long run is power.'

Mao expected his behaviour to be judged by modern, revolutionary and non-traditional rational standards, whereas the majority of his colleagues brought to these particular matters very old-fashioned ideas of personal virtue. When Mao therefore told his friends that he intended to divorce Ho in order to marry Chiang Ching, the Party was scandalized. The Central Committee withheld its approval, observing:

'Ho Tzu-chen has always been a good comrade to you, she is a reliable and faithful companion and has shown her true worth in battle and in work. Why are you no longer able to live together with a woman like this?'

To which Mao replied: 'I esteem and respect Comrade Ho, but, really, we should not think along feudalistic lines any more, where divorce is considered an injury to a woman's reputation or position.' He allegedly added that 'without Blue Apple I cannot go on with the revolution'.

Later he defined his unorthodox attitude to marriage: 'You cannot bind a man and a woman together to make them husband and wife. When someone stops caring for your place and wants to leave it, just let them go.'

Mao's case was strengthened by the erratic behaviour of Ho, who went to live alone in Sian and spurned the persuasions of Chou En-lai and his wife to return to Yenan. Chang Kuo-tao's wife briefly shared a room with her in Sian, and found her pale, sickly and adamant about not going back to Mao's quarters.

'Tse-tung', she complained, 'treats me badly. We bicker and have rows. He grabs the bench and I grab the chair! I know we're finished.'

She also developed the appalling habit of compulsively beating her children.

Of Mao, Snow wrote, 'I never saw him angry. But I heard that on occasion he has been roused to an intense and withering fury. At such times his command of irony and invective is said to be classic and lethal.' Even his humour, according to Smedley, was 'often sardonic and grim, as if it sprang from deep caverns of spiritual seclusion. I had the impression that there was a door to his being that had never been opened to anyone.'

After about a year of pressure – enhanced, according to malicious gossip, by Chiang Ching's becoming pregnant by him – Mao persuaded the special 'court' of the Central Committee, which had been set up under Chen Yun, to give him his freedom. The final arrangements were made with characteristic tact. Ho Tzu-chen was sent with her young daughter 'for medical treatment' to Russia, while Lily Wu was despatched home to Szechuan. Chiang Ching joined Mao's household in 1938, first as his secretary and then as his wife. Probably Kang Sheng, an old Party colleague of Mao who had been born in the same district as Chiang Ching, helped to arrange both the job and the marriage.

No one appears to know the date of the marriage, and there was apparently no ceremony: it may have been formalized by the mere act of Mao's telling his comrades on the Central Committee. Chiang Ching herself, giving her life story to Witke in 1972, chose not to discuss the marriage in contractual terms or in terms of dates. Her account of her first years of living with Mao made it clear that in his celebrated aloofness he did not become involved in attempting to defend her personal history against those critics in the Party who disputed her own account of her Party membership and activities. In particular, some of the people with whom she had clashed in Shanghai had now become very senior officials in the Communist establishment in Yenan.

It was later to be claimed that Mao's colleagues made it a condition of the divorce and remarriage that Chiang Ching should play no part in public or Party life. Chiang herself later denied this but, if there were such a condition, it was certainly observed for at least twenty-five years, until the Cultural Revolution.

Meanwhile, the war began to touch the Red camp. Lin Piao achieved in September 1937 the Communists' first victory over the Japanese, defeating the crack Itagaki Regiment in the battle of the Pinghsing Pass. But Mao made it clear to the various units of the Red Army as they moved off to the front that: 'The war between China and Japan has furnished the best opportunity for the development of our Party. Our policy is to devote seventy per cent of our efforts to our own expansion, twenty per cent to coping with the Kuomintang and only ten per cent to fighting the Japanese.'

But now came' yet another threat to Mao's leadership of the

Communist Party. At the end of October 1937 the only remaining man capable of offering a serious challenge to Mao's Party
supremacy suddenly arrived in Yenan. Wang Ming flew in from
Moscow on a Russian aircraft – the first to land since the Red
occupation – with instructions to the Chinese comrades from
Stalin. He was met with due ceremony at the airport by Mao and
the others, befitting his dignity as a Politburo member, as the
Party's official delegate to the Comintern and, most important,
as a member of the Executive Committee of the Comintern.

As the senior member of the Twenty-Eight Bolshevik group,
and as someone who had been in Moscow for the past twelve
years enjoying Stalin's confidence, Wang Ming presented a powerful threat to Mao. Mao must have had very mixed feelings as
he watched the Russian plane come in to land, with its welcome
anti-aircraft guns, giant radio transmitter and other items of
Soviet aid – but also with his old rival on board. All the same he
delivered at the welcoming banquet that night the expected
flowery phrases of a host: Wang's arrival was a 'heaven-sent
pleasure ... beyond all expectation ....'

Wang Ming brought a series of new instructions from Stalin
which on balance helped Mao. As always, the Russian leader
was more concerned with developments within the Kremlin than
with the realities of the world outside, and his chief command to
the Chinese comrades was to sack Lo Fu as General Secretary
because of his associations with Trotskyites at an earlier period.
This made vacant what had until recently been regarded as the
Party's most important office, and probably Wang Ming saw
himself as the right candidate for it. In the end, however, the
Politburo decided to leave it vacant.

As for the other leaders, Stalin asked that the struggle against
Chang Kuo-tao be abated (he spoke too late), and that Mao's
position as the senior Party leader be acknowledged, in view of
his successes in the past three years, but that at the same time
the Russian-trained comrades should help Mao to overcome his
theoretical mistakes and uncertain grasp of Marxism. Stalin
obviously hoped that this was the formula to bring all the war-
ring factions into one happy united Chinese Party.

So Mao had to pay a price for retaining his leadership: he had
to submit to Wang's views on the big issue of the day, the conduct of the United Front with the Kuomintang. At a Politburo
session in Yenan in December (the month of the Japanese 'Rape
of Nanking'), a political report by Wang Ming was approved
which unequivocally subordinated the Communist Party to the

Kuomintang and supported a long-term alliance between them against Japan.

But Mao secured a vital compensation for his concession. He was made Chairman of the Preparatory Committee for the next Party congress, with Wang Ming as Secretary, and this proved to be a major weapon in his final success when that congress was eventually held in 1945.

Soon after Wang Ming returned to China he visited Wuhan, the Kuomintang headquarters, to look into ways and means of improving the national status of the Communist Party. He took Po Ku, Chou En-lai, Hsiang Ying and other leaders with him, leaving Mao behind in Yenan. Mao must have realized that there was a possibility, had Chiang Kai-shek been smart enough to risk it, for a rightist Communist Party under Wang to unite with the Kuomintang in the false hope of reforming. When he came back Wang Ming said that the Reds should enter a coalition government with Chiang Kai-shek and gradually achieve power within that government through legal struggle. The underlying assumption was that Chinese society had already become capitalist, and that the proletariat would therefore be ready to rise against its enemies before very long. Mao with his peasant roots knew better.

The intellectual pre-eminence of Wang Ming was no idle consideration in Yenan. Wang's books – and those of his colleagues among the Twenty-Eight Bolsheviks – were the only Chinese books initially available in the places of study in Yenan. Hence the importance of Mao's own lectures, which he saw as the only way of breaking Wang Ming's spell and crashing through the 'ideological blockade' of the Twenty-Eight Bolsheviks.

Chiang Ching has described Mao during these years of struggle with Wang Ming as 'fitful, worried, ironic, idealistic, contriving', given to long periods of silent speculation and to wandering off among the people. Each was struggling in his own way to please Stalin, the revolutionary patriarch: each competed to impress on the Russian Pope his respective claims and gifts as leader of the Chinese revolution.

Mao's trump card was his indigenous roots. 'Speaking generally,' he later said, 'it is we Chinese who have reached an understanding of the objective world of China, not the comrades concerned with Chinese questions in the Comintern. These comrades in the Comintern simply did not understand ... Chinese society, the Chinese nation or the Chinese revolution.'

In May 1938 Mao addressed himself to the military tactics for which the war ahead would call, in a tract entitled 'Problems of Strategy in Guerrilla War Against Japan'. 'With the common people of the whole country mobilized, we shall create a vast sea of humanity in which the enemy will be swallowed up . . . .The popular masses are like water, and the army is like a fish.

Mao also gave lectures which were later developed into a long tract called 'On Protracted War'. War was a political act. After quoting Clausewitz, Mao produced his own aphorism: 'It can therefore be said that politics is war without bloodshed while war is politics with bloodshed.'

Thus the richest source of power to wage war lay in the people themselves.

It is mainly because of the unorganized state of the Chinese masses that Japan dares to bully us. When this defect is remedied, then the Japanese aggressor, like a mad bull crashing into a ring of flames, will be surrounded by hundreds of millions of our people standing upright, the mere sound of their voices will strike terror into him, and he will be burned to death.

Finally, Mao transferred the Second World War to its largest canvas.

This war, we can foresee, will not save capitalism but will hasten its collapse. It will be greater in scale and more ruthless than the war of 20 years ago, all nations will inevitably be drawn in, it will drag on for a very long time, and mankind will suffer greatly. . . . Once man has eliminated capitalism, he will attain the era of perpetual peace, and there will be no more need for war. Neither armies, nor warships, nor military aircraft, nor poison gas will then be needed. At this moment will begin the third epoch in the history of humanity, the epoch of peaceful life during which there will never be war.

While he was writing up these lectures for publication, Mao worked constantly at them for over a week, consistently leaving his food untouched. On the seventh day his bodyguard put a charcoal burner on the floor next to him because of the cold night air. Mao put his feet too near it and burnt holes in his shoes before realizing what had happened, so intense was his absorption.

When he was giving his talks in Yenan, Mao came to dominate his audience. Violet Cressy-Marcks commented that he was the only orator she had ever seen who 'made no gesture whatsoever'. She described one of his talks like this:

He kept his hands clasped behind him and he spoke for three hours. He had no notes and just looked at the audience. Outside it was very dark and inside the hall there was only a lantern or two swung over a line in front of the stage. The rest of the hall was in darkness. All around the tense faces with solemn eyes never left Mao Tse-tung's face. The silence was such that a pin could have been heard if dropped. The situation at home and abroad was reviewed, their aims, the joy and lasting internal peace created by the United Front, which, if maintained and fought for, would dumbfound the enemy, the Japanese. On and on he went. He spoke quietly but clearly, and completely dispassionately. There is no doubt whatsoever that these people all worshipped him. He was their leader, to whom they looked up, and they took unquestioningly his advice and doctrine. While Mao Tse-tung lives he will have complete control of the Communist Party in China.

Agnes Smedley wrote that Mao's lectures were 'like his conversation, based on Chinese life and history. Hundreds of the students who poured into Yenan had been accustomed to drawing their mental nourishment only from the Soviet Union or from a few writers of Germany or other countries. Mao, however, spoke to them of their own country and people, their native history and literature. He quoted from such novels as *Dream of the Red Chamber* or *All Men Are Brothers' (Water Margin)*.

Mao did endeavour to moderate his political views in line with the Party's official United Front policy, for example in his interview in 1938 with Cressy-Marcks, who questioned him keenly about collectivism.

'But do you think', she asked, 'women like cooking on one stove instead of each cooking over their own fire? And do you think Chinese farmers like sharing implements and land profits?'

'Well,' Mao replied carefully, 'if there aren't enough land implements to go round, they must share.'

'So that if you had enough, each person would have their own? Then the ideal is not communal, but individual ownership, as in capitalist countries?'

'The people themselves', Mao said, 'will settle this point.'

'Will they be allowed to?'

'Yes, but they will have to be better educated to vote. People hated machinery when it was introduced to supersede hand-weaving, and wasn't that an improvement?' The British explorer took the point that it was in fact a question of forcing.

Again, Mao wrote in surprisingly warm vein to Generalissimo Chiang Kai-shek at the end of September:

Upon their return to Yenan, Chou En-lai and other comrades spoke highly of your kindness which I have admired profoundly. All our countrymen respect your leadership of the nation in waging the unpre-

cedented war of national revolution. . . . At this juncture the Kuomintang and the Chinese Communist Party are bound together by common
interest. . . . However ferocious the enemy may be, he will be defeated
in the end, for we . . . can establish our nation as a great power in East
Asia. This is my view which I trust is also shared by you. Best wishes
for your good health and salute to the national revolution.

Yet when the news came to Yenan of the Munich pact, Mao's
opinion of British perfidy was confirmed, and he said that
Chamberlain's policy was like 'lifting a rock only to drop it on
one's own toes'.

It is hardly surprising, therefore, that Mao soon broke out of
his chains. In October, while the Japanese were taking Wuhan
and Canton in rapid succession, the Communists held a long
Central Committee meeting in Yenan. After a period in which he
had exercised public restraint, Mao now came out openly
against Wang Ming. He began by toeing the Wang-initiated
Party line on the United Front: 'In carrying out the anti-
Japanese war, and in organizing the Anti-Japanese United
Front, the Kuomintang occupies the position of leader and
framework. . . . Under the single great condition that it support
to the end the war of resistance and the United Front, one can
foresee a brilliant future for the Kuomintang . . .'

But Mao then dealt with the role of the Communists, considering first the scruples of internationalists who felt uneasy at
fighting a patriotic war against another country. 'In wars of
national liberation,' he reassured them, 'patriotism is applied
internationalism.'

Furthermore, Marxism should be placed into a genuinely
Chinese context:

Today's China is an outgrowth of historic China. We are Marxist
historicists; we must not mutilate history. From Confucius to Sun Yat-
sen we must sum it up critically, and we must constitute ourselves the
heirs of all that is precious in this past . . . . A Communist is a Marxist
internationalist, but Marxism must take on a national form before it
can be applied. There is no such thing as abstract Marxism, but only
concrete Marxism. . . .

For the Chinese Communists who are part of the great Chinese
nation, flesh of its flesh and blood of its blood, any talk about Marxism
in isolation from China's characteristics is merely Marxism in the abstract, Marxism in a vacuum. Hence the sinification of Marxism, that is,
how to apply it concretely in China so that its every manifestation has
an indubitably Chinese character, or to apply Marxism in the light of
China's specific characteristics, becomes a problem which it is urgent
for the whole Party to understand and solve. Foreign stereotypes must

be abolished, there must be less singing of empty, abstract tunes and dogmatism must be laid to rest; they must be replaced by the fresh, lively style and spirit which the common people of China love.

In a later speech Mao spoke of the military challenge. 'Every Communist must grasp the truth, "Political power grows out of the barrel of a gun." Our principle is that the Party commands the gun, and the gun must never be allowed to command the Party.'

Yet many things can be created with guns. 'We can also create cadres, create schools, create culture, create mass movements. Everything in Yenan has been created by having guns. All things grow out of the barrel of a gun . . . . We do not want war, but war can only be abolished through war, and in order to get rid of the gun it is necessary to take up the gun.'

Mao won a majority in the Central Committee for his view that the Red Army should maintain its independence from the military structure commanded by Chiang Kai-shek, although this was not publicized at the time in view of the importance of keeping it from the Kuomintang. Wang succeeded in persuading his colleagues to make political concessions for the United Front, but he was rebuffed in his demand for military concessions. The Red generals were still too important in the higher leadership, as Mao well knew. Once again, as at Tsunyi four years before, it was the soldiers who tipped the balance in Mao's favour.

The crowning triumph came when the Comintern gave its full support to the Party's United Front line as it emerged in Yenan at the end of 1938. Coincidentally, a Soviet publication in Moscow acknowledged for the first time Mao's *de facto* Chairmanship of the Chinese Politburo. Wang Ming was now on the way out.

13
FIGHT OF MAD DOGS

The aim of the bourgeois-democratic revolution which China, in Mao's view, was still undergoing, was defined in an article which he wrote in May 1939, as follows: 'To establish a social system hitherto unknown in Chinese history, namely, a democratic social system having a feudal society (during its last hundred years a semi-colonial and semi-feudal society) as its precursor and a socialist society as its successor. If anyone asks why a Communist should strive to bring into being first a bourgeois-democratic society and then a socialist society, our answer is: we are following the inevitable course of history.'

Obviously the distinction between short-term and long-term goals was difficult for many Party members, and Mao turned to the question again in another speech.

Today we are making a bourgeois-democratic revolution and nothing we do goes beyond its scope. By and large, we should not destroy the bourgeois system of private property for the present; what we want to destroy is imperialism and feudalism. This is what we mean by the bourgeois-democratic revolution . . . .

What is the goal of this revolution? To overthrow imperialism and feudalism and to establish a people's democratic republic . . . . Capitalists have no place in a socialist society, but they should still be allowed in a people's democracy.

Will there always be a place for capitalists in China? No, definitely not in the future. . . . China will certainly go over to socialism in the future; that is an irresistible law. But at the present stage our task is not to put socialism into practice. . . .

China's youth had a vital part to play, although Mao, in a passage which was deleted from the *Selected Works*, found it necessary to put a condition on this exciting role:

If the young people wish to achieve results they must . . . establish friendly relations with the adults; they must unite with the majority of the population, who are more than twenty-five years old. Do we also

need the old people? Of course we need them. Old people have experience.... Consequently, the young people must unite with the old, even
if they are a hundred, in order to struggle together against
Japan.... Old men carry out propaganda work very well; the common
people love to listen to them.... Comrades, the organization of children is also an important task.... Out there, Japanese imperialism is
busy training our children, to make of them little traitors to their country. How can we in our turn abstain from organizing the children?... Once organized, children have many advantages. They can
catch traitors, keep watch on the opium smokers, confiscate mah jong
sets, and even serve as scouts to watch the roads....

On 25 May the Russian cinematographer Roman Karmen
went to see Mao. He and his companions were 'overtaken by a
horsewoman galloping at full speed. Drawing up even with us,
she sharply reined up her horse, and with a wide gesture welcomed us gaily.' This was Chiang Ching, able to have the run of
a horse through her status as wife of the Chairman. The Russian
took colour pictures of her on horseback, managing to make her
look more Slav than Chinese.

Karmen's memoir went on to describe Chiang Ching's job as
Mao's personal secretary: 'She prepares his diary, writes down
his speeches, copies articles and takes care of miscellaneous
affairs.... She sits confidently on the small, spirited horse as it
prances and chews the bit. Two braids are bound up in ribbons
at the back of her head. She is wearing the greatcoat of a captured Japanese officer, and on her bare feet a pair of wooden
sandals.'

Chiang Ching had just finished a few months' stint at Mao's
ambitious reclamation project in the wastelands of Nanniwan,
thirty miles out of Yenan. The comrades working on this scheme
had to produce all their own food and clothing, and under this
challenge Chiang Ching's hands had for the first time become
blistered: she had never done manual work before. But she was
excused from spinning because of her tuberculosis.

On 23 August 1939 Molotov signed his pact with Ribbentrop,
and Mao welcomed it as proof of the growing strength of the
Soviet Union. Anyone who helped Japan, as Germany had done
in the past, was to be opposed. 'But from now on, it can do no
harm to us to get into closer contact with Germany and Italy if
they abandon their policy of helping our enemy. By so doing we
can weaken the strength of our enemy.' More informally, Mao
told a visitor: 'Stalin has Hitler in his pocket – but only half in.'

Two weeks later, talking to Communist officials in Yenan,
Mao defined the war as 'a fight among mad dogs'. All the

imperialist nations involved, whether on the side of Germany and Japan or on the side of Britain and France, were imperialist nations interested in counter-revolutionary plunder. Both sides 'must be equally treated as robbers, and opposition should be especially directed at the British imperialists, the ringleaders.'

Mao reserved his fiercest contempt for the British. On 14 September he lectured his colleagues on the war and told them that, 'Today England has become the most reactionary country in the world.' He condemned all parties to the European war – British, French and German – as 'unjust, predatory and imperialist'.

At this point Edgar Snow paid his second visit to the Red base. He had been told before reaching Yenan, with dark hints of corruption, that Mao now had a private motorcar. Sure enough, Mao sent his 'limousine' to collect Snow for his first interview, but when the vehicle arrived for him, the American found that it was in fact an ambulance, with the legend neatly painted on its door: 'Presented to the Heroic Defenders of China by the Chinese Hand Laundrymen's Association of New York City.'

I found Mao [Snow wrote] still living in a cave; but a modern and improved version, a three-roomed place with a study, a bedroom and a guest room. The walls were of white plaster, the floor was lined with bricks and there were some touches of feminine decoration, added by Mrs Mao. But here signs of affluence ended. . . . The years of war had changed him little. No longer on a starvation diet, he had put on some weight; his hair was clipped short. . . . He was still the student of world events and the political analyst; before he settled down to the night's tasks he read through a huge pile of the day's dispatches which were picked up by the nearby army wireless station – from the battle front in Shansi, from all over China, and from countries abroad.

On 19 October Mao spoke in commemoration of the first anniversary of Lu Hsun's death:

In my view, Lu Hsun is . . . the saint of modern China just as Confucius was the saint of old China. . . . Lu Hsun was an absolute realist, always uncompromising, always determined. In one of his essays he maintained that one should continue to beat a dog after it had fallen in water. If you did not, the dog would jump up either to bite you or at least to shake a lot of dirty water over you. Therefore the beating had to be thorough. Lu Hsun did not entertain a speck of sentimentalism or hypocrisy.

In a textbook jointly written by Mao and others under his own editorship, called *The Chinese Revolution and the Chinese Communist Party*, published in December 1939, Mao made a statement about capitalism which was to become controversial: 'As China's feudal society had developed a commodity economy, and so carried within itself the seeds of capitalism, China would of herself have developed slowly into a capitalist society even without the impact of foreign capitalism. Penetration by foreign capitalism accelerated this process.'

The imperialist powers, he added, had ' . . . never slackened their efforts to poison the minds of the Chinese people. This is their policy of cultural aggression. And it is carried out through missionary work, through establishing hospitals and schools, publishing newspapers and inducing Chinese students to study abroad. Their aim is to train intellectuals who will serve their interests and to dupe the people.'

On Stalin's sixtieth birthday, Mao drew not from the Marxist canon but from the Chinese classics to find a quotation for the occasion. 'Living in a period of the bitterest suffering in our history, we Chinese people most urgently need help from others. The *Book of Songs* says, "A bird sings out to draw a friend's response." This aptly describes our present situation.' Mao's public message ended: 'Stalin is the true friend of the cause of the liberation of the Chinese people. No attempt to sow dissension, no lies and calumnies, can affect the Chinese people's whole-hearted love and respect for Stalin and our genuine friendship for the Soviet Union.'

Mao had never met Stalin, and because of Japan's and Germany's aggression facing each end of the long Russian state, he no longer feared him. Primarily Stalin was a name, an incantatory magic name for Mao to use against his Chinese opponents.

In his speech to his comrades in Yenan on the following day, Mao was down-to-earth about the Communist patriarch: 'Comrade Stalin is the leader of the world revolution. Because he is there, it is easier to get things done. . . . If we did not have a Stalin, who would give the orders? . . . Because there is in the world a Soviet Union, a Communist Party, and a Stalin, the affairs of this world can be more easily dealt with.'

Then came the passage on which the Red Guards seized so vigorously in the 1960s. 'There are innumerable principles of Marxism, but in the last analysis they can all be summed up in one sentence: "To rebel is justified." For thousands of years everyone said: "Oppression is justified, exploitation is justified, rebellion is not justified." From the time when Marxism appeared on the scene, this old judgment was turned upside down. . . .'

Early in 1940 came the first evidence that Mao had fought through to the intellectual position, hardly Marxist in the accepted sense, that changing economic relationships would not by themselves be enough to modernize China as long as individuals had not yet altered their own cultural values and attitudes of mind. The distinctive 'cultural revolution' which was to be Mao's greatest contribution to the language of twentieth-century progress was here first mentioned. It came in a tract *On New Democracy*, produced in January 1940 as a guide to the political and cultural goals of the current stage in China's revolution.

He began uncharacteristically, and in a manner suggesting that he knew his remarks would engender opposition among the intellectuals, by saying:

I am a layman in matters of culture; I would like to study them, but have only just begun to do so. Fortunately, there are many comrades in Yenan who have written at length in this field, so that my rough and ready words may serve the same purpose as the beating of a gong before a theatrical performance. . . .

To nourish her own culture, China needs to assimilate a good deal of foreign progressive culture, not enough of which was done in the past. We should assimilate whatever is useful to us today not only from the present-day socialist and new-democratic cultures, but also from the earlier cultures of other nations, for example, from the culture of the various capitalist countries in the Age of Enlightenment.

However, we should not gulp any of this foreign material down uncritically, but must treat it as we do our food – first chewing it, then submitting it to the working of the stomach and intestines with their juices and secretions, and separating it into nutriment to be absorbed and waste matter to be discarded – before it can nourish us. To advocate 'wholesale Westernization' is wrong.

Mao's patriotic stand against Japanese aggression during these years should, perhaps, be treated with a certain reserve, precisely because of its being a logical concomitant of collaborating with Chiang Kai-shek. In 1940, if the evidence of Mao's fraternal rival Wang Ming is to be believed, Mao seriously entertained the idea of switching sides, secretly ordering one of his men, Jao Shu-shih, to negotiate with Japan and Wang Ching-wei – the Kuomintang leader at whose side Mao had worked in the 1920s but who in 1940 defected to the Japanese – for an alliance against Generalissimo Chiang. Wang Ming even recorded a conversation in which Mao justified this:

All of them – Germany, Italy, Japan – are poor [Mao is supposed to have explained]. What will we get out of fighting them? Even if we win, there'll be no profit in it. On the other hand, England, America and France are rich; especially England, which has so many great colonies. If we beat her, then just by dividing out her colonies we'll get a lot of plunder. . . . I know you will say that I'm taking up a pro-Japan line of national betrayal. But I am not afraid of that.

Mao then, according to Wang Ming, declared his intention of writing a commentary along these lines, and the Russians in 1970 alleged that he did indeed publish such an article in *New China Daily* in 1941.

The testimony of Wang and the allegations of the Russians against Mao after their break with him are not to be treated too seriously. But Mao's remarks in conversation as reported by Wang sound in character. We know that Mao was obsessed by the unjustified superiority of Britain. He may well have sensed at this juncture of the war that China was getting herself on the wrong side in terms of the struggle against European imperialism in Asia. The Kuomintang sometimes said that the Japanese problem was merely a skin disease, whereas the Communist problem was a heart disease deserving more urgent treatment. Mao may have felt the converse of this, namely that whereas the new imperialism of Japan could be relatively easily resisted when the need came, the entrenched historic imperialism of the West in Asia would need something like Japan's energy to weaken it. However, evidence is lacking for a final judgement on this question.

Meanwhile the Red Army was directed to expand its forces and to capture the area between Nanking and the sea. (The Japanese press on the same day published a report from 'unimpeachable sources' that Mao had died of tuberculosis.)

In August the Red Army had its most famous engagement against Japan, the Hundred Regiments Offensive, which General Peng Teh-huai won against Mao's advice. Instead of dispersing his men, he concentrated them, thus prematurely disclosing his strength to the enemy and allowing it to attack him more easily – or so it was afterwards alleged by the Maoists. The Red Guards in the 1960s even claimed that the battle had been launched without Mao's permission, though this is hard to believe.

More plausible, perhaps, though exaggerated, was the later Russian complaint that Mao had sought during the Japanese invasion only to conserve his own military strength, thus giving Japan a free hand and obliging the Russians to deploy along the Manchurian border men who could otherwise have been fighting

Hitler. 'Mao Tse-tung', a Russian broadcast stated in 1969, 'was just idly watching the Russians bleed. . . . This, of course, was not something expected from a man who had received cash and weapons from the Soviet Union for so many years.' In the end, the Russian commentator added, Mao had to retreat to a part of China adjoining the Russian frontier: 'As General Marshall once accurately pointed out, if the Chinese Communists had not found a sanctuary along the Russian border, Mao Tse-tung would undoubtedly have met his Waterloo.'

A year later Moscow radio pushed this interpretation even further. 'Mao Tse-tung', it insisted, 'spent his years in Yenan solely in accomplishing his monopoly of the Chinese Communist Party. Although he claimed credit for the Party's anti-Japanese operations, he merely preserved its strength for the subsequent war with the Kuomintang. Therefore, in fact, he helped the Japanese aggressor's occupation of China and caused untold sacrifices to the Chinese people.'

If justification were needed for Mao's ambivalence towards Japan, it came at the beginning of 1941 when one of the key Red Armies in Anhwei province was almost annihilated – not by the Japanese, but by Kuomintang troops, provoking a virtual collapse of the United Front against Japan. In Yenan the Communists waited to see if General Ho Ying-chin of the Kuomintang would come after them as well. The Kuomintang liaison officer at Yenan nervously asked Mao what he would do.

'You are here in Yenan all the time and you don't know?' Mao replied. 'If Ho goes for us, we'll go for him. If Ho stops, we'll stop too.'

But Mao's position in Yenan became progressively more difficult with the suspension of Kuomintang subsidies to the Red government, and a stiffening of the blockade against the Red area.

'For a time,' Mao recollected a couple of years later, 'we had a very acute scarcity of clothing, cooking oil, paper and vegetables, of footwear for our soldiers and of winter bedding for our civilian personnel. The Kuomintang tried to strangle us by cutting off the funds due to us and imposing an economic blockade; we were indeed in dire straits.'

In the spring of 1941 Mao was emboldened to become more explicit in his criticism of Wang Ming. In a preface and post-script to *Rural Surveys* he spoke again about the necessity of applying Marxism carefully and scientifically to Chinese conditions. And this meant the Chinese comrades making their own social investigations into Chinese life and China's social problems.

To this, first, direct your eyes downwards, do not hold your head high and gaze at the sky. Unless a person is interested in turning his eyes downwards and is determined to do so he will never in his whole life really understand things in China.... It has to be understood that the masses are the real heroes, while we ourselves are often childish and ignorant, and without this understanding it is impossible to acquire even the most rudimentary knowledge...

Although my assertion 'No investigation, no right to speak', has been ridiculed as 'narrow empiricism', to this day I do not regret having made it; what is more, I still insist that without investigation there cannot possibly be any right to speak.

He ended on a personal and slightly disarming note:

Today I still feel keenly the necessity for thorough research into Chinese and world affairs; this is related to the scantiness of my own knowledge of Chinese and world affairs and does not imply that I know everything and that others are ignorant. It is my wish to go on being a pupil, learning from the masses, together with all other Party comrades.

In a report in May entitled *Reform our Study*, Mao further elaborated the theme of learning with humility about Chinese conditions.

For a hundred years the finest sons and daughters of the disaster-ridden Chinese nation fought and sacrificed their lives, one stepping into the breach as another fell, in quest of the truth that would save the country and the people. This moves us to song and tears.

But it was only after World War I and the October Revolution in Russia that we found Marxism-Leninism, the best of truths, the best of weapons for liberating our nation.... As soon as it was linked with the concrete practice of the Chinese revolution, the universal truth of Marxism-Leninism gave an entirely new complexion to the Chinese revolution....

But the Communists in China still had many shortcomings.

Generally speaking, in the last twenty years we have not done systematic and thorough work in collecting and studying material.... Many Party members are still in a fog about Chinese history, whether of the last hundred years or of ancient times. There are many Marxists-Leninist scholars who cannot open their mouths without citing ancient Greece; but as for their own ancestors – sorry, they have been forgotten.... For several decades, many of the returned students from abroad have suffered from this malady. Coming home from Europe, America or Japan, they can only parrot things foreign.

But now the war took a turn which Mao had not expected. When Hitler's storm-troopers marched into Russia on 22 June 1941, in flagrant violation of the Molotov-Ribbentrop pact, Mao had to make an about-turn in his attitude to the Western powers. Now that imperialist Churchill was backing Communist Russia against fascist Germany and fascist Japan, it would be necessary for Mao to collaborate with the Britain he so distrusted. The united front which Mao was practising in China would have to be played out on an international scale, and in the world at large 'every effort must be concentrated on combating fascist enslavement', in Mao's words on the day following the invasion of Russia, 'rather than practising a socialist revolution'.

Earlier in the year the Comintern representative had asked Mao point-blank what he would do if the Japanese invaded Russia, but Mao avoided giving a direct answer. The Russians later claimed that he ignored their requests for rail sabotage in order to prevent Japanese troops from moving up towards the Russian frontier, that he 'in fact ceased fighting the Japanese troops' and kept his generals in Yenan instead of allowing them to fight the Japanese in the field. Mao, they went on, so underestimated Russian military strength that he argued for Moscow and Leningrad to be abandoned in favour of guerrilla warfare against the Germans.

The entry of Russia into the war meant that Mao had to take pressures from Moscow more seriously: his own position as an independent leader in the Chinese Communist Party was again brought into question – and a rival candidate, fully backed by the Kremlin, was sitting in a nearby cave in the person of Wang Ming. Mao's sense of insecurity came out in a remark to Wang Ming in October 1941 when, according to Wang's memoirs, Mao complained to him: 'In our Party there are three people whom the cadres love. The first is you, Wang Ming. The second is Chou En-lai, and the third is old Peng' (Teh-huai).

That was the night when Mao received a cable from Moscow formally asking the Chinese Communists to help prevent Japan from opening up a second front against Russia in the east – a request which the Politburo debated for several days. Wang said they should do something, but Mao said it was unwise.

Wang's lengthy and bad-tempered memoir, published in Moscow in 1975, waxed hysterical to the point of incredibility about the sequel to this cable. For what it is worth, he recorded that from that day onwards he ate in Mao's house at least once a day, and gradually fell victim to 'a serious stomach upset, with heavy haemorrhaging, dizziness and weakness of the heart'. It was diagnosed as 'very like poisoning'. Meanwhile under Mao's instructions building work began on the site of a new conference hall only thirty feet from Wang Ming's residence, and it went on round the clock to add to Wang Ming's discomfort.

Mao ordered Wang into hospital, where he remained until the following August. During these ten months, Wang alleged that he was systematically poisoned with mercury by the doctor in charge of him, Dr Ching Mao-yao, specifically during the period between March and May 1942 when Mao's campaign against Wang Ming and the others in the 'Moscow faction' was at its height. Wang professed to owe his life at that time to his wife, who threw away some of the medicines after observing their effect.

These medical attentions by Mao were resumed, Wang claims, in the following year after Wang Ming obtained an invitation from the Russians to fly to Moscow for treatment. In February, Wang alleged, Dr Ching prescribed for him a large dose of calomel and water, together with bicarbonate of soda and magnesium sulphate (which would have a corrosive effect). A week later he prescribed a highly concentrated solution of tannin as an enema.

Wang's wife was doubtful of these prescriptions, took other opinions and was told that they were absolutely inapplicable. Mao, in Wang's story, was obliged to agree to a committee of inquiry formed by other doctors in Yenan, including the American, George Hatem, and the Russian, Dr Orlov. They investigated throughout July and produced a report more or less corroborating Wang's version. Indeed, Wang had Dr Ching going on his knees before his sick bed and crying: 'Comrade Wang Ming, I am very guilty before you. I poisoned you. Every time I prescribed you poison I felt sick at heart.'

'Why did you do it?' Wang asked.

'Lu Fu-chung made me. He said that you were a dogmatist, someone who had opposed Chairman Mao, and so it had been decided to purge you. I was a doctor, and that is why this was entrusted to me. . . .'

Wang even described a meeting to discuss the alleged poisoning, during which Mao sat 'with his face red to the ears, a cigarette in his hand, his head hanging. . . .' Mao told the others that Wang was pretending to be ill, but was challenged by Wang's wife, and the outcome was inconclusive. Mao complained to Lu Fu-chung, in front of all the others: 'Today's meeting is full of base interests, and nothing instructive.'

Mao must certainly have been worried by this sudden upgrad-
ing of the importance of the pro-Stalin Russian-trained rivals for
the leadership. But it does not sound like him to resort to measures so patently open to discovery – and so unsuccessful. Besides,
the potential hypochondria of Wang, whose stability of temperament does not impress, should also not be underestimated.
Mao's strong card was, of course, his indigenousness and his
symbolizing of the centuries-old desire of Asians not to be told
what to do by Europeans. Whether by chance or intent, he was
able to advertise this rather brilliantly in 1941 by presiding over
an Anti-Fascist Congress of the People's East in Yenan, attended
by Vietnamese, Thais, Indonesians and Mongolians as well as
by members of Chinese minorities and overseas Chinese com-
munities. Mao's Yenan was beginning to spread its fame into
neighbouring countries.

Finally, to complete the cast in the war, the Americans were
brought in through the Japanese bombing of Pearl Harbor on 8
December. Just as Hitler's earlier march into Russia forced Mao
into the arms of Churchill, so now he had to take Roosevelt as an
ally against Japan. It made it even more certain, of course, that
the Japanese would in the end be defeated and that the major
threat to the Chinese Communists remained not Japan but the
Kuomintang.

14
LOVE IN THE ABSTRACT

In 1942 Mao felt that the conditions were at last right for a campaign of rectification within the Party, the aim of which would be to convince all its cadres to accept his point of view and leadership rather than those of Wang Ming or the other Bolsheviks. The Russian-trained faction had suffered in prestige from the incrimination of Pavel Mif, their Russian teacher and sponsor, in Stalin's purge of rightists. Stalin was in any case preoccupied with fighting Germany.

The new Comintern no longer attempted to control the Chinese Party from Moscow, and Mao was shortly to compose a resolution on its dissolution, in which he granted that, 'The Chinese Communist Party has accepted a great deal of help from the Comintern in its revolutionary struggle, but for a long time, because of the concrete situation and special conditions of its own people, it has been able to express its own line, policy and attitudes quite independently.'

The series of Japanese attacks on China had also helped Mao, giving him an excuse to keep putting off the Seventh Congress of the Party which was supposed to have been under preparation since 1937. If it had in fact been held before 1942, Mao might well have failed to consolidate his supreme position. Furthermore, many Red Army units were coming back to Yenan for retraining and to evade Japanese mopping-up operations, and this gave Mao the opportunity to stiffen up their ideology in his own inimitable manner.

He had by then gathered round him what his enemies called his 'clique', which included Ku Pai, Tan Chen-lin, Chen Cheng-jen, Teng Tzu-hui, Teng Hsiao-ping and Lin Piao (who arrived back from medical treatment in Russia at the beginning of 1942). Mao had also secured the support of Liu Shao-chi.

But open criticism of Mao's leadership was being voiced in Yenan – and not only by the Bolsheviks. Chou Yang, Chiang

Ching's old adversary from Shanghai, wrote in an article that 'every sun has some spots' – in a society where Mao's brilliance was already being compared by his supporters to that of the sun. Another writer complained in Yenan's leading newspaper of insincerity among the leadership. They did not practise sexual equality, and some of them wore clothes of 'three shades' and ate meals of 'five grades' which were unavailable to the man in the street. This was republished in a collection of essays under the title *The Wild Lily*, which was the most beautiful wild flower around Yenan but grew from a bitter-tasting bulb.

The author of *The Wild Lily* was afterwards arrested and executed, and Mao carried this on his conscience for many years. The execution, he explained to his comrades twenty years later, happened 'when the army was on the march, and the security organs themselves made the decision to execute him; the decision did not come from the centre. We have often made criticisms on this very matter; we thought that he shouldn't have been executed. If he was a secret agent and wrote articles to attack us and refused to reform . . ., why not leave him there or let him go and do labour?'

It was to address such critics and doubters that Mao launched in February 1942 his rectification campaign, to be conducted in a new Party school. His opening speech was entitled '*Rectify the Party's Style of Work.*' Mao again demanded that Marxism be put in its Chinese context.

He poked fun at intellectuals who had lost touch with real Chinese life. Many so-called intellectuals, he said, were actually quite ignorant, knowing less than a worker or a peasant. 'To this', he went on, 'some may say "Aha! You're turning everything upside down. You're talking nonsense!" But,' amid laughter, 'Comrades, don't get excited. What I say is to a certain extent reasonable. . . .' Take a man, he went on, who graduates from university but who has no trade, cannot till the land or fight, and cannot manage a job. Surely such a man should be considered at best a half-intellectual, with knowledge still incomplete? There was nothing so intrinsically special about book knowledge.

By comparison, the cook's task in preparing a meal is difficult. To create something edible, he must use a combination of wood, rice, oil, salt, sauce, vinegar, and other materials. This is certainly not easy, and to cook a good meal is all the more difficult. If we compare the tasks of the cook at the North-west Restaurant to those of the cooks in our homes, we find a great difference. If there is too much fire, the food will burn: too much vinegar and it will be sour. [Laughter.]

Cooking food and preparing dishes is truly one of the arts. But what about book knowledge? If you do nothing but read, you have only to recognize three to five thousand characters, learn to thumb through a dictionary, hold some book in your hand, and receive millet from the public. Then you nod your head contentedly and start to read. But books cannot walk, and you can open and close a book at will; this is the easiest thing in the world to do, a great deal easier than it is for the cook to prepare a meal, and much easier than it is for him to slaughter a pig ... the pig can run. ... [Laughter.] He slaughters it ..., the pig squeals. [Laughter.] A book placed on the desk cannot run nor can it squeal. You can dispose of it in any manner you wish. Is there anything easier to do?

Therefore, I advise those of you who only have book knowledge and as yet no contact with reality, and those who have had little practical experience, to recognize their own shortcomings and become a bit more humble. ... On hearing this, some people will lose their tempers, and say, 'According to your interpretation, Marx was also a half-intellectual.' I would answer that it's quite true that, in the first place, Marx could not slaughter a pig, and second, he could not till a field. But he did participate in the revolutionary movement and also carried out research on commodity production.

Marxism was a tool for China, not a religion.

Our comrades must understand that we do not study Marxism-Leninism because it is pleasing to the eye, or because it has some mystical value, like the doctrines of the Taoist priests who ascend Mao Shan to learn how to subdue devils and evil spirits. Marxism-Leninism has no beauty, nor has it any mystical value. It is only extremely useful.

It was not Mao's intention that those guilty of errors should die or be punished for them, rather that they should be educated out of them.

Our aim in exposing errors and criticizing shortcomings, like that of a doctor curing a sickness, is solely to save the patient and not to doctor him to death ...

So long as a person who has made mistakes does not hide his sickness for fear of treatment or persist in his mistakes until he is beyond cure, so long as he honestly and sincerely wishes to be cured and to mend his ways, we shall welcome him and cure his sickness so that he can become a good comrade. We can never succeed if we just let ourselves go and lash out at him. In treating an ideological or a political malady, one must never be rough and rash but must adopt the approach of 'curing the sickness to save the patient', which is the only correct and effective method.

A week later Mao delivered his second major speech on rectification, under the title, 'Oppose Stereotyped Party Writing'. The first major indictment was the way that some Party scribes filled 'endless pages with empty verbiage. Some of our comrades love to write long articles with no substance, very much like the "foot-bindings of a slattern, long as well as smelly"....'

He came close to describing his own method of writing.

Confucius advised 'think twice', and Han Yu said 'A deed is accomplished through taking thought.' That was in ancient times. Today matters have become very complicated, and sometimes it is not even enough to think them over three or four times. Lu Hsun said, 'Read it over twice at least.' And at most? He did not say, but in my opinion it does no harm to go over an important article more than ten times and to revise it conscientiously before it is published.

Two other interesting remarks made in this speech were about the study of foreign languages and on the subject of terror. The 'strategy of terror', Mao insisted, 'is not of the slightest use against the enemy: against our comrades it only does harm.... The Chinese Communist Party does not rely on terror for nourishment: it relies on the truth, on arriving at the truth by a verification of facts, and on science....'

Some Chinese were almost xenophobic about foreign languages, but in this speech Mao declared:

Let us study foreign languages. The language of the people of foreign countries is not in the least foreign formalism; it is only when the Chinese copy them and import their expressions indiscriminately that they become lifeless foreign formalism. We should ... absorb what is good and suitable for our work. Our current language had already incorporated many foreign expressions, because the Chinese language is inadequate....

Mao next addressed himself to the artists, writers and intellectuals whom he needed to gather behind him if his mission were to be successful. He prepared himself by paying visits to the Lu Hsun Academy, where his wife was an instructor. A Russian living in Yenan at this time described Chiang Ching as 'a thin woman with a lithe figure and dark clever eyes, who looked very fragile next to her husband's stocky figure'.

The same observer commented of the woman who was Mao's secretary as well as wife: 'Extreme purposefulness is her outstanding quality. Her mind has the upper hand over her temperament. She drives herself without mercy, and her career is her only concern. She is in a hurry to achieve her ends while she is still young.' Here at his wife's workplace, Mao watched rehearsals and had long talks with the actors and teachers to improve his scant knowledge of modern literature and art.

The famous Yenan Forum on Literature and Art opened on the second day of May, when, as one of the participants recalled, 'The River Yen had thawed; its muddy yellow waters rushed down the shallow bed, over sand and soil. The willow had turned green. The fragrance of the thorny-plum blossoms filled the gullies and floated into the air. It was spring . . . .' Mao arrived by car in drizzling rain and strode into an auditorium so packed that there was an overflow on the parade-ground outside.

Mao's main theme was that the artist should serve society, going out from his ivory tower to spread the word of the new culture. Chiang Ching, who attended in her capacity as Mao's secretary, felt that he was speaking not merely to an artistic minority but to 'the far wider audience who had fallen under the spell of Wang Ming, whose antagonism towards the Chairman was splashed all over the walls of Yenan'.

'The purpose of our meeting today', Mao said, 'is precisely to ensure that literature and art fit well into the whole revolutionary machine as a component part, that they operate as powerful weapons for uniting and educating the people and for attacking and destroying the enemy, and that they help the people fight the enemy with one heart and one mind.' His listeners were to be engineers of the human soul, and their works were to be cogs in the revolutionary machine.

The Chinese people, he explained, had shortcomings – backward and petty-bourgeois ideas which hampered them in their struggle. 'We should be patient, and spend a long time in educating them and helping them to get these loads off their backs. . . . They have remoulded themselves in struggle, or are doing so, and our literature and art should depict this process. As long as they do not persist in their errors, we should not dwell on their negative side and consequently make the mistake of ridiculing them. . . .'

On the last day of the Forum the discussion finished before dinner, and there was just enough light from the setting sun for a group photograph. Mao was put in the middle of the front row, but just before the shutter clicked, he stood up, walked over to Ting Ling and gave his seat to her, with the words, 'Let our woman cadre take the middle seat, we don't want to be rebuked again on 8 March' (International Women's Day). Everyone laughed.

After dinner Mao gave his concluding address, but so many people came to listen that they all moved out from the auditorium into the open air where Mao spoke under the oil lamps. He attacked the view held by some writers and artists that 'everything ought to start from "love" '. Mao insisted that

... in a class society there can only be class love – but these comrades are seeking a love transcending classes, love in the abstract and also freedom in the abstract, truth in the abstract, human nature in the abstract etc. This shows that they have been very deeply influenced by the bourgeoisie. . . .

In class society there is only human nature of a class character; there is no human nature above classes. We uphold the human nature of the proletariat and of the masses of the people. . . . The human nature boosted by certain petty-bourgeois intellectuals is also divorced from ... the masses; what they call human nature is in essence nothing but bourgeois individualism. . . .

As for the so-called love of humanity, there has been no such all-inclusive love since humanity was divided into classes. All the ruling classes of the past were fond of advocating it, and so were many so-called sages and wise men, but nobody has ever really practised it, because it is impossible in class society. There will be genuine love of humanity – after classes are eliminated all over the world. . . . We cannot love enemies, we cannot love social evils, our aim is to destroy them. This is common sense; can it be that some of our writers and artists still do not understand this?

Artists and writers should get to know the ordinary people.

China's revolutionary writers and artists ... must for a long period of time unreservedly and wholeheartedly go among the masses of workers, peasants and soldiers, go into the heat of the struggle, go to the only source, the broadest and richest source, in order to observe, experience, study and analyse all the different kinds of people, all the classes, all the masses, all the vivid patterns of life and struggle, all the raw material of literature and art. Only then can they proceed to creative work. Otherwise, you will ... be nothing but a phony writer or artist. . . .

Mao ended these talks at the Yenan Forum by giving the intellectuals advice about how to become better Communists.

A person with truly good intentions must criticize the shortcomings and mistakes in his own work with the utmost candour and resolve to correct them. This is precisely why communists employ the method of self-criticism. . . .

There are many Party members who have joined the Communist

Party organizationally but have not yet joined the Party wholly or at all ideologically. Those who have not joined the Party ideologically still carry a great deal of the muck of the exploiting classes in their heads, and have no idea at all of what proletarian ideology, or communism, or the Party is. 'Proletarian ideology?' they think. 'The same old stuff!' Little do they know that it is no easy matter to acquire this stuff. Some will never have the slightest communist flavour about them as long as they live and can only end up by leaving the Party.

Mao's gallantry in giving up his seat for the group photograph to Ting Ling could not heal the deep antagonisms which the Yenan Forum uncovered. The writers were quarrelsome about Mao's requirements of them, dividing into two main factions. One, which supported Mao's line of the artist's social duty, was led by his old friend Chou Yang, the man who had made such an enemy of Mao's wife. The other group of writers, headed by Ting Ling herself, preferred to put the emphasis on the artist's need for independence, stressing the role of imagination, aesthetics and creativity in his work.

In June 1943 came a directive which for the first time set out in detail the phenomenon which especially distinguished Mao's brand of Communism and which became known as the mass line:

On all the practical work of our Party, all correct leadership is necessarily from the masses, to the masses. This means; take the ideas of the masses (scattered and unsystematic ideas) and concentrate them (through study turn them into concentrated and systematic ideas), then go to the masses and propagate and explain these ideas until the masses embrace them as their own, hold fast to them and translate them into action, and test the correctness of these ideas in such action. Then once again concentrate ideas from the masses and once again take them to the masses so that the ideas are persevered in and carried through. And so on, over and over again in an endless spiral, with the ideas becoming more correct, more vital and richer each time.

By the summer of 1943 Mao was secure in his leadership. (The fortune-teller who had told him as a student, on his begging tour, that he would be 'safe' in his ambitions if he survived to be fifty, was thus vindicated.) He was at last elected to the new post of Chairman of the Party, thus taking formal possession of the highest seat in the hierarchy. The old post of General Secretary remained unfilled, and there was no one to challenge Mao's pre-eminence. Now that the United Front with the Kuomintang had completely broken down, the Communists needed to have a leader of national stature to offer to the public as a rival to

Chiang Kai-shek. Mao was the obvious candidate, and his eleva-
tion to this new rank no longer ran the risk of offending Stalin,
who was fully stretched on his Western front.

From now onwards the cult of Mao's personality and of his
thought began to build up. Not everyone liked it, and even Liu
Shao-chi, who became one of Mao's most enthusiastic supporters in the middle and late 1940s, was alleged to have told his
friends in 1942, 'What is a Chairman? I have never heard people
in the Soviet Union calling Lenin Chairman Lenin! ... The
Stalin of China has not yet appeared!'

The first portrait of Mao to be published in the Communist
press – a woodcut – went back to 1937, and General Lin Piao
had begun a long career of tasteless sycophancy by a report in
1938 praising Mao's 'leadership genius'. But it was not until the
rectification campaign of 1942-4 that the cult was systematically
developed. Emi Siao, Mao's childhood friend, published an article in Yenan's leading newspaper at the end of 1941 referring to
Mao as 'our brilliant great leader, our teacher and our saviour'.
This set the sickly tone for leader-writers to follow during the
years to come. Mao's colleagues began to refer to him in their
speeches as the 'wise leader' and 'standard-bearer' of the Party,
while Theodore White found them making ostentatious notes on
Mao's impromptu speeches at Yenan 'as if drinking from the
fountain of knowledge'.

Ai Ching wrote an adulatory ode entitled 'Mao Tse-tung':

> Wherever Mao Tse-tung appears,
> There the sound of clapping seethes.
>
> 'The People's leader' is no empty term of praise,
> So great is his love for them that he has the people's trust.
>
> He is rooted in a China ancient and huge,
> Bearing the weight of history on his back.
>
> His face is covered constantly with grief,
> His eyes reflect the sufferings of the people.
>
> Political analyst, poet, leader of men,
> Revolutionary – with an ideology of practice.
>
> He thinks incessantly, incessantly summarizing,
> One hand pushing aside the enemy,
>   the other gathering yet more friends.
>
> 'Concentration' is his inspired military strategy –
> Crushing his greatest enemy with his utmost strength.

A new slogan determines a new direction:
'Go all out for the death of fascism.'

In 1944 there first appeared the song which later become almost
a national anthem:

The eastern sky reddens,
The sun rises,
And in China Mao Tse-tung has come!
He strives for the welfare of the people.
He is the Great Saviour of the People!

Mao was able to attract the loyalty of a number of extremely able
young officials in Yenan who were to play key roles in Chinese
politics in the future, including Teng Hsiao-ping, Peng Chen,
Chen Po-ta, Tao Chu and Jao Shu-shih. These were to provide
the second generation of Red leadership after the war.

Liu Shao-chi consented to the build-up of Mao, and although
Chou En-lai was prevented by his United Front work in Chungking from actively lobbying for it, he had clearly come to terms
with Mao's supremacy. Only Wang Ming and Lo Fu remained
silent.

'Mao Tse-tung's personality dominated Yenan,' Theodore
White wrote after his visit in 1944. 'He was set on the pinnacle of
adoration.' A Chinese journalist found that in Yenan in 1946
portraits of Mao were omnipresent, along with his calligraphy,
and that for workers and peasants his words were 'absolute and
fool-proof'.

And yet the cult was not equally promoted throughout the
Communist areas. Mao's *Selected Works* were never published in
Yenan at all, whereas early editions were published between
1944 and 1948 in Harbin, where the eager acolyte Lin Piao was
in charge, and also in the Shansi-Chahar-Hopei area under Nieh
Jung-chen. The first collective study of Mao's three essays, 'On
Protracted War', 'On the New Stage' and 'On New Democracy',
was undertaken in the Shansi-Suiyuan area rather than in Yenan
itself.

Wang Ming claimed that Mao spoke to him on several occasions at this time about the objective necessity to create
'Maotsetung-ism', citing the examples of Marx, Lenin and Sun
Yat-sen. According to Wang, Mao conceded that people never
took to new -isms when they were first propounded, and he
declared that 'we must take our example from Mahomet, who

turned people to a new faith by force, with the sword in one hand
and the Koran in the other.'

Among Mao's own generation of fellow leaders it was Liu
Shao-chi, his fellow Hunanese who had gone to the same school
and had first collaborated with Mao in the Anyuan miners'
strike more than twenty years before, who played the most
significant role in promoting Mao's status. In 1943 Liu published an article identifying Mao's policies for the past twenty
years as being in direct succession to the Bolshevik line in Russia
– whereas those opposing Mao had been the 'Mensheviks' of the
Chinese Party. This was an important contribution to legitimiz-
ing Mao's status in terms of Russian ideology.

Liu had spoken in similar terms about Mao's opponents
(though without praising Mao) to the Party Congress in 1937,
but his analysis had been rejected then, and instead Lo Fu delivered a rival report which was accepted. As a consequence, Liu
had lost his position in the Party's North China Bureau. It was
Mao who helped him obtain a new post, and by 1940 Liu was
speaking of Mao in heroic terms: 'Only the Thought of Mao
Tse-tung is able to inspire us to go from victory to victory.... Mao Tse-tung is the great revolutionary leader of all
the people of China, and we should learn from him.'

Liu was not, of course, prepared to underwrite a dictatorship
on Mao's part. 'In our Party', he warned in 1941, 'there are no
special privileges for individuals; any leadership which is not
exercised in the name of the organization cannot be tolerated.
Comrade Mao Tse-tung is the leader of the whole Party but he,
too, obeys the Party.' Red leaders had to demonstrate their
discipline by accepting the decision of the majority even if they
knew it was wrong. But any doubts which Liu may have had
about Mao's victory were probably suppressed when Liu was
appointed to the Party Secretariat to replace Lo Fu as one of the
five-man inner circle of leadership. It was a neat revenge for his
humiliation of six years before.

Having lost his sister, Tse-hung, in the war against Japan in
1941, Mao now in 1943 lost his only remaining sibling, his middle brother, Tse-min. After rising to become the Finance Minister in Shensi in 1936, with responsiblity for the entire economy of
the Communist area, Tse-min had left in 1938 to become the
financial adviser of the warlord of Sinkiang, who was then collaborating with the Communists. Unfortunately this warlord
switched sides, and Mao's brother was thrown into gaol, where
he was killed by being given poisoned wine.

None of his family survived to see or share Mao's triumph. Tse-min's son, Yuan-hsin, now joined Mao's family in Yenan, to be looked after by Chiang Ching.

The American journalist Harrison Forman visited Mao and his wife in 1944. He described them as

... plainly dressed, she in a practical pajama-like outfit belted at her slim waist, he in a rough, home-spun suit, with baggy, high water pants. I was taken to the 'parlor' – one of the caves with a simple brick floor, white-washed walls, and solid, rather lumpy furniture. It was evening, and the only light was furnished by a single candle fixed on an up-turned cup. For refreshments I was served with weak tea, cakes and candy made locally, and cigarettes, while youngsters ran in and out during the whole conversation. They would stand and stare at me for a few moments and then, seizing a piece of candy, race out again. Mao paid no attention to them.

That July Mao talked with Gunther Stein, the correspondent for the *Manchester Guardian* and *Christian Science Monitor*, for twelve hours, starting at three in the afternoon and going on until three in the morning, in the reception room of his cave quarters. Mao, Stein wrote, 'sat on a rickety chair, lighting one cigarette after another and sucking in the smoke with the strange noise characteristic of peasants in certain parts of China.' He 'paced up and down the cave and then stood tall and massive over me for a while, his eyes fixed on mine for minutes on end, while he talked slowly and systematically with quiet emphasis.'

They had a short dinner 'under an old apple tree' and then two candles were lit in the cave, throwing

... Mao Tse-tung's huge shadow on the high vault of the cave. He noticed my struggle with the rocky little table in front of me, went out into the garden, brought back a flat stone, and stuck it under one of its legs. From time to time we had a glass of grape wine, and one pack of local cigarettes after another was exhausted as we talked on and on. During the night I made several moves to leave, although I was anxious to ask more questions. But he would not hear of it. He was going to give me more interviews, he said, but why not continue tonight and get done as much as possible?

At three in the morning, when I finally got up to go, with a bad conscience, aching limbs, and burning eyes, he was still as fresh and animated and systematic in his talk as in the afternoon.

Stein's notes were retranslated for Mao to check, and when Mao passed Stein in the street several days later he explained: 'I had to consult comrades Chu Teh and Chou En-lai about all I told you. They approved.'

'It is quite possible', he told Stein with a smile, 'that China may reach the stages of socialism and communism considerably later than your countries in the West which are so much more highly developed economically.'

'Did you ever find yourself', Stein asked, 'in a minority so that your own ideas on a subject were not carried out?'

'Yes,' Mao admitted, 'I have been in the minority myself. The only thing for me to do at such times was to wait. But there have been very few examples of that in recent years.'

The Americans, brought into the war by the Japanese attack on Pearl Harbor, had now set up their various links and missions with the Chinese national government in Chungking, and were ready to send their first observers to Yenan, since the Communists were also fighting Japan. Mao boasted to an American journalist about China's 'democracy'. On 18 July he told the *Baltimore Sun* correspondent, Maurice Votaw, that, 'Chinese history, too, has its democratic tradition. The term Republican was originated in the Chou Dynasty 3000 years ago. Mencius said: "First the people, then the state, then the Emperor." The Chinese peasant has a rich democratic tradition. . . .'

The Yenan press carried laudatory articles about George Washington, and how Roosevelt and Wallace were worthy heirs to Abraham Lincoln. On 22 July 1944 the eagerly awaited US Army Observer group, christened the 'Dixie mission', arrived at Yenan airport. Mao gave the Americans a welcoming dinner a few days afterwards. He told John Service, the diplomat in the American group, that the Americans ought to set up a consulate at Yenan which could go on functioning after the war had ended.

The Americans were cheerful, outgoing and informal, and made a surprising impact on the Chinese Communists. Gunther Stein commented that he had 'never seen large groups of Chinese and foreigners so unconventional and happy together, so completely unaware of differences of background, political creed and race – so successful in co-operating with one another and so sincere in their mutual appreciation.'

Late in August Mao had a six-hour conversation with John Service in which he called for a direct US intervention in the war. 'We think', he said, 'the Americans must land in China. It depends, of course, on Japanese strength and the developments of the war. . . . If the Americans do not land in China, it will be most unfortunate for China. The Kuomintang will continue as the government. . . . If there is a landing, there will have to be

American co-operation with both Chinese forces – Kuomintang and Communist.'

Service demurred that this would not really be necessary for winning the war, so Mao instead called on the Americans to be tougher with Chiang Kai-shek. 'Chiang', he insisted, 'is in a position where he must listen to the United States. . . . Look at the economic situation! Chiang is in a corner. Chiang is stubborn but fundamentally he is a gangster. . . . The only way to handle him is to be hard boiled. . . . The United States has handled Chiang very badly. They have let him get away with black-mail. . . .'

Mao told his unofficial American ambassador that civil war was inevitable unless the Kuomintang were restrained, and he wanted to know what US policy would be in this event: 'We can risk no conflict with the United States'. He stressed that the Communist Party's policies were merely liberal – rent reduction, interest limitation, free-enterprise industrialization with foreign capital, democracy and raising living standards. 'Even the most conservative American businessman', Mao claimed, 'can find nothing in our programmes to take exception to.'

Service afterwards recalled,

Lacking perhaps some of the suavity and urbanity of Chou, Mao could also be more lively and spontaneous. Conversations were likely to sparkle with witticisms, Chinese classical allusions and sharp and surprising statements. Apt and obvious conclusions were snapped out of the air before they seemed logically to have been reached. Conversations also wandered in unexpected and wildly diverse directions. There were few subjects in which he was not interested and few about which his omnivorous reading had not given him some knowledge.

It was normal, I suppose, that he usually seemed to be leading the conversation. You felt at times that it was you who was being interviewed. Yet this was done with a great deal of finesse. He did not monopolize the conversation, there was no 'hard sell' and you were not being overpowered. In fact, in group meetings he was usually meticulous that each person present had a chance to join in and express himself. Very often Mao would sum up the sense of the meeting. Whenever I saw this done, his summarization was masterfully fair, complete, and succinct.

On 9 October there was an impromptu dance at the Communist headquarters in the evening. Mao and Chiang Ching were both, in the words of John Service, who was also present, 'in fine humour, dancing repeatedly with each other and with most of the others present in a manner which, remembering Mao's normally quiet and reserved bearing, can only be called gay.'

At the beginning of November the Americans began their effort to bring the Communists and Kuomintang together. They sent General Hurley, who landed unannounced and unexpected on the cold bleak Yenan airfield on 7 November. Mao was told of his arrival only after the plane had landed: he gathered his senior colleagues together, piled them into his war-scarred ambulance and raced out to the runway. 'The envoy greeted them affably,' in the description of White, 'gave an Indian war whoop and climbed into the ambulance.' When they passed a shepherd with his flock, Mao recalled that he had been a shepherd boy himself, which Hurley capped by revealing that he had been a cowboy in his youth. By the time they had got through the banquet awaiting them, Mao and Hurley appeared to be bosom friends.

The bonhomie was genuine, but political understanding on Hurley's side was sadly lacking. He began his negotiations with Mao next day by pressing the Kuomintang's ideas about a rapprochement, whereupon Mao treated his American guest to a tirade against Generalissimo Chiang Kai-shek. The first day ended in furious argument.

But that evening and next morning Hurley went to the other extreme, drafting proposals for a genuine coalition government in which the Communists would share, with guaranteed freedom of speech, movement and assembly. Mao was delighted, and retained a copy of the proposals, signed by Hurley as a mark of his good faith – although he was careful to remind Mao that he could not speak for the Generalissimo. It was enough for Mao that Roosevelt's personal representative was ready to put his name to these proposals and urge them on the Kuomintang.

Wang Ming, lying on his invalid couch in the late November sun a few days later, recorded an unexpected visit by a smiling Mao. He wanted Wang to see a telegram from President Roosevelt thanking Mao for his congratulations on winning the American election. Mao appeared to believe that this missive opened up the prospect of direct personal contact with the White House.

But the Generalissimo did not, of course, accept Hurley's proposals, and the American effort to bring the two sides together failed. Mao, possibly emboldened by the telegram, decided to appeal to the only possible source of pressure upon Chiang. On 9 January 1945 he told the senior officer in the 'Dixie mission', Major Ray Cromley, that he and Chou En-lai were ready to fly to the US to meet President Roosevelt. Cromley sent a cable to the American Embassy in Chungking: 'Mao and Chou will be immediately available either singly or together for exploratory conference at Washington should President Roosevelt express desire to receive them at White House as leaders of a primary Chinese party.'

Complete secrecy was requested so that the move would not spoil the Communists' negotiations with Chiang Kai-shek. A second cable was addressed to General Wedemeyer, the American military representative, to the effect that Chou had asked that Ambassador Hurley be left out of this, 'as I don't trust his discretion'. Even in normal circumstances Mao was probably pushing his luck to hope for the accolade of a White House audience, but two quite separate and unforeseen pieces of bad luck made his failure certain.

In the first place General Wedemeyer was away in Burma, and had asked Ambassador Hurley to deal with his mail, so that Hurley read Chou's comment on himself. In the second place Hurley had become angry over two apparent offers of military aid to the Communists by US army officers without any prior consultation with him. In the event he sat on the request for a time, eventually tacking it on to a message to Washington advising against military help to the Communists. The White House was thus left in a position where it did not feel that it had to give a view one way or the other on Mao's offer. It was never acknowledged, let alone answered.

During these exchanges with the Americans, Mao's eldest son returned from Russia. It was fifteen years since his father had seen him. Mao An-ying, now a young man of twenty-five, had been arrested by the Kuomintang in 1930, along with his mother, Yang Kai-hui. After her execution he and his middle brother, An-ching, had been smuggled to Shanghai where they lived under false names and in desperate straits in the care of members of Mao's family in exile from Changsha. After Russia entered the war the boys had been sent to the USSR to study at the Comintern School at Ivanovo.

An-ying took the Russian alias of Sergei. He was good at Russian but began to forget his Chinese. The Russians found him modest, likeable, a little spoiled but never one to mention his father. He fought on the East European front in a tank unit, and Stalin gave him a pistol.

The younger boy, An-ching, had followed a similar career under the name of Nikolai. He studied engineering and made an impression on his Russian comrades as an intense and oddly behaved character, subject to sudden enthusiasms which never lasted. Mao once disclosed that An-ching had mental health problems, and it was probably An-ying and An-ching who were meant in the note appended to one of Mao's speeches in the 1950s to the effect that 'one son was killed, one went mad'.

The Red Guards had claimed that An-ching had been mis-treated by the bourgeois family which had looked after him when his mother was arrested. Some Russian specialists thought he was schizoid, another believed that his behaviour was caused by his having been hit over the head with a stick by a Western missionary. In Russia he played chess and fell in love with a Russian blonde, and appears to have been something of a minor playboy.

When Mao An-ying returned to Yenan in the winter of 1944-45, the younger boy was left in Russia. Mao evidently felt that his eldest son needed to be re-Sinified after his Russian experi-ence, and he sent him to live several miles away with the famous labour hero, Wu Man-yu, who had come to Yenan before the war as a hungry refugee, was given a little land by the Commun-ists and built it up very successfully as a date garden. According to a pro-Russian member of the Chinese leadership the young man objected to his father's order and told him afterwards: 'I did not "learn" from this kulak. I am deeply opposed to every facet of the lives of this big kulak family. I shall forever remain a Marxist-Leninist, a pupil of Soviet educational institutions. I shall never consider this a disgrace, on the contrary I am proud of it!'

It was, after all, in the tradition of the Mao family that the son should turn against the father. But there was some justice on Mao's side. Later, after a year on the farm growing calloused hands, when the young man was given a job translating between Russian and Chinese, a Chinese comrade asked him in front of a Russian: 'Have you learned any Chinese yet?'

The family also retrieved Mao's teenage nephew, Mao Chu-hsiung, the son of Tse-min, who had been brought up by his maternal grandmother since the poisoning of his father in Sin-kiang. But he lasted little more than a year, being buried alive by opponents in the civil war.

Meanwhile Mao tried to get to the bottom of the mysteries of American policy. On 13 March he invited John Service for another long conversation in which he assured the American that Chinese Communist policies threatened no interest of the US. Mao declared:

Between the people of China and the people of the United States there are strong ties of sympathy, understanding and mutual interest. Both are essentially democratic and individualistic. Both are by nature peace-loving, non-aggressive and non-imperialistic. China's greatest post-war need is economic development. She lacks the capitalistic foundation to carry this out alone. Her own living standards are so low that they cannot be further depressed to provide the needed capital.

America and China complement each other economically; they will not compete. China does not have the requirements of a heavy industry of major size. She cannot hope to meet the United States in its highly specialized manufactures. America needs an export market for her heavy industry and these specialized manufactures. She also needs an outlet for capital investment.

China needs to build up light industries to supply her own market and raise the living standards of her own people. Eventually she can supply these goods in other countries in the Far East. To help pay for this foreign trade and investment she has raw materials and agricultural products. America is not only the most suitable country to assist this economic development of China, she is also the only country fully able to participate.

For all these reasons there must not and cannot be a conflict, estrangement or misunderstanding between the Chinese people and America. . . .

Soon afterwards, Service was ordered to return to Washington. Mao received him for the last time on 1 April. Mao 'was in exceptionally good spirits,' Service reported, 'getting out of his chair to act out dramatic embellishments of his talk, and diverging to recall amusing anecdotes.' He repeated his hopes for a continued constructive American policy in China.

Service reached Washington on 12 April, the day Roosevelt died. He quickly became involved in the FBI investigation into the *Amerasia* case and was arrested for allegedly passing on diplomatic secrets to the press on 6 June. The combination of these events led Mao to give up his hopes of American assistance and goodwill, and he regarded the arrest of Service as a turning-point in US policy towards China.

Outwardly, Mao kept up his hopes for American understanding and help. He gave a banquet of pork dumplings, panther meat, hundred-year-old eggs and fiery bygar wine for seven American airmen who had parachuted from a disabled B-29 just before it crashed in North China. The Communists led them through Japanese lines to safety via Yenan, and Mao presented each one of them with a gift – in one case of a heavy wool blanket made in the Red area. They had seen Mao himself walking and

talking with comrades while moving his fingers in a rapid
mechanical pattern, carding wool – the nearest he ever came to
Gandhi's spinning-wheel.

'The American people,' Mao observed in a speech in April,
'whom the Chinese people used to regard as living in a faraway
place, now seem next-door neighbours. The Chinese people will
work together with the people of the great nations – America,
Great Britain, the Soviet Union and France – and also with the
peoples of all nations to create a "firm and lasting" world peace.'
But the disillusion soon came into the open, and by July Mao
was boasting to non-Communist Chinese visitors that 'Since I
have been able to fight Japan with these few rusty rifles, I can
fight the Americans too. The first step is to get rid of Hurley,
then we'll see.'

Meanwhile Mao was preparing for the long-delayed Seventh
Party Congress, the so-called 'Congress of Victors', which
opened in Yenan in April 1945. The curtain-raiser for this was a
long text written by Mao and adopted by the Central Committee
a few days before the Congress opened, as 'A Resolution on
Certain Questions in the History of Our Party'. This was an
unabashed rewriting of history with the aim of propelling Mao
into the key role in the success of the Chinese Communist
movement: 'Representing the Chinese proletariat and the Chinese people, Comrade Mao Tse-tung has creatively applied the
scientific theory of Marxism-Leninism, the acme of human wisdom, to China . . . and he has brilliantly developed the theories
of Lenin and Stalin. . . .'

In Mao's own words in this amazing 'Resolution',

. . . we rejoice especially in the fact that in those ten years [1927-37]
our Party, with Comrade Mao Tse-tung as its representative, made
very great advances in creatively applying to Chinese conditions the
revolutionary theories of Marx, Engels, Lenin and Stalin. At last,
towards the end of the Agrarian Revolutionary War, our Party
definitely established the leadership of Comrade Mao Tse-tung in the
central leading body and throughout the Party. This was the greatest
achievement of the Communist Party of China in that period, and it is
the surest guarantee of the liberation of the Chinese people.

Self-congratulation could be carried no higher. In this document Mao set out his case against his critics from left and right,
both in the area of military strategy and in politics. He quoted
Stalin for the thesis that the correct direction of tactics requires a
correct analysis of the situation, and then went on to say that

'one of the best models is Comrade Mao Tse-tung's direction of the Chinese revolutionary movement'.

This was the only quotation from Stalin in the entire Resolution, and it was a back-handed one, since foresight had been the one quality singularly lacking in Stalin's perception of the Chinese situation. The Resolution made clear in fact that Mao had scant respect for Stalin's foresight, and that Stalin's guidance played little or no part in the development of Mao's theories about the right course of the Chinese revolution. The text in fact was not published until just before Stalin's death, eight years later.

Guidance on how to arrive at a correct subjective judgement cannot, of course, be codified, and all the Resolution could say on this was: 'Comrade Mao Tse-tung provided us with a model of how to combine perseverance in truth as a matter of principle with submission to organization as a matter of discipline, a model of how to conduct inner-Party struggles in a correct way while maintaining inner-Party unity in a correct way.'

'From the very day he embraced the cause of the Chinese revolution', the author went on without apparent embarrassment, 'Comrade Mao Tse-tung has devoted himself to applying the universal truth of Marxism-Leninism to the investigation and study of the actual conditions of Chinese society. . . . Indeed, the political, military and organizational lines then laid down by Comrade Mao Tse-tung were brilliant achievements. . . .'

At the end the Central Committee, adopting this Resolution in which the hero hymned his own praises, recognized 'with unprecedented unanimity . . . the correctness of Comrade Mao Tse-tung's line and with unprecedented political consciousness rallies under his banner.'

The Seventh Congress, which opened on 23 April, was thus a triumph for Mao. Its highlight was the report on 14 May by Liu Shao-chi on the new Party constitution, in which it was stated that the Party 'guides its entire work . . . by Mao Tse-tung's theory of the Chinese revolution.' In the course of his report Liu referred to Mao or his Thought no fewer than 105 times. 'Mao Tse-tung', Liu's wife later told her daughter, 'had no prestige until the Seventh Congress. Your father and other leaders established the prestige for him.'

The fact that the gesture was not whole-hearted was confirmed in a remark later made by Liu's brother: 'Liu Shao-chi graduated from the Soviet Marxist-Leninist Academy. It was

Liu Shao-chi who gave Chairman Mao his position; Liu Shao-chi could have won the first election.' This was, of course, an exaggeration: no one could have challenged Mao by 1945. But Mao was building his triumph on insecure foundations, as the 1960s were to prove.

Liu nevertheless chose in 1945 to merge the Party apparatus which he had so carefully built up in the cities and trade unions with Mao's peasant armies from the rural areas (the Party now boasted more than a million members), on the basis that he was the deputy and ultimate heir. His praise of Mao to the Congress was unstinting:

Mao Tse-tung's great accomplishment has been to change Marxism from a European to an Asian form. . . . Mao Tse-tung is Chinese; he analyses Chinese problems and guides the Chinese people in their struggle to victory. He uses Marxist-Leninist principles to explain Chinese history and the practical problems of China. He is the first that has succeeded in doing so. . . . He has created a Chinese or Asian form of Marxism. China is a semi-feudal, semi-colonial country in which vast numbers of people live at the edge of starvation, tilling small bits of soil. . . . In attempting the transition to a more industrialized economy, China faces . . . the pressures . . . of advanced industrial lands. . . . There are similar conditions in other lands of south and east Asia. The courses chosen by China will influence them all.

On 11 June the new constitution was agreed and Mao was confirmed as Chairman of the Party and of its principal organs, with Liu as his first deputy. Even so there was evidence of Mao's reservations about the coalition he had built against the Bolsheviks. According to one colleague Mao blocked the candidature of a certain comrade for the Central Committee because he would not say 'even one word against the address of Chou En-lai and Wang Ming, therefore he is a dogmatist . . .' It would seem that Mao was still jealous, even suspicious, of Chou En-lai.

At the end Mao sent stretchers for two sick leaders, one of them Wang Ming, so that their presence could demonstrate the unity of the conference. Wang described the scene:

Mao Tse-tung was standing alone on the stage and energetically waving his hands to invite the members of the Praesidium to join him. . . . Liu Shao-chi, Chou En-lai, Chu Teh and Jen Pi-shih climbed up to the stage and stood with him at the long Praesidium table. The other ten members of the Praesidium remained sitting in the hall. Gesticulating with his arms and nodding with his head, Mao now invited them to come on to the stage. At last they did so, one by one, slowly as if they were embarrassed, going into the right-hand corner to sit down at the edge of the stage a long way from the Praesidium, so that even the delegates sitting in the front rows could not see them. This left the five men standing on their own at the Praesidium table. Mao anxiously wandered around them, looking at each one. The other four, their faces red with mortification, fussed and nudged each other just like children on a visit. They did not even know where each was supposed to sit.

The 'unity' had been achieved at a price.

The Japanese war was now approaching its end, and Mao observed with distaste the busy preparations by the Kuomintang, with American support, for the civil war which was to follow. 'The American government', he predicted in the middle of July, 'will fall hopelessly into the deep, stinking cesspool of Chinese reaction.' The Mao who had once sought to see Roosevelt now sent a fraternal telegram instead to Comrade William Z. Foster, leader of the American Communist Party.

At the beginning of August the atom bombs fell on Hiroshima and Nagasaki. A few days later Mao reassured his cadres that such weapons did not by themselves decide wars. 'Some of our comrades ... believe that the atom bomb is all-powerful. ... These comrades show even less judgment than ... a certain British peer called Lord Mountbatten. He said the worst possible mistake is to think that the bomb decides the war. These comrades are more backward than Mountbatten.'

Generalissimo Chiang cabled Mao immediately after the Japanese surrender inviting him to Chungking for peace negotiations. For almost two weeks the telegrams flew back and forth, but Mao made conditions. At the end of August Ambassador Hurley flew to Yenan to urge Mao to come down and talk with his rival. Mao was persuaded. He cabled to Chiang: 'My humble self is most willing to come to Chungking to discuss national peace and reconstruction. ... Your younger brother is preparing to come. ...' On 28 Augut he flew to sup with the man who he knew was bent on destroying him.

15

SUP WITH THE DEVIL

Generalissimo Chiang Kai-shek gave a dinner for Mao on the night of his arrival in Chungking on 28 August 1945. It was their first meeting for eighteen years. 'Chiang lifted a toast to him,' an observer noted, 'but only touched the cup to his lips.' For the first two days Mao stayed as a guest at his deadly enemy's summer home outside the city, while Chou En-lai tasted his drinks first in case of poison.

Backed by Chou and Wang Jo-fei, who had also flown with him from Yenan, Mao plunged into discussions with the Kuomintang leadership. 'Chiang talked about peace . . .,' he later recollected, 'but he also gave underhand orders. During the negotiations he carried out a campaign against our Party and annihilated three divisions. . . .' On 4 September Mao and Chiang had their first tête-à-tête without any aides. But the differences persisted: Chiang would have no more than twelve Communist divisions in a coalition China, whereas Mao wanted twenty or twenty-four.

Meanwhile Mao went the rounds of tea parties, cocktails, receptions and press conferences, putting the Communist point of view to uncommitted Chinese and to foreigners of various persuasions in the city which was then acting as the capital of China. He met the Russian, American, British, Canadian and French ambassadors as well as leading members of the Aid-China organizations of various countries. He gave a copy of his poem 'Snow' to the Ta Kung Pao to publish, thus helping to overcome his image as a rude and uncultured peasant leader. 'The people throughout China want peace,' he told the assembled foreign correspondents, 'and I have come to Chungking to make every effort to achieve it.'

Mao was particularly keen to meet progressive Americans, and he received William Hinton and Gerald Tannebaum in what was known as the Eighth Route Army Office, a white stucco house on one of Chungking's narrow, dirty streets which acted as the Communist 'embassy'. Both Americans, then in China with the

US government, were surprised to find Mao taxing them in detail about Truman and the American labour movement.

'What is the difference', he wanted to know, 'between the Farm Bureau and the Farmers' Union?. . . . Why are most of the workers in America unorganized?. . . .'

He also met three young American airmen, Howard Hyman, Edward Bell and Jack Edelman. These three sympathizers with the Chinese Communists knew that Mao was a heavy smoker but that cigarettes were short in Yenan, 'So we took a few cartons of American cigarettes from our rations and wrote a short note voicing our hopes for a prosperous and peaceful future for the people of China,' leaving them at Mao's headquarters.

They were rewarded with a dinner at which Private Hyman observed how, 'The interaction between Mao and the workers, leaders, cooks and waiters was one of affection and warmth. I could not detect even a hint of pompousness, protocol, patronizing or any other affectation.' It is not known if Mao smoked the cigarettes, but not long afterwards a former Chinese acquaintance of his staying in Chungking was sent some Lucky Strike cigarettes with Mao's compliments, so perhaps the gifts were used as gifts again.

After five weeks the two sides began to patch up an understanding. On 8 October Mao went to a Kuomintang reception and spoke optimistically about China's future. 'Long live new China!' was his toast. 'Long live Chairman Chiang!' Two days later he signed a provisional agreement with the Generalissimo, and in the evening Chiang Kai-shek invited him to the opera. Mao's car was bombed in the car park while he was inside the building, a reminder if it were needed that, whatever the Generalissimo's intentions (and the Communists had good reason from their experiences in the 1920s to doubt them), there were some elements in Kuomintang China which did not wish to collaborate with Mao. On this uneasy note Mao flew back to Yenan on 11 October.

He returned out of sorts and in bad health. 'My nerves were too tense', he reported to his comrades, 'during my stay in Chungking. Now I feel dreadfully tired. I've lost strength and I often have palpitations, dizziness, insomnia and sweating in my sleep.' According to one colleague, he suffered from nervous exhaustion for more than six months.

He explained the understanding which he had brought back from Chungking:

The Kuomintang has accepted the principles of peace and unity, recognized certain democratic rights of the people and agreed that civil war should be averted and that the two parties should co-operate in peace to build a new China. On these points agreement has been reached.

There are other points on which there is no agreement. The question of the Liberated Areas has not been solved, and that of the armed forces has not really been solved either. The agreements reached are still only on paper. Words on paper are not equivalent to reality. . . .

The prospect was one of continuing to talk on the one hand, but continuing to fight on the other. 'The arms of the people, every gun and every bullet, must all be kept, must not be handed over.'

When no public statements or appearances were made by Mao for several months, the rumours began to spread, including a story that he had gone to Russia to plan with Stalin for the Communist take-over of China. Ironically this was just when Stalin came to the conclusion that the Chinese Communists were too weak to win a civil war against the Kuomintang, and that he should not therefore encourage them. Towards the end of 1945 the Russians had handed over the impregnable town of Shanhaikwan near the Russian border to the Red Army, only to see the Kuomintang smartly defeat the Chinese Communists and take it over.

Four of Mao's fellow leaders were killed in April 1946 when an American transport plane crashed between Sian and Yenan. They included one of his old rivals for the leadership, Po Ku, and a newer potential candidate, his fellow negotiator in Chungking, Wang Jo-fei. At the same time, however, another ghost from the Communist leadership's past suddenly reappeared in China after fifteen years in Moscow. Li Li-san showed up in Harbin amid speculation that he might have been sent by Stalin to take Mao's place. But the Mao cult in the Red areas continued. Chang Ju-hsin, one of Mao's most eager supporters, declared in 1946:

Some people say that Mao Tse-tung is a genius, a wise man. Certainly, he is the greatest genius since the beginning of the history of China. But it must be pointed out that his genius is neither a mystery nor the result of some inborn qualities. His genius, wisdom, and intelligence are the concentrated reflection of those of the Chinese people. Mao Tse-tung is the most outstanding descendant of the Yellow Emperor, the most distinguished representative of the Chinese people. At the same time, he is also a leader of the people of the world, a scientist, a genius, and a revolutionary – a faithful disciple of Marx, Engels, Lenin and Stalin.

In May the Kuomintang and Western press again insisted that Mao had gone to Moscow, but the rumours were vigorously

denied. Ten years later Mao was publicly to chide Stalin for his
half-heartedness at this crucial stage in the history of the Chinese
revolution. 'Stalin', he declared in 1956, 'first enjoined us not to
press on with the revolution, maintaining that if the war flared up,
the Chinese nation would run the risk of destroying itself. Then
when fighting did erupt, he took us half seriously, half sceptically.'

Robert Payne, the British writer, saw Mao in Yenan in June, in
a bare room adorned by portraits of Sun Yat-sen, Chiang Kai-
shek, Truman, Stalin and Attlee. Things were improving slightly
in Yenan as compared with the 1930s. There was electric light by
courtesy of the 'Dixie mission' power plant, and among the films
that were shown in 1946-7 were *The Bandit of Sherwood Forest* and,
less appropriately, *The Dolly Sisters*.

Payne declared that photographs failed to give a true impression of

... the man with the long streaming blue-black hair, the round silver-
rimmed spectacles, the fine cheek-bones, the pursed, almost feminine
lips, and the air of a college professor. . . . One moment he giggles like a
boy, and the next moment the soft voice takes on depth and authority
and a quite extraordinary resonance. He is fifty-three and looks
thirty. . . . He wore black cotton slippers and a brown woollen Sun
Yat-sen uniform. When he shook hands, he lifted his elbow to the height
of his shoulder, an odd gesture. . . .

The Kuomintang, all pretence of collaboration abandoned,
now launched a full military offensive against the Communists.
Mao had to face an armed struggle in which he would get help
neither from the Russians nor from the Americans. Yet he
seemed to know that he would win. As he told the American
writer, Anna Louise Strong, in August,

We have only millet plus rifles to rely on, but history will finally prove
that our millet plus rifles is more powerful than Chiang Kai-shek's
aeroplanes plus tanks. Although the Chinese people still face many
difficulties and will long suffer hardships from the joint attacks of US
imperialism and the Chinese reactionaries, the day will come when
these reactionaries are defeated and we are victorious. The reason is
simply this: the reactionaries represent reaction, we represent progress.

This was the interview in which Mao elaborated his famous
dictum on the atom bomb. Strong wanted to know what would
happen if the Americans used the new bomb against the Russians. 'The atom bomb', Mao replied, 'is a paper tiger which the
US reactionaries use to scare people. It looks terrible, but in fact
it isn't. Of course, the atom bomb is a weapon of mass slaughter,

but the outcome of a war is decided by the people, not by one or two new types of weapon.' He also foreshadowed his later analysis of the zonal division of the world. 'The United States and the Soviet Union', he told Strong, 'are separated by a vast zone which includes many capitalist, colonial and semi-colonial countries in Europe, Asia and Africa,' and he predicted growing reaction in this zone against super-power oppression.

At the end of August Mao went up to Harbin to plan with Lin Piao how the Red Army in the north-east would cope with the Kuomintang attacks. Li Li-san, fresh from Russia, was already there and was reported to have gained the political protection of Lin Piao. To the world at large Li presented an apologetic face. 'The facts of history', he told the *New York Herald Tribune* at the beginning of September, 'show Mao was right and I was wrong. I am happy to be back under Comrade Mao's leadership.' But a *New York Times* correspondent reported that Li was forming a counter-group in the north to blunt Mao's leadership, with a view to setting up – with Russian help – autonomous regions in both north-east China and Mongolia.

In October A. T. Steele of the *New York Herald Tribune* interviewed Mao. Steele wanted to know if Mao considered Chiang as China's 'natural leader'. 'There is no such thing in the world', Mao replied, 'as a "natural" leader.' He was bitter about the insincerity of American mediation in China.

Mao had good reason to be grim about the civil war. Reporting to his comrades on the fighting with the Kuomintang a year after Japan's surrender he said, 'The experience of the past three months has proved that in order to wipe out 10,000 enemy troops we have to pay a price of 2000 to 3000 casualties of our own. This is unavoidable.' The Kuomintang was four times stronger than the Communists and in the opening phase of the 1946–9 civil war it knocked the Red Army for six between the Great Wall and the Yangtze.

At the end of 1946 he received a group of Western journalists at Yenan. 'He is apparently virtually recovered from the overwork', one of them reported, 'which kept him inactive last winter. He laughed often. . . .' A *New York Times* correspondent described him as a 'rather effeminate-looking man in . . . brown home-spun suit and black cloth cap, sitting in an unheated cave cracking water melon seeds expertly between his teeth. . .' A few days later Gerald Samson of the *News Chronicle* spoke to Mao over dinner about the Russian removal of industrial equipment from north-east China. 'The Russian army', Mao explained, 'have not taken it to kill the Chinese people, but if General Chiang had it he would use it for this purpose.' Some observers believed, of course, that Stalin was deliberately denying assistance to the Chinese Communists. As for the future, Mao assured Samson, 'an era of industrialization and capitalism is the first stage towards a Communist China.'

That Mao was deeply conscious and resentful at this time of the opposition to his leadership, both within the Chinese Party and outside, seemed clear from a scroll of a Tang Dynasty poem which he copied for a friend:

> To win and lose battles is a soldier's lot,
> But it takes a brave man to bear insult and disgrace.
> Strong and talented are the youth of Kiangtung,
> Who knows but that I may ride again!

Mao was indeed in the early weeks of 1947 to 'ride again', but this was to be the last lap in his laborious journey to power in Peking. On 12 March the Kuomintang launched a prolonged air attack on Yenan which compelled the Communists to evacuate their capital. During the tense days leading up to the evacuation, Mao spent more time than usual playing with his children, apparently to give the appearance of being relaxed.

More than twelve inches of snow covered the ground when the Red Army set off at dusk on 18 March, leaving behind them a ghost town reduced to rubble by enemy bombs. Kuomintang troops took over Yenan almost immediately.

Mao rode in a jeep which was struck by machine-gun fire from enemy aeroplanes only a few miles out of Yenan. A Western press report said that he had received a bullet wound in the left chest. In fact the passengers in Mao's jeep were not injured, although the roof was perforated: for the rest of the journey they camouflaged it with foliage.

At this point Mao and his wife realized to their horror that they did not have their children with them. Mao's little boy Mao-mao had been lost in the confusion of the sudden evacuation from Yenan, and was never heard of again. But an urgent search found Li Na in a peasant house, happily innocent of what had been happening. To keep her safe, the little girl was sent to join Chou En-lai's wife, Teng Ying-chao, who had been assigned to a different area which was militarily safer. The girl stayed in Teng's custody for several months, and even in the 1970s was still calling Chou's wife 'Mama Teng'.

The trek which began in March 1947 became another Long

March of two years, with Mao moving almost constantly from place to place to dodge Kuomintang troops. Because of the danger and harassment, it became the habit of Mao's men to march through the night from dusk to dawn, and to sleep through the day – a habit which they afterwards found difficult to give up. Wherever they were able to camp for a few days they stocked up on the 'three treasures' necessary for the journey in those parts – fur, herbs and salt. In order to minimize the enemy's chances of finding them, the leaders took on aliases. Mao became Li Teh-sheng – meaning 'Determined to be victorious'. The rumour in some Chinese newspapers was that Mao had gone to North Korea.

The Communist leaders had split on abandoning Yenan. Most of the Central Committee Secretariat, including Mao and Chou En-lai, struck north towards the Great Wall, while remaining within the Shensi-Kansu-Ninghsia region, while Liu Shao-chi and Chu Teh headed east to establish an alternative Working Committee in Hsipaipo in Hopei. Mao himself 'took personal command in the North-west theatre' as well as having the responsibility of directing the war on all fronts.

Mao's detachment had to take a tortuous route to Ching-yangcha, where on 9 April Mao composed a circular informing the rest of the Party about what had happened. He ordered them to defend the Communist areas in the north-west 'with a firm fighting spirit; it is entirely possible to achieve this objective', and explained that the Central Committee and army headquarters would remain in the Shensi region – 'an area where we have a favourable mountainous terrain, a good mass base, plenty of room for manoeuvre and full guarantee for security'.

They then set off for Wangchiawan in difficult conditions. Mao had to eat gruel 'made of flour and elm seeds', and his bodyguard noticed him swaying in his saddle from hunger and fatigue as soon as he mounted his horse. His aides hurriedly brought up a stretcher.

'What's this?' laughed Mao. 'You want me to get on the stretcher again?'

'You're too tired,' his bodyguard said. 'The comrades are all willing to carry you.'

'Everyone else is very tired too,' Mao commented, continuing to ride.

From Wangchiawan, where they rested for almost two months, Mao issued orders to General Peng Teh-huai and other commanders in the field. 'Our policy', he wrote, 'is to keep the enemy on the run in this area for a time (about another month) ... to tire him out, to reduce his food supplies drastically and then look for an opportunity to destroy him. ... This may be called the tactics of "wear and tear". ...'

Wangchiawan was a tiny village of ten families living on the side of a mountain, and the enemy's camp was only about six miles away. An old peasant lent the Communist leaders his ramshackle cave quarters, looking out on to a courtyard filled with the acrid smell of pickled-vegetable vats.

There were two adjoining caves, Mao and his wife taking the inner one, Chou En-lai and two other Central Committee members the outer. When the four men needed to confer, Chiang Ching had to leave the cave and move into a donkey shed. She recollected afterwards how she had to live with donkeys for days on end with nothing to do, becoming infested with lice and fleas, and losing weight.

It was here that Mao had an unusual chance to play his beloved schoolmaster's role. One day his 'landlord', the old man from the village whose cave Mao had borrowed, came in while they were listening to their radio. He had never seen a radio before, and was amazed. After looking at it from all sides, he said: 'What is this? Is there someone inside?'

Everyone laughed.

'Don't laugh,' Mao said. 'If any of you understand the principle of the thing, explain it to old uncle.'

But none of them could, and so after an embarrassed pause Mao brought over a stool for the old man to sit on and then, in a casual conversational way, began to explain what a radio was all about. 'He talked of the echoes in the mountain valleys,' one of the participants later recalled, 'of the vibrations in the air, and finally of the various principles governing electro-magnetic waves. The more we heard, the more interested we became. It was like attending a fascinating lecture.'

The old man was thrilled with his new discovery, saying that if he'd found one in the past he would probably have chopped it up for firewood. But if he found one in the future he would keep it 'to hear our Chairman Mao speak!'

At this there was a hush, for the old man did not realize the true identity of his new teacher, knowing him only by his alias of 'Li Teh-sheng'.

After Mao had left Wangchiawan, the old man finally learned who it was that had been living in his cave. Later, when the Kuomintang occupied the village, they tried to force out of him

the whereabouts of Mao, even chopping two of his fingers off to encourage him. But the old man never told them.

The Central Committee meetings in the Wangchiawan cave were intense and argumentative. Nobody knew from which direction and in what strength the enemy would approach. Mao's view was that the Communists should maintain a flexible strategy of constantly evading the enemy within the north-western territory which they knew so well. Others argued for a retreat to the other side of the Yellow River and a quick march eastwards. Mao often finished these meetings angry and exhausted, and Chiang Ching later recalled that she did not at first understand what made him so bad-tempered.

Mao's more optimistic outlook was vindicated by the battle of Panlung on 4 April, in which the Red Army eliminated a Kuomintang division and took over a vast quantity of supplies as well as prisoners. But in June, Mao had to lead his men out of Wangchiawan as enemy troops approached the village, taking a western route in the shadow of the Great Wall. The Kuomintang was chasing them all the way, and they had to keep up an uninterrupted march through thunder, lightning and blinding rain. At one point their guide lost his way and they had to retrace their steps within earshot of the enemy, communicating only by hand signals.

Chiang Ching deliberately let her horse fall behind the leaders in the van, in order not to burden them with having to look after her in these circumstances, and she soon found herself the only rider among foot soldiers. One of them dragged her off the saddle on to the muddy ground to avoid the danger of the horse bolting or slipping in the mud and throwing her. These men had to join hands in a human chain in order to keep on the right track. Towards dawn, Mao passed a message back for her to rejoin him at the front.

That night they managed to throw off the enemy and turned eastwards to spend the second half of June and July in Hsiaoho. From here Mao launched the Red Army on a country-wide offensive and also put his stamp of approval on a report from Liu Shao-chi about the slow progress of land reform. The two leaders were still working in harness, although Liu's reservations occasionally came out, as when he told a Party meeting: 'There is no perfect leader in the world. This was true of the past as it is of present, in China and other countries. If there is one, he only pretends to be such, just like thrusting leeks up a pig's nose to make it look like an elephant.'

Enemy pressure had Mao on the run again at the beginning of August, and for three weeks he was on a steady daily march towards the Yellow River. He was now in the thick of the fighting, riding on a black horse, taking out a cigarette to fondle, and then regretfully putting it back in his pocket because the 'no smoking' order was out, rolling up his trouser legs to wade through streams, sticking branches into rivers to see how fast they were flowing, putting a crown of willow tendrils on his hat as camouflage against the enemy planes overhead, and then, when camp was struck, setting up the radio, endlessly reading telegrams and sending messages to the other commanders to control the campaign, sometimes coming out to listen for the gun-fire from distant hills and valleys which told them whether or not his plans were succeeding.

They headed toward Chiahsien, on the banks of the Yellow River, where Chiang Ching was able to buy some crab-apples for Mao. The enemy was in hot pursuit. Word came to Mao at the head of the column that Chou En-lai was ill. Mao sent his stretcher back for his comrade, who was sitting exhausted on the grass with a bleeding nose. He resisted the stretcher at first, only giving in when Chiang Ching came back to investigate. Once he was laid out on it, the underneath of his shoes came into full view, and Chiang Ching exclaimed: 'Vice-Chairman Chou, your socks are showing through the soles of your shoes!'

'Showing, are they?' Chou laughed. 'No wonder my feet felt the bumps on the road when I walked.'

On another occasion, when Mao had already retired, Chou En-lai saw a fire which the enemy had lit on a nearby mountain. After discussing it with the senior officer on the watch, Chou said: 'Don't tell the Chairman; let him have a good sleep. He's too tired.'

But Mao heard them from his quarters and called out: 'Don't worry. Today the world is not theirs, it is ours.'

From Chiahsien the Kuomintang forced Mao westwards yet again, as far as Liangchiacha, where he directed by radio-telephone in the third week of August the crucial battle of Shachiatien. The Communists' victory in this battle marked the end of their defensive phase in the civil war and heralded the Red Army counter-offensive. Chiang Kai-shek had over-extended his lines to Manchuria, and under estimated the extent to which the Red Army had been able to acquire rifles and material from the Russians – as well as from Kuomintang prisoners. The peasants were also responding to the Communist rallying cry of land reform. Mao now marched eastwards at Chiahsien again, but then turned about to go south to a temporary winter headquarters at Yangchiakou in north Shensi, from mid-November to late March 1948.

During this stage of the march Chiang Ching left her husband and crossed the Yellow River to the ancient city of Shuangta in order to be reunited with her daughter Li Na after eight months of being parted. Chou's wife had left the girl there after seeing her out of Yenan in the spring. From the city wall Mao's wife caught a last glimpse of the city of Yenan, far to the west, and felt a pang of nostalgia. She and her daughter quickly rejoined Mao and his detachment.

In December Mao composed one of his important speeches entitled 'The Present Situation and Our Tasks', dictating it to Chiang Ching who took it down word by word. 'At that time,' Mao recollected, 'I had contracted a disease whereby I could not write.'

The speech was delivered to the Central Committee at Yangchiakou on Christmas Day, 1947. Mao emphasized the importance of a lenient land reform policy. The Outline Land Law of September 1947 provided for equal distribution of land per head: for this to be implemented properly the Party should organize not only peasant associations but also 'poor peasant leagues composed of poor peasants and farm labourers and their elected committees; and these poor peasant leagues should be the backbone of leadership in all rural struggles.' At the same time 'there should be no repetition of the wrong ultra-Left policy, which was carried out in 1931-4, of "allotting no land to the landlords and poor land to the rich peasants".'

In fact Mao was crying for the moon in hoping that the Communist Party could at one and the same time redistribute land in equal portions and preserve the middle peasant economy so essential to the country as a whole. What he said to the Central Committee at Yangchiakou that Christmas Day was an assertion, so typical of the man, that impossibly conflicting goals could be achieved if only everyone were clever, careful, imaginative, thorough and honest enough to implement policy that way. In the real world the outline Land Law was being implemented by thousands of Party cadres, each possessing varying degrees of these qualities.

Another new problem was the huge new membership of the Communist Party, which had grown in the past decade by almost a hundred-fold to reach three million. This had enabled

the Party to do well against both the Japanese and the Kuomintang, but

... shortcomings have also cropped up. Many landlords, rich peasants and riffraff have seized the opportunity to sneak into our Party. In
the rural areas they control a number of Party, government and
people's organizations, tyrannically abuse their power, ride roughshod
over the people, distort the Party's policies and thus alienate these
organizations from the masses and prevent the land reform from being
thorough.

Mao ended his report with a stirring rallying cry, linking
China's situation with the destiny of the whole world:

All the anti-imperialist forces in the countries of the East ... should
unite together, oppose oppression by imperialism and by their domestic
reactionaries and make the goal of their struggle the emancipation of
the more than 1000 million oppressed people of the East.... This is
the historic epoch in which world capitalism and imperialism are going
down to their doom and world socialism and people's democracies are
marching to victory. The dawn is ahead, we must exert ourselves.

Those three months in Yangchiakou were ones of almost continuous writing for Mao. His output ranged from overall questions of military strategy to the problems of dealing with the
bourgeoisie in the liberated areas, land reform, economic policy,
democracy within the army and administrative efficiency within
the Party. When his hand became numb with writing he would
exercise his fingers by squeezing a rock.

Mao's flexible approach to class status was vividly illustrated
in his ruling about landlords. Landlords in the old liberated
areas who had changed their mode of life while the Party was
reducing rents and interest, provided they had engaged in physical labour for at least five years, 'may now have their class status
changed in accordance with their present condition, as long as
their behaviour has been good.' In this same directive of January
1948, Mao dealt with the question of punishment.

After the people's courts have given the handful of arch-criminals
who are really guilty of the most heinous crimes a serious trial and
sentenced them, and the sentences have been approved, it is entirely
necessary for the sake of revolutionary order to shoot them and
announce their execution. That is one side of the matter. The other side
is that we must insist on killing less and must strictly forbid killing
without discrimination. To advocate killing more or killing without
discrimination is entirely wrong; this would only cause our Party to
forfeit sympathy, become alienated from the masses and fall into isolation.

Once the land struggle had reached its height in each locality,

... we should teach the masses to understand their own long-term interests – to regard those landlords and rich peasants who do not persist in wrecking the war effort or the land reform and who number tens of millions in the country as a whole (as many as 36 million out of a rural population of about 360 million) as a labour force for the country and to save and remould them. Our task is to abolish the feudal system, to wipe out the landlords as a class, not as individuals.

16
LAST LAP TO PEKING

Late in March 1948 Mao left Yangchiakou for the penultimate stage on his long march to power in Peking. He led his men eastwards across the Yellow River near Chaitseshan, and then wound north to cross the Great Wall, just for one day, into Inner Mongolia before coming down into Hopeh. They had to cross the snow-covered Wutai Mountains at a height of 10,000 feet, which took the breath out of many of them. Mao and Chiang Ching went to the summit of one peak in a jeep which had been captured from the enemy a few days before, to enjoy a magnificent panorama. A little further on they were attacked from the air for several days running.

During the journey Mao dispensed wisdom to the liberated areas. In April he berated the Communist journalists for their shortcomings, in a talk to the editorial staff of the *Shansi-Suiyuan Daily*. In particular, some of them were not thoroughly carrying out the mass line:

They still rely solely on a handful of people working coolly and quietly by themselves. One reason is that, whatever they do, they are always reluctant to explain it to the people they lead and they do not understand why or how to give play to the initiative and creative energy of those they lead. Subjectively, they too want everyone to take a hand in the work, but they do not let other people know what is to be done or how to do it. That being the case, how can everyone be expected to get moving and how can anything be done well?' . . .

Our papers talk about the mass line every day, yet frequently the mass line is not carried out in the work of the newspaper office itself. For instance, misprints often crop up in the papers simply because their elimination has not been tackled as a serious job. If we apply the method of the mass line, then, when misprints appear, we should assemble the entire staff of the paper to discuss nothing but this matter, and tell them clearly what the mistakes are, explain why they occur and how they can be got rid of and ask everyone to give the matter serious attention. After this has been done three times, or five times, such mistakes can certainly be overcome.

All the same, Mao wanted his newspapers to retain their punch and thrust.

You must retain the former merits of your paper – it should be sharp, pungent and clear-cut and it should be run conscientiously. We must firmly uphold the truth, and truth requires a clear-cut stand.... Newspapers run by our Party and all the propaganda work of our Party should be vivid, clear-cut and sharp and should never mutter and mumble.... A blunt knife draws no blood.

At the end of May Mao arrived in Hsipaipao, which was to remain his headquarters for the next ten months, until his triumphal 200-mile ride into Peking the following March.

Mao had some difficulty imposing his pattern on distant battlefields. One of his colleagues went into his office late in 1948 to find him angry. Asked what was the matter, Mao replied: 'Lin Piao won't obey orders! I have already ordered him several times to take Changchun by storm, but he won't obey! He wants to starve them out, to force the garrison to capitulate.'

A few days later the same colleague found Mao again angry, because General Lin had ignored Mao's order to send an ultimatum to one of the leading Kuomintang generals calling on him to surrender immediately or else face annihilation. Lin believed that the general might defect, but never surrender.

Mao had a long argument with Wang Ming around this time in which he apparently wrung his hands, metaphorically speaking, about the way in which the Party under his own leadership had committed itself to a line hostile to the Russian-backed comrades. He even blamed some of the mistakes in political line on Liu Shao-chi. At the same time he berated Wang for not wanting China to have its own '-ism' to set alongside Leninism.

'You still want to raise Russian Marxism', he said, 'to a governing position in the Chinese Party....'

Eventually Wang's wife came in and said, 'I've been looking for you all over, and it turns out that you two are arguing again. Better come home for supper.'

Chiang Ching, who had been sitting in the corner listening to the argument, agreed: 'How marvellous that you've come.... These two old cockerels are impossible; they no sooner meet than they start to fight; and when the fight starts, you can never see an end to it. Get hold of yours and take him for his supper, and I'll get hold of mine and take him for his supper, so they can't fight any more.'

The Communists now controlled the whole of north China

above the River Yangtze, and it remained to prepare the campaign for taking over the southern half of China. Mao devoted his New Year message for 1949 to this theme. He attacked the faint-hearted: 'If the revolution is abandoned halfway, it will mean going against the will of the people, bowing to the will of the foreign aggressors and Chinese reactionaries and giving the Kuomintang a chance to heal its wounds, so that one day it may pounce suddenly to strangle the revolution and again plunge the whole country into darkness.'

Yet Stalin had argued precisely in that way, wanting Mao to have a People's Republic north of the Yangtze, and let south China go its own way. He may have feared the consequences of a Chinese Communist regime unsympathetic to Russia and controlling the resources of the entire Chinese nation. He may have been right, though, for the wrong reason; Mao now went on to sweep into south China to absorb populations and territory not in the least prepared for Communism, whose social and political indigestibility was to be one of his main problems afterwards. Some people would say that he took on too much.

Liu Shao-chi would certainly have preferred the slow option. If the revolutionary situation were to develop too fast, he said at the end of 1948, 'we will have many difficulties. It is better if it goes a bit slower so that we can make thorough preparations.'

When Chiang Kai-shek rebuffed Mao's peace terms, Mao made his own call to the millions of Chinese living south of the Yangtze River:

All you broad masses of the people of the Yangtse valley and the South – workers, peasants, intellectuals, urban petty bourgeoisie, national bourgeoisie, enlightened gentry and Kuomintang members with a conscience – your attention please! The days of the Kuomintang die-hards who have been riding roughshod over you are numbered. You and we are on the same side. The handful of die-hards will soon topple from their pinnacle, and the people's China will soon emerge.

As the glint of final victory grew brighter on the horizon, Mao began to come to terms with the fact that he, his soldiers and his Party would increasingly have to act in the cities, so different from the rural areas in which they had gained their entire experience. He dwelt on the various aspects of this in a report to the Central Committee in Hsipaipao on 5 March 1949.

From 1927 to the present the centre of gravity of our work has been in the villages ... using the villages in order to surround the cities and then taking the cities. The period for this method of work has now ended. The period for the city to lead the village has now begun. . . . In the South the People's Liberation Army will occupy first the cities and then the villages. . . . Under no circumstances should the village be ignored and only the city given attention; such thinking is entirely wrong. Nevertheless, the centre of gravity of the work of the Party and Army must be in the city; we must do our utmost to learn how to administer and build the cities. . . .

It was in this address that Mao spelt out his national economic policy for a Communist-ruled China. 'China already has a modern industry constituting about 10 per cent of her economy; this is progressive . . .' But China also had 'scattered and individual agriculture and handicrafts, constituting about 90 per cent of her entire economy; this is backward . . . not very different from ancient times. . . . There will be need, for a fairly long period after the victory of the revolution, to make use of the positive qualities of urban and rural private capitalism as far as possible, in the interests of developing the national economy.'

During this initial period capitalist elements which were not harmful would be allowed to exist and even expand. But capitalism would be restricted and curbed by government regulation, by tax policy and by the fixing of market prices and labour conditions.

As for the scattered, individual agriculture which accounted for almost 90 per cent of the national economy, this would have to be 'led prudently, step by step and yet actively to develop towards modernization and collectivization. . . . It is necessary to organize producers', consumers' and credit co-operatives. . . .'

This speech ended with a ringing call for pride:

Very soon we shall be victorious throughout the country. This victory will breach the eastern front of imperialism and will have great international significance. To win this victory will not require much more time and effort, but to consolidate it will. The bourgeoisie doubts our ability to construct. The imperialists reckon that eventually we will beg alms from them in order to live. With victory, certain moods may grow within the Party – arrogance, the airs of a self-styled hero, inertia and unwillingness to make progress, love of pleasure and distaste for continued hard living. With victory, the people will be grateful to us and the bourgeoisie will come forward to flatter us.

It has been proved that the enemy cannot conquer us by force of arms. However, the flattery of the bourgeoisie may conquer the weak-willed in our ranks. There may be some Communists, who were not conquered by enemies with guns and were worthy of the name of heroes for standing up to these enemies, but who cannot withstand sugar-coated bullets; they will be defeated by sugar-coated bullets. . . .

We can learn what we did not know. We are not only good at destroying the old world, we are also good at building the new. Not only can the Chinese people live without begging alms from the imperialist, they will live a better life than that in the imperialist countries.

According to Wang Ming, there was also an exchange at this Central Committee meeting in Hsipaipao about the leadership. Wang had accused Mao of plotting through the rectification campaign to become leader of the Party – to which Mao, according to Wang, made a good reply:

'I say that it was not a secret plot, but an "open" plot. I said openly at the time that I wanted to replace Wang Ming and take over his position, and I wrote the "Resolution on Certain Questions in the History of Our Party": in the future I will write more history. How can you call that a secret plot?'

'What "place" of mine did you want to take?' Wang said. 'After all, I was not General Secretary.'

'Po Ku and Lo Fu', Mao answered, 'were only nominally General Secretary. After the Fourth Plenum of the Sixth Central Committee' (in 1931) 'the main commander in the Party in reality was Wang Ming.'

Peking was now captured, and the Communists were ready to move their government apparatus into this historic city. 'When I was young and read novels,' Mao joked to Wang Ming, 'I often thought: how unusual and marvellous to be an emperor! But I didn't know how to become an emperor. Now I understand. Soon we will enter Peking. And as soon as we enter Peking I'll be an emperor, won't I?'

The next big prize in the Red offensive was the city of Nanking, prompting Mao to a poem on the significance of the military victory that was unfolding.

Over Chungshan swept a storm, headlong,
Our mighty army, a million strong, has crossed the Great River.
The City, a tiger crouching, a dragon curling, outshines its ancient
glories;
In heroic triumph heaven and earth have been over-turned.
With power and to spare we must pursue the tottering foe
And not ape Hsiang Yu the conqueror seeking idle fame.
Were Nature sentient, she too would pass from youth to age,
But Man's world is mutable, seas become mulberry fields.

Mao took up residence in Peking where previous rulers of China had reigned, behind the red walls of the Forbidden City. He chose a modest but exquisite bungalow among pine trees in the Chungnanhai (South Lake Park) area of the Forbidden City, surrounded by a moat. There were two separate but connected suites for himself and Chiang Ching, marked off by intricately carved and painted pillars in the Ming style. Mao and Chiang Ching were also given a small villa in the Western Hills outside Peking near the Jade Fountain Pagoda.

As at Yenan, Mao had a little garden in Chungnanhai, where he and Chiang Ching grew jasmine, herbs and vegetables. 'I have managed also', she said later, 'to raise a plot of rice . . .' and a cotton patch.

Within days of her arrival in Peking, however, Mao's wife was packed off to Moscow for medical treatment. She was, in her own words, 'all skin and bones, reduced to 90 pounds'. The rigours of the two-year march from Yenan had defeated her, just as the strains of the Long March fifteen years earlier had defeated her predecessor, Mao's second wife.

In Moscow Russian surgeons took Chiang Ching's tonsils out and sent her to Yalta, the sunny Black Sea holiday resort, to put on weight. When she returned to Moscow, Stalin invited her to call, under the apparent misconception that Mao had entrusted her with a message. In fact, Mao did not leave Peking to pay tribute at Stalin's court until after Chiang Ching had returned to China in the autumn.

His wife's recollection of her early days with Mao in Peking was that most of their time was spent in reading, studying current affairs and writing. They rarely went out together, and almost never did they go out to dinner in a restaurant just for the fun of it. Chiang Ching described Mao as 'not very careful about what he ate'. He was a fast eater, and was usually full by the time the last course arrived. By then he had usually forgotten about it anyway.

It reminded Chiang Ching of the Sung statesman who always used to eat the dishes nearest to him, ignoring the others on the table. The cook thought that it was the particular dish he liked, and was disillusioned to learn from his wife that he merely ate indiscriminately from whichever dish was nearest to hand.

'That's all you know about history,' Mao chuckled to Chiang Ching when she mentioned this story, 'and you tease me about it!'

Mao did not often speak about his own standard of living, but he did confess to his Central Committee comrades in the early 1960s, 'It is primarily people like us who have cars, houses and steam heat, and chauffeurs. I have only 430 *yuan*. I can't afford to hire secretaries, but I must.' His monthly salary was sometimes quoted during the 1950s at 600 *yuan*, the equivalent of £90, and at the beginning of 1970 he was said to have taken a 20 per cent cut in his salary. But he was also said to have become wealthy, by Chinese Communist standards, from the royalties on his books.

His bodyguards mourned after his death: 'The house you lived in was old, but you declined all offers to have it repaired.... Your shirts, blankets and shoes were worn thin from many years of use. We suggested many times that they be changed, but you would not allow it.' The quilt which he had used since 1942 lasted until 1962 and was then lodged in a museum. The pair of leather lace-up shoes which Mao began to wear when he first entered Peking were still available for exhibit after his death almost thirty years later, along with his bathrobe conspicuously patched at the elbow.

These men in the Army Unit 8341, whose responsibility it was to look after Mao, came eventually to play a controversial political role. They painted Mao as a model employer:

You often came to our dormitories to see us, enquired about our families and asked how things were with us. You wanted to know whether we had received letters from home and if all was well there.... You sent us tickets for model revolutionary operas. In summer you asked whether we were troubled by mosquitoes and ordered our rooms to be sprayed. In winter, you stroked our hands to see if we were cold, and you came often to our kitchen to check on our food....

Mao's working hours were unusual. He would rise at eleven in the morning, take lunch at three and dinner at half-past seven, but would not retire to bed until five in the morning. When there was a crisis, or a particularly demanding piece of work, he used to work 'for several days and nights on end...,' his guards remembered, 'forgetting to go to bed or eat his meals. Sometimes his food became cold and had to be re-heated again and again.' His diet was claimed to be simple, 'including coarse grains and portulaca and other wild vegetables'.

In his early years as Chairman in Peking Mao was reputed to smoke about fifty cigarettes a day, preferring the British brand of State Express 555 – though by the early 1960s he was rumoured to have cut down to twenty a day, and to be smoking Chinese brands. It was said that smoking exacerbated his coughing, which in turn inhibited his public speaking in later life. He was seen in the late 1960s holding a small cigar instead of his usual cigarette, possibly for health reasons.

One of Mao's relaxations was a regular, though unadvertised excursion to his favourite barber's shop on the street leading to the Drum Tower. Here he liked to reminisce and gossip with his old cronies. At home he would usually play table-tennis every evening. It was said that he seldom missed the ball, made fast and powerful returns and 'often wins the game'.

He loved walking in the snow, 'kicking the snow with great joy, as if nothing were more pleasant'. One of his guards confessed: 'We know the Chairman's weakness for snow, and every time it snows we make a point of not sweeping it away in the courtyard.' Mao went on to the end sleeping on a springless wooden bed, of the kind to which he was accustomed.

Mao's family situation had by this time become somewhat complicated, and must have been occasionally distressing – to the extent that Mao ever allowed his emotions to be played upon his relatives. During the initial months in Peking his wife was away in Russia having treatment, while his former wife, Ho Tzu-chen, flew back from Russia uncured and was installed in a mental institution in Shanghai. Their daughter Li Min, who came back from Russia with her mother, was re-united with her father in the Forbidden City and began to be brought up by Chiang Ching as a stepdaughter, along with her own daughter by Mao, Li Na.

The atmosphere was supposed to be emancipated, but was in fact difficult. 'Our children', Chiang Ching later recalled, 'are allowed to talk back to their father; sometimes we even make them talk back on purpose!'

Mao's two sons by his first wife, An-ying and An-ching, were also back in China. Russian friends observed the latter in Harbin soon after 1949, living in the style to which he had become accustomed in Russia, and which Chinese comrades doubtless found affected and extravagant: there was a report that he went back to Russia in 1950 for further psychiatric treatment.

One gets an impression of these two young men as disoriented drifters who could not find a suitable role to play in their father's new China. Mao probably despised them for having become so Russified, forgetting that the reasons for their going to Russia were partly of his own making. He evidently felt that the boys should make their own way in the world, and that for them to rely on his help would be to ruin their possibilities of development. He did have at home his two daughters, one a teenager and the other about to become one; rumour had it that they both yearned to be ballet dancers.

In August Changsha was liberated, and the family of Mao's first wife, Yang Kai-hui, was able to cable him through the Red Army radio station. Mao sent a reply on 8 August about Yang's two boys: 'An-ying and An-ching are in Peking. An-ching is attending school. Maybe An-ying can go back to work in Hunan. They all want to see grandmother very much.' Mao also broke it to the family, which had been cut off from the north for so many years, that his and Yang's daughter, Yang Chan, had 'died a glorious death for the country eight years ago in the war of resistance against Japan in north-east China.'

It was perhaps with thoughts of his family that Mao wrote another poem in April, replying to a verse from his old scholar friend Liu Ya-tzu, which had hailed him as 'the maker of a new epoch'. Mao's reply suggested the personal grief which he was suppressing in the context of his political triumph:

> I still remember our drinking tea in Kwangchow
> And your asking for verses in Chungking as the leaves yellowed.
> Back in the old capital after thirty-one years,
> At the season of falling flowers I read your polished lines.
> Beware of heartbreak with grievance overfull,
> Range far your eye over long vistas.
> Do you say the waters of Kunming Lake are too shallow?
> For watching fish they are better than Fuchun River.

At the end of June Mao replied to a number of his critics. He began with a discussion of aims: 'For the working class, the labouring people and the Communist Party the question is ... one of ... working hard to create the conditions in which classes, state power and political parties will die out very naturally and mankind will enter the realm of great Harmony.'

This was the goal set by the nineteenth-century Chinese thinker Kang Yu-wei, in his famous work *Ta Tung Shu*, or the *Book of Great Harmony*. In this way did Mao carefully root Communist objectives in the indigenous Chinese intellectual tradition rather than in an imported Western ideology, hoping to reassure the non-Marxists who represented the majority of thinking people in China.

He then listed what his critics complained of, one by one. 'You are leaning to one side,' they said. 'Exactly.... All Chinese without exception must lean either to the side of imperialism or to the side of socialism. Sitting on the fence will not do, nor is there a third road. . .'

'You are dictatorial.' To which Mao replied: 'My dear sirs,

you are right, that is just what we are. All the experience the Chinese people have accumulated through several decades teaches us to enforce the people's democratic dictatorship, that is, to deprive the reactionaries of the right to speak and let the people alone have that right.'

'Don't you want to abolish state power?' Yes, was the answer to this, but not now.

The state apparatus, including the army, the police and the court, is the instrument by which one class oppresses another.... The people's state protects the people. Only when the people have such a state can they educate and remould themselves on a country-wide scale by democratic methods and, with everyone taking part, shake off the influence of domestic and foreign reactionaries (which is still very strong, will survive for a long time and cannot be quickly destroyed), rid themselves of the bad habits and ideas acquired in the old society, not allow themselves to be led astray by the reactionaries, and continue to advance ... towards a socialist and communist society.

Mao concluded this heartfelt talk, entitled 'On the People's Democratic Dictatorship', with a word on the alteration of the challenge which the Party faced. The fighting was behind it, the unknown work of construction lay ahead.

We shall soon put aside some of the things we know well and be compelled to do things we don't know well.... We must learn to do economic work from all who know how, no matter who they are. We must esteem them as teachers, learning from them respectfully and conscientiously.... If we dig into a subject for several months, for a year or two, for three or five years, we shall eventually master it.

In August Mao's scorn was particularly aroused by the American *White Paper* on US relations with China, which wrote off China to Communism with regret and called the outcome of the civil war 'ominous'. In the final weeks before the proclamation of the People's Republic, Mao shouted his angry contempt for the Americans. In a newspaper commentary on 18 August, he wrote:

The Americans have sprinkled some relief flour in Peking, Tientsin and Shanghai to see who will stoop to pick it up ..., they have cast the line for the fish who want to be caught. But he who swallows food handed out in contempt will get a bellyache. We Chinese have backbone.... What matter if we have to face some difficulties? Let them blockade us! Let them blockade us for eight or ten years! By that time all of China's problems will have been solved.

On the *White Paper's* gloomy predictions for China, Mao's comment was:

Of all things in the world, people are the most precious. As long as there are people, every kind of miracle can be performed under the leadership of the Communist Party. . . . We believe that revolution can change everything, and that before long there will arise a new China with a big population and a great wealth of products, where life will be abundant and culture will flourish. All pessimistic views are utterly groundless. . . .

In September Mao convened the Chinese People's Political Consultative Conference in Peking, and in his opening address he declared to the outside world:

Our work will go down in the history of mankind, demonstrating that the Chinese people, comprising one quarter of humanity, have now stood up. The Chinese have always been a great, courageous and industrious nation; it is only in modern times that they have fallen behind. . . . From now on our nation will belong to the community of the peace-loving and the freedom-loving nations of the world and work courageously and industriously to foster its own civilization and well-being and at the same time to promote world peace and freedom.

Ours will no longer be a nation subject to insult and humiliation. We have stood up. Our revolution has won the sympathy and acclaim of the peoples of all countries. We have friends all over the world. . . . The era in which the Chinese people were regarded as uncivilized is now ended. We shall emerge in the world as a nation with an advanced culture.

On 30 September the Conference elected Mao Chairman of the government of the People's Republic of China. Just before the election some of the non-Communist delegates asked him about it in the corridor.

'Anyone', Mao mischievously explained to them, 'has the freedom to vote for anyone whose name is printed on the ballot, but of course he mustn't cross out all the names on it and write in the name of Hsi-men Chin.' Hsi-men Chin is a character in the erotic novel *Ching Ping Mei*, the Chinese *Decameron*, to whose sexual debauchery Mao was fond of referring.

That day he read, in his thick southern accent, an epitaph to the martyrs of the civil war – including his own wife, brothers and sister – and what he said was recorded for the radio, one of the few such instances.

On 1 October 1949 Mao ceremonially proclaimed the foundation of the People's Republic of China from Tienanmen, the Gate

of Heavenly Peace. Canton and Chungking were still not liberated, but the Generalissimo had fled to Taiwan and there was no
doubt of the issue in the civil war. Mao, at the age of fifty-five –
an age considered in some modern societies as suitable for
retirement – had indeed become a people's emperor.

PART THREE
POWER

17
MEAT FROM THE
TIGER'S MOUTH

Mao's first challenge as head of the Chinese People's Republic
was the need to make things up with Stalin. This was an
extremely awkward duty for him, since he had arrived in his
pre-eminent position largely on the platform of not following the
Russian model. But now, as the first Communist ruler of China,
he had to go to Moscow to make his peace with the acknowledged head of the international Communist movement. He no
doubt hoped that Stalin would agree to open a new chapter and
forget the past, building on the significance to them both of the
world's largest nation's joining the Communist ranks.

Mao knew full well the doubts which Stalin had about him.
After the victory of the Chinese Communists, Stalin 'suspected
China of being another Yugoslavia', Mao recalled thirteen years
later, 'and that I would become a second Tito.'

By the time he was ready, in December, to go to Moscow for
the first time and meet Stalin, he was also aware that one of his
colleagues had preceded him and was apparently, with Russian
support, consolidating his hold on the strategic region of Manchuria. This was Kao Kang, the man who had received Mao in
Shensi at the end of the Long March and enabled him to survive
the ordeal.

During the final phase of the civil war, between 1946 and
1949, Kao had built up his position as leader in Manchuria with
its crucial control of China's railway link to the Soviet Union,
and its heavy industries which were vital to the Chinese Communists. He was thinking of himself as an alternative leader to
Mao, saying, according to later allegations: 'I am an international Communist whereas Mao Tse-tung and his group are
native Communists of Chingkangshan.' Kao did not overtly seek
Mao's position as Chairman of the Party, but was angling for
Liu Shao-chi's position as Secretary-General and Chou En-lai's
post as Premier. All this was supposedly with Russian support.

Mao said later that 'Stalin was very fond of Kao Kang and made him a special present of a motor car.' Khrushchev remembered how much of the information which the Kremlin received about the mood of the leaders in Peking came from Kao Kang, 'Governor in Manchuria, where he'd been on close terms with our own representatives.'

In July 1949, only weeks before Mao proclaimed the People's Republic in Peking, Kao had led an independent trade mission to Moscow as 'the representative of the North-east People's Democratic Government in China', signing a trade agreement with Stalin over Mao's head.

According to a version of a report made by Chen Yi later, Kao 'invited experts from the Soviet Union and sent students there by simply requesting *ex post facto* approval of the Central government'. Kao's Manchuria even had its own separate currency until 1952.

Mao therefore went to Moscow on 16 December 1949 with some misgivings about the role of his former friend and saviour, and he must have been surprised when Stalin took Mao into his confidence. 'Stalin', Khrushchev recalled later, 'decided he wanted to win Mao's trust and friendship so he took the Russian Ambassador's reports about his conversation with Kao Kang, and handed them over to Mao, saying, "Here, you might be interested in these." God only knows what Stalin thought he was doing.' Khrushchev then offered his own explanation:

Why did Stalin betray Kao Kang? I think he was motivated by his own suspiciousness. He figured that sooner or later Mao would have learned on his own that Kao Kang had been informing on him – and, if that had happened, Mao could have accused Stalin of fomenting opposition to the Chinese government. So Stalin decided it would be better to sacrifice Kao Kang and thereby earn Mao's trust. However, I don't think Mao ever really trusted Stalin.

Khrushchev was right. Mao had no reason before his visit to suppose that Stalin had good intentions towards him, and the outcome of his negotiations left in his heart a deep-rooted mistrust. For this reason, the presence and activities of Kao in Manchuria must have become increasingly intolerable. But Mao would have to wait until Stalin's death before he could deal with this dangerous rival.

There is a strange reticence on both sides about Mao's nine-week stay in Moscow, with a two-day interlude in Leningrad. He turned up at the party for Stalin's seventieth birthday, and was entertained to dinner several times by the Russian leader. But they found it difficult to engage with one another.

According to Khrushchev, Stalin had been extremely worried about China's new ruler. 'What kind of man is this Mao Tse-tung?' he had asked his colleagues beforehand. 'I don't know anything about him. He's never been to the Soviet Union.'

Stalin suspected that Mao had the outlook of a narrow peasant, that he was afraid of urban workers and was building his Red Army on an isolated basis, taking no account of the working class. He felt confirmed in these beliefs by the way Mao had held back from taking Shanghai after the Kuomintang could no longer defend it. This was one of the first things Stalin put to Mao.

'Why didn't you seize Shanghai?' he asked.

'Why should we have?' Mao replied. 'If we'd captured the city we would have had to take on the responsibility for feeding the six million inhabitants.'

This answer only strengthened Stalin's suspicions: rather than enter Shanghai and enlist the support of the proletariat there, Mao had worried lest the job of providing food for the city would detract from his struggle against Chiang in the rest of the country.

'What kind of a man is Mao anyway?' Stalin said to his colleagues when recounting this conversation afterwards. 'He calls himself a Marxist, but he doesn't understand the most elementary Marxist truths. Or maybe he doesn't want to understand them.'

Once the preliminary calls had been made, the steam went out of the negotiations. Stalin would sometimes not see Mao for days at a stretch, and, as Khrushchev put it, 'since Stalin neither saw Mao nor ordered anyone else to entertain him, no one dared to go and see him.' Rumours spread that Mao was unhappy, that he felt confined and ignored, and that if this treatment continued, he would leave. Whereupon, Stalin would throw another dinner for him, to keep him stringing along. Some Russians attributed the length of Mao's stay to the fact that he was often ill in Moscow, turning pale and being unable to speak at meetings.

Stalin, for his part, aggravated Mao's fears by asking for concessions in China very similar to those which China had been forced to give to Westerners in the past. He proposed a joint-stock company, for example, for exploiting natural resources in Sinkiang, and he also asked Mao for territory to set up a rubber plantation – both ideas being highly reminiscent of capitalist European imperialism in the bad old days.

The memory of those sessions with Stalin remained vivid in Mao's mind. Eight years later, he told his comrades at home:

I argued with Stalin in Moscow for two months. On the questions of the Treaty of Mutual Assistance, the Chinese Eastern Railway, the joint-stock companies and the border, we adopted two attitudes: one was to argue when the other side made proposals we did not agree with, and the other was to accept their proposal if they absolutely insisted. This was out of consideration for the interests of socialism. Then there were the two 'colonies', that is the North-east and Sinkiang, where people of any third country were not allowed to reside. . . .'

'We wanted', Mao recollected in another conversation in 1957, 'to sign a Sino-Soviet Treaty of Amity, but he didn't want it. We asked for the return of the Chinese Eastern Railway but he was reluctant to give it up. However, there is still a way to get a piece of meat from the mouth of a tiger.'

After a fruitless month in the bitter winter cold of the Russian capital, Mao summoned Chou En-lai from Peking to salvage the negotiations. The myth that the two supremos could settle their problems face to face was shattered, and Mao's prestige in China fell as a result. Three weeks later, on 14 February 1950 (St Valentine's Day), a Treaty of Friendship, Alliance and Mutual Assistance was ceremonially signed, along with an agreement for only $300 million of Russian credits for China over five years, and other economic pacts. It was clear to everybody that Stalin had been notably ungenerous, by the yardstick either of what he was doing for the East European countries or of what the Americans were doing for their allies in Asia.

There was also a discussion about events which were soon to take place in Korea, the significance of which Mao evidently failed to appreciate at the time. Stalin asked him about the plan of Kim Il-sung, the North Korean leader, to invade South Korea.

'Mao . . . approved Kim Il-sung's suggestion,' Khrushchev reported, 'and put forward the opinion that the USA would not intervene, since the war would be an internal matter which the Korean people would decide for themselves.'

A few days later Mao travelled back through Siberia and the Chinese north-east to Peking, where he made a tight-lipped speech about the 'eternal and indestructible' friendship between the two countries. Pictures of the 'Great Meeting' of Stalin and

Mao began to appear all over China, and a new song began to go round praising them in extravagant terms: 'Mao Tse-tung! Stalin! They are shining as bright as the sun in the sky!' But the inner circle in Peking knew that Mao had been rebuffed.

To the extent that Mao had stood up for Chinese pride and self-respect in his dealings with Stalin, his Chinese comrades no doubt admired his performance. But to the extent that he failed to come back with the goods needed for China's economic development, in a situation where Russia had the technological know-how and finance to offer which China would take decades to build up on her own, they must have been bitterly disappointed.

His minimal reconciliation with Stalin achieved, Mao settled down to the domestic problem of applying the Yenan formula to a heterogeneous country of 600 million people. As Chiang Ching bluntly put it, 'Now that the people have given us high positions, good pay and great authority, if we fail to make new contributions could the people want us for long?'

In February and March, after his return from Russia, Mao went on a tour of the urban and industrial North-east, going to factories and enterprises in such cities as Harbin, Changchun and Shenyang. The local officials tried to make him comfortable and provide good food, but Mao discouraged any special arrangements. Seeing a spring bed in his room in one city, he told his bodyguard: 'We are not used to such a bed. You'd better use our own.' The spring bed was taken away, and Mao's simple bedding was laid out on a wooden board.

'It is good', Mao observed at the Harbin railway works, 'that you have many veteran workers. We don't have the knowledge and should rely on the veteran workers in running the factory.'

To one of the men in charge he said: 'Do you know how to manage a factory?'

'No,' the official replied, 'I don't. I was transferred to the factory only recently.'

'If you don't know,' Mao commented, 'you should learn. None of us knows, and we should all learn.'

The problem of land reform in the south was particularly difficult, and early in 1950 Mao circularized Party leaders in the southern provinces suggesting that they slow down the redistribution of land. It would have to be on an extremely large scale, which would invite excessive zeal on the part of the Party officials. It would not have the wartime background which had enabled people in the north to see it in perspective, and so the

shock to society would be all the more severe. Finally, it would
upset the national bourgeoisie with whom the Party was trying
to collaborate. Mao therefore urged that the rich peasants in
south China should not be touched for the time being in spite of
the Communist victory.

'The view held by certain people', he declared in June, 'that it
is possible to eliminate capitalism and realize socialism at an
early date is wrong, it does not tally with our national condition.'
The Party had already done wonders, but what the Communists
should now avoid was impulsiveness. 'It is undesirable to hit out
in all directions and cause nationwide tensions. We must
definitely not make too many enemies, we must make concessions and relax the tension a little in some quarters. . . .'

The intellectuals should be persuaded to study materialism in
order to shed their idealism. 'Let them say that man was created
by God, we say man evolved from the ape.'

During this unsettling interlude came a poem on the first
anniversary of the Communist victory, composed during the
dances performed in the centre of Peking for the occasion:

> The night was long and dawn came slow to the Crimson Land.
> For a century demons and monsters whirled in a wild dance,
> And the five hundred million people were disunited.

> Now the cock has crowed and all under heaven is bright,
> Here is music from all our peoples, from Yutien too,
> And the poet is inspired as never before.

But tragedy was to strike from an unexpected quarter, tragedy
both for China and for Mao himself. At the end of June Kim
Il-sung marched across the Korean demarcation line, and the
Korean war broke out. President Truman responded on the
assumption that the war had been planned with the support of
both Russia and China. The Chinese themselves knew that
Mao's visit in Moscow had been a not very successful begging
mission, but for Western statesmen in Washington and London
it had looked more like a journey of submission to Russian control, and the Korean thrust was seen as the first move in a
campaign to spread the Communist writ further across parts of
Asia.

Mao had been wrong. The Americans – and not only the
Americans – did intervene to support the South Korean regime,
and by October the United Nations' forces under General
MacArthur had crossed the Yalu River and looked like heading
for the Chinese frontier. On the day after the crossing, overcom-

ing his own strong misgivings about provoking the Americans, Mao issued an order to the Red Army: 'I hereby order the Chinese People's Volunteers to march speedily to Korea and join the Korean comrades in fighting the aggressors and winning a glorious victory.'

During the early weeks of the Chinese military involvement in Korea Mao arranged for the speedy departure of Wang Ming, his old pro-Russian rival, by train to Moscow. Wang, paranoid to the end, alleged that this was a plot to have him die in an American air attack on the railway between China and Russia. He had already complained about being given, by Mao's direction, lysol instead of medicinal soap to wash out his bowels in one of the Chinese Communist hospitals. But he was to reach Russia safely, to live there for many years, writing his memoirs and cataloguing Mao's alleged misdeeds.

One of the officers to go with the Volunteers to Korea was Mao's eldest son, An-ying. After completing his period of farmwork this young man had first been assigned to translation duties in Peking, and then gone on to do military training. He was said to have commanded a division in Korea, although this sounds unlikely. He was only thirty at this time.

In November 1950, either in an American air raid or in the crash of a Chinese aircraft, An-ying was killed. The news as received by Mao was, in Chiang Ching's understated comment, 'deeply unsettling' to their personal lives. It was later said that during the campaign in which An-ying had become a casualty, General Peng Teh-huai had disregarded Mao's orders, with the inference that, but for Peng, the young man might have survived.

After the war was over, Kim Il-sung used to send a wreath every year to be laid at An-ying's grave in the Chinese cemetery in Hoechang, for his remains were, 'at the request of the Korean people', in one account, never brought back to his homeland.

The Korean War interrupted Mao's plans for developing the Chinese economy and introducing socialism. It also provided an incentive for the Kuomintang, still alive and kicking in Taiwan, to redouble, this time with full-scale American support, its efforts to sabotage and subvert the mainland which it had so recently vacated. In 1951 much of Mao's time and energy was spent in directing campaigns against counter-revolutionaries and other delinquents and miscreants. The so-called Three-Antis campaign (against corruption, waste and bureaucracy), followed by the Five-Antis (against bribery, tax evasion, fraud, theft of government property and theft of state economic secrets), together with a campaign for thought reform among recalcitrant intellectuals, were all inaugurated at this time.

It was these campaigns, along with the land reform, which provoked so much bloodshed. Only the minority, Mao instructed in May, roughly between 10 and 20 per cent, of counter-revolutionaries who had committed extremely serious crimes should be executed. They should include those who 'owed blood debts or who have committed other major crimes which have provoked public indignation such as frequent rape or the plundering of large amounts of property, or who have done extremely serious harm to the national interest.'

The others, even if they had committed capital offences, should be given lighter forms of punishment. 'If we have such people executed, it will not be easily understood by the masses, nor will the response from public figures be so favourable; at the same time it will deprive us of a large pool of labour-power and will not serve to split the enemy ranks; besides we may make mistakes on this question.'

Meanwhile Mao's wife was edging her way into his political life. In mid-1950, with the help of Chou En-lai, she was given a seat on the Film Steering Committee of the Ministry of Culture, and a few months later she found an issue on which she could prove herself to Mao as standard-bearer of his ideas. The occasion was the release of a film called *The Life of Wu Hsun*, a famous nineteenth-century beggar who had saved and invested some money in order to set up schools to educate the poor. The film glorified him, so Chiang Ching complained that it was encouraging people to be timid do-gooders rather than thoroughgoing radical revolutionaries. The Communist officials in charge of cultural affairs, notably her old enemy from Shanghai days, Chou Yang, now the Vice-Minister for Culture, took no notice of her. Even Mao showed little interest, and after a long argument she walked out on him.

For several days she failed to put in an appearance in his suite, and Mao eventually went to her study where she was engrossed in her research, offering the grumpy comment: 'So you're still up to this.'

She told Mao that she wanted to go to Wu Hsun's home district in Shantung to get more data. Mao objected, but Chiang Ching went there in spite of him, using a pseudonym, and came back triumphantly with material showing that Wu Hsun had in fact become a landlord and a supporter of the landlord class. Mao was at last convinced, and helped her to write some of her reports. He himself wrote in the *People's Daily*:

Certain Communists who have allegedly grasped Marxism merit special attention. They have studied the history of social development – historical materialism – but when it comes to specific historical events, specific historical figures (like Wu Hsun) and specific ideas which run counter to the trend of history (as in the film *The Life of Wu Hsun* and the writings about Wu Hsun), they lose their critical faculties. . . . Where on earth is the Marxism which certain Communists claim to have grasped?

Later in 1951 Chiang Ching went incognito into central China to help in the land reform, and Mao sent on her greatcoat at her request when the cold weather set in. But he also agreed with his colleagues that she should resign her offices, as chief of his secretariat and also director of the cinema department – because, it was said, of her ill health.

Many of Mao's comrades were not impressed by Chiang Ching's qualifications for political or even cultural responsibility. Khrushchev correctly captured this sentiment when he ungenerously wrote that, 'some people say she was once a talented actress, while others say her only talent was in serving as a nice mattress for Mao to sleep on'.

At the end of 1952, complaining of liver pains, she set off for her second visit to Russia for medical treatment. The Russian surgeons operated to explore her liver, but were not able to pinpoint the trouble. Instead she was sent once more to Yalta where she had a massive course of penicillin. Only in the autumn of 1953 was she allowed to return to China, still not cured.

According to Chiang Ching, one of Stalin's suggestions to Mao was that he should publish his collected works. Certainly, soon after Mao's return from Moscow in 1950, the process began of revising and editing those pieces of writing which he wished to preserve for posterity. There were many reasons for revision. Obviously he wanted to put right the more blatant theoretical mistakes in his earlier compositions. Secondly, some of the ideas which he had expressed before gaining the Party leadership at Tsunyi needed to be substantiated, even though they had been rejected by the Party at the time.

At the same time, Mao did not wish to leave open any grounds for political rivals to attack him as disobedient to the Party before 1935. Finally, it was expedient for Mao in the early 1950s to play down the extent to which the Chinese Party had rejected Stalin's ideological authority.

As a result of all these criteria, the texts were very extensively modified in the course of revision, by way of both additions and deletions, as well as various modifications. A leading Western scholar, Stuart Schram, has concluded that, 'One cannot accept even a single sentence as being identical with what Mao had actually written without checking it against the original version.'

The first volume of *Selected Works of Mao Tse-tung* appeared in October 1951, the second in April 1952 and the third in May 1953. There was then a gap until September 1960, when the fourth volume was published, and the fifth appeared only post-humously.

The purpose of the *Selected Works* was to establish a canon of doctrine unique to China, as Mao had explained to Wang Ming and as he restated in 1960:

It will not do for any country to rely on old things alone at any time. If we had Marx and Engels alone, and not the writings of Lenin, such as his *Two Strategies*, we could not have resolved the new problems which have appeared since 1950. If we had the 1907-published *On Materialism and Empirical Criticism* alone, it would not have sufficed to deal with the new problems which cropped up before and after the October Revolution. To conform with the needs at that time, Lenin wrote *On Imperialism, The State and the Revolution*, etc.

After the death of Lenin, it became necessary for Stalin to write *The Basis of Leninism* and *The Question of Leninism* to cope with reactionaries in defence of Leninism. We wrote *On Practice* and *On Contradiction* during the closing stage of the Second Civil War and the early days of the anti-Japanese war. These were writings we had to turn out in order to meet the needs of that time.

It is in this context that the profusion of Chinese quotations in Mao's writings should be judged. Mao was writing for Chinese, not Western readers. It has been calculated that of all the references in Mao's writings, 22 per cent were to Confucian sources, 12 per cent to Taoist or Mohist works, and 13 per cent to Chinese legends or belles-lettres. Almost half of his quotations, in other words, were familiar to Chinese readers. By contrast, only 4 per cent came from Marx or Engels, 24 per cent from Stalin and 18 per cent from Lenin.

This reflects Mao's own reading. While he was a compulsive reader, he was also a highly selective one. The comment by a Russian visitor to Yenan in the early 1940s that Mao read only antique encyclopedic dictionaries, ancient philosophical treatises and old novels, and was ignorant of Western classics and scornful of all that was not Chinese, was exaggerated – but not com-

Above: With British Labour delegation in Peking

Below: With Khrushchev in Peking, 1958

Iconography

Right: Peking poster

Below: Peng Teh-huai created marshal

Far right: Preparing for Russian visitors

Above: Mao at home

Left: With Red Guard

Opposite above left: Gang of Four effigy hanging 1977

Opposite above right: Lin Piao addressing Red Guards in Peking 1969. (Left to right: Chiang Ching, Chou En-lai, Lin Piao, Mao)

Right: Mao and Nixon, Peking, 1976

Mao in 1933

Mao in 1975

Mao's funeral

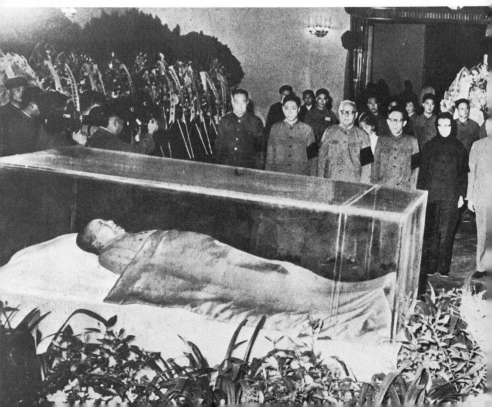

pletely wide of the mark. Mao's own ambivalence about literature was undisguised. 'If one believes everything in books,' he
once told a meeting of comrades, 'it is better not to read books at
all.' He was so fond of saying, 'The more books one reads, the
more stupid one gets', that the line recurs in several places.

How Marxist are the *Selected Works*? One of Mao's pro-Russian
colleagues was highly critical of his philosophical essays. They
included, he declared, serious mistakes in theory (being 'anti-
materialist, subjectivist, idealistic and voluntaristic') as well as
method (being 'anti-dialectical, contradictory to scientific
methodology and sophistical'). As for Mao's *On Dialectical Materialism*, it had so many mistakes and naive arguments that anyone understanding Marxism would, on reading this work, 'laugh
till his teeth fell out'.

Mao conceded publicly that some of his comrades said 'that I
did not have even a modicum of Marxism'. He furthermore
confessed how his Marxism had developed in the field rather
than in the classroom: 'I had all sorts of non-Marxist ideas
before, and it was only later that I embraced Marxism. I learnt a
little Marxism from books and so made an initial remoulding of
my ideas, but it was mainly through taking part in the class
struggle over the years that I came to be remoulded. And I must
continue to learn if I am to make further progress, or otherwise I
shall lag behind.'

There are many characteristic themes which emerge from the
Selected Works, such as the methodological desirability of the middle path – a highly Chinese formulation. Take Mao's advice
about dealing with the Kuomintang at the end of the civil war:
'We should not refuse to enter into negotiations because we are
afraid of trouble and want to avoid complications, nor should we
enter negotiations with our minds in a haze. We should be firm
in principles; we should also have all the flexibility permissible
and necessary for carrying out our principles.'

Another idea which runs through the *Selected Works* is that
instability and imbalance are normal. 'Wind will not cease, even
if trees want rest,' Mao said in one article. 'No need to be afraid
of tidal waves; human society has been evolved out of "tidal
waves".' Mao put the matter unequivocally in the sentence:
'Balance, qualitative change and unity are temporary and relative – while imbalance, sudden change and disunity are absolute
and permanent.'

Then there was the populist streak in Mao's writings. 'We
Communists are like seeds and the people are like the soil.

Wherever we go we must unite with the people, take root and blossom among them.' Hence the need for any Communist leader to maintain contact with the masses and derive nourishment from them. 'The masses are fair-minded, they won't write off our record.'

At the same time Mao's ideas about class were unusual. In a directive on class he once wrote:

It is ... important to distinguish between class background and one's own performance, with emphasis on the latter.... The question is whether you take the stand of your original class or take a changed class stand, that is, taking the side of workers and poor and lower-middle peasants.... If we consider only the background, even Marx, Engels, Lenin and Stalin would be unacceptable.

The Chinese bourgeoisie could thus be admitted to the exclusive club of 'the people', provided they behaved well and changed their thinking. But whether you have changed your mind is, of course, a highly subjective question. And Mao admitted in the end that he had been deceived on this question by many of his closest comrades. 'Peng Chen's essence', he complained of the Mayor of Peking in 1966, 'has been hidden for thirty years.'

Mao could never bring himself to like the intellectuals. In a speech he made in 1968 to the Red Guards, young revolutionaries from universities and factories trained by the army to carry out the Cultural Revolution, he said, 'I think the intellectuals are most uncivilized. I think the unsophisticated soldiers are most civilized.' Yet for all his materialism, there is an overt acceptance, even glorification of the role of the subjective in life. He quoted Confucius, 'What the superior man seeks is in himself.'

Early in the 1960s he wrote: 'We cannot take the view that spontaneity and the *laissez-faire* spirit do not exist in a socialist society.' He strongly believed in the capacity of subjective forces to change objective reality, in the power of voluntarism. He set this out very clearly in a tract of 1938:

When we say we are opposed to the subjective approach to a problem, we mean that we must oppose ideas of individuals not based upon or not corresponding with objective facts.... But everything must be done by man; the protracted war and final victory will not take place without human action. And action presupposes ideas, arguments, opinions, plans, directives, policies, strategies and tactics....

People who direct a war cannot strive for victories beyond the limit allowed by the objective conditions, but within that limit they can and must strive actively for victory. The stage of action for these commanders in a war must be built upon objective conditions, but on this stage, they can direct the performance of many living dramas, full of sound and colour, of power and grandeur. . .

These ideas – and more – were brought together in the *Selected Works* to present a coherent exposition of Maoism, or of Mao Tse-tung's Thought, almost as scholars in the distant past had collated the teachings of Confucius and other sages. Mao Tse-tung Thought was described as 'a precious ideological asset' and an 'inexhaustible theoretical treasure-house'. A little verse was put about:

> Chairman Mao's works are a fine treasure-chest,
> To be drawn upon always and always for the best,
> One word is worth gold piled as high as your head,
> Once learnt, then your heart and mind are dyed red.

Mao himself was sometimes modest about his intellectual achievements. 'The *Selected Works of Mao Tse-tung*, how much of it is mine? It is a work of blood. . . . These things in *Selected Works of Mao* were taught to us by the masses and paid for with blood sacrifices.'

Besides circulating to almost every Party member and beyond in China, the *Selected Works* were translated into dozens of languages and distributed throughout the world. They made their appeal at various levels. They caused *The Times* in an editorial for his seventieth birthday to call Mao 'China's Philosopher King', and yet one of his young African visitors once told him, 'Your works are much easier to understand than those of Marx, Engels and Lenin. . . . Your works are very readable.' There was an element of common sense and Victorian self-help moralizing of the Samuel Smiles brand in Mao's works, along with the philosophical discussions and advice on waging revolution, which enhanced their popularity.

18
WIELDING THE WHIP

So far no foreign leaders had come to Peking to make a state visit and pay respects to the new government. Tsedenbal, the Party leader of the Mongolian People's Republic, was the first to do so, in September 1952 – three years after Mao had proclaimed his own Republic. What is surprising is the failure of the Russians to make this gesture. It was perhaps too much to expect in the closing years of Stalin's life. The old Russian dictator died in March 1953, and Mao wrote a surprisingly fulsome obituary: 'Everyone knows that Comrade Stalin had an ardent love for the Chinese people and believed the might of the Chinese revolution to be immeasurable. To the problems of the Chinese revolution he contributed his sublime wisdom.'

Kim Il-sung of North Korea was the next foreign statesman to call on Mao, in November 1953 – the least that he could do in view of China's contribution to the Korean War, including the sacrifice of Mao's eldest son. The first non-Communist states-man to pay tribute was Jawaharlal Nehru of India, who came in October 1954 in spite of the message which Mao had sent to the Indian Communist Party a few days after establishing the Chinese People's Republic, when he had told Nehru's domestic antagonists: 'India, relying on the brave Communist Party of India ... will certainly not remain long under the yoke of imperialism. ... Like free China, a free India will one day emerge in the socialist and people's democratic family. . .' In the interim, Nehru had proved himself genuinely independent of world blocs in arranging the ceasefire in Korea in the summer of 1953.

The Korean War had been costly to China. In a speech in the summer of 1952, Mao revealed that in the previous year, 'What we spent on the war ... more or less equalled our expenditures for national construction; it was fifty-fifty.' In 1952 the cost would be only half as much, but this was still a huge amount.

The Chinese had been able to stand up to the Americans, Mao added, because the Americans were 'rich in metal but poor in morale'.

Mao renewed his complaints about the lack of democracy among his own comrades in the Communist Party. In his closing speech to the People's Consultative Conference – which included many non-Communist delegates – in February 1953, Mao urged his hearers to oppose bureaucracy among the officials, a theme which would lead ultimately to the nation-wide chaos of the Cultural Revolution fourteen years later.

Take the organs at the Central government level: even there many leading cadres in many departments are quite satisfied with sitting in their offices and writing decisions and issuing directives. Attention is paid only to arranging and assigning work; no attention is given to going down among the rank-and-file to learn the real situation and check up on the work. And so their leadership constantly results in isolation from the masses and from reality. . . .'

This was to establish a new pattern in his attempt to discipline his own Party, in which he invited those outside the Party to criticize members of his Party for not living up to its high ideals – something which his critics within the Party felt to be inexcusable. The dirty washing, they felt, should be kept at home.

But there were also differences of substance building up within the leadership which were going to become highly destructive. Land reform was complete and China's peasants were being introduced to the virtues of co-operative agriculture as a first step towards collectivization. But Liu Shao-chi, Mao's deputy, took the view that China would have to industrialize and mechanize its agriculture first, before being able to take the land effectively into public ownership.

Liu had declared as early as the summer of 1951, in words which were later to be interpreted by the Red Guards as a criticism of Mao, that, 'There are some comrades who hold that the countryside, relying on mutual aid teams and co-operatives . . . can carry out the collectivization of agriculture, the socialization of agriculture. This is a kind of utopian-agrarian socialism: it is erroneous.' He circulated a comment behind Mao's back setting out arguments against the swift spread of co-operatives in the countryside, but had to give way to Mao at the end of 1951 when the Politburo accepted a resolution pressed by Mao to speed up the formation of co-operatives.

Mao delivered a stinging public rebuke to Liu:

From now on, all documents and telegrams sent out in the name of the Central Committee can be dispatched only after I have gone over them, otherwise they are invalid. Please take note.

On several occasions resolutions adopted at meetings called by the Central Committee, which I had not gone over, were issued without authorization. This is a mistake and a breach of discipline.

Later Mao again attacked the conservative caution of his deputy and pushed through the Politburo a decision further to accelerate both nationalization and collectivization.

In August 1953 he again attacked the moderates in the Party's leadership, especially Liu's protégé, Po I-po, then Minister of Finance. The tax system involving 'equality between public and private enterprises' proposed by Po 'would have led inevitably to capitalism', Mao claimed. Po had 'bourgeois ideas which are favourable to capitalism and harmful to socialism.' Po was not the only one.

At this conference [Mao said] Liu Shao-chi said that he had made mistakes of a sort, and Comrade Teng Hsiao-ping said he too had made some mistakes. Whoever makes a mistake must make a self-criticism.... Throughout the country there are quite a number of people who thrive on anarchy, and Po I-po is one such person. To some extent he has been corrupted both politically and ideologically and it is absolutely necessary to criticize him.

Mao closed his harangue with a memorable call for Party discipline and modesty, recalling regulations which had been adopted at earlier meetings but never put into writing.

The first is a ban on birthday celebrations. Birthday celebrations don't beget longevity.... The second is a ban on gifts, at least in the Party. The third is to keep toasts to a minimum.... The fourth is to keep applause to a minimum. There should be no ban and no pouring of cold water on the masses who applaud out of enthusiasm. The fifth is a ban on naming places after persons. The sixth is a ban on placing Chinese comrades on a par with Marx, Engels, Lenin or Stalin. Our relationship is one of pupils to teachers and that is how it should be. Observance of these regulations is true modesty.

In the summer of 1953 Mao had his celebrated clash with the renowned old non-Communist philosopher Liang Shu-ming. Liang had been a progressive reformer since the revolution of 1911, active in agricultural affairs and rural self-government. He had striven very hard in 1945 for an agreement to avoid the civil war, and after 1949 he became a member of the People's Political Consultative Conference.

It was at a meeting of this conference in Peking that Liang urged a better deal for the peasants, who were faring so much worse than the factory workers of the cities. If the urban workers were in the 'ninth level of heaven' in the Buddhist hierarchy, he said, the peasants were in the 'ninth level of hell'.

Chou En-lai quickly rebutted what Liang had said, and so Liang passed a note to Mao asking to speak again. Permission was given, and Liang Shu-ming walked calmly to the platform.

'I am speaking again', he said, 'because first, I want to test myself, and second, I want to test the fairness of the Communist Party.'

At this point Mao lost his temper and seized the microphone.

'I suppose', he interrupted, 'you think you are very beautiful, more beautiful than Hsi Shih, more beautiful than Kuei-fei' (two famous beauties of historical times) 'but to me, you stink!' Liang was speechless with surprise and the meeting bristled with tension.

'The radio in Taiwan', Mao went on, pointing his finger at Liang, 'says that you are a man of character and principles. But to me, you stink! You have stinking bones!'

Liang was then hounded off the platform by Maoist members of the audience, but a respected old ex-Kuomintang general stood up, bowed to Mao and said: 'May I ask the Chairman whether what happened just now is a question of Liang's thought, or of his politics?'

The purpose of this intervention was that thought, in the Communist view, can be corrected by education, whereas political mistakes are far graver. There was a long pause until Mao at last replied:

'It is a question of his thought.'

'In that case. . . .', said the old general reprovingly, 'I think we should not have become so excited today.'

Later in the year Mao got his own back on Liang Shu-ming, describing him at a large meeting in Peking as 'an assassin with a pen'. He made fun of Liang's famous metaphor about the ninth hell, as well as his views that 'China is without classes' or that China's problem was one of cultural maladjustment needing not an ideological but 'a colourless transparent government'. Liang, Mao insisted, was 'an ambitious schemer, a hypocrite', who 'only talks drivel'.

Nevertheless, Mao did not want Liang out of the way. He wanted the Party to go on debating with him in order to clarify the problems, and presumably in the hope of remoulding him.

Mao also, though he did not say this, relished opposition and debate and was getting too little of this from his own comrades, who tended either to be sycophantic or else to conspire behind his back.

Mao's wife was now back in Peking convalescing from her illness, and so Mao used to sit at her bedside every day while she read him newspapers and telegrams and selected things for him to read, including new books, from the incoming mail.

But there is a curious lacuna about the son of Mao whose custody she lost. The boy was Ho Tzu-chen's child, and had apparently been in Moscow with her during the early 1940s but had returned, it was said, to Shanghai where he was put in the care of a priest, whose family beat the lad so hard that he never recovered his sense of balance. The boy used to rock crazily to left and right, often tripping or falling to the ground.

At some point after the Communist victory the boy was reunited with his father, and Chiang Ching reared him as her own son and came to love him. But when she had to undergo radiotherapy for cancer the boy was taken away by Mao's aides and she never found out where he had been taken. Nor, according to her, did Mao himself. The whole affair was a great tragedy, for the boy was intelligent. He was said to have been able to sing the *Internationale* from beginning to end at the age of three!

This is an extraordinary story, from Chiang Ching's own mouth. How could Mao have been incapable of controlling what was done with his own children in his own house? Could he have been so distressed at the daily sight of the boy's nervous disorder that he asked others to remove him? Was the boy taken for treatment? Why was he never heard of again? The whole episode is riddled with implausibility. And yet Chiang Ching has declared very definitely that this is what happened.

In the following year she was able to resume her political collaboration with Mao. She noticed, reading avidly from her sickbed, an article in a specialist journal about the famous eighteenth-century novel *Dream of the Red Chamber*, the classical masterpiece of Chinese literature. 'I have read *Dream of the Red Chamber* five times,' Mao once said – adding hastily, 'but I have not been influenced by it, as I regard it as history.'

An old university professor who had made his name in the 1920s and 1930s as a commentator on the book had recently written about it again in laudatory tones, but without reading into it the lessons of class struggle. Two young Marxist students now took him to task for this, and Chiang Ching showed their criticisms to Mao, who agreed that they should be widely read. Once again, as in the Wu Hsun affair three years earlier, the Communist officials in charge of culture showed themselves to be palpably less revolutionary than the Chairman. The leading official publications had rejected this iconoclastic article until Mao, at his wife's prodding, insisted.

In the summer Mao and his wife used to go from Peking to the seaside at Peitaiho, and in 1954 he wrote a poem there:

> A rainstorm sweeps down on this northern land,
> White breakers leap to the sky.
> No fishing boats off Chinwangtao
> Are seen on the boundless ocean.
> Where are they gone?
>
> Nearly two thousand years ago
> Wielding his whip, the Emperor Wu of Wei
> Rode eastward to Chiehshih; his poem survives.
> Today the autumn wind still sighs,
> But the world has changed!

Meanwhile, Mao tried to consolidate his position against some of his long-time rivals, making at the end of 1953 his move against Kao Kang. Nothing had happened in the preceding four years to dull his suspicions about Kao's ambition. The Korean War had made China even more dependent than ever upon Manchuria, the immediate rear area for the fighting. The death of Stalin in the spring of 1953 had removed Kao's outside backer, however, and from then on Mao prepared his strategy for dealing with him.

On Christmas Eve of 1953, the day on which Beria was convicted of treason in Moscow, Mao proposed to the Politburo a resolution on Party unity which set out criticisms of Kao. 'I said', he later recalled, 'there were two headquarters in Peking. The first headed by me stirred up an open wind and lit an open fire. The second headed by others stirred up a sinister wind and lit a sinister fire; it was operating underground.'

A few weeks later Liu Shao-chi moved a resolution in the Central Committee on Mao's behalf, pointing out that some Party leaders were 'going so far as to regard the areas or agencies under their charge as their private possessions or independent kingdoms.' It was difficult for Mao to appear publicly to take the lead in denouncing his old comrade, and so he diplomatically 'went on leave' at the time of this Central Committee meeting in

Peking. According to a non-Communist politician then in Peking, Mao 'purposely went back to his native place, and said he was going to spend the Chinese New Year there, thus pretending to be a bystander.'

Mao later admitted the supreme importance he attached to the meeting. 'We did right to ... adopt the resolution. Otherwise Kao Kang would have remained rampant for another year – an unimaginably dreadful situation.' But Liu Shao-chi did not proceed fast enough for Mao's taste, and the final chapter in the Kao Kang story had to wait until the following year.

The undaunted Wang Ming revisited China, like the proverbial bad penny, at the end of 1953. Within three months he was in hospital in Peking with liver and gall bladder trouble, predictably rejecting the very strong advice of his physicians to undergo surgery. Even after returning to permanent exile in Russia soon afterwards, he claimed to have received poisoned food packets from Mao's agents in China, which he was wise enough to test first on his cat. The cat, he claimed, died.

In 1954 a new constitution was drafted for the People's Republic. In the course of commending the draft Mao revealed his ideas about China's development:

I think for us to build a great socialist country, about fifty years, or ten five-year plans, will probably be enough. By then China will be in good shape and quite different from what it is now. What can we make at present? We can make tables and chairs, teacups and teapots, we can grow grain and grind it into flour, and we can make paper. But we can't make a single motor car, plane, tank or tractor. So we mustn't brag and be cocky.

Mao had already put in train some major reforms dear to his heart, including the simplification of the Chinese characters (he rejected the Writing Reform Committee's proposals on this subject in 1953 as not sufficiently radical). In 1956 he said:

I am of the opinion that foreign alphabets are better. ... Foreign alphabets contain few letters, incline to one-sided writing and surpass the Chinese characters. However, some professors say 'Chinese is the best of all languages in the world.' I do not think so. Therefore, we should adopt romanization. Haven't we adopted the arabic numerals which were invented by foreigners? Roman numerals first appeared in Rome. Aren't Britain, America and Russia using them?

Later Mao talked to a group of musicians about borrowing from the West. He rounded upon those who blindly worshipped Western music as better than Chinese. Complete Westernization, he warned, was impracticable:

It will not be accepted by the common people of China. The arts and
the natural sciences differ in this respect. For example, removing the
appendix and taking aspirin have no national form. This is not the case
with the arts: with them the question of national form does arise.

But in the end Mao conceded the cause of the musicians' dis-
orientation.

We must acknowledge that in respect of modern culture the standards
of the West are higher than ours. We have fallen behind. . . . We must
be good at absorbing the good things from foreign countries in order to
make good our own shortcomings. . . . We learn from the ancients in
order to benefit the people of today, and we learn from foreigners in
order to benefit the people of China.

The second half of 1954 was the season for distinguished visitors. Nehru had come, and on 25 August 1954 Mao received a
British Labour Party delegation led by Clement Attlee, the
former Prime Minister, and including Aneurin Bevin and Edith
Summerskill. The Britons described him afterwards as tanned
and confident, monopolizing the discussion in spite of the presence of Liu Shao-chi and Chou En-lai during the three-hour
session. Mao wanted to know why the British Labour government had not been able to eliminate the bourgeoisie. Attlee and
his lieutenants countered by boasting of the living standards of
the majority of the British people, but Mao said that this was a
product of the exploitation of colonies.
   'When I asked them', Attlee wrote afterwards, 'to explain how
Denmark, Sweden and Norway were also high in the scale,
though they had no colonies, they could not answer.'
   In September Mao met for the first time the Dalai Lama, the
traditional leader of Tibet. He expressed his pleasure that Tibet
had 'come back to the motherland' and explained that China's
mission was to bring progress to Tibet by developing its natural
resources: the Chinese generals who were in command in Lhasa
were there to help the people of Tibet and not to exercise authority over them.
   He then asked the Dalai Lama point-blank whether they had
in fact done anything against his wishes. The Tibetan leader felt
himself placed 'in a very difficult position', as he afterwards
recollected. He gave a diplomatic reply. He was equally diplomatic during his next interview with Mao, which went on for
three hours with only an interpreter present. The Dalai Lama
tried to remove Mao's suspicions, convinced that he would not

get rid of the Chinese by opposing them, and could only hope
patiently to improve his situation.

A few days later Mao called in person on the Dalai Lama.
'Something', the Tibetan recalled, 'made him say that Buddhism
was quite a good religion, and Lord Buddha, although he was a
prince, had given a good deal of thought to the question of
improving the conditions of the people. He also observed that the
Goddess Tara was a kind-hearted woman.' After a few minutes
of such talk, Mao left again, leaving the Tibetan bewildered.

On a later occasion the Dalai Lama was invited to a meeting at
Mao's house attended by about twenty senior officials. He sat next
to Mao and was greatly impressed by his personality. The topic
was the rural standard of living in China. Mao 'spoke bluntly
... saying that he was not yet satisfied with what was being
done . . .; he quoted letters from his own village saying that Communist officials were not doing all they should to help the people.'

After a while Mao turned to the Dalai Lama and said that,
'Tibetans were firm or stubborn in their ideas, but after twenty
years Tibet would be strong; now, China was helping Tibet, but
after twenty years Tibet would be helping China.' He mentioned a
famous Chinese general who, after many victories elsewhere, had
finally met his match against the Tibetans.

Mao's final interview with the Dalai Lama took the form of a
long lecture about democracy, and how the Tibetan leader should
come closer to public opinion. Mao then edged closer to the Dalai
Lama on his chair and whispered confidentially:

'I understand you very well. But of course, religion is poison. It
has two great defects. It undermines the race, and secondly it
retards the progress of the country. Tibet and Mongolia have both
been poisoned by it.'

The Dalai Lama was puzzled by these tactless remarks addressed to a religious leader. But his over-all impression of Mao was
favourable.

His appearance gave no sign of his intellectual power. He did not look
healthy, and was always panting and breathing heavily. His dress was
just the same style as everybody else's, although it was usually a different
colour; but he did not pay much attention to his clothes, and once I
noticed that the cuffs of his shirt were torn. His shoes looked as though
they had never been polished. He was slow in his movements, and slower
still in speech; he was sparing of words and spoke in short sentences, each
full of meaning and usually clear and precise; and he smoked incessantly
while he talked. Yet his manner of speech certainly captured the minds
and imagination of his listeners, and gave the impression of kindness and
sincerity.

Mao convinced the Dalai Lama that he would never use force to convert Tibet to Communism, and the Tibetan leader believed until the end that Chinese persecution and oppression could not have Mao's approval or support – whereas Chou En-lai appeared to him far more ruthless. His comment on Chou was that, 'I was not in the least surprised, as I would have been with Mao Tse-tung, to learn later that he approved the policy of oppression in Tibet.'

The Dalai Lama celebrated the Tibetan New Year in Peking with a traditional party where Mao was offered a piece of cele-bratory cake, which it was the Tibetan custom at the New Year to throw up to the ceiling as an offering to Buddha. When Mao was told of this, he duly threw his piece of cake to the ceiling, but then, 'with a mischievous expression, he threw another piece down on the floor.'

More significant than any other foreign delegation, however, was the trio of Russian leaders who came to celebrate the fifth anniversary of Mao's Republic on 1 October 1954 – Khrushchev, Bulganin and Mikoyan. For Nikita Khrushchev it was the first of three visits which he was to make to Peking, and the most forma-tive. He found that he was greeted with courtesy, but not sincerity:

After I had arrived Mao and I embraced each other warmly and kissed each other on both cheeks. We used to lie around a swimming pool in Peking, chatting like the best of friends about all kinds of things. But it was all too sickeningly sweet. The atmosphere was nauseating. In addi-tion, some of the things Mao said put me on my guard. I was never exactly sure that I understood what he meant. I thought at the time that it must have been because of some special traits in the Chinese character and the Chinese way of thinking. Some of Mao's pronouncements struck me as being much too simplistic, and others as being much too complex.

Mao had just been able to resume regular swimming after a thirty-year interruption. One of the universities in Peking opened a new indoor swimming pool in 1954. 'I went there every evening with my bag,' Mao recalled, 'changed my clothes, and for three months without interruption I studied the nature of the water.' Soon afterwards a splendid pool was constructed for him in his garden, and it was at this pool that he entertained Khrushchev, but it was said that he was so distressed at the expense incurred by the Party that he insisted on paying for it himself out of his royalties.

One conversation while 'Mao and I were lying next to the swimming pool in our bathing trunks discussing the problems of war and peace' remained in Khrushchev's memory.

'Comrade Khrushchev,' Mao began, 'what do you think? If we compare the military might of the capitalist world with that of the socialist world, you'll see that we obviously have the advantage over our enemies. Think of how many divisions China, USSR and the other socialist countries could raise.'

'Comrade Mao Tse-tung,' Khrushchev replied, 'nowadays that sort of thinking is out of date. You can no longer calculate the alignment of forces on the basis of who has the most men. Back in the days when a dispute was settled with fists or bayonets, it made a difference who had the most men and the most bayonets on each side. Then when the machine gun appeared, the side with more troops no longer necessarily had the advantage. And now with the atomic bomb, the number of troops on each side makes practically no difference to the alignment of real power and the outcome of a war. The more troops on a side, the more bomb fodder.'

'Listen, Comrade Khrushchev,' Mao responded. 'All you have to do is provoke the Americans into military action, and I'll give you as many divisions as you need to crush them – a hundred, two hundred, one thousand divisions.'

Khrushchev tried to explain that a few nuclear missiles could turn all the divisions of China to dust, but Mao did not want to listen and obviously thought he was a coward.

Further misunderstanding was caused because Khrushchev wanted a million Chinese workers to be sent to Siberia to help the USSR exploit its vast timber resources there.

Mao's response ... was typical ... and indicative of what was to come. He really knew how to put us down. First, you have to imagine what Mao was like in person. He moved as calmly and slowly as a bear, swaying from side to side. He would look at you for a long time, then lower his eyes and begin talking in a relaxed quiet voice:

'You know, Comrade Khrushchev, for years it's been a widely held view that because China is an underdeveloped and overpopulated country, with widespread unemployment, it represents a good source of cheap labour. But you know, we Chinese find this attitude very offensive. Coming from you, it's rather embarrassing. If we were to accept your proposal, others might get the wrong idea about the relationship between the Soviet Union and China. They might think that the Soviet Union has the same image of China that the capitalist West has.'

There could hardly have been a better example of mutual misunderstanding between Marxist-Leninist comrades. A curious feature of Khrushchev's visit was his abortive encounter with Chiang Ching. Premier Chou En-lai was about to introduce them as they stood on the rostrum of the Gate of Heavenly Peace reviewing the parade for the fifth birthday of the People's Republic. According to his wife's later account, Mao saw what was about to happen, walked over to her and brusquely escorted her away to a side alley, evidently to prevent her meeting the Soviet leader – whom in the end she never did meet in her life.

19
CATCHING THE HIGH TIDE

Mao found himself in the spring of 1955 rid of one rival in his own Party. Teng Hsiao-ping moved a resolution at a Party conference on the 'Kao Kang – Jao Shu-shih Anti-Party Alliance', declaring that a group of Communists including Kao had rebelled against the senior Party leadership and that Kao had 'attempted to make an independent kingdom of Manchuria'. He had 'not only refused to bow to the Party and admit his guilt, but even made his last expression of rebellion against the Party by killing himself.'

Khrushchev was one of those who questioned this official version of Kao's end, commenting, 'I doubt very much whether Kao Kang committed suicide, most likely Mao had him strangled or poisoned.' But there seems no good basis for such doubt. One version of the events leading up to Kao's death includes an incident where he took out a pistol during an interrogation and cried: 'If you comrades distrust me so much I'll kill myself before you.' He was disarmed on that occasion by the nearest Politburo member, but there is no reason to think that Kao did not try again, this time with success. Suicide is the traditional final act of protest in China.

The Kao affair had constituted a major threat to Mao's leadership. 'The Kao – Jao affair', he later observed, 'was an earthquake of the eighth degree of magnitude.' But whatever Kao's ambitions may have been, Mao also had his motives for moving against him. It was alleged by his enemies that Mao wanted to use the Kao episode in order to promote Teng Hsiao-ping at the expense of Liu Shao-chi, who had been reluctant all along to proceed against Kao and who was now beginning to argue against Mao's socio-economic policies.

It was also said that Mao wanted to put one of his own followers into Kao's place as boss of Manchuria, and that he wanted to eliminate Jao Shu-shih, the man in charge of Shanghai at this time, and others around him because they were the only surviving witnesses of Mao's alleged secret move during the war to sound out Japan about an anti-Kuomintang alliance.

In his own speech at the conference which carried the anti-Kao resolution, Mao suggested some of his own personal problems – as well as those of other Long Marchers who had found haven in the Shensi base in 1935 – when he lectured his comrades on how they should take issue with wrong ideas even coming from somebody you were fond of.

We should keep a certain distance from whatever is inconsistent with Party principles. . . . We should not fail to keep this distance merely because someone is an old friend, an old superior, an old subordinate, an old colleague, a schoolmate or a fellow townsman. We have repeatedly had this experience in the current anti-Party case of Kao and Jao. . . .-
When on account of an old and intimate relationship with certain people you find it difficult to speak out and fail to keep a certain distance, give any rebuff and draw a clear line of demarcation, you'll find yourself more and more deeply involved and haunted by their 'ghosts'. Therefore we must take a stand and adhere to principles. . . . Identify by name the person and the department involved. You have done a poor job and I am not satisfied, and if you feel offended, so be it. Fear of offending others is only fear of losing votes and of an uneasy relationship in work. Will I lose my rice-bowl if you don't vote for me? Nothing of the kind. Actually, if you speak your mind and lay the issues on the table sharply, you'll find it easier to get along with others.

But that same conference in March 1955 rebuffed Mao's ideas on the economic front: most comrades preferred the more cautious approach of Liu Shao-chi. Mao accordingly took steps to create his own counter-party to circumvent the majority of his colleagues on the Politburo and Central Committee who were blocking his policies. He did what almost every ruler has done in such circumstances, he formed his own 'praetorian' guard.

The Central Committee already had its own General Office, which served the secretarial needs of Mao, while the army supplied a special unit, later known as Unit 8341, to act as Mao's personal bodyguard. Veteran members of this unit recalled after his death that:

To better acquaint himself with the concrete details of the movements for agricultural co-operation and the state monopoly of the purchase and marketing of grain, Chairman Mao ordered us to select one man from each prefecture to work in his bodyguard unit. He regarded investigation by these comrades back in their home villages as one of his methods to keep in contact with the rural areas and grasp the situation there.

In May 1955 Mao instructed these men to take on a new political assignment.

'All of you', he said, 'are doing security work. Now I'd like to give you an extra job, that is to make investigations. . . . You have three tasks, security work, study and investigation to boot. . . .'

'Let's make it a rule,' he told these men who would be going back to their native places for investigations: 'Be modest to others, respect your parents and the district and township cadres, and don't put on airs. Modesty will help get good results from investigations.'

The men duly went out and came back with a mass of information to which Mao listened.

When the first group of comrades returned towards the end of 1955, Chairman Mao spent over ten hours in three days to listen to their reports and dined with these comrades at his home. He enquired in detail about production and living conditions in the villages, read the investigation reports word by word and even corrected the wrong wordings and punctuation marks. . . . Some comrades brought millet cakes, a staple food of the peasants of their native villages, to Chairman Mao when they were reporting to him. Chairman Mao tasted some and told the comrades around him that they should all eat a bit. . . .'

One day, when comrades from Hunan and Hupeh provinces finished reporting about their home villages, Chairman Mao said gladly that it took only three hours to learn the conditions of the 60,000,000 people in the two provinces.

'This is indeed an excellent method. You have served as a link between me and the peasant masses.'

Gesticulating with three fingers, he went on: 'You have seen the peasants and I have seen you, thus I have seen the peasants indirectly within this bit of distance. You are peasants with arms and class consciousness.'

These security men were not only sent back for investigation but also were required to write letters home.

'If you each write a letter', Mao told them, 'every two months, or four or five letters every year, to ask whether the peasants have enough food to eat and about production and co-operatives, and show me the replies from home, I will be well-informed.'

What was at issue between Mao and his colleagues was the wisdom of taking the Chinese peasants wholesale into the first stage of collectivization, by setting up co-operatives on a large scale. Earlier attempts to do this had not succeeded, but Mao wanted to try again. There was opposition from many peasants, who were also oppressed by the quotas for grain set by the government. Lacking a sufficient incentive, production declined, ultimately affecting industry and construction as well as agriculture. The officials in charge of rural affairs, notably Teng Tzu-hui, an old collaborator with Mao, decided to go slow on cooperatives. Liu Shao-chi presided over a meeting in the early part of 1955 accepting Teng's view.

But Mao would not bow to the majority, even among his own colleagues. He convened a conference of regional Party secretaries in July and persuaded them to accept his plans for accelerating the collectivization of agriculture. 'A new upsurge', he insisted, 'in the socialist mass movement is imminent throughout the countryside. But some of our comrades are tottering along like a woman with bound feet, and constantly complaining, "you're going too fast".'

Mao saw no reason why the programme for creating co-operatives could not be maintained or even accelerated, or why the building of socialism could not be basically completed by 1967.

The bourgeois-democratic revolution against imperialism and feudalism, which had already been consummated, took the land from the landlords and distributed it to the peasants. 'But this revolution has passed and feudal ownership has been abolished. What exists in the countryside today is capitalist ownership by the rich peasants and a vast sea of private ownership by the individual peasants. As is clear to everyone the spontaneous forces of capitalism have been steadily growing in the countryside. . . .'

Against the advice of the technocrats and of most of his senior colleagues, Mao thus by-passed and flouted his own faint-hearted Central Committee and plunged China into a fast completion of co-operativization, under which peasants were made to see the advantages of sharing their agricultural equipment and even their labour and land.

Afterwards Mao's comrades agreed that he had been right, had recognized the high tide. When the Central Committee met in October, Liu confessed his mistaken judgement: 'I failed to promote and study seriously the Agricultural Producers' Co-operatives. . . . This was wrong.'

Mao summed up the vigorous and wide-ranging discussion which had taken place in the Central Committee. 'We now have two alliances,' he went on, 'one with the peasants and the other with the national bourgeoisie. Both are indispensable to us. . .' But whereas the alliance with the peasants was basic and permanent, 'the alliance with the bourgeoisie is a temporary one, because the bourgeoisie is to be liquidated. In the future, the ranks of the proletariat will be augmented by several million members of the bourgeoisie. . . .'

On this matter we are quite heartless! On this matter Marxism is indeed cruel and has little mercy, for it is determined to exterminate imperialism, feudalism, capitalism, and small production to boot. In this respect, it is better not to have much mercy. Some of our comrades are too kind, they are not tough enough, in other words they are not so Marxist. . . .

Our aim is to exterminate capitalism from the face of the earth and make it a thing of the past. What emerges in history is bound to die out. Everything in the world is a historical phenomenon; as there is life, so there must be death. As a historical phenomenon, capitalism must also die out, and it has a very nice place to go to, that is, underground, there to 'sleep'.

Mao then spoke of the campaign against counter-revolutionaries. 'This year and the next,' he said, 'we will carry out suppression of counter-revolutionaries among eleven or twelve million people. Counter-revolutionaries cannot be seen. But once you investigate you will find out. . . . All over the country 110,000 counter-revolutionaries have been discovered from among 2.2 million people. There are 50,000 major suspects still around.' Such was the price of progress.

It was on this occasion that Mao gave his most celebrated definition of what was meant by left and right deviations.

It is a 'Left' deviation if your judgment is premature, and it is a 'Right' deviation if your judgments lag behind. . . . We should . . . achieve our aims naturally instead of forcing their attainment. Take childbirth for instance. It requires nine months.

If, in the seventh month, the doctor should exert pressure and force the child out, that would not be good, that would be a 'Left' deviation. If, on the other hand, the unborn child is nine months old and very much wants to come out and yet you won't allow it, that would be a 'Right' deviation. In short, everything moves in time. When the right time comes for something to be done, it has to be done. If you don't allow it, that is a 'Right' deviation. If the right time has not come, yet you try to force it through, that is a 'Left' deviation.

Meanwhile Mao was involved in compiling and analysing reports on co-operativization from all over the country: 'I spent eleven days', he told the Central Committee in October, 'reading 120-odd reports, making corrections and writing notes to them. In this manner I have "travelled all the kingdoms" and gone farther than Confucius, "travelling" as far as Yunnan and Sinkiang.'

These reports were published first in September and again in December, under the title *Socialist Upsurge in China's Countryside*. In his preface to the second edition Mao described the 'fundamental change' in the second half of 1955. More than half of China's peasant households had by then joined co-operatives.

This is a tremendous event. This event makes it clear to us that we need only the calendar year 1956 in order basically to complete the semi-socialist co-operative transformation of agriculture. In another three or four years, that is, by 1959 or 1960, we can in the main complete the transformation of semi-socialist co-operatives into fully socialist ones. . . .

This event makes it clear to us that in scale and tempo China's industrialization . . . can no longer proceed exactly in the way previously envisaged, but must be appropriately expanded and accelerated. . . .

When three five-year plans are completed, that is, by 1967, the production of grain and many other crops will double or treble the highest annual output before the founding of the People's Republic.

The reason for this infectiousness of optimism from the grass roots up to the level of Mao himself was clear from the many reports between the covers of *Socialist Upsurge in China's Countryside*. Many had notes written by Mao.

One case was the co-operative in Nantsuichuang village, where the Party had backed the poor peasants in establishing a co-operative in spite of the jeers of the middle peasants, who mocked their aspirations: 'Chicken feathers can't fly up to heaven.' But the co-operative did succeed, and Mao commended their example.

'The poor are turning their past upside down,' he commented. 'The old system is dying, a new system is being born. Chicken feathers really are flying up to heaven. In the Soviet Union, this has already happened. In China, it is happening now. And it is going to happen all over the world.'

The most famous commentary of Mao in this remarkable compilation was the one where he committed himself to incredible heights of optimism.

Nineteen fifty-five has been the decisive year for the struggle between socialism and capitalism in China. . . . In the first half of 1955 the atmosphere was foul and dark clouds theatened. But in the second half of the year there has been a complete change and the climate is entirely different; in response to the call of the Central Committee tens of millions of peasant households have swung into action and gone co-operative.

At the time the editor is writing these lines, over sixty million peasant households have joined co-operatives all over the country. This is a raging tidal wave sweeping away all demons and monsters. People of all sorts in our society have been clearly revealed for what they are. It is the same in the Party. By the end of this year the victory of socialism will be largely assured.

Two or three years later Mao wrote an 'explanation' of this, in which he confessed to have been over-optimistic. It had not been 'proper', as he put it, for him to say that socialism had won basic victory in 1955.

This is the way it should be put: 1955 was the year in which basic victory was won as regards the aspect of ownership in the relations of production, while in the other aspects of the relations of production as well as some aspects of the superstructure, namely, on the ideological and political fronts, either a basic victory was not won, or, if won, the victory was not complete and further efforts were required.

We did not anticipate that such a great storm would burst upon the world in 1956 [a reference to Suez and Hungary] nor did we anticipate that a campaign of 'oppose rash advance' would occur in the same year in our country, a campaign which dampened the enthusiasm of the masses. Both events gave a considerable stimulus to the Rightists in mounting their wild attacks.

Mao was also pondering how to speed up the nationalization of industry. One night in early December in 1955, about eighty leading businessmen in Shanghai were told to go to the Sino-Soviet Friendship Hall where, to their surprise, Mao appeared to speak to them. He was introduced all round by Chen Yi, then the Mayor of Shanghai. One of them afterwards described the scene.

Mao, he said, was 'tall for a Chinese; he is a heavy soft-looking man who appears younger than his pictures usually suggest. He is very slow. He walks with his toes pointed out; he takes short steps and swings his arms more than seems necessary for his ponderous gait. His face is animated. . . . A cigarette is almost always held between his pudgy fingers, and his teeth are stained black from chain-smoking.'

The eighty bourgeois businessmen stiffened and gasped with surprise when they realized who it was. Mao sat down at the speaker's table.

'Why don't you smoke?' he asked them calmly, 'It won't hurt you. Churchill has smoked throughout his long life and he is in good health. In fact, the only man I know who doesn't smoke but has lived long is Chiang Kai-shek.'

Everybody laughed and the tension dissipated. Mao praised the contribution which the 'national capitalist friends' had already made.

'Now,' he went on pleasantly, 'I have come from Peking to seek your advice.' Many businessmen had been urging that the nationalization of private enterprise should be hastened, 'lest the national bourgeoisie lag behind in the progress towards socialism'.

'I don't think that I can agree with that,' he added, 'but I am not well informed on the subject. I want to listen to your opinions. I have brought only my two ears to this meeting, and if you expect to hear more from me, you will be disappointed. . .'

The member of his audience who afterwards described the evening noted that in a formal address to a large gathering, Mao spoke poorly, but his slow drawl was remarkably effective in a small casual group such as this one.

The businessmen hastened to enter their (insincere) agreement about hurrying up the transformation to socialism which they knew Mao wanted to hear. One of them reckoned that at the existing rate more than twenty years would be needed, which was far too slow. Some suggested that it might be achieved in five years. For two hours Mao listened attentively, then, when the speeches were over, he thanked them all and said that he would give serious thought to their opinions. After he had gone they discussed this remarkable meeting in the knowledge that they would have to become self-supporting labourers much sooner than they had anticipated, perhaps within the next six years.

A few weeks after this courteous talk it was announced that the transformation would be accomplished within the next six days. The former businessmen then had to exist on modest wages and fixed interest.

As the Shanghai capitalists competed with each other to profess enthusiasm for their socialist transformation, a story went round their dinner tables illustrating the different approaches of Mao and his two senior colleagues, Liu Shao-chi and Chou En-lai. Mao, this tale went, once asked Liu and Chou how they would make a cat eat pepper.

'That's easy,' Liu replied, ' . . . you get somebody to hold down the cat, stuff the pepper into its mouth, and push it down with a chopstick.'

'No, no!' Mao raised his hands in horror. 'Never use force, that is undemocratic. Everything must be voluntary. How would you do it?' he asked, turning towards Chou.

'I would starve the cat,' replied the Premier. ' . . . Then I would wrap the pepper in a slice of meat. If the cat is hungry enough it will swallow it whole.'

But Mao still shook his head. 'One must not use deceit either,' he declared. 'Never fool the people.' The other two looked questioningly at him. What would he do?

'It's so easy,' Mao explained. 'Rub the pepper thoroughly into the cat's arse. When it begins to burn, the cat will lick it off – and be happy that it is permitted to do so.'

Mao also extended socialism to the handicraft trades, but with a few reservations based on his own appreciation of their wares. In instructions which he issued in March 1956 he explained that these private operators performed various useful services, including the production of food and clothing.

They also produce arts and crafts such as cloisonné or the glass grapes blown by 'the five spinsters of the Chang family'. Besides, the technique of roasting Peking duck is exportable. People in some service trades make their rounds of the streets and villages, fixing all sorts of things as in the play *Mending Jars for Aunty Wang* – these people travel around and are well-informed. The Dawn-in-the-East Market displays more than six thousand kinds of articles for sale.

Mind you, don't let our fine handicraft products be discarded. Pock-marked Wang's and Chang Hsiao-chuan's kitchen knives and scissors must not be discarded, no, not even ten thousand years from now. Anything good and characteristically Chinese that has been discarded must be restored and even improved. [It is] a good idea ... to look after the old master craftsmen.... Yang Shih-hui, the ivory carver, is actually a very fine artist. Once he and I ate at a table together, and while observing me he was able to carve my likeness. I could have observed him for several days without being able to draw a picture of him, I'm afraid.

Meanwhile Mao had been consulting with Party leaders in the provinces on the forward planning for agriculture, and in December he drafted a circular for the Central Committee setting out the seventeen articles which had been agreed, asking for reactions of lower-level cadres by the New Year so that the programme could be finalized in January. This was the germ of what later became known as the Twelve-Year Plan for Agriculture, although at this stage it lacked the comprehensiveness and specific detail of a plan.

The seventeen articles called for the nation-wide establishment of advanced co-operatives with pooled land by 1960. They laid down that only well-behaved landlords or rich peasants could be admitted into co-operatives, and that the leadership should come primarily from poor peasants.

As for industry, Mao's ideas at this stage were somewhat

unformed. 'In the realm of industry,' he told the Central Committee in January 1956, 'we are dependent ... on foreign machinery import.'

We are able to build neither large machines nor small high precision machines.... Some comrades pour forth insane talk such as this: 'Let's do without foreign help, we are revolutionaries.' This is absurd. We are now in a time of cultural revolution, a revolution of techniques, a revolution which attacks ignorance and stupidity; without foreign help, by pretending to rely on our own forces, we will never succeed. This is sensible talk, it must be explained to the vast majority of cadres.

Right now, planes fly at altitudes around 60,000 feet, and one must therefore have supersonic planes: the time when one went to war on horseback is over. We have a vital need for top level brains. I think we should make a decision on this subject. To have a number of high quality intellectuals, we must have a multitude of ordinary intellectuals. Later, everybody must reach the mathematical level of Hua Lokeng [China's most famous mathematician, trained at Cambridge], everybody must be able to read *Das Kapital*. This is possible within thirty years, if not twenty years, or at any rate in the next century. What else would communism mean? China must be among the first countries of the world in the realm of civilization, science, techniques and industry.

In spite of his heavy preoccupation with domestic problems, Mao spared time to receive foreign dignitaries – Ho Chi Minh and Sukarno in 1955 and the Indonesian leader again the next year.

'Brother Mao,' Sukarno told him before boarding his plane home at the end of his first visit, 'I hope it will not be long before I see you in Indonesia. The people of Indonesia are waiting to see you.'

Mao accepted the invitation, but never took it up. Sukarno complained eleven years later that he had already invited Mao eight times.

On the second visit Mao pooh-poohed the impression given by Chou at the Bandung Afro-Asian conference in 1955 that China welcomed conciliation with the Americans. 'I said to Sukarno', Mao told his own people afterwards, 'that we need not be anxious to join the United Nations or to establish diplomatic relations with the US. Let the US appear like a villain internationally and be deprived of its political capital domestically and isolated at present....' Yet the secret ambassadorial talks between the US and China had already begun in Warsaw.

To Latin American Communist leaders he stressed the need

for each Party to be independent. 'It seems to me that the parties in some Asian countries, such as India and Indonesia, have not done so well in rural work. . . . I beg to advise you not to transplant Chinese experience mechanically. Experience of any foreign country can serve only for reference and must not be regarded as dogma.' Communists, he concluded, should not be afraid of making mistakes. 'Failure is the mother of success.'

20
THE NIGHT OWL

Now came an unexpected distraction. In the middle of February 1956, the Russian Communists opened their Twentieth Congress in Moscow, and ten days later Khrushchev delivered his astonishing posthumous attack on Stalin. According to Khrushchev himself, Mao's immediate reaction was favourable: 'Comrade Khrushchev has opened our eyes and given us light that we might see. He has told us the truth at last. We will reform.'

But Khrushchev had in fact gone too far for Mao's liking. 'When Stalin was criticized in 1956,' Mao afterwards recalled, 'we were on the one hand happy, but on the other hand apprehensive. It was completely necessary to lift the lid, to break down blind faith, to release the pressure and to emancipate thought. But we did not agree with demolishing him at one blow.' For all Stalin's blindness and obduracy, the old man had leadership qualities which were not yet visible among his successors.

Mao redoubled his efforts to play down the cult of personality in China. One comrade who happened to be sitting nearest to the door of a meeting hall recounted how a zealous aide of Mao had once told him, 'When the Chairman enters, you should be the first to stand up and clap your hands.' But after Khrushchev's speech, Chou En-lai told cadres: 'In future, when the Chairman comes into a room, you must not stand up and clap. This is not a good thing.'

A few weeks later Mao issued his considered judgement on Stalin, differing from Khrushchev in several important respects. Stalin had 'erroneously exaggerated' his own role, and 'counterposed his individual authority' to the Russian collective leadership. Leadership was needed by Communists, but when a leader 'alienates himself from the masses' his usefulness was reduced.

Stalin had made numerous serious mistakes, notably about agriculture, on the question of Yugoslavia and in advising the international Communist movement. But he was not wrong in everything. For all his errors, 'Stalin was a great Marxist-Leninist.'

In this same newspaper editorial Mao repeated his thesis, so provocative to the Russian comrades, that contradictions do not end with socialism. Innovations and social change go on under socialism, humanity being still in its youth.

The day after this editorial Mao received the Russian envoy Anastas Mikoyan, and criticized to his face the way in which Khrushchev had handled de-Stalinization. The implications were clear to both sides, because Mikoyan had come to Peking to sign an agreement about Russian economic aid to China, and Mao had asked for double what Russia had given for China's First Five-Year Plan. The Russian-Chinese alliance was heading for disaster.

The quarrel over de-Stalinization coincided with Chinese disenchantment about Russian technical advice. 'In the early stages of nation-wide liberation,' Mao later recalled, 'we lacked the experience to administer the economy of the entire country. Therefore during the first five-year plan [1952–6] we could only imitate the methods of the Soviet Union, though we always had a feeling of dissatisfaction with them. . . .'

These doubts were clearly set out in Mao's most famous post-1949 essay, *On the Ten Major Relationships*. The shock of Khrushchev's speech at the Twentieth Congress had set Mao to re-thinking the premises of what he was trying to do in China. 'On impulse,' he explained afterwards, 'I held a discussion with thirty-four ministers. Ten principal relationships were considered, my head swelled, and I "boldly advanced".' The result was a text for China's first turning away from the Russian industrial model.

This celebrated restatement of Mao's political platform in the light of seven years of power and disillusion with Moscow was delivered to the Politburo on 25 April 1956. Everybody wanted China's heavy industry to develop fast, but too much investment had been put into it at the expense of light industry and farming – and it was the farms which gave the country its foodstuffs and raw materials for light industry, together with its source of accumulated capital. Similarly, inland industry had been developed at the expense of coastal industry, out of fear of American attacks, but this had been overdone.

More planes and artillery and atom bombs were needed. But the best way to achieve this was to cut military expenditure from the one-third of state spending which it represented in the first five-year plan, down to about one-fifth, in order to help build the industrial base.

The standard of living of workers should be raised, and wages increased. In Russia the peasants were squeezed too hard by compulsory sales at low prices. China should avoid that mistake.

'You want the hen to lay more eggs and yet you don't feed it, you want the horse to run fast and yet you don't let it graze. What kind of logic is that!'

'We need a further extension of regional power,' and China should abandon the Russian example of shackling local authorities and putting everything in the hands of the centre. 'I consider that to restrict local powers too narrowly is not so beneficial. We still have little experience, and little maturity on the question of the state's handling of the relationship between the centre and the regions.'

The chauvinism of the Han people, who constituted the vast majority of the population, towards the national minorities, should be opposed.

'We say China is a country vast in territory, rich in resources and large in population; as a matter of fact, it is the Han nationality whose population is large, and the national minorities whose territory is vast and whose resources are rich – or at least in all probability their resources under the soil are rich.'

To suppress counter-revolution and build socialism, the regime had to be 'highly coercive'. Nevertheless, it was no good having too much cumbersome bureaucracy. 'I propose that the Party and government should be thoroughly streamlined and cut by two-thirds, provided that no person dies and no work stops.'

It must be rare in history for a head of state publicly to call for the axing of two out of three civil servants and ruling Party officials.

'It is wrong to say that counter-revolutionaries have been completely eliminated and that we can therefore lay our heads on our pillows and just drop off to sleep. As long as class struggle exists in China and in the world, we should never relax our vigilance.'

But arrests should be few in future and executions should be avoided. If one political criminal were executed, others would be compared with him and many heads would begin to roll.

Second, people may be wrongly executed. Once a head is chopped off, history shows it can't be restored, nor can it grow again as chives do, after being cut. . . .

The third point is that you will have destroyed a source of evidence. . . . Often one living counter-revolutionary serves as living witness against another. . . .

The fourth point is that killing these counter-revolutionaries won't (1) raise production; (2) raise the country's scientific level; (3) help do away with the four pests;* (4) strengthen national defence or (5) help recover Taiwan. . . .

But 'people who have made mistakes, provided they are good at drawing lessons from their mistakes, will, if they take care, make fewer mistakes in future. . . . It is those who have not made mistakes who are in danger and should be on their guard, because they do not have this immunity and so easily become overconfident.'

Finally, the right balance between copying and not copying must be found. 'Some of us in the past had learnt bad things from abroad. They were as pleased as punch with what they had learned, but meanwhile the people from whom they had learned these useless things had already discarded them.'

'In the Soviet Union, those who once extolled Stalin to the skies have now in one swoop consigned him to purgatory. . . . Stalin's mistakes amounted to only 30 per cent of the whole and his achievements to 70 per cent.'

China should firmly reject the decadent bourgeois system, but at the same time learn from the advanced science and technology, and even management, of capitalist countries. 'In the industrially developed countries they run their enterprises with fewer people and with greater efficiency and they know how to do business. . .'

The Chinese, Mao said in this seminal speech, must learn to lose their feeling of inferiority. At the same time, China had no claim to be proud of a revolution that had come more than thirty years later than the Russian one. 'Although our revolution is one step ahead of a number of colonial countries, we should resist the temptation to be proud of that too.'

Chou En-lai and his technocrats were unconvinced by Mao's economic arguments. The planners believed that a crash campaign to develop the economy by methods untried elsewhere would fail. Mao conceded afterwards that 'no clear resolution was made' about launching a leap forward in industry, although he claimed there was 'a gentleman's agreement' to that effect.

---

*These were rats, sparrows, flies and mosquitoes. The killing of sparrows resulted in a plague of caterpillars; subsequently, sparrows were removed from the category of pests, and bedbugs substituted in their place.

The most significant impact of de-Stalinization in China was Mao's decision to allow more freedom of expression to the non-Communists in order to keep pace with what was happening in other socialist countries and avoid an explosion of the kind which eventually happened in Eastern Europe. In May he launched a new slogan, 'Let a hundred flowers bloom, let a hundred schools contend.'

'Criticism must be allowed,' Mao told Edgar Faure, the former Premier of France, on a visit to Peking soon afterwards. 'If not, centres of irritation and incomprehension are created. Men must be allowed to say what they have in their hearts. . .' At the same time, however, 'One must take account of special conditions. With a people like this it is necessary to observe certain limits.'

At the end of their conversation, Faure spoke of Mao's poems.

'That is an old story,' Mao said. 'Once I composed poems, it is true. That is when I lived in the saddle. On horseback, one has the time. One can search out rhymes and rhythms; one can reflect. It was good, that life on horseback. Sometimes, these days I look back on it with regret.'

A few days later Mao was swimming across the River Yangtze in white trunks with a dozen youngsters, taking two hours to cover the twelve miles. In the next three days Mao made two more separate crossings with these local swimmers, sometimes floating on his back, sometimes on his side and sometimes doing the back stroke. Occasionally he cradled the back of his head in his hands and talked to his companions. At the end of one crossing he remarked: 'If I had something to eat, I could have stayed in the water for another two hours.' His delight was expressed in a poem, entitled 'Swimming'.

> I have just drunk the waters of Changsha
> And come to eat the fish of Wuchang.
> Now I am swimming across the great Yangtse,
> Looking afar to the open sky of Chu.
> Let the wind blow and the waves beat,
> Better far than idly strolling in a courtyard.
> Today I am at ease.
> 'It was by a stream that the Master said –
> "Thus do things flow away!" '
>
> Sails move with the wind.
> Tortoise and Snake are still.
> Great plans are afoot:
> A bridge will fly to span the north and south,

Turning a deep chasm into a thoroughfare;
Walls of stone will stand upstream to the west
To hold back Wushan's clouds and rain
Till a smooth lake rises in the narrow gorges.
The mountain goddess if she is still there
Will marvel at a world so changed.

The bridge over the Yangtse was opened by Mao a few months later. He named it, 'Iron and Steel Rainbow'.

The slowcoaches in the Politburo had been busy meanwhile. An editorial inspired by Chou En-lai opposed 'hasty bold advances', and Mao refused to read it through. 'It seemed to be impartial,' he recalled later, 'but, actually, the emphasis was on opposition to bold advances. . . . On this editorial I noted 'Will not read'. Why should I read something that attacks me? It was so frightening, it has such power to sway.' The technocrats gathered their forces to oppose what they called impetuosity, adventurism and attempts to do everything overnight.

As an example of the cost of too much speed, the editorial cited the case of the double-bladed, double-wheeled ploughs which had been manufactured in numbers far exceeding the need, so that 700,000 of them now had to be scrapped. Cash crops for industry had been neglected, and livestock had been slaughtered because of the forcible co-operativization under Mao's insistence.

Chou En-lai later took the blame for this opposition to Mao in the summer of 1956. 'I bore the responsibility', he confessed during the Cultural Revolution, 'for the opposition to adventurism in 1956, and I made a self-critical examination.' But there were many others who also crossed Mao at this time, including Li Fu-chun, Chen Yun, Li Hsien-nien, Teng Tzu-hui and Po I-po.

Mao was unrepentant and told a preparatory meeting for the Eighth Party Congress at the end of August 1956 why speed was of the essence:

The United States has a population of only 170 million, and as we have a population several times larger, are similarly rich in resources, and are favoured with more or less the same kind of climate, it is possible for us to catch up with the United States.

Oughtn't we to catch up? Definitely yes. What are your six hundred million people doing? Dozing? Which is right? Dozing or working? If working is the answer, why can't you with your 600 million people produce 200 million or 300 million tons of steel, when they with their population of 170 million can produce 100 million tons? If you fail to catch up, you cannot justify yourselves, and you will not be so glorious or great. . . .

You have such a big population, such a vast territory and such rich resources, and what is more, you are said to be building socialism, which is supposed to be superior; if after working at it for fifty or sixty years you are still unable to overtake the United States, what a sorry figure you will cut! You should be read off the face of the earth. Therefore, to overtake the United States is not only possible, but absolutely necessary and obligatory. If we don't, we, the Chinese nation, will be letting the nations of the world down and we will not be making much of a contribution to mankind.

This progress would be achieved with the Soviet alliance, which Mao defended.

As some mistakes have occurred in the Soviet Union and there is so much talk and gossip about them, it might seem that these mistakes were terrible. It is wrong to take this view. No nation can be free from mistakes, and since the Soviet Union was the first socialist country in the world and went through so much for so long, it was impossible for it not to make mistakes. . . . In the Soviet Union the main trend, the principal aspect, the major part, has been correct. . . .'
The slogan we have advocated all along is to draw on the advanced Soviet experience. Who told you to pick up its backward experience? Some people are so undiscriminating that they say a Russian fart is fragrant. That too is subjectivism. The Russians themselves say it stinks.

When the Eighth Party Congress began in September 1956, Mao took a surprisingly self-effacing role, reflecting the fall in his prestige as a result of the failure of his 'little leap forward', and also the effect of the de-Stalinization campaign in Russia. In the need publicly to exempt the Chinese Party from the sort of criticism now being aimed at Stalin's Party, the Chinese leaders sought to show that there was no cult of the personality in China. No doubt those who were already irked by Mao's behaviour and performance in the first seven years of the People's Republic took a certain relish in thus down-grading his official status.

Peng Teh-huai, who could claim almost equal seniority with Mao in the Party's history, was probably one of these. He proposed that the new Party constitution should omit the references to 'the Thought of Mao Tse-tung' which had been in the 1945 constitution.

'I was opposed', he explained afterwards, 'to the cult of personality.'

Liu Shao-chi agreed with the suggestion with the words: 'It is probably better to excise it'.

Liu in his political report argued that the credit for the Party's successes should be better distributed:

The reason why the leader of our Party, Comrade Mao Tse-tung, had played the great role of helmsman in our revolution and enjoys a high prestige . . . is not only that he knows how to integrate the universal truth of Marxism-Leninism with the actual practice of the Chinese revolution, but also that he firmly believes in the strength and wisdom of the masses, initiates and advocates the mass line of Party work, and steadfastly upholds the Party's principles of democracy and collective leadership.

This was the first time that Mao's name had been linked with a respect for collective leadership, and Mao himself must have been reminded of his efforts the previous year to side-step his colleagues in order to prove that he was right on the agricultural co-operatives. Did he take the hint that readiness to defer to the majority was as important an element in his leadership, from his colleagues' point of view, as the correctness of his ideas? His own speech, in which he stressed the need for co-operation with non-Communists, got more applause for its international affairs than its domestic passages.

Mao afterwards took Liu to task for declaring at this Congress that 'the contradiction between the proletariat and the bourgeoisie in our country has been basically resolved', and 'that the history of the system of class exploitation, which lasted for several thousand years in our country, has on the whole been brought to an end. . . .'

Another feature of the Eighth Congress was Mao's decision to stand down from the front line of leadership, to enable his senior colleagues to deal with day-to-day affairs and establish their claim to the succession. This followed the shock of the ineptitude of the Soviet leadership after Stalin. One of the innovations of the new Party constitution was the provision for an honorary chairmanship of the Central Committee, obviously with Mao in mind. The Secretariat of the Party was also reorganized and strengthened to enable it to operate effectively without Mao, with Teng Hsiao-ping as the new Party General Secretary.

The consequence of all these moves was that delegates to the Eighth Congress were given the impression that Mao was no longer the supreme figure that he once had been. Explaining why Mao Thought was left out of the Constitution, Liu Shao-chi told delegates that Mao's leadership had been established in 1945: 'Even if we don't talk of it now, everyone will still know about it. Besides, if one is always repeating something so that people get accustomed to hearing it, it does not serve any purpose.'

The drift in Mao's reputation had gone quite far, and he must have been uncomfortably aware that many of his colleagues, particularly Liu Shao-chi and Peng Teh-huai, were not repeating in their public speeches the ritual invocations of his name and thought that had been mandatory in the past. Were they merely drawing the lesson of de-Stalinization? Or were they genuinely weary of him? He was to brood on this for many years.

Chou En-lai's report to the Congress on the economy stressed the need to avoid impetuosity and adventurism. Financial limitations should not be ignored. Liu and Mao were both irritated by the slowdown which the technocrats had imposed in the summer on 1956, but at the Eighth Congress they had to bow to the majority, including especially the provincial Party secretaries, who supported Chou and the planners.

On 23 October 1956 the Hungarian rising broke out. Before this, Mao had shown understanding for the Polish desire for greater independence of Moscow, and he said as much to Anastas Mikoyan and Edward Ochab when they came to represent Russia and Poland at the celebrations of the seventh anniversary of the Chinese People's Republic. Mao defended the Pole against Mikoyan's criticisms, and followed this with a letter to Ochab which probably played an important part in inducing the Polish leader to back the liberal Gomulka as the man to cope with Poland's problems. But after the Hungarian rising Mao's attitude hardened. Liu Shao-chi flew to Moscow to confer with the Russian leadership, consulting frequently with Mao.

'It was no problem', Khrushchev recalled, 'for Liu to get in touch with him on the telephone because Mao is like an owl; he works all night long. Mao always approved whatever Liu recommended. . . .'

In November Mao spoke from the heart to the Central Committee on the major issues confronting it. He began with the widespread doubts about economic policy.

Our planned economy is at once in equilibrium and in disequilibrium. Equilibrium is temporary and conditional. . . . We Marxists hold that disequilibrium, contradiction, struggle and development are absolute, while equilibrium and rest are relative. Relative means temporary, conditional. Viewed in this light, is our economy advancing or retreating? We should tell the masses and the cadres that it is both advancing and retreating, but mainly advancing, though not in the straight line but in a wave-like manner. [Hardly a very encouraging analysis.]

Mao called for much more discussion before the final decision on each annual budget, in order to allow 'all of us to get to understand the contents of the budget'. And this was the cue for a lecture on the way the experts were treating the politicians like himself.

> Otherwise it will always be the comrades in charge who know them better while we on our part will just raise our hands. . . . They are like opera singers on the stage, they know how to sing, we are like the audience, we don't know how to sing. But if we go to the opera often enough, we shall be able to tell good singers from poor ones more or less correctly. After all, it is up to the audience to pass judgment on the singer's performance. And it is with its help that the singer corrects his mistakes. This is where the audience is superior. An opera can continue to run if people like to see it over and over again. Operas which people don't like very much have to be changed. Therefore inside our Central Committee there is the contradiction between experts and non-experts.

Diligence and thrift must be the watchwords.

> Some comrades have suggested that factory directors and heads of colleges and schools might live in sheds, and this, I think, is a good idea, especially in hard times. There were no houses whatsoever when we crossed the marshlands on the Long March, we just slept where we could. . . . We all came through. Our troops had no food and ate the bark and leaves of trees. To share happiness and suffering with the people – we did this in the past, why can't we do it now? As long as we keep on doing so, we shall not alienate ourselves from the masses.

Mao then turned to the international scene and to the dramatic events in East Europe and Russia. 'It was . . . a shock when Beria was uncovered. How could a socialist country produce a Beria?' In Mao's view, 'the sword of Lenin' had been discarded to a considerable extent by some Russian leaders.

> Is the October Revolution still valid? Can it still serve as the example for all countries? Khrushchev's report at the Twentieth Congress of the Communist Party of the Soviet Union says it is possible to seize state power by the parliamentary road, that is to say, it is no longer necessary for all countries to learn from the October Revolution. Once this gate is open, by and large Leninism is thrown away.

Finally Mao came to the subject of 'great democracy' – or more freedom of speech, foreshadowing the convulsions of the Cultural Revolution.

> If great democracy is now to be practised again, I am for it. You are afraid of the masses taking to the streets, I am not, not even if hundreds and thousands should do so. . . . If some people grow tired of life and so become bureaucratic, if, when meeting the masses, they have not a single kind word for them but only take them to task, and if they don't bother to

solve any of the problems the masses may have, they are destined to be overthrown.

Now this danger does exist. If you alienate yourself from the masses and fail to solve their problems, the peasants will wield their carrying-poles, the workers will demonstrate in the streets and the students will create disturbances. Whenever such things happen, they must in the first place be taken as good things, and that is how I look at the matter.

He cited a case where villagers had suddenly been made to move out, without consultation or proper arrangements, to make way for a new airfield. They had complained that 'even the birds will make a few squawks if you go poking with your pole at their nest in a tree and try to bring it down.' 'Teng Hsiao-ping,' Mao accused, 'you, too, have a nest, and if I destroyed it, wouldn't you make a few squawks?' Mao similarly complained about his comrades preventing a hundred students coming up by train from the south to lodge complaints in Peking.

It is my opinion and Premier Chou's that the students should have been allowed to come to Peking and call on the departments concerned. The workers should be allowed to go on strike and the masses to hold demonstrations. Processions and demonstrations are provided for in our constitution. In the future when the constitution is revised, I suggest that the freedom to strike be added, so that the workers shall be allowed to go on strike.

Mao played down the numbers involved in the various suppression campaigns. Since the previous year more than four million people had been investigated, of which only 38,000 – or 1.2 per cent – had been found to be counter-revolutionaries. The previous estimate of 5 per cent was inaccurate because it was based 'on subjective observation, not on objective fact'.

On another occasion Mao invited officials and democratic party leaders to meet him for four hours. In the course of this he held his cigarette up in the air, about a foot above his head, and said:

The masses and cadres have had a hard time of it these past years with our movements, and we ought to give them a chance to take a breath. They ought to have a chance to express their views about the conduct of the government and the Party. I think we will all benefit from hearing their opinions. I know that there is friction between Party and non-Party members, and in all the Party organizations as well. I hope that everybody will express his opinions openly. It's no crime to talk, and nobody will be punished for it.

'We must let "a hundred flowers bloom and a hundred schools

of thought contend"',' Mao said, 'and see which flowers are the best and which school of thought is best expressed, and we shall applaud the best blooms and the best thoughts.'

At the end of the year, Mao, preparing for the Hundred Flowers movement which he was planning for 1957, courted the businessmen and non-Communist intellectuals. He addressed a conference of the factory-owners, businessmen and shopkeepers who were collaborating so nervously with his government.

'I am nobody,' he told them. 'I don't even have a degree.' But he proceeded to give them a long lecture on how to run their businesses. He began by congratulating them on undertaking individual political reform. 'Even you yourselves had not expected that you would have reformed so quickly, and that the tide of learning would be so high. Are you going to develop self-criticism?' To which the eager reply came from the hall, 'We will.'

He went on to talk about Hungary, saying, 'Soviet Russia is a socialist country, and yet she is trying to grab territory from brother nations. This is contrary to the principle of socialism.' He thus convinced them that he was a liberal.

Meanwhile Mao maintained his record of domestic misfortune. Illness struck his wife again that winter. In the previous year, 1955, she had gone back to Russia for an inconclusive check-up: as usual, the Russian and Chinese specialists disagreed with each others' diagnoses. This time, in 1956, Chiang Ching had a complete physical relapse, running a continuously high fever and losing weight suddenly.

Her gynaecologist diagnosed cervical cancer, for which there were two possible treatments, surgery or radiation therapy. She was still feeling the pain of the after-effects from her earlier operation for liver disease and would not tolerate more surgery. The Chinese doctors therefore tried radium implants as well as cobalt 60, but both treatments proved intolerable. The doctors said in desperation that she must go back to Moscow. She suffered agonies in Moscow with successive rounds of cobalt treatment so massive that she spent a lot of time under an oxygen mask.

When Premier Chou was in Moscow in January 1957 to negotiate with the Kremlin, he visited Chiang Ching in hospital and told her that Mao wanted her to stay there until she was clearly on the mend. He condition, however, deteriorated and she developed paralysis. Eventually the Russian doctors in their turn gave up and sent her back to Peking. On the aeroplane subcutaneous bleeding broke out all over her body. There seemed little hope, but eventually she made a complete recovery.

21

THE HUNDRED
FLOWERS

At the beginning of January 1957 Mao made a gesture to China's old-fashioned intellectuals and artists which perhaps spoke more loudly than a hundred speeches. He informed the editor of the monthly magazine *Poetry* that it could publish his classical poems.

'Up to now,' he explained, 'I have never wanted to make these things known in any formal way, because they are written in the old style. I was afraid this might encourage a wrong trend and exercise a bad influence on young people. Besides, they are not up to much as poetry, and there is nothing outstanding about them.'

Private editions of Mao's poems had already been circulating, but Mao had always been diffident about them. 'Whatever you said about his poetry,' Robert Payne had reported from Yenan, 'he had one final, absolute answer – it was shockingly bad, and he would be ashamed to have it seen. It was nonsense, but the kind of nonsense which gave him pleasure, for he giggled again, knowing only too well that the poetry was good.'

Mao's poems mostly followed the *tzu* form, which had been first developed in the late Tang (ninth century AD) period and flowered in the Sung (eleventh and twelfth centuries). 'Just as you', he wrote to Chen Yi, the Foreign Minister, in 1965, 'are good at writing unorthodox verse, I know a little about *tzu* with lines of different lengths. . . . I think both of us are still beginners. . . .'

Mao was aware of the irony of a revolutionary writing classical poetry, which does not lend itself to the modern themes of class struggle and revolution. His old antagonist Wang Ming was very stern about this in his memoirs: of all Mao's thirty-seven poems, he admonished, 'there is not one which glorifies Marxism-Leninism, the Communist Party, the working class, not one which expresses the life of the workers, peasants and soldiers. . . .'

Mao was also aware that by publishing his poems he courted misunderstanding. 'Of course,' he wrote to the prospective publisher, 'our poetry should be written mainly in the modern form. We may write some verse in classical forms as well, but it would not be advisable to encourage young people to do this because these forms would restrict their thought and they are difficult to learn.'

In a speech a year later Mao gave a blunter opinion of the modern poetry being written in China: 'The new poetry of today is formless. Nobody reads it. Anyway I would not read it, not unless you gave me a hundred dollars.'

Among those qualified to enjoy them, opinions differ about Mao's poems. One respected classical scholar from Hunan declared that they were 'certainly not to be considered seriously. . . . There is a dash of audacity in his poems, but I surely cannot agree with the claim that they are unprecedented in the past, or cannot be equalled in the future.' Kuo Mo-jo, the poet in Mao's cabinet, claimed that: 'Chairman Mao's poems have been repeatedly steeled so that they are noble in spirit and harmonious in melody, vigorous in tone and yet lovable in their simplicity. They are loved by everyone and recited everywhere. Yet the fact is', he added engagingly, 'that not everyone really understands them fully, and not every poem is understood by all.'

Jerome Chen, Mao's Chinese biographer who lives in the West, concluded that his poetic abilities, 'although they are uneven, are of no mean order and would have secured him a place in contemporary Chinese literature independent of his pre-eminent position in the political sphere.' Fou Ts'ong, the pianist who fled from Mao's China, nevertheless held him to be a 'great poet'.

Mao had used his poetry as a formidable political weapon in 1945, when he had disarmed Chungking opinion with his poem *Snow*, and he equally disarmed China's intellectuals at the beginning of 1957 by having his classical poems published on the eve of his biggest experiment with free speech – or, as he preferred to call it, 'great democracy' – the Hundred Flowers movement.

Mao explained to provincial and municipal Party secretaries at the beginning of 1957 that he proposed to allow free debate among the intellectuals. He indicated the sort of target he had in mind by attacking the grading of Party officers, a sensitive issue in the Party. 'Some cadres now scramble for fame and fortune and are interested only in personal gain. . . . This business of grading cadres, have done with it! Let wages be roughly evened out, with slight differences here and there. . . .'

Mao then turned to his new theme of great democracy.

There is nothing terrifying about great democracy. On this score I do not see eye to eye with some comrades among you, who seem scared of it. In my view, should great democracy come about, first, you should not be scared of it, and second, you should make an analysis of the words and deeds of its advocates. In pushing their so-called great democracy, those bad types are bound to say or do something wrong, which will only expose and isolate them. . . . In Hungary, great democracy toppled the Party, the government and the army once it was set in motion. This will not happen in China. If a handful of school kids can topple our Party, government and army by a show of force, we must all be fatheads.

In another talk, Mao again defended the place of public argument, first of all in the Sino-Soviet context.

In my view, wrangling is inevitable. Let no one imagine that there is no wrangling between communist parties. How can there be no wrangling in this world of ours? Marxism is a wrangling -ism, dealing as it does with contradictions and struggles. . . .

Truth must out.

It is a dangerous policy to prohibit people from coming into contact with the false, the ugly and the hostile, with idealism and metaphysics and with the twaddle of Confucius, Lao Tzu and Chiang Kai-shek. It will lead to mental deterioration, one-track minds, and unpreparedness to face the world and meet challenges.

You should learn this art of leadership. Don't always try to keep a lid on everything. Whenever people utter queer remarks, go on strike or present a petition, you try to beat them back with one blow, always thinking that these things ought not to occur. . . . Disturbances having good grounds ought to occur; groundless ones will get nowhere. Life should have some complication, otherwise it would be too monotonous.

Meanwhile Chou En-lai had interrupted a tour of several Asian countries in order to rush to Moscow, Budapest and Warsaw, to help in the latest crisis there. 'I told comrade Chou En-lai over the phone', Mao later explained, 'that these people are blinded by their material gains and the best way to deal with them is to give them a good dressing down.'

On 27 February he delivered his famous speech outlining the Hundred Flowers concept for the first time outside the Party – to a large audience of 1800 leading citizens, many of whom were non-Communist, under the title 'On the Correct Handling of Contradictions Among the People'. Once again, Mao jumped the gun on his own colleagues, omitting to clear his new programme of accelerated rectification and free speech through the Central Committee.

The leadership presented a ragged picture at the session when Mao spoke. Liu Shao-chi, who disapproved of the whole idea, was conspicuously absent from the platform, as well as Peng Teh-huai and Lin Piao, who was ill. Lin Po-chu and Chu Teh both stayed away to advertise their dissent and even Lo Jung-huan, one of Mao's own followers, did not show up. Most of the Chinese leaders who had been following the disturbing events in Eastern Europe felt that they made it all the more necessary for the Communist world to maintain unity within itself in the face of US imperialism: 'Don't weaken the socialist camp' was the common theme. Chou had brought back a slightly different message, saying that internal reform was the key to the survival of Communism, and Mao thoroughly agreed with this.

As Mao went through his long speech, according to one of the student leaders, 'eighty per cent of the high-ranking cadres disapproved, and some of them even got up and walked out of the meeting.' Mao had gone too far.

In the weeks that followed, tape recordings of Mao's four-hour speech were circulated around the country for select audiences. A Shanghai businessman was among one of them, and he afterwards described it as delivered in 'Chairman Mao's slow calm voice', beginning by discussing the Hungarian rising and its repercussions in China, and admitting that strikes, student unrest and peasant discontent had taken place.

One highly placed official had worked hard at night, Mao revealed, to prepare and distribute anti-Soviet posters. A well-known scholar had called publicly for the killing of thousands of Communists 'for the good of the people'. Most such people were not counter-revolutionaries, and the trouble should really be laid at the door of 'bureaucratism' among the Communist Party cadres. They had suppressed some of the people's legitimate dissatisfaction instead of educating and persuading, so now they needed to be shown their mistakes so that they could correct them.

Some of the campaigns against counter-revolutionaries had been carried too far, resulting in injustices. These errors would be corrected. But the imperialist claims that twenty million people had been killed as counter-revolutionaries were quite false. The true number was 'not much greater than 700,000'.

A Party rectification campaign would now be inaugurated throughout China which, for its success, needed the support of everybody. The people were to help the Party by criticizing it, speaking out freely and airing their grievances. There would be no retaliation. Indeed, those who would not voice their criticisms 'are not our friends'.

As for Mao himself, he was like a leading character in a well-known opera, now growing too old to play the star's part. He might soon step down to a secondary role. There was no mention of any criteria by which 'poisonous weeds' could be distinguished from 'fragrant flowers'. The impression made on this listener was of a sincere leader making a dramatic change in policy.

Once the *New York Times* had printed, from East European sources, extracts from his speech of 27 February introducing the Hundred Flowers campaign, Mao obviously wanted to publish his own approved version in Peking, but this could not be done until the Party had agreed on what criteria should be inserted to limit the freedoms which had originally been open-ended. When the speech was eventually published on 19 June in the *People's Daily*, three months after it had been delivered, it left out the figure of 700,000 counter-revolutionaries who had been executed, but put in six ways of distinguishing between acceptable and unacceptable criticisms – fragrant flowers from poisonous weeds. They all boiled down to the same thing: 'They should help to strengthen, and not discard or weaken, the leadership of the Communist Party.'

'After the events in Hungary,' Mao put it a few years later, 'we allowed scattered free expression of opinion, and tens of thousands of little Hungaries appeared ... over four hundred thousand rightists had to be purged.'

The published version of *On The Correct Handling of Contradictions Among the People*, when it was eventually put out, stated that China faced two kinds of social contradictions, those between the people and 'the enemy', and those among the people themselves. Who were 'the people'?

At this point of time in China, during the period of building socialism,

... the classes, strata and social groups which favour, support and work for the cause of socialist construction all come within the category of the people, while the social forces and groups which resist the social revolution and are hostile to or sabotage socialist construction are all enemies of the people. ...

Our People's government is one that genuinely represents the people's interests, it is a government that serves the people. Nevertheless there are still certain contradictions between the government and the people. These include contradictions among the interests of the state, the interests of the collective and the interests of the individual; between democracy and centralism; between the leadership and the led; and the contradiction arising from the bureaucratic style of work of certain government workers in their relation with the masses.

The contradiction between the bourgeoisie and the workers was one between exploiter and exploited and was therefore by nature antagonistic. 'But in the concrete conditions of China, this antagonistic class contradiction can, if properly handled, be transformed into a non-antagonistic one, and be resolved by peaceful methods.'

The people's democratic dictatorship 'led by the working class and based on the worker-peasant alliance' was built on the concepts of freedom and democracy. 'But this freedom is freedom with leadership and this democracy is democracy under centralized guidance, not anarchy. Anarchy does not accord with the wishes or the interests of the people.'

Mao then alluded to the Hungarian incident which had made such an impact upon China. 'Certain people in our country were delighted by the events in Hungary. They hoped that something similar would happen in China, that thousands upon thousands of people would demonstrate in the streets against the people's government.' But the Hungarian demonstrators had been misled and had wrought great harm. 'The damage done to the country's economy in a few weeks of rioting will take a long time to repair.' What then was the role of force?

We cannot abolish religion by administrative decree or force people not to believe in it. We cannot compel people to give up idealism any more than we can force them to believe in Marxism. The only way to settle questions of an ideological nature or controversial issues among the people is by the democratic method, the method of discussion, of criticism, of persuasion and education, and not by the method of repression or coercion. . . .

If one persists in using the methods of terror in solving internal antagonisms, it may lead to transformation of these non-antagonistic contradictions into antagonistic ones, as happened in Hungary. . . . He who does not allow himself to be criticized during his life will be criticized after his death. . . . Often correct and good things have first been regarded not as fragrant flowers but as poisonous weeds. Copernicus' theory of the solar system and Darwin's theory of evolution were once dismissed as erroneous and had to win through over bitter opposition. . . .

The class struggle between the proletariat and the bourgeoisie . . . will continue to be long and tortuous and at times will even become very acute. The proletariat seeks to transform the world according to its own world outlook, and so does the bourgeoisie. In this respect, the question of which will win out, socialism or capitalism, is still not really settled. Marxists are still a minority among the entire population as well as among the intellectuals. Therefore, Marxism must still develop through struggle.

What about the role of Marxism? Could it be criticized, even though it was claimed by the Party to be the guiding ideology?

Certainly it can. Marxism is scientific truth and fears no criticism. If it did, and if it could be overthrown by criticism it would be worthless. . . .

Marxists should not be afraid of criticism from any quarter. . . . Plants raised in hot-houses are unlikely to be sturdy.

What, finally, about the danger of strikes and demonstrations of the kind that had been carried out by small numbers of workers and students the year before? 'In a large country like ours, there is nothing to get alarmed about if small numbers of people create disturbances' – a hint of the Cultural Revolution to come in the 1960s.

Mao then travelled to Tsinan and Nanking to lecture the provincial cadres on how they should 'persevere in plain living and struggle' and 'maintain close ties with the masses'. He berated them again for making so much fuss about their own grading, and set out his impossibly high standards for a self-respecting Communist:

I have heard that during the grading of cadres last year, some people burst into tears and made terrible scenes. . . . When the grading doesn't meet their wishes, tears begin to stream down their cheeks. They never shed a single tear during the war against Chiang Kai-shek, the movement to resist US aggression and aid Korea, the agrarian reform and the suppression of counter-revolutionaries, nor have they shed a tear during the building of socialism, but as soon as their personal interests were affected, rivers of tears began to flow. . . .

There is much that is unfair in this world, and maybe you have been improperly graded, but even so there is no reason to make a fuss about it. . . . A Communist is supposed to work hard and to serve the people with his whole heart, not with half or two-thirds. Those whose revolutionary will has been waning should have their spirits revived through rectification.

By April 1957 Mao had retired to Hangchow, the beautiful semi-tropical city south-west of Shanghai which had been the capital of the effete Southern Sung Dynasty in the thirteenth century. For the remaining two decades of his life he spent at least as much time here, away from the hated protocol, bureaucracy and intrigue of Peking, as in the capital itself. Hangchow was humid in the late summer, with temperatures going up to 106°, so that at the height of one summer even the air conditioning could not bring the temperature down below 86°. As a native of Hunan, this suited Mao admirably.

From Hangchow Mao complained about the sabotage of his Hundred Flowers campaign by the Party newspapers (which had failed to carry reports of the relevant decisions) and by other Party leaders. Speaking to local cadres he conceded that he was in a minority on the issue, and that the army propaganda chief who was complaining openly in the press about the unhealthy effect of the liberal policies of the Hundred Flowers, 'represents ninety per cent of the comrades within the Party, so I have no mass base'. He nevertheless insisted that the Party would have to 'open wide' for a time and accept criticism, although he claimed defensively: 'I do not encourage the people to make trouble; I am not holding riot-promoting conferences.'

In this kind of mood, his talk about the future development of the Chinese revolution became wild and speculative. 'I once said that there will still be revolution in one thousand years. But this is not certain. After ten thousand years production relationships will definitely be transformed. In the future it will not be a matter of nationalization but of globalization.' An article in the *People's Daily* a few days later stated that the intellectuals were uncertain whether the call to bloom and contend was sincere, or else a trap to uncover their wrong thinking.

Eventually, after pulling out all his guns, Mao bullied the Central Committee to agree, with evident reluctance, to a new rectification campaign of 'gentle wind and fine rain'. Even so there was confusion over the priorities. Liu Shao-chi set out the targets of the campaign as being, firstly subjectivism, secondly bureaucratism and thirdly sectarianism. But Mao put bureaucratism firmly at the head of the list, thus justifying the need to bring in people from outside the Party to join in the criticism of Party members. This was the feature which Mao's comrades most fiercely resented, his showing them up to outsiders.

Peng Chen, the outstanding second-generation Communist leader and Mayor of Peking, resisted for several days Mao's call for self-criticism and ideological education. He particularly disliked the non-Communist intellectuals, and the feeling was mutual.

But on 30 April Mao's directive went out ordering 'a movement of ideological education carried out seriously, yet as gently as a breeze or mild rain. . . . Comradely heart-to-heart talks in the form of conversations, namely exchange of views between individuals, should be used more and large meetings of criticism or "struggle" should not be held.'

The campaign lasted from 1 May to 7 June. Mao had expected

it to go on for much longer, possibly for several months, but in the end he had to bow to his comrades' reservations. Artists, intellectuals, democratic politicians and students were satisfied that they could speak their minds freely, and they poured out their long bottled-up grievances against the Communists.

On 19 May the campaign of free speech suddenly ran into fast gear at Peking University where hundreds of posters were being stuck up every day enlarging the targets of criticism and rubbing the Party's nose in the dust. On 23 May a young woman lecturer spoke at Peking University's 'democratic plaza', contending that Mao's talks on literature and art at the Yenan forum in 1942 were no longer applicable.

One student gained nation-wide fame by writing a poster every day, each provocatively called a 'poisonous weed'. The first quoted Heraclitus: 'In Ephesus all adult men should die, and government of the city should be handed over to beardless young men.' The *People's Daily* was 'the Great Wall sealing off the truth.'

This fearless youth called on the younger generation to show that, 'Besides those "Three-Good students" (or morons, model students, or "small nails" or "sons and daughters of Mao Tsetung" or whatever you call them, it's just the same) who have annihilated their thinking faculties, there are still among Chinese youth thousands of talented and remarkable persons.' This poster was signed: *'Puer Robustus Sed Malitiosus'*.

Another one who 'bloomed and contended' was the veteran ex-Kuomintang general who had intervened four years earlier in the confrontation between Mao and the old philosopher Liang Shu-ming. He now referred to Mao as 'hot-tempered', 'impetuous' and 'reckless', qualities which had 'often affected his decisions in matters of policy, causing unnecessary deviations in the implementation of government policy'.

In the midst of all the furore, Mao was calmly composing what was to become his most famous poem, the only one in which he referred openly to his personal life. Called *The Immortals*, it recalled the memory of Yang Kai-hui, Mao's first wife, and her martyrdom a quarter-century earlier. 'I lost my proud Poplar and you your Willow. . .'*

Not long after this, the aide who had stayed with Yang Kai-hui in Changsha when Mao left the city in 1927 came to see Mao in Peking. This was the person who had been with her right to the end, and his visit was a poignant reminder to Mao after a thirty

*See page 145 supra.

years' interval of all the dreams and heartbreaks of those early days of his career. When his visitor began to talk of Yang's courage and loyalty and of her hopes for the boy An-ying, Mao burst into tears. 'Kai-hui was a good person,' was all that he could say. 'An-ying was a good son.'

On 15 May, after only two weeks of blooming and contending, Mao applied the brake on his political campaign. 'Over the last few months', he ordered, 'people have been criticizing dogmatism but have allowed revisionism to go unchallenged. Dogmatism should be criticized, or else many mistakes cannot be rectified. Now it is time to direct our attention to criticizing revisionism.'

The Marxists comprised only 'the majority' within the Communist Party, and some bourgeois intellectuals who had agreed earlier to accept socialism and Communist Party leadership now wanted to go back on their word. 'This will not do,' Mao declared. 'Once they back out, there is no place for them in the People's Republic of China. Your ideals are those of the Western world (also known as the free world), you might as well go there.' Many did so, like the pianist Fou Ts'ong who went officially to study in Warsaw and then went on, less officially, to England where he married Yehudi Menuhin's daughter. Thousands of others went, via Hong Kong, to North America, Europe, South-East Asia and Australia.

Ten days later Mao hemmed in the Hundred Flowers campaign even more, telling young non-Communists that the Communist Party was 'the core of leadership of the whole Chinese people', without which the cause of socialism could not be victorious. 'Any word or deed at variance with socialism is completely wrong.' Meanwhile extracts from Khrushchev's secret speech denouncing Stalin, translated from the *New York Times*, were being posted up at Peking University.

One of the leading non-Communist ministers in the government said that 'venerable' Mao had assumed that democratic parties would put forward criticisms politely. 'But the estimate was incomplete,' he explained. 'It was not thought that the Party could have committed so many mistakes.' Telegrams of complaint from Party officials in the provinces demanding that the campaign be stopped were said to be 'coming in like snowflakes'.

On 8 June Mao threw in his hand, issuing a directive to muster forces to repel the 'wild attacks of the rightists'. Those who had spoken out were now attacked as bourgeois rightists, just as the perceptive non-Communists had feared from the outset. Leaders of the student riot in Wuhan were actually executed.

Mao's support in the Politburo was now down to a bare majority, vulnerable to only one or two waverers. This kind of situation had not excessively worried him before, for example in 1955 when he had pressed ahead for collectivization. But then his ideas had worked. Now his Hundred Flowers movement was in trouble. Peng Chen, the Mayor of Peking, rubbed Mao's nose in the dirt. He told his men in Peking,

Stalin considered himself perpetually and absolutely correct. The result was that he was ... smashed to smithereens. ...

All men make mistakes; what matters is the size and nature of the mistakes. ... The cadres in our Party are all tools of the Party. The problem is, how should a tool like comrade Mao Tse-tung be better used. ...

But the students were bitter. One of the last posters to go up at Peking University, signed by 'a group of first year students in the department of history', read:

Intelligent friends! Everybody has been cheated! The goal of the Rectification Campaign of the Communist Party was not the removal of the three evils, the solution of the contradictions among the people or the improvement of the style of work, but the acquisition of even greater power, to be able better to rule over the 'stupid' Chinese people. Isn't that clear? Even after the Emperor has ordered the Party to mend its ways, the mandarins of all degrees are nevertheless still in place, everything remains just as before. Lately, the Emperor has discovered some 'right-wing elements' and he now uses them to frighten the 'stupid' Chinese people!

In a July newspaper editorial Mao sought to defend himself from the charge of having misled democrats about the Hundred Flowers movement.

The purpose was to let demons and devils, ghosts and monsters 'air views freely' and let poisonous weeds sprout and grow in profusion so that the people, now shocked to find these ugly things still existing in the world, would take action to wipe them out. In other words, the Communist Party foresaw this inevitable class struggle between the bourgeoisie and the proletariat.

The bourgeoisie and bourgeois intellectuals were allowed to start this war. ... Some people say this was a covert scheme. We say it was an overt one. For we made it plain to the enemy beforehand: only when ghosts and monsters are allowed to come into the open can they be wiped out; only when poisonous weeds are allowed to sprout from the soil can they be uprooted.

But Mao was for obvious reasons unready to see the leading

rightists whom he had led on at the beginning of May punished by
his Communist critics, and Chou En-lai supported him in this.
The Party establishment, however, led by Liu and Peng Chen,
wanted to deal harshly with the democratic politicians. One result
of this was a series of published self-criticisms by such politicians
in which attacks on Mao himself were allowed to be circulated.
One rightist was quoted as saying that collectivization had been
badly done: 'The peasants are cursing Chairman Mao.' Another
damned Mao's temperament as tempestuous and Bismarckian.
Mao was accused of favouring non-Marxist flatterers and time-
servers over his own Party colleagues.

Mao's defence was to go round the country giving his own
version of events, as he did to cadres in Shanghai on 9 July.

I'm the kind of person who consults the workers and peasants before I do
anything significant or make decisions on major issues, talking over and
discussing things with them and with the cadres close to them to see if my
ideas are all right. This makes visits to various places necessary. Staying
put in Peking could be fatal. It is a barren place where you can't get any
raw material.

It all rested on Mao's optimism about the people. 'All wisdom
comes from the masses. I have always said that it is intellectuals
who are most ignorant. This is the heart of the matter.' But it was
necessary to 'set a fire going' every two or three years.

In Yenan we were not so daring, we did not forbid but we also did not
express. We had not carried out the socialist revolution and had no
experience, and this episode of frank and loud airing of views has
increased our experience. In future we shall still wish to have a frank
airing of views. Let a hundred flowers blossom does not embrace
counter-revolution, however. We are able to have a frank airing of views
once a year. To suppress the people as though they are enemies is very
dangerous. . . .

Mao had lost none of his optimism, and now directed this
towards the economy again. Two days later, speaking to the
Central Committee on the population question, he remarked:

In my opinion China must depend on intensive cultivation to feed
itself. One day China will become the world's number one high-yield
country. . . . I think an average of half an acre of land per person is more
than enough and in future one-sixth of an acre will yield enough grain to
feed one individual. Of course birth control will still be necessary, and I
am not encouraging more births. . . . There should . . . be a ten-year
programme for family planning. . . . As far as procreation is concerned,
the human race has been in a state of total anarchy and has failed to
exercise control.

Mao suggested that the steel target would be reached faster if there were more small plants. He asked for the slogan of 'greater, faster, better and more economical results', which had been dropped in the second half of 1956 by 'a gust of wind', to be restored. 'Is this possible?' he asked. 'Please consider the matter.'

Mao also spoke of his ambitions to change the physical face of China, referring in a later speech to the campaign to eliminate the 'four pests'.

I am very interested in this matter. I don't know how you feel about it. But I assume you are interested too. Doing away with the four pests is a big public health campaign and a campaign to destroy superstition. Eliminating them is not easy. To exterminate the four pests also calls for free airing of views, great debate and big-character posters.

If the entire nation is mobilized to do this and achieve some success, I believe there will be a change in the mentality of the people and the morale of the Chinese nation will be given a big boost. We must invigorate this nation of ours. The prospects for the success of family planning are good. There should be a great debate on this matter too, and there should be periods of trial, expansion and popularization, each lasting several years. . . . I say this country of ours is full of hope.

22
THE EAST WIND PREVAILS

While the state of Communism in China thus seesawed up and down, the position of international Communism was definitely improving. In August 1957 the Russians acquired their first inter-continental ballistic missile. In October they launched their Sputnik satellite into space, and agreed to supply Mao with nuclear know-how for national defence, including a sample atom-bomb and technology for its manufacture.

With this pact in his pocket Mao went to Moscow in November 1957 to attend the world conference of Communist Parties on the Soviet Union's fortieth anniversary. He had two themes in his mind for the Moscow 'summit'. One was the importance of maintaining the unity of the socialist camp, the other was how best to exploit its new technological superiority (something which he in fact overestimated).

At Moscow airport Mao gave praise to the Russians, which, given their past disagreements, was generous: 'There is no force on earth which can separate us.'

Khrushchev was surprised to find that Mao turned down his idea for a division of labour within the international movement, whereby the Chinese would concentrate upon establishing closer contacts with the countries of Asia and Africa, especially India, Pakistan and Indonesia – leaving the Russians to deal with Western Europe and the Americas.

'No,' Mao replied when this idea was put to him in Moscow, 'it's out of the question. The leading role in Africa and Asia should belong to the Soviet Union. . . . The Communist Party of the Soviet Union should be the one and only centre of the international Communist movement, and the rest of us should be united around that centre.'

'I think', Mao told Khrushchev on another occasion, 'if the imperialists were to attack China, you shouldn't intervene. We should fight them by ourselves. Your job would be to survive. Let us watch out for ourselves. What's more, if you were attacked, I don't think you should retaliate.'

'And what should we do?' Khrushchev asked.

'Retreat'.

'Where to?'

'You've retreated before,' Mao pointed out. 'You retreated all the way to Stalingrad during World War Two, and if you're attacked again you could retreat all the way to the Urals and hold out for two or three years. You'd have China at your back.'

'Comrade Mao Tse-tung,' Khrushchev replied, 'if a war started now, how long do you think it would last? It wouldn't be like the last war. That was a war of air forces and tanks. Now there are missiles and atomic bombs. What makes you think we'd have three years in which to retreat to the Urals? We'd probably have only a few days, and after that there would be nothing left of us but a few tattered remnants scratching along. If we told the enemy that we won't retaliate, we'd be inviting them to attack.'

In Moscow Mao addressed the Supreme Soviet, the first time a Chinese head of state had ever addressed the law-making body of one of the great European powers. While praising Russia's accomplishments since 1917, and its help to China, Mao made it clear that his revolution had its own characteristics and that China would follow her own star.

For thousands of years the working people of the world and all progressive humanity have dreamed of building a society in which there would be no exploitation of man by man. This dream was realized on one-sixth of the earth's land surface for the first time in history by the October Revolution....

The Chinese people are fortunate in having the experience of the October Revolution and of the socialist construction in the Soviet Union, which enables them to make fewer mistakes, to avoid many others and to pursue their course fairly smoothly, although they still face many difficulties.

It is clear that, after the October Revolution, if a proletarian revolutionary of any country should overlook or not seriously study the experience of the Russian revolution, of the proletarian dictatorship and of socialist construction of the Soviet Union, and should fail to use these experiences analytically and in a creative way in the light of the specific conditions in his own country, he would not be able to master Leninism, which represents a new stage in the development of Marxism, and he would not be able to solve the problems of revolution and construction in his own country correctly. He would either commit doctrinaire or revisionist mistakes. We must oppose both these deviations simultaneously, but at present, to oppose revisionist deviation is a particularly urgent task....

Ten days later, Mao put in an unexpected appearance at a
conference of the Chinese students in Russia. Greeted with shouts
of, 'Long live Chairman Mao, Long long life to Chairman Mao!'
he responded: 'Please don't say that. I am making only a five-year
plan for my personal future.' He sat on the rostrum, lit up a cigar
and addressed them on the new superiority of the socialist camp.
They reported afterwards that:

Chairman Mao pointed out . . . that the appearance in the heavens of
two artificial satellites and the coming to Moscow of delegates from the
sixty-four communist and workers' parties to celebrate the holiday of the
October Revolution mark a new turning point. The forces of socialism
surpass the forces of imperialism. . . .

Chairman Mao said that the direction of the wind in the world had
changed. In the struggle between the socialist and capitalist camps, it
was no longer the West wind that prevailed over the East wind, but the
East wind that prevailed over the West wind [a classical phrase from
Dream of the Red Chamber]. The whole world now has a population of 2.7
billion, of which the various socialist countries have nearly one billion,
the independent, former colonial countries more than 700 million, the
countries now struggling for independence or for complete independence
plus the capitalist countries with neutralist tendencies 600 million, and
the imperialist camp only about 400 million, besides which they are also
divided internally. Earthquakes are likely to occur over there.

Next day, on 18 November, Mao spoke at last to the Moscow
Conference of Communist Parties, elaborating these themes. He
explained his differences with Khrushchev, but in a mild and
mostly reasonable manner.

Some seem to think that, once in the Communist Party, people all
become safe with no differences or misunderstandings, and that the
Party is not subject to analysis, that is to say, it is monolithic and
uniform, hence there is no need for talks. It seems as if people have to be
one hundred per cent Marxist once they are in the Party. Actually there
are Marxists of all degrees, those who are one hundred per cent, ninety,
eighty, seventy, sixty or fifty per cent Marxist, and some who are only ten
or twenty per cent Marxist. Can't two or more of us have talks together in
a small room? Can't we proceed from the desire for unity and hold talks
in the spirit of helping each other? . . .

Any kind of world, and of course class society in particular, teems with
contradictions. Some say that there are contradictions to be 'found' in
socialist society, but I think this is a wrong way of putting it. The point is
not that there are contradictions to be found, but that it teems with
contradictions.

Mao then went on to deliver what became, for the international
community, one of the most famous remarks he ever made. He

talked about the possibility of a new world war, in which atomic bombs might be dropped. He had already, three years earlier, in a conversation with the first Finnish Ambassador, revealed a certain wildness on this question.

Even if the US atom bombs were so powerful, that when dropped on China they would make a hole right through the earth or even blow it up, that would hardly mean anything to the universe as a whole though it might be a major event in the solar system. . . . The sooner they make war the sooner they will be wiped from the face of the earth. Then a people's United Nations would be set up, maybe in Shanghai, maybe somewhere in Europe, or it might be set up again in New York provided the US warmongers had been wiped out.

At the Moscow conference in 1957 Mao was not so reckless, but his words were widely misunderstood, causing alarm on both sides of the Iron Curtain.

At present another situation has to be taken into account, namely, that the war maniacs may drop atomic and hydrogen bombs everywhere. They drop them and we drop them too; thus there will be chaos and lives will be lost. . . . How many people will die if war should break out? Out of the world's population of 2700 million, one third – or, putting the figure a bit higher, one half – may be lost. . . .

I debated this question with a foreign statesman [Nehru]. He believed that if an atomic war was fought, the whole of mankind might be annihilated. I said that if the worst came to the worst and half of mankind died, the other half would remain while imperialism would be razed to the ground and the whole world would become socialist. In a certain number of years, there would be 2700 million people again and definitely more.

This was how the *People's Daily* reported his speech, but Khrushchev reported it more colourfully. His paraphrase of Mao's argument was this: 'As for China, if the imperialists unleash war on us, we may lose more than three hundred million people. So what? War is war. The years will pass, and we'll get to work producing more babies than ever before.'

Mao had put the reproduction sequel more crudely than this, however, according to Khrushchev: 'He allowed himself to use an indecent expression. . . .' Khrushchev was sitting next to Soong Ching-ling, the non-Communist widow of Sun Yat-sen, who had joined Mao's government and was in his delegation to Moscow. 'She burst out laughing at Mao's racy language. Mao laughed, too, so we all joined in with laughter.'

The speech met with an indignant reception in Moscow. Gomulka, the Polish leader whose rise to power on a platform of more freedom from Soviet control had been supported by Mao, spoke out strongly against Mao's nuclear analysis. 'Mao Tse-tung', the Czech leader, Anton Novotny, said, 'says he's prepared to lose three hundred million people out of a population of six hundred million. What about us? We have only twelve million people in Czechoslovakia. We'd lose every last soul in a war. There wouldn't be anyone left to start over again.'

Mao was simply attempting to bolster his international audience in the way that he would a Chinese audience, by speaking out what the worst might be (and thereby reducing its terror), asserting that it would never happen anyway, but asserting also that if it did happen life would still go on and all would not be lost. The East Europeans took him more literally than he intended, and Mao acquired an unjust international reputation, which he never completely threw off, for blustering belligerence.

On returning to Peking he plunged into his crusade to accelerate the development of both socialism and modernization in China, ready bluntly to criticize the USSR where its leadership had proved wrong.

He turned on his domestic critics and on those who resisted his unorthodox methods of speeding up things, at a conference in 1958 at Nanning. He attacked the Politburo which, 'like the United Nations of Dulles ... has become a voting machine. You give it a perfect document and it has to be passed. ... The document does not go into textual research and analysis, and it also has foreign words. I too have a method, and that is passive resistance. I will not read it. For two years I have not read your documents and I do not expect to read them this year either.'

Mao made fun of the typical procedure: 'Ten minutes before the conference opens the document is produced for resolution without any consideration being given to people's state of mind. You are experts, and also reds. The majority in the Politburo are red but not expert.' Mao sympathized with the desire of bureaucrats to put the best face on things and pretend to a perfection thay might not actually possess. 'It is like Marguerite, the heroine of the novel, *La Dame aux Camélias*, who felt it necessary to put on make-up when she saw her lover, although she was dying.' Mao wanted administration to be conducted in a more open and candid manner. 'What is wrong with seeing people in a dishevelled, ungroomed condition?'

His way of developing policy ideas was this:

You write them down one at a time as they come to your mind, setting forth opinions which are not yet well defined in your mind and ideas which are not yet crystal clear, and discuss them with others. Don't treat everything that has been issued as an 'imperial edict', so that once it has been discussed it becomes inflexible.

(The informal versions of Mao's speeches are indeed full of references to his having changed his mind since an earlier speech or statement.)

Mao insisted that the disagreements be argued out within the Politburo or Central Committee:

It just will not do without having a tit-for-tat confrontation. It will either be your persuading me or my persuading you. Or be a middle-of-the-roader. Some people are just that; they will not take a stand on major issues. Marxism is supposed to teach us not to camouflage one's own view, isn't it?

He complained of the way his fellow politicians had treated him:

I was only an actor playing the part of an old retainer, while they were the stars. Anyway, I do have some seniority, and I should be informed. I am rather disappointed.

I stand for the theory of permanent revolution. Do not mistake this for the Trotskyist theory of permanent revolution. In making revolution one must strike while the iron is hot – one revolution must follow another, the revolution must continually advance. The Hunanese often say, 'Straw sandals have no pattern – they shape themselves in the making.' . . .

At the end of January 1958 Mao succeeded in getting a very broad programme of faster economic development accepted within the Party, in a document which came to be known as the *Sixty Points on Working Methods*. It was a compromise formulation in which several leaders had participated, but Mao personally approved or modified each paragraph in it.

The burden of the *Sixty Points* was that the next three years would be crucial in China's economic advance, and the people's energy should therefore be mobilized 'in an entirely uninhibited manner'. Experimental fields would be popularized in agriculture, and all Party Committee members should 'leave their offices for four months every year, to investigate and study at a lower level.'

On 10 March Mao ridiculed at Chengtu the immaturity of Chinese attitudes in the earlier 1950s.

I couldn't have eggs or chicken soup for three years, because an article appeared in the Soviet Union which said that one shouldn't eat them. Later they said that one could eat them. It didn't matter whether the article was correct or not, the Chinese listened all the same and respectfully obeyed. . . . In short, the Soviet Union was tops.

The significance of this in the economy was obvious.

We couldn't manage the planning, construction and assembly of heavy industrial plants. We had no experience, China had no experts, the Minister himself was an outsider, so we had to copy from foreign countries, and having copied we were unable to distinguish good from bad. Also we had to make use of Russian experience and Russian experts to break down the bourgeois ideology of China's old experts. . . .

When Chinese artists painted pictures of me together with Stalin, they always made me a little bit shorter, thus blindly knuckling under to the moral pressure exerted by the Soviet Union at that time. Marxism-Leninism looks at everyone on equal terms, and all people should be treated as equals. . . .

There are two kinds of cult of the individual. One is correct such as that of Marx, Engels, Lenin, and the correct side of Stalin. These we ought to revere and continue to revere for ever. It would not do not to revere them. As they held truth in their hands, why should we not revere them? We believe in truth; truth is the reflection of objective existence. A squad should revere its squad leader; it would be quite wrong not to.

Then there is the incorrect kind of cult of the individual in which there is no analysis, simply blind obedience. This is not right. . . . The question at issue is not whether or not there should be a cult of the individual, but rather whether or not the individual concerned represents the truth. If he does, then he should be revered. If truth is not present then even collective leadership will be no good.

Now was the time to apply analysis to Stalin, the 'old ancestor' (he used the term *lao tsu-tsung*, which had commonly been applied when he was a young man to the Dowager Empress Tzu-hsi), separating his faults from his virtues.

The Chinese revolution won victory by acting contrary to Stalin's will. . . . When our revolution succeeded, Stalin said it was a fake. We did not argue with him, but as soon as we fought the war to resist America and aid Korea our revolution became a genuine one in his eyes.

In a second talk at Chengtu a few days later, Mao threw out his ideas on the new Chinese development model. China, he insisted, could do better than the Russians, 'for there are more of us, and the political conditions are different, too: we are livelier, and there is more Leninism here. They, on the other hand, have let part of Leninism go by the board, they are lifeless and without vitality.'

At the same time, the speed of construction was something 'that exists objectively', and China should not attempt the impossible. 'We must get rid of the empty reports and foolish boasting, we must not compete for reputation, but serve reality. Some of the targets are high, and no measures have been taken to implement them; that is not good. . . .'

Mao then held forth for a very long time on the need to accept the tensions generated by fast progress. The Russians did not talk about the contradictions between leaders and led, but, 'if there were no contradictions and no struggle, there would be no world, no progress, no life, there would be nothing at all. To talk all the time about unity is "a pool of stagnant water"; it can lead to coldness.'

On this question Mao directly challenged the Russian theorists, including the philosopher Yudin whom Stalin had sent as his first ambassador in Peking to tutor him. *The Concise Philosophical Dictionary*, which Yudin had co-authored in the 1930s and had been translated into Chinese in the 1940s, 'makes a specialty of opposing me. It says the transformation of birth into death is metaphysical, and the transformation of war into peace is wrong.'

In the last analysis, who is right? Let me ask; if living beings do not result from the transformation of inanimate matter, where do they come from? All living substances result from changes in twelve elements such as nitrogen and hydrogen. . . . Sons are transformed into fathers, fathers are transformed into sons: women are transformed into men, men are transformed into women. Such transformations cannot take place directly, but after marriage, sons and daughters are born; is this not transformation?

The universe, too, undergoes transformation, it is not eternal. Capitalism leads to socialism, socialism leads to communism, and communist society must still be transformed, it will also have a beginning and an end. . . . Monkeys turned into men, mankind arose; in the end, the whole human race will disappear, it may turn into something else, at that time the earth itself will also cease to exist. The earth must certainly be extinguished, the sun too will grow cold.

After the philosophy, back to the steel industry.

There remains a question in my mind, about producing, in the course of the second five-year plan, twenty million tons of steel. Is this a good thing, or will it throw everything into confusion? I'm not sure at present, so I want to hold meetings.

In a final talk at Chengtu in March, Mao dwelt on the cultural aspect of the Chinese revolution and the need for open debate.

Under socialism private property still exists, the small group still exists, the family still exists. The family, which emerged in the last period of primitive communism, will in future be abolished. It had a beginning, and will come to an end. Kang Yu-wei perceived this in his book, *Universal Harmony*. Historically, the family was a production unit, a consumption unit, a unit for the procreation of the labour force of the next generation, and a unit for the education of children. . . .

But in future the family could impede the development of production.

Under the present system of distribution of 'to each according to his work', the family is still of use. When we reach the stage of the communist relationship of distribution of 'to each according to his need', many of our concepts will change. After maybe a few thousand years, or at the very least several hundred years, the family will disappear. Many of our comrades do not dare to think about these things. They are very narrow-minded. . . .

Professors – we have been afraid of them ever since we came into the towns. We did not despise them, we were terrified of them. When confronted by people with piles of learning we felt that we were good for nothing. . . .

This attitude is another example of the slave mentality, a relic from the time of 'gratitude for His Majesty's favours'. We must not tolerate it any longer. Naturally we cannot go out tomorrow and beat them up. We have to make contact with them, educate them, and make friends with them.

Here Mao went into his oft-repeated set-piece on the capacity in history of the young and uneducated to create new schools of thought.

Confucius started at the age of twenty-three; and how much learning did Jesus have? Sakyamuni founded Buddhism at the age of nineteen. . . . What learning did Sun Yat-sen have in his youth? He only went through higher middle school. Marx was also very young when he first created Dialectical Materialism.

The Chinese Communists should not feel diffident about their theory. 'Now we want to run journals and to prevail over the bourgeois intellectuals; we only need to read a dozen or so books and we can beat them. . . .' The people in history who had been genuinely inventive were relatively unlearned, and were always opposed by the 'old fogies'.

The inventor of sleeping-pills was not even a doctor, let alone a famous doctor; he was only a pharmacist. At first the Germans did not take him seriously, but the French welcomed him. That was how sleeping-pills started.

I am told that penicillin was invented by a man who worked as a laundryman in a dyer's and cleaner's. Franklin of America, who discovered electricity, began as a newspaper boy. Later, he became biographer, politician and scientist. Gorki had only two years of elementary schooling. Of course some things can be learnt at school; I don't propose to close all the schools. What I mean is that it is not absolutely necessary to attend school.

So it was with Mao and his fellow Communists in China: 'When we started to make revolution, we were mere twenty-year-old boys, while the rulers of that time ... were old and experienced. They had more learning, but we had more truth.'

But the major criticism of the opponents of the Great Leap Forward, like Chang Hsi-jo, the non-Communist who had studied under Laski at the London School of Economics and served as China's Minister of Education in the 1950s, was rebutted by Mao:

Chang Hsi-jo criticized us for 'craving greatness and success, being impatient for quick results, scorning the past and putting blind faith in the future'.

This is just what the proletariat is like! Irrigation, rectification, anti-rightism, 600 million people engaged in a great movement. Isn't this 'craving for greatness and success'? In setting average advanced norms for workers, aren't we 'being impatient for quick results'? Unless we despise the old system and the old reactionary productive relationships, what do we think we are doing? If we do not have faith in socialism and communism, what do we think we are doing?

Mao went through the country encouraging the local Party cadres to shed their doubts and hesitations and release a new upsurge of economic activity.

Throughout the country, the communist spirit is surging forward.... In view of this, our country may not need as much time as previously thought to catch up with the big capitalist countries in industrial and agricultural production.

All decadent modes of thought and other unsuitable parts of the superstructure are crumbling daily. It will still take time to clear this refuse away completely, but there can be no doubt that the influence of these things has disintegrated.

Apart from their other characteristics, China's 600 million people have two remarkable peculiarities; they are, first of all, poor, and secondly, blank. That may seem like a bad thing, but it is really a good thing. Poor people want change, want to do things, want revolution. A clean sheet of paper has no blotches, and so the newest and most beautiful words can be written on it, the newest and most beautiful pictures can be painted on it.

The people's commune, named after the Paris Commune which so fascinated Mao, emerged during the spring and summer of 1958. The first hint of it came in articles by Chen Po-ta setting out Mao's desire to see co-operatives transformed into comprehensive organizations for industrial and agricultural co-operation, to constitute also the nation's basic social unit. Co-operatives were already amalgamating in order to facilitate the building of large-scale dams and irrigation works, but now they learned of Mao's ideas on integrating industry, commerce, education and government into one large social framework.

Mao toured three provinces in the summer to see for himself how they were going, and finally gave his blessing to the Chili-ying commune. 'It looks very hopeful,' he declared. 'I wish all of Honan were as good as this. . . . If there is a Commune like this, then there can be many more.' Two or three days later he declared his approval in more general terms, and this was taken as the signal for rural cadres to follow throughout the country even though the communes had not yet been endorsed by the Party's Central Committee. Through the communes, and by dint of hard work, China could reach Communism in six or seven years.

But Mao's critics were still vocal. On 24 April Mao's fellow Hunanese and old comrade from Chingkangshan, Peng Teh-huai, led, as Minister of Defence, a Chinese military goodwill mission to the capitals of the Warsaw Pact countries. He may well have travelled in the same aircraft as the senior Vice-Minister of Foreign Affairs, Lo Fu, who was going to Warsaw as the Chinese observer at the Warsaw Pact Foreign Ministers' Conference. They probably exchanged views on the recent dramatic developments in policy under Mao's leadership. As former Chinese representative on the Comintern and ex-Ambassador in Moscow, Lo Fu deplored Mao's quarrel with the Kremlin.

Peng had come to question Mao's concept of a nation in arms as expressed in the creation of a mass-scale amateur militia. He believed that China would do better with a fully professional army, employed in the barracks rather than in the rice-fields, supplied with nuclear arms by the only available ally, Russia. Hence Peng disapproved of Mao's divergence from Moscow.

In May, during the Eighth Party Congress, in spite of widespread doubts, Mao finally gained endorsement for the Great Leap Forward. He made four speeches ranging over all the important issues and hitting at several targets. One was the diffidence of the Chinese in following such a demanding foreign tutor as Karl Marx, who 'lived in a very tall building, and one had to climb many flights of stairs to reach him, something unattainable in a lifetime. . .' But 'stairs can be made and so can elevators', and this led to the flourish of a pedagogical device much favoured by Mao, that of looking through the other end of a telescope. He made the Chinese see themselves through foreign eyes.

I once asked some comrades around me whether we lived in heaven or on earth. They all shook their heads and said that we lived on earth. I said no, we live in heaven. When we look at the stars from the earth, they are in heaven. But if there are people in the stars, when they look at us, wouldn't they think that we are in heaven? Therefore I say that we live in heaven while also on earth at the same time.

The Chinese like the gods. I asked them whether we were gods. They answered no. I said wrong. The gods live in heaven. We live on earth, but also in heaven; so, why shouldn't we be considered gods also? If there were people in the stars, wouldn't they also consider us as gods?

My third question was whether the Chinese were also foreigners? They said no, only the foreigners were foreigners. I said wrong, the Chinese were also foreigners, because when we consider the people of foreign countries as foreigners, wouldn't they also consider us as foreigners?'

Mao admitted his own ignorance on many subjects:

'Neither do I understand industry. I know nothing about it, yet I do not believe that it is unattainable. I discussed the subject with several persons in charge of industry. It seems to be incomprehensible at the beginning, but becomes comprehensible after a few years of study. There's nothing much to it!

Having quoted so many famous names from Chinese history, Mao could not resist invoking the name of the most famous emperor of them all, in a context where he was explicitly inviting comparison. The emperor Chin Shih-huang, founder of the Chin dynasty in the first century BC, had been an expert in 'respecting the modern and belittling the ancient', Mao said.

'Chin Shih-huang', Lin Piao interrupted, 'burned the books and buried the scholars alive.'

'What did he amount to?' Mao went on, stimulated by this interjection.

He only buried alive 460 scholars while we buried 46,000. In our suppression of counter-revolutionaries, did we not kill some counter-revolutionary intellectuals? You accuse us of acting like Chin Shih-

huang, but you are wrong; we surpass him one hundred times. You
berate us for imitating Chin Shih-huang in enforcing dictatorship. We
admit them all. What is regrettable is that you did not say enough. We
have had to say it for you.

At which there was laughter in the hall.

So brimming with optimism was Mao at this moment that he
was able to envisage China's achievement of big-power status. 'I
feel that after fifteen years we will become cocky, and big-nation
chauvinism may appear.' Things were at last beginning to go in
the right direction in China: 'Confidence has increased because
of the Great Leap Forward in agricultural production. . . . I feel
our communism may arrive in advance of schedule.'

Mao reprimanded the speaker from the previous day who had
said that one couldn't go wrong if one followed 'a certain individual'.

By 'a certain individual', he meant me. This statement needs mod-
ification. One should follow and yet not follow. An individual is sometimes right and sometimes wrong. Follow him when he is right and do
not follow when he is wrong. One must not follow without discrimination . . . wherever truth is, we follow. . . . One must have independent
thinking.

Optimism oozed from almost every line of Mao's speech to the
heads of delegations to the congress on 18 May. 'With 11 million
tons of steel next year and 17 million tons the year after, the
world will be shaken,' he boasted. 'If we can reach 40 million
tons in five years we may possibly catch up with Great Britain in
seven years. Add another eight years and we will catch up with
the US.'

Nor should China be afraid of the population doom-watchers.

We are not afraid of a population of 800 millions or one billion.
American reporters say that, after one hundred years, the Chinese
population will constitute fifty per cent of the world population. By that
time our cultural level will be high. When all the people are college-
educated they will naturally practise birth-control.

He also defended his impulsiveness: 'I consciously used the
rightists to carry out the rectification. Turn it loose first before
thinking of a method. Struggle a few rounds and see.'

At the Eighth Party Congress Mao was able to reverse the
alignments which he had faced over his Hundred Flowers campaign. Because the Hundred Flowers had threatened Liu Shao-
chi's Party organization, he and his group opposed it, whereas
Chou En-lai, with nothing equal at stake, was ready to support

Mao. This time it was the economic planning apparatus of Chou's technocrats in the State Council which was threatened by Mao's unorthodox intervention in the economy, and so Chou opposed it. But Liu, perhaps getting his own back on Chou, was ready, with some reluctance, to fall in behind Mao on the Great Leap Forward. Perhaps he guessed – even hoped – that Mao would over-reach himself.

Just after the Eighth Congress had given Mao his head, Peng Teh-huai on his East European tour had a meeting with Khrushchev in Tirana, the Albanian capital. It was afterwards alleged that he delivered to the Russian leader a catalogue of the complaints which he and others in the Chinese Party had against Mao's leadership.

In June Mao spoke at a forum of the Military Affairs Committee, trying to shock the soldiers out of their debilitating dependence on the Russians. The question of producing a book of combat regulations had come up.

When the Soviet comrade advisers saw that we were not copying theirs, they made adverse comments and were displeased. We might ask these Soviet comrades: Do you copy our regulations? If they say they don't, then we will say: If you don't copy ours, we won't copy yours. . . .

We have rich experience, more than the Soviet Union. We should not regard our own experience as worthless. This is wrong.

'Our experience', Lin Piao, ever the parrot, interjected, 'is very rich. We must not throw gold away as though it were yellow dust.'

At the end of June Mao read in the *People's Daily* a news report about the extinction of leeches and the elimination of schistosomiasis in a particular locality. The news 'excited me so much that I was unable to sleep that night. When the next morning came, the breeze rose and the sun shone upon my windows, I was still gazing at the southern sky and happily writing these lines.' The lines were the poem called 'Farewell to the God of Plagues':

So many green streams and blue hills, but to what avail?
This tiny creature left even Hua To powerless!
Hundreds of villages choked with weeds, men wasted away;
Thousands of homes deserted, ghosts chanted mournfully.
Motionless, by earth I travel thirty thousand miles a day.
Surveying the sky I see a myriad Milky Ways from afar.
Should the Cowherd ask tidings of the God of Plague,
Say the same griefs flow down the stream of time.

The spring wind blows amid profuse willow wands,
Six hundred million in this land all equal Yao and Shun.
Crimson rain swirls in waves under our will,
Green mountains turn to bridges at our wish.
Gleaming mattocks fall on the Five Ridges heaven-high;
Mighty arms move to rock the earth round the Triple River.
We ask the God of Plague: 'Where are you bound?'
Paper barges aflame and candle-light illuminate the sky.

A month later Khrushchev flew in on an unexpected visit, apprehensive lest the Russians become involved in a rash Chinese entanglement with the Americans in the Taiwan Straits. He had a conversation with Mao which echoed the one which Mao had had with Stalin nine years earlier about the capture of Shanghai. This time, Khrushchev was puzzled to know why the Chinese had not taken from the Kuomintang the off-shore islands of Quemoy and Matsu when it seemed they were able to do so.

'Comrade Mao,' he asked, 'why did you stop just as you were within reach of victory?'

'We knew what we were doing,' said Mao.

'What do you mean, you knew what you were doing? You started the operation in the first place in order to seize the islands, and you stopped just short of your objective. What did that prove? Are you now trying to tell me you never intended to go through with your plan?'

'All we wanted to do,' Mao replied, 'was show our potential. We don't want Chiang to be far away from us. We want to keep him within our reach. Having him on Quemoy and Matsu means that we can get at him with our shore batteries as well as our force. If we'd occupied the islands, we would have lost the ability to cause him discomfort any time we want.'

Khrushchev did not understand the strategy. He proposed joint naval arrangements with China, which Mao interpreted as 'unreasonable demands designed to bring China under Soviet military control'.

In a speech four years later, Mao complained that in 1958 'our attention was diverted to opposing Khrushchev. From the second half of 1958 he wanted to blockade the Chinese coastline. He wanted to set up a joint fleet so as to have control over our coastline. . . .'

23
THE GREAT LEAP FORWARD

Mao spent the second half of 1958 touring the country to whip up enthusiasm for economic advance, interspersed with high-level political conferences, usually packed with his own supporters to ensure his majority, to gain the necessary Party imprimatur. He praised the new people's commune which now sprang up all over China as a successor to the co-operative.

'It is better', he said during an inspection tour of Shantung in August, 'to set up People's Communes. Their advantage lies in the fact that they combine industry, agriculture, commerce, education and military affairs. This is convenient for leadership.' The early examples included the sequestration of sexes, and of children from parents, in separate dormitories to allow the commune leaders the maximum opportunity to mobilize labour on a large scale for agriculture and public works: this was indeed convenient for leadership, but not so pleasant for the led.

At Tientsin University in the same month Mao declared: 'From now on the schools must establish factories and the factories schools. The teachers must take part in physical labour. They should not move their mouths only; they should move their hands too.' As he was to sum it up proudly to his Central Committee at the end of the year,

... a form to build socialism was found, facilitating the transition from collective ownership to ownership by the people, and from socialist ownership by the people to the Communist ownership by the people, making life easier for the workers, peasants, merchants, students and soldiers and rendering possible many undertakings on a large scale and by many people.

After a tour of central China in September, Mao returned to Peking to call for mass mobilization to build backyard steel furnaces – 'Samovar steel furnaces', Khrushchev called them – in the effort to boost production while at the same time spreading

technology into the countryside. China was going to industrialize
without urbanizing, and would double its grain harvest simply
by working harder.

He put in a long word for the pig, dispensing advice on hog
husbandry.

The main source of our fertilizers is pig and big animal farming. If we
can achieve a pig a man or six pigs an acre, our fertilizer problem would
be solved. It is ten times better than any inorganic chemical fertilizer. A
pig is a small chemical fertilizer plant. Furthermore, it has meat, bris-
tle, hide, bones, and entrails which have medicinal use. Pig farming
and other animal farming on a big scale are decidedly justifiable. It
seems possible to fulfil this glorious and great task in one or two five-
year plans.

The Peking press was delirious with joy. The *People's Daily*
proclaimed on 1 October,

In agriculture the Red flag is flying ... emerging into the red flames
coming from the steel plants: the sky has turned red.... The Greek
mythology of ancient times was only a tale, a dream, an ideal. Today,
in the era of Mao Tse-tung, heaven is here on earth.... Once the Party
calls, tens of millions of the masses jump into motion. Chairman Mao is
a great prophet. Through scientific Marxism-Leninism he can see the
future.... Each prophecy of Chairman Mao has become a reality.

By now there was a 'third generation' of Communist leadership, radical in outlook, converging around Mao in his battle
against his more cautious contemporaries and always ready to
offer a theoretical justification for Mao's ideas. One of them was
Chang Chun-chiao, who wrote an article urging the reintroduc-
tion of equal wages and part-payment for work by free supply of
goods, as had been done in Yenan. Mao wrote an editorial for
the *People's Daily* supporting this.

At a conference in Chengchow, in November, Mao expounded
his ideas about the communes, in the context of a thorough-
going criticism which he delivered of one of Stalin's books,
Economic Problems of Socialism in the Soviet Union. 'This book by
Stalin', he complained, 'has not a word on the superstructure
from beginning to end. It never touches upon man. We read of
things but not man.... His basic error is his distrust of the
people.' The Russians 'walk on one leg while we walk on two
legs. They believe technology and cadres decide everything.
They emphasize specialization but not redness, cadres but not
the masses.' However, Mao conceded that China 'is still backward in commodity production, even behind Brazil and India.'

But by the time the next high-level conference was held, in Wuchang at the end of November, modifications of the beautiful dream had to be imposed. Mao explained why. 'For a time I was in favour of producing thirty million tons of steel next year. Upon arrival at Wuchang I thought it was not such a wonderful idea after all.' His gullibility in having accepted such impossible targets and claims was now exposed.

In a talk on 30 November to directors of co-operative organizations Mao showed his first signs of uncertainty. 'We should follow the plan for a while and see what happens. We will decide by 1 July next year.' He expressed his first reservations about the vast claims being made for the increase in the grain harvest. 'Just how much is the grain output? Has it been doubled more or less? Probably it is better to record a ninety per cent increase.'

To cover up his uncertainties, Mao treated the co-operative directors to a rambling exposition of international affairs. He compared Dulles with the British.

The English are sly and cunning. The Americans are relatively short-tempered. The English constantly make strategic and tactical moves. Dulles discusses the five big issues in the world: nationalism, bipolarism, atomic energy, outer space and communism. He is a thinking man. To understand his statements, one must study them word by word and resort to the English dictionary.

Mao talked to another group of co-operative directors a fortnight later, and explained why he was planning his resignation as head of state.

In regard to the resignation issue, there has to be an 'idol'. A class must have a class leader. The Central Committee must have a first secretary. Without the atom as the nucleus there would not be rain. Rather than chaos after death, it is better to have chaos now, while the person is there. It would be impossible to be without a nucleus. There must be consolidation. After a while, an 'idol' emerges and it becomes relatively difficult to eliminate him. This is a psychological condition of long standing. In the future, my duties may increase or decrease. . . . Actually, I am only serving as half a Chairman, without charge of daily affairs.

He also made plain his sturdy disrespect for constitutional legalities. 'The issue of integrating politics and the commune . . . was not passed by the People's Congress, nor is it in the Constitution. Many parts of the Constitution are obsolete, but it cannot be revised now. After surpassing the US we will formu-

late a written constitution. . . . What we have is an unwritten
constitution. . . .'

When the full Central Committee assembled at Wuchang in
December in a mood to indict his mistakes, Mao pleaded eloquently for his policies, defending his positive lead both at home
and abroad – in his risky provocation of the Americans over the
battle for the off-shore islands of Quemoy and Matsu in the
Taiwan Straits. He also gave his critics his definitive answer to
the question whether imperialism and reaction were real or
paper tigers.

Mao wanted it both ways: they were both at once, and were 'in
the process of being changed from real into paper tigers'. Mao's
real message was to

... despise the enemy strategically and take full account of him tacti-
cally. But why take full account of him if he is not a real tiger? Apparently there are still people around who still do not get the point so we
must do some more explaining. . . .

The destruction of the rule of imperialism, feudalism and
bureaucrat-capitalism in China took the Chinese people more than one
hundred years and cost them tens of millions of lives before victory in
1949. Look! Weren't they living tigers, iron tigers, real tigers? On the
other hand they eventually changed into paper tigers, dead tigers,
bean-curd tigers. These are historical facts. Haven't people seen or
heard about these facts? There have been thousands and tens of
thousands of them! Thousands and tens of thousands!

At last Mao came to the burning issue of the Great Leap
Forward. He began with a revealing comment on the appearance
of the people's commune in Honan. 'We once said that we must
be prepared for unlucky happenings ... but there are also
unexpected good things. We did not expect the formation of the
people's communes in April, and a resolution was not made until
August. . . .'

A little later in his speech Mao talked about the necessity to
'avoid certain impractical ideas that emerged from the 1958
Great Leap Forward'. He admitted that he had once favoured a
steel target of thirty million tons for 1959.

At that time I was only concerned with the question of demand. I was
worried over the problem of who would be using this steel, but did not
think of the problems of whether it is possible.

Now our goal should be small. We should not set it too high and
leave a margin for safety. . . . It would not look right for China to enter
Communism ahead of the Soviet Union.

Mao had been stopped by the economy itself, which refused to move ahead as fast as he wanted, and was outflanked at Wuchang by Chou En-lai. Chou rallied leading military figures (including Chu Teh and Peng Teh-huai) who thought it unwise of Mao to provoke both the Russians and the Americans at the same time, to back the technocrats against Mao's economic utopianism. Although Liu Shao-chi and Teng Hsiao-ping remained faithful to him, the Wuchang conference forced Mao to back down on his commune policy and his headlong rush to Communism within six years. Afterwards Mao complained:

I was not satisfied with the Wuchang conference; I could do nothing about the high targets. So I went to Peking to hold a conference, but although you had met for six days, you wouldn't let me hold mine even for a single day. It's not so bad that I am not allowed to complete my work, but I don't like being treated as a dead ancestor.

His efforts to reverse the verdict were unsuccessful. Following the Wuchang conference, the construction of one-sex barracks in the more radical communes was halted, and the private ownership of houses, gardens and small domestic animals was guaranteed. The ambitious claims which had accompanied the first burgeoning of the people's commune were dropped.

The arrangements were also finalized for Mao's retirement from the first line of leadership. Mao was anxious to make it clear afterwards that this was his own idea.

I am responsible for ... the division into first and second lines. Why did we make this division. . .? The first reason is that my health is not very good; the second was the lesson of the Soviet Union. Malenkov was not mature enough, and before Stalin died he had not wielded power. Every time he proposed a toast he fawned and flattered.

Many things are left to other people so that other people's prestige is built up, and when I go to see God there won't be such a big upheaval in the state. Everybody was in agreement with this idea of mine.

At Wuchang itself Mao tried to allay any fears that might be caused about a change or a split in the leadership. He told the Central Committee:

Things are really odd in this world! One can go up but not come down. I expect that a part of the people will agree and another part disagree. People do not understand, saying that while everyone is so full of energy in doing things, I am withdrawing from the front lines. It must be clearly explained. This is not true. I am not withdrawing.

For the first time he bared intimations of his own mortality.

He told the comrades at Wuchang:

Death has benefits, fertilizer is created. You say you don't want to become fertilizer, but actually you will. You must be mentally prepared. . . . Death is inevitable. One cannot live 10,000 years. One must be prepared at all times. My words are depressing. Every man dies, individuals will always die, but mankind will always continue to live. . . . If one must die, one dies. As for socialism, I would like to devote myself to it for a few more years. After surpassing the US, we can go and report to Marx. . . . I am not willing to die, but strive to live on. But if I must die, then let it be so.

Liu Shao-chi's prize for supporting Mao during this Party debate over the Great Leap Forward was to inherit his position as head of state, leaving Mao to work more comfortably in his own way behind the scenes as Chairman of the Party.

In a speech to Party secretaries in February 1959, Mao sought to salvage the idea of the Great Leap. The Leap should not be abandoned, he insisted. He accepted that there was some 'cutting back' in the last two months of 1958. 'The people needed a rest. It is nothing unusual to relax a little, but we must exert efforts again.' There would be another leap forward in 1959, even if it were only a small one.

If not a great leap forward, we will make a small leap forward. Most likely it will be a great leap forward every year. Is a Great Leap Forward situation unfolding? I hope you will all think it over whether we will have great, medium or small leaps forward in the future. I am inclined to leaping forward.

He readily agreed that 'economic work is very complicated.'

Naturally we have defects and mistakes. Tackling one side and overlooking another, causing waste in labour, the tense situation in supplementary foods, the still unsolved light industrial raw material problem . . ., the lack of adjustment in transportation, undertaking too many projects in capital construction – all these are our defects and errors. Like a child playing with fire, without experience, knowing pain only after getting burned. In economic construction, like a child without experience, we declared war on the earth, unfamiliar with the strategy or tactics. We must frankly admit such defects and errors . . . just what is planned and proportionate development? We have just begun to come into contact with this problem. . . .

In those early months of 1959 Mao fought a stubborn rearguard action to save what he could of the Great Leap Forward, giving speeches, writing circulars, and sending them desperately round the country in an attempt to keep up some of the momentum. 'In 1959,' he recalled afterwards, 'I put out thirty or forty thousand words of material, but it is clear that a mere "battle on paper" is useless. . . .'

In April he tried to defend his Leap before the Central Committee in Shanghai, conceding at the outset that he had not planned it well enough. 'We often did a great deal of planning with people of the same opinion but little with people of differing opinions; we planned much with the cadres but little with the production personnel. Inadequate discussion and arbitrary decision means that affairs will not be managed well.' But he refused to bow down to his critics even if they formed a majority in the Party committees.

'An individual sometimes wins over the majority. This is because truth is sometimes in one person's hands only. Truth is sometimes in the hands of a minority, as when Marxism was in Marx's hands alone. Lenin said that you had to have the spirit of going against the current.' Mao also refused to accept that the experience of 1959 was a defeat for the Great Leap Forward, taking refuge in a theory derived from physics.

All movements consist of waves; in natural science there are sound waves and electro-magnetic waves. That all movements advance in wave-like fashion is a law of the development of motion; it is objective and does not change in response to human will. In our work we always go from point to area, from small to large, and always in wave-like fashion and not as a continuously rising line.

But history was obviously marching past him. At the end of April the National People's Congress elected Liu Shao-chi as Chairman of the Republic instead of Mao, under the arrangement which had been made within the leadership almost three years earlier as a means of improving the Party's image in the post-Stalin era and also to suit the personalities involved. It was ironic that the change took effect at a time when Mao's star was obviously waning and his credibility reduced.

The Party's propaganda department put out equal-sized photographs of Liu and Mao to be displayed side by side on big occasions, and the word was spread that it was now permissible to call Liu Mao's 'closest comrade-in-arms'.

'Daddy's very busy,' Liu's wife told her children, 'and has not time for rest. Chairman Mao has now washed his hands of the concrete affairs of state, and handed them all over to your father. You must not disturb him.'

Realizing that he had been let down by over-optimistic or

over-ambitious local cadres reporting exaggerated harvests, Mao threw out yet another *cri de coeur* to all the Party secretaries at provincial and lower levels pleading with them not to kill the Great Leap Forward by over-enthusiasm or hubris. Rice targets should be based on reality:

Just do not pay any attention to those stipulations made in the instructions from higher level. Ignore them and simply concentrate on practical possibilities. For instance, if production per acre was actually only one ton last year, it would be very good indeed if production could be increased by a quarter-ton or half a ton. Elevating it to two, three or four tons and even more is mere bragging and cannot be achieved at all. So what is the use of exaggerating? . . .

State exactly how much you have harvested and refrain from making false statements which are contrary to facts. . . . An honest man has the courage to speak the truth and, in the end, it will be beneficial to the people's cause and to himself . . . it should be said that many of these false statements were the result of pressure from above.

In May Mao circulated a new quantitative definition of his Great Leap Forward idea. 'Whenever the rate of increase of production is up to ten per cent, it is a leap forward. If it is twenty per cent, it is a great leap forward. If it is thirty per cent, it is a sustained great leap forward.' It was a far cry from the heady days of fifteen months earlier, when production was to be doubled.

In June 1959 Khrushchev made the decisive break in Chinese-Russian relations by reneging on his promise made only two years earlier to supply nuclear know-how to China. China's programme to build her own nuclear weapons and industry suffered a crippling blow, while Khrushchev flew to Camp David to see President Eisenhower. General Peng Teh-huai saw Khrushchev in Moscow just before his journey to the US, and was afterwards alleged to have spoken again to the Russian leader about the dissatisfaction with Mao in China. Perhaps Khrushchev calculated that his actions would encourage Mao's colleagues to dump him.

Mao chose this moment, when everything seemed to be going against him, to visit his birthplace – his first for the incredibly long period of thirty-two years. In his earlier civil war days he had gone home at moments of crisis to revive his spirits, and this may have been his instinct now. He reached Shaoshan on 25 June. After stepping through the door of his house, he gazed for a while in silence at the picture of his dead parents before observing to his companions that they would not have died in the medical conditions of today. Next morning he went to a hill to see his parents' graves, taking a pine twig which he 'offered ... before the graves in a dignified and respectful manner', in the words of somebody present. With head bowed, he said: 'The ancestors suffered hardships, whereas the descendants enjoyed happiness.'

The occasion stimulated Mao to write a poem with the title 'Shaoshan Revisited':

> Like a dim dream recalled, I curse the long-fled past –
> My native soil two and thirty years gone by.
> The red flag roused the serf, halberd in hand,
> While the despot's black talons held his whip aloft.
> Bitter sacrifice strengthens bold resolve
> Which dares to make sun and moon shine in new skies.
> Happy, I see wave upon wave of paddy and beans,
> And all around heroes home-bound in the evening mist.

In the light of what was to happen seventeen years later, it is interesting that on this visit to Hunan Mao appointed Hua Kuo-feng as secretary of the provincial committee, and received the family of Yang Kai-hui, his first wife, in Changsha in Hua's company. (To everyone's great surprise, Hua became the man who eventually succeeded Mao as Chairman of the Party after his death.)

If Mao did receive solace and nourishment from returning to his roots, he was not allowed much time before it was tested. On 1 July he flew to the mountain resort of Lushan on the west bank of Lake Poyang for the most vitriolic Politburo and Central Committee meetings in his experience. He arrived in Lushan apprehensive but philosophical, as his poem written on that day shows:

> Perching as after flight, the mountain towers over the Yangtze;
> I have overleapt four hundred twists to its green crest.
> Cold-eyed I survey the world beyond the seas;
> A hot wind spatters raindrops on the sky-brooded waters.
> Clouds cluster over the nine streams, the yellow crane floating,
> And billows roll on to the eastern coast, white foam flying.
> Who knows whither Prefect Tao Yuan-ming is gone
> Now that he can till fields in the Land of Peach Blossoms?

Both this poem and 'Shaoshan Revisited' were designed, Mao afterwards asserted, as 'replies to those bastards' opposing him in the Politburo.

The atmosphere at Lushan was highly charged. Tao Chu, the Party's overlord in Canton and a supporter of Mao, remarked defensively in an article circulated in his own province that 'we can say that a man is great not because he is "consistently correct" – which is impossible to be – but because he can size up the situation and make decisions at the opportune moment in the light of it.'

The national media were still heavily underpinning Mao's reputation. 'In the absence of Comrade Mao Tse-tung and his thinking,' a *People's Daily* article insisted, 'our revolution will fail.'

But some people wanted the mighty Mao brought down. Lo Fu and Peng Teh-huai agreed, talking between the sessions of the Lushan conference, that the pressure at the conference was very great: 'The participants were forced to say only nice things, they were not allowed to criticize.' They assessed Mao as smart and ruthless, like Stalin in his declining years. Peng commented that 'The first emperor of any dynasty is always sharp and brilliant.'

This was the meeting at which Peng declared his hand. Outspoken, warm-hearted and yet truculent, Peng was one of the few of the first-generation Communists to retain after 1949 all his old frugality of lifestyle. He used to share with his soldiers with none of Mao's aloofness, and for some Chinese he was an alternative hero to Mao. He now submitted a resolution attacking the Great Leap and read out a long memorandum supporting his criticisms. He claimed that whereas in the earlier years of the People's Republic Chinese adults were getting over 20 ounces of rice a day, by 1956 this had fallen to 15 ounces, and by 1958 to 10 ounces – not enough for a man to survive on, so that people were reduced to eating algae, cotton leaves and mustard plant leaves. Peng was supported by another army veteran, Lin Po-chu, by Lo Fu, and by two more leading Hunanese, General Huang Ko-cheng (the Chief of Staff) and Chou Hsiao-chou (Party Secretary in Hunan).

Peng was particularly censorious about the wastage incurred by the building of small blast furnaces even in areas where coal was unobtainable, so that trees had to be cut down to feed them. The argument was acrimonious. Mao demanded the disgrace of Peng. When it was put to him that this might spark off a revolt among the armed forces because of Peng's popularity, Mao declared with tears in his eyes that if the army revolted, he would go back to the villages and recruit another one – whereupon the other generals present at the meeting all stood up in turn to pledge their loyalty to Mao.

There were two votes in the Politburo on Peng's resolution. On the first time round it won a majority. Mao would not leave it there, however, resorting to the old Leninist technique of getting reinforcements to come in and sit on an enlarged Politburo meeting, where the vote was reversed.

Some of the leaders who had voted against him the first time probably switched their vote on the second occasion, either because they saw that continued opposition was useless, or because they felt that the inner knowledge of the result of the first vote might suffice to restrain Mao from doing this kind of thing again. For the remainder of the long meeting, the battle between Mao and Peng degenerated to arguing over the extent of Peng's punishment. Mao later blamed Peng for this:

'The first Lushan conference of 1959 was originally concerned with work. Then up jumped Peng Teh-huai and said; "You fucked my mother for forty days, can't I fuck your mother for twenty days?" ' (This was a reference to Peng's self-criticism in 1945 over his conduct of civil war battles, when there had been "forty days of struggle" between him and Mao.) 'All this fucking messed up the conference and the work was affected. Twenty days was not long enough and we abandoned the question of work. . . .'

During these distasteful exchanges at Lushan Mao wrote letters to his wife, who was convalescing in their seaside villa at Peitaiho, giving her a blow-by-blow account. Chiang Ching telephoned him in reply to say that she was flying to Lushan immediately to join him. He would not allow it: 'The struggle's too acute,' he said. But she defied him and sat in on the meetings, confirming afterwards that they were more violent than she had expected.

Mao had already begun to confess his errors in a series of instructions sent out at the beginning of July. One of the major lessons, he said, of the Great Leap Forward was 'the lack of balance. When we walk, both legs should move, but we did not do so.' He also accepted the criticism of his order of priorities – first heavy industry, second light industry and then agriculture. 'Henceforth we may have to reverse the order.'

On another occasion Mao attempted a technical defence:

We organized the Great Leap Forward not in accordance with the requirements of the law of value, but in the light of socialist basic economic laws and our requirements for expanding production. If you look at it from the viewpoint of the law of value alone, the conclusion that you would inevitably draw is that we lost more than we gained in the Great Leap Forward. You would inevitably describe last year's all-out campaign for smelting steel and iron as ineffectual labour, low-quality steel produced by indigenous methods, big country and many subsidies, indifferent economic results, etc.

From the partial, short-term viewpoint, the all-out campaign for smelting steel and iron seems to have cost us dear. However, viewing the situation as a whole in the long term, it is worthwhile because the all-out campaign for smelting steel and iron has opened up a new phase in the overall economic construction of our country. The establishment of a large number of new steel and iron bases and other industrial points throughout the country will make it possible for us to go a long way to speed up our tempo.

At his Lushan 'trial' Mao said:

Now that you have said so much, let me say something, will you? I have taken sleeping-pills three times, but I can't get to sleep. . . . They all say we are in a mess. Even if it is hard to listen to it, we must listen to it and welcome it. As soon as you think in this way, it ceases to be unpleasant to the ears. Why should we let the others talk? The reason is that China will not sink down, the sky will not fall. We have done some good things and our backbones are straight. . . .

Just because for a time there were too few vegetables, too few hair-pins, no soap, a lack of balance in the economy and tension in the market, everyone became tense. . . . I did not see any reason for tension, but I was also tense nevertheless; it would be untrue to say I wasn't. In the first part of the night you might be tense, but once you take your sleeping-pills the tension will go away for the rest of the night.

The fact was that Mao, whatever the chaos, was thrilled to have been able to spread the debate about socialism so widely and so deeply among the Chinese population: 'Where else can one find such a school . . . which will enable a population of several hundreds of millions as well as several millions of cadres to be educated?'

Mao could profit, as always, from the inability of his col-leagues to agree among themselves. At the beginning of the Great Leap Forward, Chou En-lai was against Mao, while Liu Shao-chi was for him. But during the post-mortem after its fail-ure, the positions became somewhat reversed. Chou began to defend Mao once he was down, whereas Liu turned on him for his mistaken lead. Chou's instinct was to make the best of things, and to restore some face to their leader, whereas Liu anticipated Mao's expulsion from the magic circle of decision-makers.

Mao intimated almost exactly the extraordinary course which he would take in acting against his own government only seven years later:

If we do ten things and nine are bad, and they are all published in the press, then we will certainly perish, and will deserve to perish. In that case, I will go to the countryside to lead the peasants to overthrow the government. If those of you in the Liberation Army won't follow me, I will go and find a Red Army, and organize another Liberation Army. But I think the Liberation Army would follow me.... [They did.]

Everybody has faults. Even Confucius made mistakes. I have also seen Lenin's handwritten manuscripts which had been altered so much that they looked a real mess.

But Mao confessed in a moving passage his own mistakes in economic planning:

Coal and iron cannot walk by themselves; they need vehicles to transport them. This I did not foresee. I and ... the Premier did not concern ourselves with this point. You could say that we were ignorant of it. I ought not to make excuses, but I shall too, because I am not the head of the Planning Commission. Before August of last year my main energies were concentrated on revolution.

I am a complete outsider when it comes to economic construction, I understand nothing about industrial planning.... Comrades, in 1958 and 1959 the main responsibility was mine, and you should take me to task....

If you don't agree with me then argue back. I don't agree with the idea that the Chairman cannot be contradicted.... Anyway the fact is that you have been contradicting me one after the other, though not by name.... I do not claim to have invented the people's communes, only to have proposed them.

But he could not resist a resentful dig at the press.

It was as though I had found a treasure in the regulations of the Chayashan Commune. When I was in Shantung a reporter asked me: 'Are the people's communes good?' I said: 'They are good,' and he published it in a newspaper. There was a spot of petty-bourgeois fanaticism there, too. In future reporters should keep away.

Mao's defence concluded with lame bravado and coarse invective:

Have we failed this time? All the comrades present say there have been gains; it has not been a complete failure. Is it mainly a failure? No, it's only a partial failure. We have paid a high price. A lot of 'communist wind' has blown past, but the people of the whole country have learned a lesson....

The chaos caused was on a grand scale and I take responsibility.
Comrades, you must all analyse your own responsibility. If you have to
shit, shit! If you have to fart, fart! You will feel much better for it.

But now the battle was over the fate of Peng, who made a
self-criticism to the Central Committee, dating his errors back to
the battle of Kanchow where he had failed to capture the town.
'It was very wrong of me', he admitted, 'to argue with comrade Mao Tse-tung in such a bad manner. This argument consequently brought about my personal prejudice against comrade
Mao Tse-tung.'
Peng had also opposed Mao at the Lochuan conference in
1937 and he admitted failing to defer to headquarters during the
battle of the Hundred Regiments in 1940, through 'blatant
over-enthusiastic patriotism'.
Peng wrote to Mao in September abasing himself and
apologizing for his errors.

I now fully realize that my bourgeois world outlook and methodology
were deep-rooted, and my individualism most serious. . . . In the past,
because of my bourgeois stand, I considered all your well-intentioned
and sincere criticisms as blows at me. . . . I have been unworthy of your
teaching and patience with me for the past thirty years, I am filled with
indescribable shame and remorse. . .

Mao distributed the letter within the Party and welcomed it.
'If he thoroughly changes and makes no more major vacillations
he will "instantly become a Buddha", or rather a Marxist. . . . Let us severely criticize the mistakes he has made and at
the same time welcome every improvement he has made. We
should take this two-sided attitude to help an old comrade who
has been with us for thirty-one years.'
Peng asked to be rehabilitated by working as a peasant. But
Mao sent him on a tour of Chinese factories and then, displaying
a keen sense of humour, had him installed to run the 'Sino-Soviet
Friendship' state farm in Heilungkiang.
On 11 September 1959 Mao delivered the second of his major
speeches in defence of his mishandling of the Great Leap Forward to survive in the public record, this time to the Military
Affairs Committee. Like his performance at the Lushan conference seven weeks earlier, it was a maudlin mixture of petulance,
self-abasement and mockery.

If there is not enough pork, not enough vegetables, not enough soap,
they seize the opportunity to say, 'You have done things badly!' They
say it is your affair and not theirs. There was a shortage of umbrellas in

Chekiang and they called it a 'maladjustment of proportions', 'petty-bourgeois fanaticism', etc. It will be very difficult for this small minority of people to enter Communism to become real Marxists.

In a revealing citation from the classics, Mao claimed that 'Even the sages made mistakes' with this quotation from the *Analects*:

'The faults of the superior man are like the eclipses of the sun and moon. He has his faults, and all men see them; he changes again, and all men look up to him.' . . .
My words are also directed to all of us comrades, including myself. There are many things I haven't studied. I am a person with many shortcomings. I am by no means perfect. Very often, there are times when I don't like myself.
I have not mastered all the various domains of Marxist learning. And, for example, I don't know foreign languages well either. I've only just begun recently to study economic works. But, comrades, I study with determination, and I will go on studying until I die.

In September 1959 Mao received Khrushchev on his third and last visit to China. Tactlessly, the Russian leader came directly from Camp David where he had been having another *tête-à-tête* with Eisenhower. Since his last visit he had further irritated Mao by his attitude to the Indian border problem. As China and India had both gradually extended through the 1950s their military control of border regions which were often uninhabited and desolate, they came hard up against differences of idea about the actual line of their Himalayan frontier, which until then had been academic. Border skirmishes and a war of words now poisoned Sino-Indian relations, and Mao expected Russian support.

'In September 1959,' Mao later recalled, 'during the Sino-Indian border dispute, Khrushchev supported Nehru in attacking us, and *Tass* issued a communiqué. Then Khrushchev came to China and at our tenth anniversary banquet in October, he attacked us on our own rostrum.'

Khrushchev, who had been so perceptive in noting Stalin's insensitivity to Mao's nationalism, now committed a similar mistake. The Russians had put long-range submarines into service, and asked if they could operate a radio station on Chinese territory in order to maintain contact with them. The Chinese refused, but Khrushchev brought it up again with Mao during this visit.

'Comrade Mao Tse-tung,' he urged, 'we will give you the money to build the station. It doesn't matter to us to whom the station belongs, as long as we can use it to keep in radio contact with our submarines. . . . Comrade Mao Tse-tung, couldn't we come to some sort of agreement, so that our submarines might have a base in your country for refuelling, repairs, shore leaves, and so on?'

'For the last time, *no*, and I don't want to hear anything more about it.'

'Comrade Mao Tse-tung, the countries of the Atlantic Pact have no trouble cooperating and supplying each other, and here we are – unable to reach an agreement on so simple a matter as this!'

'No!'

'If you want, you can use Murmansk as a port for your submarines.'

'No!' Mao replied. 'We don't want anything to do with Murmansk, and we don't want you here. We've had the British and other foreigners on our territory for years now, and we're not ever going to let anyone use our land for their own purposes again.'

After the euphoria of the Great Leap Forward there came now the heartbreak of food shortages and industrial breakdown. For three successive years, 1959 to 1961, severe unseasonal drought and floods devastated the Chinese peasants in their new communes. The superstitious saw it as heaven's retribution to Mao for his sacrilegious 'war on the earth', which ran so counter to the Confucian tradition. He never fully recovered from this loss of prestige.

24
A WORN-OUT OLD GALOSH

In 1960, while Liu Shao-chi, Chou En-lai and Teng Hsiao-ping struggled to put China back on its feet again, Mao migrated southwards, disengaging from the day-to-day affairs of the capital, to spend more time reflecting and writing. In the aftermath of the Great Leap Forward China's gross national product slumped by about a quarter. Income per head of population fell by one-third, and industrial production by more than 40 per cent. Much of this was attributable to the three consecutive years of bad weather which afflicted China from 1959, but some of the responsibility attached to Mao's own policies in the Great Leap.

Mao preferred the more temperate climate of Hangchow and Shanghai to the cold winters of Peking with their dust storms and snow, and he enjoyed missing the ceremonial rituals of formal dinners for visiting dignitaries. In Hangchow he lived in a new villa in the hills at the west side of the scenic lake. In Shanghai he stayed at the building which used to be the French Club, with a good swimming pool. In this semi-retirement he saw less and less of his fellow Politburo members, more and more of his own circle of friends sympathetic with his views, notably his former secretary, Chen Po-ta, his wife, Chiang Ching, and her old ally Kang Sheng.

From his southern retreat Mao would issue policy statements which were dutifully echoed in newspaper editorials and speeches by Party officials, discussed at work conferences and supposedly implemented through the bureaucratic apparatus. But Mao became less and less happy with the efficiency and sincerity of the bureaucracy.

The extravagant claims for his genius which began to be made in 1958 during the Great Leap Forward, for the first time since Yenan days, continued to be made. The *People's Daily* had hailed Mao in 1958 as the foremost living Marxist-Leninist theoretician. Anastas Mikoyan was asked about this in Washington, and after some hesitation gave the diplomatic reply, 'Mao remains as good a theoretician as he always was.'

In the winter of 1959-60 Mao was said in the *People's Daily* to 'have solved problems which Marx, Engels, Lenin and Stalin could not, or did not have time to, solve during their lifetimes.' In a radio talk it was said that 'Mao Tse-tung's ideology glows 100,000 feet high.' Khrushchev, goaded by these remarks, told a meeting of the Warsaw Pact in February 1960 that Mao was 'a worn-out old galosh, which can only be put in a corner of a room to be admired.'

But Mao had no intention of being ignored. After a six-month absence he put in a public appearance at the National People's Congress in the spring of 1960 and received numerous delegations from the Third World in various parts of central China in May. At the end of that month he received Viscount Montgomery, the British general, in Shanghai over dinner, and was obviously puzzled as to why this politically conservative figure was so interested in him.

'I suppose you know', Mao taunted him over the meal, 'you are talking to an aggressor. I have been branded as such in the United Nations. Do you mind talking with an aggressor?'

After dinner Mao talked admiringly of Cromwell, and Montgomery spoke warmly about the French, American and Chinese revolutions.

'You seem to be very enlightened,' Mao commented in surprise.

Montgomery wanted to know what China's ultimate aims would be when she was strong again.

'Ah!' Mao replied. 'You obviously think China will then practise aggression outside her borders.' He offered what Montgomery found to be a rational and realistic exposition of the fact that temptation might well come in the future when Mao would no longer be able to do anything about it, but that in his own lifetime he would do his utmost to prevent anything of the kind.

Montgomery asked Mao why China was such a closed shop to Western visitors. 'He said a major reason was, the Western peoples brought with them a laxity in moral standards which might impede the high standards he was trying to reach in China – adding that where the Westerner goes, moral standards deteriorate.' Montgomery did not reply, but admitted afterwards that the remark was difficult to refute.

Khrushchev stepped up his offensive against Mao at the Bucharest conference in June, where, according to Mao, he 'tried to encircle and annihilate us'. Khrushchev attacked Mao by name, accusing him of being merely another Stalin, 'oblivious of any interests other than his own, spinning theories detached from the realities of the modern world'. Mao had become 'an ultra-leftist, an ultra-dogmatist, indeed, a left revisionist'.

Khrushchev spoke at length, and somewhat defensively, about the Indian border question. The Chinese dispute with India

... had nothing to do with capitalism and socialism: it was a purely nationalist dispute and it had done the socialist cause untold harm, quite apart from such details as losing Kerala to communism. ...

Why ... should the Chinese, who are always boasting of their colossal population, need support from the Soviet Union, whose population was less than the population of India? And what would happen to this frontier dispute when the day came, as it would, when India was a socialist country. . .?

Khrushchev complained that the Chinese had hindered Soviet defence measures on the Manchurian border by preventing the installation of a radio transmitter 'for use against our enemies' and preventing reconnaissance flights by Russian aircraft. And Mao had 'sent Peng Teh-huai to a labour camp' because he had dared to criticize the policy of the communes in a letter to the Soviet Communist Party.

Khrushchev recalled all the Russian experts, with their precious blueprints and formulae, from China in July, and it took the Chinese economy five years to recover. Mao later declared, with slight exaggeration, 'We spent the whole of 1960 fighting Khrushchev.'

In fact Mao spent some of his time in 1960 giving a critical reading to a Russian textbook on political economics. By making absolute 'the concern for personal material interests' as a means of increasing production, the Russians were courting 'the danger of developing individualism'. To treat the question of the distribution of consumer goods as 'a decisive motivating force' amounted to the 'erroneous viewpoint of distribution determinism', constituting a revision of the correct viewpoint of Marx and 'a theoretical error'. The book

... talks as if the creative activity of the masses has been dependent on material motives for inspiration. Whenever an opportunity arises, this book will talk about personal material interests as if it always wants to utilize this thing to tempt people. ... If they publicize material interest like this, capitalism will become invincible.

The Russian textbook did not explain that 'when the interests of all the people are resolved, personal interests will also be resolved. The personal material interests stressed by them are in reality short-sighted individualisms.' And Mao indulged here in a reminiscence of the ideologically formative days of Yenan.

When we were in the base areas, we enforced a free supply system. People were a little healthier then. They did not quarrel on account of their wages. After liberation, we instituted a wage system and arranged all personnel in order of rank. . . . More troubles arose. Many people frequently quarrelled in their fight for a higher rank.

Another example of this Russian error was the primacy given to piece-work over time-rate wage systems, which 'will promote the psychology of a section of workers to struggle for the purpose of scrambling for big pieces of work. They will not be concerned first for the collective enterprises, but rather for personal income.'

Reverting frequently to this theme, Mao finally asked the question why things had gone so wrong in Russia. 'There must be a reason for putting special emphasis on material interests nowadays. In the Stalin period, they placed far too much emphasis on collective interests and paid little or no attention to personal income. . . . Today, they have gone to the opposite extreme.'

Contradictions would thus continue under socialism, and even under Communism – something to which the Russian textbook did not address itself. 'The transition from socialism to communism is a revolution. . . . Furthermore, there are technical revolutions and cultural revolutions. Communism is bound to go through many stages. It certainly will have many revolutions.' By way of an aside, and one which carried personal implications, Mao spoke of the second generation: 'The children of our cadres are a source of deep concern to us. They have no experience in life and in society. Yet they put on airs and think highly of themselves. We must educate them not to rely on their parents and on martyrs, but entirely on themselves.'

There were also international questions on which the Russian book had gone wrong. It advocated, for example, division of labour, economic specialization and submission of individual socialist countries to a mutual economic system. Mao came out very strongly against this:

This is not a good proposition. We will not even go so far as to propose it to our provinces. We advocate overall development. We will not say that there is no need for each province to produce goods which it can depend on other provinces to supply to meet its needs. We want all provinces to do as much as possible in developing all kinds of production. . . . One good thing about Europe is that all its countries are independent. Each of them does its own thing and makes it possible for the economy of Europe to develop at a fast pace.

Since the Chin Dynasty, our country has taken shape as a big nation. Over a long period of time, the whole country has more or less kept a unified appearance. One of its defects was bureaucratism. It kept the country under very tight control. Each locality could not develop independently. Procrastination was rampant and economic development was at a slow pace. Today, conditions are completely different. We want to attain unification for the whole country and independence for the different provinces. . . .

Every country should develop its industry to the fullest extent so as to strive for regeneration through its own efforts, and do it independently as much as possible so that it will not depend upon others, as a matter of principle. It will not handle what it actually cannot do. Particularly in agriculture we should do everything possible in order to develop production well. It is very dangerous to depend upon foreign countries or other provinces for the things that you eat.

Again, peaceful competition between the two world systems of capitalism and Communism was advocated in the Russian book, which would be to change 'two *de facto* world markets into two economic systems inside a unified world market. It is a retrogression from the views of Stalin.' It was the struggle, not the co-existence, between the two systems that should be emphasized.

Finally, there were numerous doctrinal points on which Mao faulted the Russian book. It wrongly made industrialization a prerequisite for the collectivization of agriculture. It wrongly argued that revolution was more difficult in backward countries. Mao countered this by saying that the bourgeoisie was actually *less* powerful in a country like China:

In our country there have been only three generations of bourgeoisie. However, in such countries as Great Britain and France the bourgeoisie have existed for scores of generations. The development of their bourgeoisie has a history of 250 or 260 years to more than 300 years. The ideology and working style of the bourgeoisie are having an effect on all fields and on all levels. Hence the British working class does not follow the communist party, but the Labour party.

On the withering away of the state, the Russian view was perhaps too optimistic. Mao had a reservation. 'However, one more international condition is required before the state can die out. It is dangerous for others to have a state apparatus while you don't.'

In September Volume IV of Mao's *Selected Works* was published, giving Lin Piao an excuse to indulge in a farrago of
flattery and exaggeration.

Like a beacon, this brilliant thesis [of paper tigers] of comrade Mao
Tse-tung's illuminated the road of our advance.... This penetrating
analysis and great foresight by comrade Mao Tse-Tung gave tremendous inspiration to the whole Party, the whole army and the whole
people, so that, at times when the sky became overcast, we were able to
see that the darkness would soon end and that the light of the dawn
showed ahead.

But when Edgar Snow came to see him again in October, Mao
conceded that the Chinese people were not yet getting enough to
eat. He predicted that it would take another sixty years for China
to catch up with the Gross National Product of the United
States.

Snow asked Mao to say something about China's long-term
construction plans.

'I don't know,' Mao confessed, to Snow's surprise.

'You are being too prudent,' Snow insisted.

'It's not a question of being too prudent,' Mao said. 'It's just
that I really don't know, we just haven't any experience, that's
all.'

Mao was uncharacteristically defensive about the economy.

'So what if the Chinese masses should not have the material
comforts of the European bourgeoisie for another fifty years?
Deprivation, austerity, struggle makes self-reliance. Obsession
with comforts makes men decadent and spiritually barren. Isn't
it likewise with nations?'

Mao revealed his ambition to swim the Potomac or Missis-
sippi, hinting at the détente to come in the 1970s.

To the Central Committee at the beginning of 1961, Mao
confessed his perplexity about China's setback, again conceding
that in the early years of the People's Republic, 'We had no deep
understanding of conditions.' Nor would China be able to modernize as quickly as he had originally hoped. 'We cannot transform what we do not know about.'

As for the break with the Soviet Union, 'Marxism-Leninism is
basically one with different twigs and leaves, like a single tree
that has many twigs and leaves.' But China would have to do
without Soviet aid and be fully self-reliant. In the past the communes had 'built their house with others' work', equivalent to
'getting it through exploitation, and ... contrary to Marxism-
Leninism.'

A month later the Central Committee approved a watered-down version of the Sixty Rules for the people's communes, prepared by Teng Hsiao-ping. Mao was annoyed at being asked to rubber-stamp something he didn't agree with. 'Which emperor', he is alleged to have demanded, 'decided this?'

But for the most part he was left undisturbed, and in a poem written at this time referred to himself as 'lost in dreams':

> White clouds are sailing above Mount Chiuyi;
> Riding the wind, the Princesses descend the green hills.
> Once they speckled the bamboos with their profuse tears,
> Now they are robed in rose-red clouds.
> Tungting Lake's snow-topped waves surge skyward;
> The long isle reverberates with earth-shaking song.
> And I am lost in dreams, untrammelled dreams
> Of the land of hibiscus glowing in the morning sun.

Browsing in the Central Revolutionary Museum with time on his hands, he came across an old and forgotten article of his opposing book-worship, which he had not read for thirty years. 'I find that it still has some use,' he commented, 'so I have had printed a good many copies as a reference for comrades.' But the comrades were not bothering to read him any more.

He wrote a verse about the women militia:

> How bright and brave they look, shouldering five-foot rifles
> On the parade ground lit up by the first gleams of day.
> China's daughters have high-aspiring minds,
> They love their battle array, not silks and satins.

But it was inspired by a photograph, not the reality.

At meetings called by his colleagues, he continued to make heavy weather of his errors. During a Peking conference in June,

I talked about my own shortcomings and mistakes. I said I wanted the comrades to convey what I said to their various provinces and districts. I found out later that many districts did not get my message, as if my mistakes could be hidden and ought to be hidden. Comrades, they mustn't be hidden. Any mistakes that the centre has made ought to be my direct responsibility, and I also have an indirect share in the blame because I am the Chairman of the Central Committee.

Western reports said in July that Chou En-lai had quarrelled with Mao over the policy to be adopted towards the Russians. Mao certainly continued to preach a hard line about the short-comings of the Kremlin, while the technocrats in the Chinese government, struggling to do without Russian technical aid, would have preferred a more conciliatory approach. At one of the Politburo meetings, incidentally, held in Mao's residence late at night, Mao told his aides to prepare for the participants a meal of one bowl of noodles each.

'Let them eat only half their fill,' he ordered 'and they will know how the common people feel when there isn't enough to eat.'

His wife had now become a professional photographer under her maiden name, and Mao was particularly taken with one of her shots of scenery at Lushan. He wrote a poem about the photograph, and copied it on the back for her:

> Amid the growing shades of dusk stand sturdy pines,
> Riotous clouds sweep past, swift and tranquil.
> Nature has excelled herself in the Fairy Cave,
> On perilous peaks dwells beauty in her infinite variety.

In the autumn of 1961 Mao had his second encounter with Montgomery, talking with him this time for nine hours. At five o'clock Mao said that he was going to swim in the Yangtze River and that Montgomery should go with him. They drove to a launch from which Mao, in Montgomery's account, 'swam and floated downstream for about an hour', in a four-miles-per-hour current surrounded by about sixty youngsters and aides. Afterwards Mao took a shower. Montgomery gave Mao some English cigarettes, which he passed on to his interpreters because he only smoked Chinese. The British visitor noted that Mao ate only sparingly, and that he took no alcohol, only water and tea, and no pills.

'In another fifty years,' Montgomery observed, 'you will be terrific.'

('What he meant', Mao explained to a Party work conference a few weeks later, 'was that after fifty years we might become powerful and 'invade' other countries.')

Mao's reply was different from his earlier answer:

We are Marxist-Leninist, our state is a socialist state not a capitalist state, therefore we wouldn't invade others in a hundred years or even ten thousand years. In your country the development of capitalism took several hundred years. We won't count the sixteenth century which was still in the middle ages. From the seventeenth century to now is already three hundred and sixty years. In our country, the construction of a great and mighty socialist economy I reckon will take more than one hundred years.

Later Mao went to see an opera on a traditional theme about

the monkey subduing the demon. Challenged by Kuo Mo-jo, he composed a comment in verse:

> A thunderstorm burst over the earth,
> So a devil rose from a heap of white bones.
> The deluded monk was not beyond the light,
> But the malignant demon must wreak havoc.
> The Golden Monkey wrathfully swung his massive cudgel
> And the jade-like firmament was cleared of dust.
> Today, a miasmal mist once more rising,
> We hail Sun Wu-kung, the wonder-worker.

A few days afterwards Mao wrote another poem in response to a fellow poet's composition on the plum blossom:

> Wind and rain escorted Spring's departure,
> Flying snow welcomes Spring's return.
> On the ice-clad rock rising high and sheer
> A flower blooms sweet and fair.

> Sweet and fair, she craves not Spring for herself alone,
> To be the harbinger of Spring she is content.
> When the mountain flowers are in full bloom
> She will smile mingling in their midst.

Mao's lowest point in his career came in January 1962, when he had to face his critics at a meeting of 7000 cadres. This was the occasion when Liu Shao-chi made his strongest attack on Mao's policies during the Great Leap Forward. He quoted Hunanese peasants – a particularly bitter twist for Mao – for the proposition that the economic difficulties following the Great Leap had been only 30 per cent the fault of nature, and 70 per cent the fault of man.

The Great Leap Forward, Liu declared bluntly, had been

... carried out somewhat too fast, for equilibrium was destroyed so that after three years of leaping, it will take eight to ten years, starting from the present, to put things in order. This doesn't add up. . . . When the Chairman says the situation is very good, he is referring to the excellence of the political situation. One can't say that the economic situation is very good; on the contrary it is very ungood.

Before the entire élite of the Party, going down well below the level of the Central Committee, Mao's chosen successor publicly took Mao to task. 'In the past several years,' Liu said, 'many shortcomings and mistakes have occurred in our work. The cadres and members of the whole Party and even the great majority of the people all have had painful personal experience of this. They have starved for two years.'

Mao was pushed aside like an over-enthusiastic ignoramus, and the 'right opportunists' whom he had brought down in 1958 were now rehabilitated. One of the jokes circulating among the cadres was that, 'When Mao does not study for three days, he can't catch up with Liu Shao-chi.'

To all of this Mao replied that the masses would have the last word. He agreed that the Party's leaders would have to expose themselves to the verdict of the masses, even if this meant being 'thrown out'.

What is so impossible about that? Why should a person only go up and never go down? ... I think that demotion and transfer, whether it is justified or not, does good to people. They thereby strengthen their revolutionary will. ... I myself have had experience in this respect and gained a great deal of benefit. ...'

I am not advocating the indiscriminate wrong-treatment of our cadres, our comrades, or anybody else, in the way in which the ancients detained Wen Wang, starved Confucius, exiled Chu Yuan, or cut off Sun Tzu's kneecaps. I'm not in favour of this way of doing things – I oppose it.

What I am saying is that in every stage of mankind's history there have always been such cases of mishandling. ... Even in a socialist society such things cannot entirely be avoided either. ...

Mao claimed that the Party's collective leadership operated on highly democratic lines.

For example, in the standing committee and the Politburo situations like this often arise: when I say something, no matter whether it is correct or incorrect, provided that everyone disagrees with me, I will accede to their point of view because they are the majority.

Those of you who shirk responsibility or who are afraid of taking responsibility, who do not allow people to speak, who think you are tigers, and that nobody will dare to touch your arse, whoever has this attitude, ten out of ten of you will fail. People will talk anyway. You think that nobody will really dare to touch the arse of tigers like you? They damn well will!

But in the end he had to come back to his own self-criticism.

Let everybody criticize us. As for me, I will not go out during the day; I will not go out to the theatre at night. Please come and criticize me day and night.

The audience laughed at that.

'Then,' Mao went on, 'I will sit down and think about it carefully, not sleep for two or three nights, think about it till I understand it, then write a sincere self-examination. Isn't that the way to deal with it?

That summer Liu was so emboldened in his *de facto* succession to Mao's mantle that he reissued his old book, *How to Become a Good Communist*. One of the passages in this work referred to

> ... certain representatives of dogmatism who at one time ... regarded themselves as China's 'Marx' or China's 'Lenin' and had the impudence to require that our Party members should revere them as Marx and Lenin were revered, support them as 'the leaders' and accord them loyalty and devotion. ... No member of our Party has any right to demand that the rank-and-file should support or keep him as a leader.

This was originally aimed at the Twenty-Eight Bolsheviks in the 1940s, but in 1962 it must have been read as a *double entendre*.

'I've read Liu Shao-chi's *How to Become a Good Communist* several times,' Mao commented later. 'It is anti-Marxist-Leninist.'

'Liu', said someone who knew them both in the 1920s and 1930s, 'was never much of an admirer of Mao. He once told me that, in his opinion, Mao was somewhat illogical in his approach to problems, stubborn, indiscriminate in his choice of means, and lacking in self-cultivation.' Liu's strength was in organizing and administering. It was this quality of his which became so valuable during these bitter years of economic chaos.

Liu had a more constructive view of the role of the middle classes than Mao. 'It is also good', he remarked towards the end of 1960, 'to have some bourgeoisie in a society. These people are most energetic, and they are capable of crawling through cracks. ... They are able to crawl through a crack to make money because they have discovered our shortcomings in planning. Our cracks are thus filled. When they start anything, we should also start the same thing.'

'It is good', he wrote a year later, 'to have underground factories where these do not cheat their customers; the things they produce are useful.' In 1962 Liu even declared that 'All methods conducive to the mobilization of the peasants' enthusiasm for production during the transition period may be adopted. ... Industry must retreat to a sufficient extent and so must agriculture, by fixing quotas based on the household and allowing individual farming.'

At the September 1962 meeting of the Central Committee Peng Teh-huai, who had submitted five reports on his field investigations in the countryside during his punishment in 1960 and 1961, tabled a self-vindicatory document of 80 000 words in criticism of Mao, and he was supported this time by both Liu Shao-chi and Teng Hsiao-ping.

Mao, who was, ironically, in the chair of the meeting, bowed his head to the criticisms but gave no ground on the question of reinstating Peng Teh-huai.

He registered his dissent over the rehabilitation of cadres who had gone down during the Great Leap Forward. 'The recent trend towards the reversal of verdicts is incorrect.'

Mao chose, understandably, to dwell on international affairs in his speech to the Committee, for here there was something positive to say. In the early 1950s he had been unduly pessimistic about the Third World. Mao had believed at that time that 'the parties and trade unions of Asia and the parties of Africa might suffer serious damage', but it did not turn out that way.

'Since the second world war, thriving national liberation has developed in Asia, Africa and Latin America year by year. . . .'

China's task was to support these national liberation movements. 'We want to unite with so many people. But they do not include the reactionary national bourgeoisie like Nehru, nor the reactionary bourgeois intellectuals like the Japanese Communist Shojiro Kasuga, who supports the theory of structural reforms. . . .'

Chiang Ching was by now cured of her cancer, and fully recovered from her protracted illness. This she had achieved by undergoing a series of acupuncture treatments and a rigorous programme of exercise, including swimming, Chinese shadow-boxing and table tennis. In September she broke out of the cocoon which Mao and the Party had wound around her and made her first public appearance, at a reception for the visiting President Sukarno of Indonesia, as Mao's wife.

The *People's Daily*, in a subtle piece of newspaper politics, published on 30 September the first official photograph of Mao and his wife, posing with the two Sukarnos, ever to be seen by the Chinese public. It was on page one, whereas the photograph of Liu Shao-chi and his wife, also with the Sukarnos, published five days earlier, had been on page two. Chiang Ching was angry that Liu's wife had got in first, while her rival complained that Chiang Ching's photograph had been better displayed. The bitching between these rival first ladies was to be heard over and over again in the years to come.

Mao professed to stay above such petty arguments. During 1962 his first mother-in-law, the widow of his beloved teacher,

Professor Yang Chang-chi, died, and Mao wrote to the family: 'As regards the funeral arrangements, bury her with my dear wife, comrade Yang Kai-hui, in the same tomb.... Our two families are one, just one family, and there is no need to say what's mine and what's yours.'

Mao ended the year by writing a poem on his seventieth birthday in the traditional Chinese system (whereby the first birthday is the actual day of birth). It suggested that the old man was not yet to be written off.

> Winter clouds snow-laden, cotton fluff flying,
> None or few the unfallen flowers.
> Chill waves sweep through steep skies,
> Yet earth's gentle breath grows warm.
> Only heroes can quell tigers and leopards
> And wild bears never daunt the brave.
> Plum blossoms welcome the whirling snow;
> Small wonder flies freeze and perish.

Signs of a resurgence were even strong in the anti-Russian poem which he wrote for Kuo Mo-jo at the beginning of 1963:

> On this tiny globe
> A few flies dash themselves against the wall,
> Humming without cease,
> Sometimes shrilling,
> Sometimes moaning,
> Ants on the locust tree assume a great-nation swagger
> And mayflies lightly plot to topple the giant tree.
> The west wind scatters leaves over Changan,
> And the arrows are flying, twanging.
> So many deeds cry out to be done,
> And always urgently;
> The world rolls on,
> Time presses.
> Ten thousand years are too long,
> Seize the day, seize the hour!
> The Four Seas are rising, clouds and waters raging,
> The Five Continents are rocking, wind and thunder roaring.
> Our force is irresistible,
> Away with all pests!

Mao continued his old habit of commenting on documents passing over his desk, and one such note in May 1963 gave a clear hint of the struggles still to come.

'Class struggle, the struggle for production and scientific experiment', he wrote, 'are the three great revolutionary movements for building a mighty socialist country. . . .' If these three movements were not carried out, 'then it would not take long, perhaps only several years or a decade, or several decades at most, before a counter-revolutionary restoration on a national scale inevitably occurred, the Marxist-Leninist Party would undoubtedly become revisionist or fascist, and the whole of China would change its colour.'

Mao set out on his road to political recovery by launching an entirely new campaign on this theme, the socialist education movement. He told the Central Committee that it would have to be an almost permanent movement, 'requiring five or ten generations', to clean up the Communist Party. He described it as 'the first great struggle since land reform. There has not been this sort of scope, breadth or pervasiveness for several years.' But it would only succeed if the ranks of the Party were purified. 'There are some cadres who eat more and take more advantages, and there are some who illicitly cohabit with the daughters of landlords and rich peasants.'

The Central Committee at Hangchow accepted Mao's ten-point programme for the spreading of socialist education, but four months later Liu Shao-chi rewrote it in what Mao regarded as a revisionist manner, in order to emphasize the role of incentives in production, encourage private plots and accommodate the enterprising and advanced 'rich peasants'.

It was not much consolation for Mao to be able to issue in August, at the request of the Black American leader, Robert Williams, then in exile in Cuba, a declaration of support to American blacks. This was the first of eight calls which Mao was to make during the 1960s for a Third World upsurge against American imperialism.

I call upon the workers, peasants, revolutionary intellectuals, enlightened elements of the bourgeoisie, and other enlightened personages of all colours in the world, white, black, yellow, brown, etc., to unite to oppose the racial discrimination practised by US imperialism and to support the American Negroes in their struggle against racial discrimination. In the final analysis, a national struggle is a question of class struggle. In the United States, it is only the reactionary ruling clique among the whites which is oppressing the Negro people. They can in no way represent the workers, farmers, revolutionary intellectuals, and other enlightened persons who comprise the overwhelming majority of the white people.

In August Mao told some African visitors:

Racial discrimination is found in Africa, in Asia, and in other parts of the world. The racial question is in essence a class question. Our unity is not one of race; it is the unity of comrades and friends. . . .

In the fight for thorough emancipation the oppressed peoples rely first of all on their own strength and then, and only then, on international assistance. The people who have already won victory in their revolution should help those who are still struggling for liberation. This is our internationalist duty.

Mao also condemned in August the persecution of Buddhists by the anti-Communist regime in South Vietnam and the American breach of the Geneva Accord commitments. 'No one', he declared, 'will assert that a treaty can make US imperialism lay down its butcher's knife and suddenly become a Buddha, or for that matter behave itself even a little better.'

On 6 September came the first of nine lengthy polemics addressed by the Chinese Communist Party to the Communist Party of the Soviet Union, parts of which were written by Mao with the help of Kang Sheng and Chen Po-ta.

What Mao really thought about Khrushchev's Russia came out in some of his comments on Yugoslavia, the lesson of which, he wrote at the end of September,

. . . shows that not only is it possible for a working-class party to fall under the control of a labour aristocracy, degenerate into a bourgeois party and become a flunky of imperialism before it seizes power, but even after it seizes power it is possible for a working-class party to fall under the control of new bourgeois elements. . . . It shows that a restoration of capitalism in a socialist country can be achieved . . . through the degradation of the leading group in that country.

Khrushchev sent Mao a personal letter in November in the hope of persuading him to make a new start in jointly opposing US imperialism. Mao had already declined an invitation to visit Moscow, and he took the struggle with the Russians sufficiently seriously to go to the airport in July to meet his two insubordinate lieutenants, Teng Hsiao-ping and Peng Chen, on their return from ineffectual negotiations in Moscow. Mao made no known answer to Khrushchev's *billet doux*, although the Central Committee eventually replied unhelpfully, with such remarks as: 'If you should feel the need for the help of Chinese experts in certain fields, we would be glad to send them.'

In December Mao wrote again at length about the need for Communist cadres to behave properly. He praised the work of two Hunan leaders, including Hua Kuo-feng, for their style of work, comparing so favourably with other comrades who 'welcomed praise but not criticism', took little interest in studying what was being done elsewhere and confined their vision to their own area or unit, 'which is sheer parochial arrogance.'

When people see only what is under their feet, not what lies above the mountains and beyond the seas, they are likely to be as boastful as 'the frog at the bottom of a well'. But when they raise their heads to see the immensity of the world, the kaleidoscope of man's affairs, the splendour and magnificence of the cause of humanity, the richness of man's talents, and the breadth of knowledge, they become modest. What we are dedicated to is a world-shaking task. We must focus not just on the work and happiness in front of our eyes, but also on the work and happiness of all of us in the distant future. Marxism-Leninism helps us to overcome the self-satisfaction of a small producer due to a small success or a small achievement. . . .

Modesty and self-abasement are not synonymous. Modesty does not mean belittling oneself; it is an expression of a realistic attitude and the progressive spirit which enables one to see facts objectively, whereas self-abasement is an expression of unrealism, a lack of self-confidence, and a fear of difficulty. Self-abasement and self-advertisement or a feeling of superiority are based on subjectivism and are wrong. They represent two extreme and erroneous subjective estimates of oneself. The boastful person detaches himself from reality and overestimates himself, exaggerates his actual ability and role. . . . The self-abasing person is apparently the opposite of the boastful, but he is just as unrealistic. He underestimates himself, forgets that he can be improved and disciplined in his work, and belittles the part he has played and will play in the revolution. Consequently, he loses his courage and confidence in making progress and relaxes his fighting spirit.

Mao was here writing from the nadir of his own fortunes as ruler of China, but he was keeping his eyes firmly on the longer perspective of what was to follow the economic recovery.

25
ALONE WITH THE MASSES

At seventy Mao was still ebullient enough to declare that he proposed to lead a group of experts on foot or horseback to survey the Yellow River from its estuary to its headsprings, instructing his aides to practise their riding and read up the background materials in preparation. Mao was fascinated by the Yellow River, 'the cradle of our Chinese nation', as he called it, and issued many directives for harnessing it. This particular project never materialized, but others, more dramatic and wide-ranging in their consequences, were to shake the world. During the two years, 1964 and 1965, he lay low, giving Liu Shao-chi head to run China on conservative lines, while Mao planned a spectacular come-back. He was now in fair health and soon after his seventieth birthday he commented:

I have a gentlemen's agreement with my doctor: When I have a fever I will call you, and when I do not have one I will not bother you and you will not bother me. I said that if I did not have to call on him for an entire year, that would be testimony of his great merit. If I had to bother him every month, this would be proof that he had failed in his work. I only follow half of what the doctor says and expect him to follow me in the other half. If we abide by everything the doctors say sickness will multiply and life will be impossible.

I have never before heard of so much high blood pressure, and liver infections. If a person doesn't exercise but only eats well, dresses well, lives comfortably and drives wherever he goes, he will be beset with a lot of illnesses. Excessive attention to food, clothing, housing, and means of transportation are the four underlying causes of illness among high-level cadres.

While chiding his colleagues for corrupt living, Mao also warned them against any lowering of China's guard against Russia, He pursued the same theme at a meeting a few weeks later. 'In the final analysis,' he asked, 'are some people ill or is their revolutionary will declining? Or did they go dancing six times a week? Or is it love of beauty not country? Some say they are so sick they cannot do their work. Can an illness be that bad?'

Mao now had the unexpected experience of fellow Asian Communist leaders calling on him to try to mediate his quarrel with the Russians. Le Duan of Vietnam and a Japanese Communist Party delegation led the field in this endeavour at the beginning of 1964. They got short shrift.

A major reason for Mao's obstinacy which had not until then been revealed came out into the open when he met a Japanese socialist delegation in July and said to them, apropos of the four small northern Japanese islands occupied by the USSR:

> The areas occupied by the Soviet Union are really too many. By the Yalta Agreement, under the guise of making her independent, Mongolia actually came under the control of the Soviet Union. . . . In 1954 when Khrushchev and Bulganin came to China, we raised the territorial question, but they turned us down. . . . Wherever they can detach, they have done so to the limit. It is said that Sinkiang and north of the Amur River must be incorporated into the Soviet Union. . . .
>
> The Soviet Union has an area of 8½ million square miles and a population of only 200 million. It should stop its activities of annexation. . . . About 100 years ago the areas east of Baikal came under Russian occupation, and since then Vladivostok, Khabarovsk, Kamchatka, and so on became Soviet territory. We have not yet had the reckoning for this account.

Mao began to develop his concept of the intermediate countries standing between (and against) the two super-powers. He told a group of French Deputies: 'France, Italy, Germany, Britain (if she can cease to be America's agent), Japan and ourselves – that is the third force.' This was a quite unorthodox analysis for a Communist leader, and it aroused the utmost interest in other capitals.

He evidently enjoyed dealing with bourgeois Westerners after his stormy experiences with the Russians. Commenting on Khrushchev's proposals for improving relations in 1964, Mao agreed that the border problem could be discussed, and 'a little commercial business can be done, but not too much, as Soviet products are heavy, clumsy, expensive, and they always hold back in giving us what they have. . . . It is not as easy as working with the French bourgeoisie. At least they have some business ethics.'

Mao cultivated his 'liberal' image by looking after his predecessor, the former boy emperor, Hsuan-tung, better known as Henry Pu Yi. On the tenth anniversary of the People's Republic

Mao had issued pardons to some political prisoners, including Pu Yi, who duly came out of prison and began a new life as a gardener in his former palace. 'We should maintain good solidarity', Mao told a meeting in February 1964, 'with Emperor Hsuan-tung. He ... is my superior. Hsuan-tung's salary of 100-odd *yuan* is too small. He is, after all, an emperor.'

His unaccustomed leisure while his juniors governed the country allowed him to speak out on his favourite topic, education:

Our present method of conducting examinations is a method for dealing with the enemy, not a method for dealing with the people. It is a method of surprise attack, asking oblique or strange questions. . . . I do not approve of this. . . . I am in favour of publishing the questions in advance and letting the students study them and answer them with the aid of books. . . .

Whispering in other people's ears and taking examinations in other people's names used to be done secretly. Let it now be done openly. If I can't do something and you write down the answer, which I then copy, this is all right. Let's give it a try.

Mao also had more time for his own family. Both his 'niece' and nephew were now studying for their professions and in the summer of 1964 he had long and revealing conversations with them. Transcripts of these talks were later circulated among the Red Guards as 'texts' for the Cultural Revolution.

On 24 June he talked to his 'niece', Wang Hai-jung – actually his young cousin on his mother's side. She was then studying English at the Institute of Foreign Languages: later she became a Vice-Minister for Foreign Affairs.

'The class struggle in our school', Wang began, 'is acute. I have heard that reactionary slogans were found written on the blackboard of our English language department. All were in English.'

'What did these reactionary slogans say?' Mao asked.

'I only know one,' the girl replied ... ' "Long live Chiang".'

'What else?' Mao insisted.

'I don't know. I only know this one. . . .'

'Good!' Mao replied. 'Let whoever it is write more slogans and post them outside for all the students to read. Did he kill anyone?'

'I don't know if he has killed anyone,' the girl replied. 'But if we find him, I think we should dismiss him from the Institute and reform him through labour.'

'There's no need to dismiss him,' Mao commented, 'as long as he hasn't killed anyone, nor should we send him to reform through labour. Let him stay at school to continue his studies. You can call a meeting and let him tell the students why Chiang Kai-shek is good and what are the good things that Chiang Kai-shek has done. You can also tell him why Chiang Kai-shek is no good. How many people are there in your Institute?'

'About three thousand including staff and faculty,' the girl replied.

'Among three thousand people, it's best to have seven or eight pro-Chiang elements.'

'One is too many,' the girl protested. 'If there are seven or eight such people, I don't know what will become of us!'

'Oh no,' said Mao. 'You shouldn't get nervous at seeing one reactionary slogan.'

'Why do we need seven or eight such people?'

'If there are several such people,' Mao explained, 'we have an opposition group. So long as they don't kill people they can serve as an example of negative education.'

'Our Institute', Wang went on, 'has thoroughly followed the class line. In the latest enrolment, seventy per cent of the students admitted are from families of workers and poor and lower-middle peasants. The remaining thirty per cent are from children from families of cadres and martyrs.'

'How many students in your class', Mao asked, 'are from worker-peasant families?'

'Besides me, there are two from cadre families. The rest are children from workers, poor and lower-middle peasants. All of them behave well, and I have learned a great deal from them.'

'Do you have good relations with them?' Mao asked. 'Do they like to make close friends with you?'

'I think our relations aren't bad,' she cautiously replied. 'I can get along with them very well; so can they.'

'That's good.'

'One student in our class from a cadre family doesn't behave well. He is inattentive in class and doesn't study after class. He reads novels all the time. Sometimes he sleeps in the dormitory during class sessions, and sometimes he doesn't attend our meetings on Saturday afternoons. Nor does he get back to the campus on time on Sundays. He is often absent from our class meetings or the Communist Youth League committee. None of us approves his behaviour.'

'Do your teachers allow you students to sleep,' Mao asked, 'or read novels in class?'

'No.'

'They should,' Mao declared. 'Teachers should allow students to read novels and sleep in class and take good care of their health. Teachers should talk less and let students read more. I believe that the student you have just mentioned has promise, since he dares to stay away from meetings and not return to campus on time on Sundays. When you go back to your Institute please tell that student that eight or nine o'clock in the evening is too early to return to the campus. He may return at eleven or twelve o'clock. By the way, who told you to hold meetings on Sunday evenings?'

'When I was attending the normal college,' the girl explained, 'the college authorities didn't allow students to use Sunday evenings for meetings and students were usually free on Sunday evenings. At one meeting of the Youth League branch committee, several cadres proposed that we live an organization life one Sunday evening. Many members opposed this proposal; some even went to talk to the political adviser, insisting that Sunday evenings should remain free and that we should be permitted to be out during the evening. Later the political adviser went along with their opinion and asked us to hold meetings some other time.'

'The political adviser was right,' Mao said.

'Here in this Institute we always have meetings on Sunday evening. It is either a class meeting, or a meeting of the Youth League branch committee, or a meeting of all classes of the same grade, or a seminar for the study group of the Party course. Since the start of this semester, there has not been a single Sunday evening not spent on a meeting.'

'After your return to school,' Mao told her, 'you should lead a rebellion by not returning to school and not attending any more meetings on Sundays.'

'I wouldn't dare!' she exclaimed. 'School regulations say that students must return to school on Sunday. If I don't obey, others will say that I am disrupting the school's system.'

'What system is that?' Mao asked. 'Don't bother with it. You can just stay away from school and tell the others that you want to disrupt the school system.'

'I couldn't,' the girl protested. 'I would be criticized if I did.'

'I don't think you'll be able to achieve much success in the future', Mao warned her, 'if you are afraid of being responsible for disrupting the system, being criticized, being punished, being dismissed from the Institute and being refused admission into the Party. What should you be afraid of? The worst that could happen is that you'd be dismissed from school. But the school should allow students to rebel. After you get back to school you must lead the rebellion.'

'But I am a relative of the Chairman,' the girl said. 'If I don't listen to him and take the lead in disrupting the school system, others will criticize me for arrogance, conceit and disregard for organization and discipline.'

'Here you go again. You are afraid of being criticized for arrogance and conceit and for disregard for organization and discipline. Why? You may say that you are inspired by the words of the Chairman before you rebel. I believe the student you've just mentioned will accomplish greater success than you in the future, for he dares to disobey the school system. . . . I can see that you are somewhat metaphysical. . . .'

'What questions', the girl went on to ask, changing the subject, 'should I pay attention to? I suppose I should take some vaccine to avoid infection.'

'How metaphysical you are! Why do you need vaccine? No, it's good for you to be somewhat infected. You should go into the work deeply and play the part, and then come out. . . . Does your school ask you to read the bible or the scriptures?'

'No,' the girl replied. 'What is the use of reading such things?'

'If you want to be a translator but haven't read the bible or the scriptures, how can you carry out your duties? . . . By the way, how do you say *chih-shih fen-tzu* in English?'

'I don't know,' the girl confessed.

'Oh you! You've studied English for such a long time and yourself are an intellectual, but you don't know how to say 'intellectual' in English!'

'Let me consult the Chinese-English dictionary.'

'Please do,' Mao said. 'Is the word there?'

'Too bad,' the girl replied after a while, 'it's not in this Chinese-English dictionary.'

'Let me have a look,' Mao said, ' . . . It's true. This Chinese-English dictionary is useless, and it omits many other words. Ask your school to compile a good quality Chinese-English dictionary after you go back. The new dictionary should include all the political terms, and it had better include examples of usage under every entry.'

'With so little time and qualified people, how can our school compile such a dictionary?'

'Your school', Mao insisted, 'has so many teachers and students. Why can't it compile a dictionary? . . .'

'OK,' the girl said. 'I will mention it to the school leadership. I think we can manage it.'

Mao ended the conversation with some advice and a warning.

'You should go back,' he told her, 'and read ten or twenty classical Marxist-Leninist works and some books concerning materialism. As far as I can see, your level of theoretical study is not very high. And so, you should not try to achieve one hundred per cent in your studies. Nor should you make less than forty per cent. Sixty or eighty per cent is right for you.'

'Why not one hundred per cent?' the girl asked.

'One hundred per cent is too much. Don't read too much. Too much study will kill people. . . . I am very worried about the children of our cadres. They don't have much experience of life or society but they are arrogant and give themselves superior airs.'

A fortnight later on 5 July Mao had the first of three long conversations with his nephew, Yuan-hsin. The young man was at this time a gifted student at the Harbin Military Engineering Institute. He had been taken into Mao's family after the execution of his father in the early 1940s, and Mao took in this conversation an appropriately paternal tone.

'Have you made any progress', he began, 'in the course of the past year? Have you raised your level?'

'I'm a bit mixed up about it myself,' the nephew faltered. 'I wouldn't venture to say that I have made any progress; if I have, it is merely superficial.'

Mao professed to draw some comfort from this.

'I think you have after all made some progress, your way of looking at problems is no longer so simple. . . .'

'Are you going to study Marxism-Leninism, or revisionism?' Mao went on, aggressively.

'Naturally,' Yuan-hsin replied, 'I'm studying Marxism-Leninism.'

'Don't be too sure, who knows what you're studying? Do you know what Marxism-Leninism is?'

'Marxism-Leninism', the nephew suggested, 'means that you must carry on the class struggle, that you must carry out revolution.'

'It has not been finally determined who, in the end, will overthrow whom,' Mao commented. 'In the Soviet Union . . . is not the bourgeoisie in power? We, too, have cases in which political power is in the grip of the bourgeoisie; there are production brigades, factories, and county committees, as well as district and provincial committees, in which they have their people, there are deputy heads of public security departments who are their men. Who is leading the ministry of culture? The cinema and the theatre are entirely in their service, and not in the service of the majority of the people. . . .'

His nephew talked about the kind of political training given at the Institute, and Mao urged him to take proper exercise.

'You have already come to know water, and have mastered it, that is excellent. Do you know how to ride horseback?'

'I don't know how to ride,' Yuan-hsin confessed.

'To be a soldier, and not to know how to ride – this should not be. . . . Have you done any rifle shooting or not?'

'I haven't touched a gun for four years,' the young man admitted.

Mao wondered what kind of soldier he was who did not know how to shoot. His nephew recalled that once he had gone swimming in cold weather, so that it was warmer in the water than outside. Afterwards, coming out and feeling the cold air, he had said: 'It is after all a bit more comfortable in the water.'

Mao stared angrily at his nephew on this disclosure.

'In fact,' he remonstrated, 'you like comfort and fear difficulties. You know how to think about yourself, you spend all your time pondering your own problems. Your father was dauntless and resolute in the face of the enemy, he never wavered in the slightest, because he served the majority of the people. If it had been you, wouldn't you have got down on both knees and begged for your life? Very many members of our family have given their lives, killed by the Kuomintang and the American imperialists. You grew up eating honey and thus far you have never known suffering. In future, if you do not become a Rightist, but rather a Centrist, I shall be satisfied. You have never suffered, how can you be a Leftist?'

'Is there still some hope for me?' the young man asked.

'Well yes, there is hope. . . . You must especially learn to work with people who disagree with you. If you like to have people praise you, if you like to have honey on your lips, and songs to your glory in your ear, that is the most dangerous thing, and that is exactly what you do like. Is it not the case that you spend your time with the sons and daughters of cadres, and look down on other people?'

Under questioning, the nephew revealed that his lessons did not allow him much time either for politics or for meeting ordinary people.

'That is wrong,' Mao reproved. 'The class struggle is your most important subject, and it is a compulsory subject. . . . Only when you have completed a course of political training can I consider you a university graduate. Otherwise, if the Military Engineering Institute lets you graduate, I won't recognize your diploma. If you don't even know about the class struggle, how can you be regarded as a university graduate?'

The conversation ended on the same point where it had begun.

'Why', Mao insisted, 'are you interested in your professional speciality, but not in Marxism-Leninism?'

All the nephew could say, however, about his exposure to Marxist theory was:

'I've read only very little, and I didn't understand much of what I did read.'

It was from conversations like these that Mao conceived the determination to rebel against his colleagues in order to check the visible embourgeoisement of his Party.

It was Chiang Ching, Mao's wife, who was to give him his pretext. She was beginning to come into her own as a reformer of the traditional Chinese opera, and Mao spent considerable time in 1964 seeing new operas and making suggestions about them. But some of Mao's comrades were not as enthusiastic as he about Chiang Ching's interfering with the traditional opera.

Peng Chen, the Peking Party boss, commented that revolutionary operas were 'still at the stage of wearing trousers with a slit at the seat, and sucking the fingers'. Chiang Ching sought the support of Teng Hsiao-ping for her work, but his only response was to say, 'For her drama reform I would raise two hands to show my approval, but I would not care to watch the show.'

It was Teng who voiced openly that summer the resentment which many of Mao's colleagues felt about the growing political role of Mao's wife. 'Some people', he remarked, 'try to gain publicity for themselves just by criticizing others. They step on the shoulders of others just in order to mount the stage. . .' No one doubted that it was to Chiang Ching that he was referring. Yet she was elected a deputy to the National People's Congress at the end of 1964, standing ready to support her husband when the moment came.

Mao told a philosophy conference in August that class education should be extended by students going down to the farms – even if they were not in good health.

People won't die by going down to the countryside. There may be some flu but it will be all right when they put on more clothes. . . . College students, those in the liberal arts, should begin to go down to the countryside this winter.

Those who are studying the sciences need not move now, though they may move once or twice. But all liberal arts students, students of history, or political economics, literature and law must go. Everybody should go: professors, instructors, administrative workers and students, for a period of five months at a time. They should spend five months in the rural areas and five months in factories to acquire some perceptual knowledge. They should take a look at horses, cows, sheep, chickens, dogs and pigs, as well as rice, kaoliang, legumes, wheat and millet.

Kang Sheng interrupted to complain that one of the leading economists in Peking had been 'fooling around with Liberman's works and with capitalism'. To this Mao replied with a surprising defence of capitalism. 'It is all right to engage in some capitalism. Society being so complex, wouldn't it be too monotonous to engage only in socialism to the exclusion of capitalism? Wouldn't that be too one-sided an approach without any unity of opposites? Let them engage in it.'

Mao went on to bemoan what relatively little impact he had yet been able to make on Chinese capitalism.

To distribute land to the peasants is to transform feudal landlord ownership into the ownership of individual peasants, which is still under the domain of bourgeois revolution. It is by no means strange to distribute land, since MacArthur has distributed land in Japan and Napoleon also distributed land. Land reform cannot eliminate capitalism, and thus will never enable us to reach socialism.

In our nation now, about one-third of the power is controlled by the enemy or by those who sympathize with the enemy. We have been here fifteen years and have two-thirds of the domain. Today a Party branch secretary can be bribed with a few packs of cigarettes and there's no telling what you might achieve by marrying your daughter off to such a person.

A French delegation spent two and a half hours with Mao at his country house in Hangchow in September, and found him failing in health. One of the Frenchmen thought he recognized the early stages of Parkinson's disease, while others thought he might have suffered a stroke. When he went from one room to another, an aide escorted him, guiding him lightly by the elbows.

'Mao smoked incessantly,' one Frenchman wrote. 'From the number of cigarettes he lit during the evening it was obvious that he was a three-pack-a-day man, and he had a bad case of smoker's cough: he breathed heavily with a distinct wheeze.

'He also had some slight difficulty in co-ordinating his gestures. To light a cigarette, Mao, who is left-handed, held the match-box in his right hand and struck the match with his left. To get a better grip he steadied himself by bearing down with both elbows on the armrests of his chair.'

One of the Frenchmen began to speak about France's 'new role' in South-East Asia, but Mao interrupted.

'Since Dienbienphu,' he said, 'France has had no role in Asia. And let me tell you something you may or may not know: many of the gunners at Dienbienphu were Chinese.'

Replying to questions about the economy, Mao said flatly that, 'China does not have an economic plan. . . . We did have a long-term plan but it went wrong. Too much was borrowed from abroad. We have less experience in this domain than you and we have not put everything right yet.'

Another visitor in October was Nehru, to whom Mao explained that China did not want war and did not have atom bombs, although if other countries wanted to fight there would be catastrophe in the whole world and many people would die. Mao did not believe that one atom bomb would destroy all mankind, so that you would not be able to find a government to negotiate peace. Nehru replied that he was Chairman of the Atomic Energy Commission in India and knew about the destructiveness of atomic power. He was convinced that no one could survive a nuclear war. Mao demurred that it would probably not be so. Existing governments might disappear, but others would arise to replace them.

China's first nuclear test in fact took place on 16 October 1964, representing a triumph both for Mao's determination to 'go it alone' after the Russian nuclear advisers had left China five years earlier, but also, and more particularly, for the Western-trained Chinese atomic scientists who had done it. Later, at a discussion on economic planning, somebody said that China would have to catch up with the technology of other countries. Mao concurred: 'Yes, we must. . . . No matter what country, no matter what missiles, atomic bombs, hydrogen bombs, we must surpass them.'

At a forum on Central Committee work on 20 December, Mao summed up fifteen years of Communist rule in the remark: 'Landlords and rich peasants are the masters backstage. On the stage are the corrupt elitist cadres.' In order to reform rural society itself, the political instruments through whom that reform was being conducted had to be purified. It was necessary to show the poor peasants that they could struggle against bad cadres just as much as they had earlier struggled against rich landlords. As for the most 'vicious' elements, 'we should give them the label of new bourgeoisie'.

Another participant suggested leaving it to the ordinary peasants to decide how to deal with corrupt cadres, since they would be understanding and reasonable. To which Mao retorted: 'Sometimes this isn't so. Once the masses are aroused, they become blind, and we have our own blindness too.'

Defections of artists did not escape Mao's notice, 'The musician Fou Ts'ong', he told the same conference, 'has fled to England. I say this is good. What's the use of keeping this kind of person in the country?'

In January 1965 Mao had a four-hour conversation over dinner with Edgar Snow. Mao ate moderately of a hot peppery Hunanese meal, Snow reported, and 'drank a glass or two of Chinese grape wine, rather perfunctorily as of yore. He smoked perhaps a dozen cigarettes during the evening.'

Mao revealed that he had read General Maxwell Taylor's book, *The Uncertain Trumpet*. The USA could not win the war in Vietnam, and yet it had fought a progressive war of independence from British imperialism and then fought a civil war to establish a free labour market. Washington and Lincoln had been progressive men of their day, and when the USA first established its republic it was hated and dreaded by all the crowned heads of Europe. Then the Americans were revolutionaries, now they needed to struggle for liberation from their own monopoly capitalists.

Was there any justification in the Russian criticism that China fostered a 'cult of personality'? Mao thought that there was. Stalin had been said to be the centre of such a cult, whereas Khrushchev had none at all. Probably Khrushchev fell because he had no cult of the personality. . . .

Mao said that he had been reading reports of an American investigation in the Bikini Islands six years after the nuclear tests there, which had shown that mice, fish, birds and plants were growing happily. For the bacteria, the birds, the mice and the trees, the atom bomb really was a paper tiger. Possibly for man himself it was different. . . . Mao said that he had heard that there was an American film called *On The Beach* which showed nuclear war bringing the world to an end. Was it a scientific film?

Snow asked about the size of the population. Mao replied that he really did not know. Some said that there were 680 or 690 million Chinese but he did not believe it. How could there be so many? The peasants had sometimes confused the picture.

Asked whether Snow could take any message from Mao to President Johnson, the reply came, after a pause: No! Mao did anticipate an improvement in Sino-American relations, though not necessarily within his own lifetime. He was getting ready to see God very soon. He recalled in this conversation how both his brothers, his first wife and their son had been killed, and how odd it was that death had so far passed him by. He had been prepared for it many times, but death just did not seem to want him.

China would be in the hands of later generations which ought to be more knowledgeable than Mao's. They would assess the work of the revolution in accordance with their own values. Man's condition on this earth was changing more and more rapidly. A thousand years from now, all of us, even Marx, Engels and Lenin, would probably appear rather ridiculous.

Mao did not talk much to Snow about current Chinese politics, and six years later, when they met again, he explained that a great deal of power had slipped from his control in 1965. But he was preparing his come-back, initially through an innocuous-sounding campaign.

He presented to his colleagues a twenty-three-article programme for developing the socialist education movement. Liu Shao-chi's response was distinctly negative, and Mao later revealed that it was at this time that 'my vigilance was aroused' about Liu.

The first of Mao's twenty-three articles was the necessity to rectify 'those people within the Party who are in authority and are taking the capitalist road...' Liu Shao-chi doubtless saw in this the threat of a needlessly divisive witch-hunt within the Party leadership. But his strenuous objection to it inevitably laid him open to self-identification as a 'capitalist-roader'. By the end of January Mao had decided that Liu would have to go.

He had also concluded that the bureaucracy had in fact become a new ruling class. 'The bureaucratic class', he wrote, 'is ... sharply opposed to the working class and the poor and lower-middle peasants. These people have become or are in the process of becoming bourgeois elements sucking the blood of the workers. How can they have proper understanding?' Mao asked everyone in China to learn from the model agricultural brigade

at Tachai, which had immunized itself against these diseases.

In March Mao gave some candid military advice to visitors from the Palestine Liberation Organization. 'There are some foreigners studying military science in China. I advise them to go back, and not to study too long. A few months will do. There is only lecturing in the class room, which is of no use.... You should spend most of your time in your own country. Perhaps there is no need to go abroad, and you will still learn it all right.'

In the spring of 1965 Mao went on a long tour of central and southern China to prepare his moves against Liu and the others, but also intensifying foreign speculation about his health. In May he returned for the first time in almost forty years to the mountain stronghold of Chingkangshan, where he had founded the formula which he was now attempting to spread all over China. On the morning of 27 May he climbed up the slope to the summit and took in the scenes which had then been his daily life. He poured his feelings into a poem:

> I have long aspired to reach for the clouds
> And I again ascend Chingkangshan.
> Coming from afar to view our old haunt,
> I find new scenes replacing the old.
> Everywhere orioles sing, swallows dart,
> Streams babble
> And the road mounts skyward.
> Once Huangyangchieh is passed
> No other perilous place calls for a glance.

> Wind and thunder are stirring,
> Flags and banners are flying
> Wherever men live.
> Thirty-eight years are fled
> With a mere snap of the fingers.
> We can clasp the moon in the Ninth Heaven
> And seize turtles deep down in the Five Seas:
> We'll return amid triumphant song and laughter.
> Nothing is hard in this world
> If you dare to scale the heights.

The Western press reported rumours that Mao had had a stroke, and was in hospital in Shanghai or Hangchow. It was said that he walked with difficulty on a public occasion and failed to speak, and Mao himself admitted that he was not up to doing all his own writing. 'Now, when I want something written, it is all done by a secretary, not by my hand.' He added wryly that, 'If you never take the initiative and rely on a secretary, it is just like having a secretary assume your responsibility for leadership work' – a reflection perhaps on Chiang Ching or Chen Po-ta.

Mao was certainly seeing doctors in 1965, for he was stimulated to issue a sarcastic directive about them:

Tell the Ministry of Public Health that it only works for fifteen per cent of the total population of the country and that this fifteen per cent is mainly composed of gentlemen, while the broad masses of the peasants do not get any medical treatment....

The Ministry of Public Health is not a Ministry of Public Health for the people, why not change its name to the Ministry of Urban Health, the Ministry of Gentlemen's Health, or even to Ministry of Urban Gentlemen's Health? ...

There is another peculiar thing. Whenever the doctor makes an examination he always has to wear a mask no matter what the illness is.

Is this because he is afraid of catching a disease and transmitting it to others? I am afraid that it is primarily because he is afraid of catching an illness himself. But different diseases should be dealt with separately. If he wears a mask no matter what the illness, this creates a distance between doctor and patient from the start.

We should leave behind in the city a few of the less able doctors who graduated one or two years ago, and the others should all go into the countryside.

In August a publication which was to become the manifesto of Mao's return to power and a world best-seller, the 'Little Red Book' of *Quotations of Chairman Mao,* made its first appearance. The history of this went back to 1960 when Lin Piao, as Mao's new Minister of Defence, produced a set of sayings which were read and revised by Mao and disseminated in the army. A year or two later Lin began the custom of printing quotations from Mao, boxed and in bold type, in the army newspaper *Liberation Army Daily.* He went on to produce in 1964 a pocket edition of passages from Mao's writings for soldiers to carry about in their packs, and this was the predecessor of the first regular edition of the *Quotations* to appear on 1 August 1965 and to be frequently reissued in subsequent years, edited by the General Political Department of the Army.

On 3 August 1965 Mao dropped his most open hints of what was to come. André Malraux delivered to Mao a letter from Charles de Gaulle and they had a long conversation in the presence of Liu Shao-chi, the French Ambassador and other Chinese leaders. Mao spoke of the bad influence of the intellectuals, especially among the young: the Ambassador, Lucien Paye, protested that China's students, as far as he had been able to see, were committed to Mao's vision. Mao looked sceptical.

'Youth', Mao said, 'must be put to the test. . . .' – a hint of what was to come in the Cultural Revolution. Malraux noticed that Mao spoke as if he were addressing an imaginary contradictor, as if he were saying, 'This is how it will be, whether you like it or not' – even as if he were speaking through Malraux to Liu.

'Soviet revisionism', Mao declared, 'is an . . . apostasy. It is moving towards the restoration of capitalism, and one wonders why Europe isn't satisfied with it.'

'I don't believe', Malraux differed, 'they are contemplating a return to private ownership of the means of production.'

'Are you sure? Look at Yugoslavia!'

Malraux found Mao stiff and slow in walking, but he commented: 'Mao is not stricken: he has the uncertain equilibrium of the statue of the Commendatore, and walks like a legendary figure risen from some imperial grave.'

'Khrushchev', Mao observed, 'seemed to think that a revolution is done when a Communist party has seized power – as if it were merely a question of national liberation.'

Mao went on to mock Kosygin's message that, 'Communism means the raising of living standards.' Mao commented:

Of course! And swimming is a way of putting on a pair of trunks! . . . It isn't simply a question of replacing the Tsar with Khrushchev, one bourgeoisie with another, even it it is called communist. It's the same as with women. Of course it was necessary to give them legal equality to begin with! But from there on, everything still remains to be done. The thought, culture and customs which brought China to where we found her must disappear, and the thought, customs and culture of proletarian China, which does not yet exist, must appear. The Chinese woman doesn't yet exist either, among the masses; but she is beginning to want to exist. . . . Revolution . . . isn't a victory, it is a mixing of the masses and the cadres over several generations.

They had been walking to the steps where Malraux's car was waiting. 'But in this battle', Mao added, 'we are alone.'

'Not for the first time,' Malraux suggested.

'I am alone with the masses. Waiting.' The Frenchman found bitterness, irony and especially pride in Mao's tone. He had not spoken these words for the benefit of his colleagues, since he had left them behind, out of earshot. But it was only after leaving them that he had begun to speak with passion, and he walked more slowly than his condition required him to, in order to prolong these private moments with an outsider who had sympathetic insight into his situation.

Revisionism, Mao went on, was the death of the revolution. 'I have told you that the revolution is also a feeling. . . . Men do not like to bear the burden of the revolution throughout their lives.' Only one per cent of China's Communists were in the countryside. The survivors of the old guard of the Party had been moulded by action. 'On the other hand, there is a whole generation of dogmatic youth, and dogma is less useful than cow dung. . . . Whatever your Ambassador may think, this youth is showing dangerous tendencies. . . . It is time to show that there are others.'

At last the moment came for farewells.

'I am alone,' Mao repeated. Suddenly he laughed: 'Well, with a few distant friends: please give General de Gaulle my greetings.'

Soon afterwards Mao satirized the Russian version of Communism, against which he felt himself called to struggle, in a poem:

> The roc wings fanwise,
> Soaring thirty thousand miles
> And rousing a raging cyclone.
> The blue sky on his back, he looks down
> To survey Man's world with its towns and cities.
> Gunfire licks the heavens,
> Shells pit the earth.
> A sparrow in his bush is scared stiff.
> 'This is one hell of a mess!
> O I want to flit and fly away.'

> 'Where, may I ask?'
> The sparrow replies,
> 'To a jewelled palace in elfland's hills.
> Don't you know a triple pact was signed
> Under the bright autumn moon two years ago?
> There'll be plenty to eat,
> Potatoes piping hot,
> Beef-filled goulash.'
> 'Stop your windy nonsense!
> Look, the world is being turned upside down.'

Lin Piao was the only one to give unflinching support to the Chairman, whose efforts in September and October to bring his colleagues round to a new rectification campaign within the Party were unsuccessful. The others were still critical of Mao.

Liu Shao-chi and Peng Chen were even urging that the treaty with the Russians be reactivated in order to protect China against the American bombings in Vietnam.

Mao put his foot down, however, and insisted that China would have to defend herself by self-reliance. In turn, the others rejected his call for an upheaval in cultural and educational policy. Peng Chen declared that, 'Even if the Chairman is wrong, then he too must be criticized.' And Teng Hsiao-ping was alleged afterwards to have 'coldly dissociated himself from Mao'.

Mao recognized that there was no hope for him in Peking, where the campaign for socialist education was being carried out in a deliberately half-hearted way. In a characteristic gesture, he left Peking for the south and turned in despair to his wife's group of political friends. He was not to return to the capital for nine months, after planning the details of his last big campaign.

26
THE CULTURAL REVOLUTION

The immediate issue which Mao now took up against the conservatives in his own Party as a prelude to the big shake-up
which he wanted was a play written by Wu Han, the deputy
mayor of Peking and Peng Chen's protégé, called *Hai Jui Dismissed from Office*. Based on an obscure event of the Ming Dynasty,
this was in fact a thinly disguised commentary on the Peng
Teh-huai affair in 1959. Its timbre can be judged from one of its
lines where a minister, Hai Jui (i.e. Peng Teh-huai), says to his
emperor (i.e. Mao):

In earlier times you did quite a few good things, but how about now?
Your mind is deluded, and you are too dogmatic and prejudiced. You
think you are always right and refuse criticism. Your faults are too
numerous. The whole country has been dissatisfied with you for a long
time and the inner and outer ministers and officers all know it.

No Chinese reader would miss the analogy.

Mao explained afterwards to friends in Peking that he 'suggested to comrade Chiang Ching that she organize some articles
to criticize *Hai Jui Dismissed from Office*. But this was impossible to
accomplish here in this Red metropolis, and there was no alternative but to go to Shanghai to organize it.' Chiang Ching complained that the rightists in the Party kept a close watch on this
development through agents who had sneaked into her group.

'Wherever I went, they tailed me; they installed detecta-
phones. They spied on ... the Chairman, Vice-Chairman Lin,
the Premier and me!' But the literary work was done, by Chiang
Ching, Chang Chun-chiao and Yao Wen-yuan, with the help of
the Shanghai Party boss, Ko Ching-shih.

The first article was published in Shanghai on 10 November
1965, but the *People's Daily* in Peking took no notice of it whatsoever. Indeed, Peng Chen had one of his aides telephone
Shanghai on the following day to find out who had authorized

them to attack Wu Han without consulting his own group of five in Peking who were supposed to be in charge of the campaign to reform cultural affairs. Chang Chun-chiao replied, 'Mao', whereupon Peng's aide hung up without a word. For the rest of December a battle of wills was fought between the two cities over the issue of national publication of the article. Towards the end of the month Peng Chen asked one of his colleagues at a meeting of the Peking Party:

'How is Wu Han now?'

'Wu is nervous,' came the reply, 'for he is aware that this criticism originates from a source.'

'Source or not,' Peng replied, 'we seek only the truth. In truth, everyone is equal.'

On 29 November Mao forced the issue by publishing the article in *Liberation Army Daily*, the army newspaper controlled by his ally Lin Piao, as well as having it read over the radio, so that Peking had no option but to follow suit. Up to this point it would have been possible for Peng Chen to have surrendered Wu Han to Mao as a scapegoat, in which case he might well have retained his position and power. But he chose to back his subordinate and thus elevated the struggle into one between Mao and himself.

Mao was making full use of his 'secret weapon' in the form of his personal and bodyguard staff, especially Unit 8341. He had already instructed them in the summer to go down to the rural areas and factories to explain and implement the socialist education movement.

According to Red Guard information, Mao's office was being bugged by one of the leaders close to Peng Chen, and information gained from this eavesdropping was supplied not only to Peng but even to the Russians. It was rumoured in Peking, however, that Mao's chief bodyguard, Wang Tung-hsing, detected the surveillance devices and persuaded Mao to feed false information to his opponents in order to mislead them.

Mao took up his offensive against revisionism in science and culture in a speech to a Party conference in Hangchow – in the presence of Peng Chen, who was now Mao's chief antagonist. Mao drew attention to the appalling chasm which was growing between the cadres, the students and the peasants.

'I said to my own child, "You go down to the countryside and tell the poor and lower-middle peasants: My dad says that after studying a few years we became more and more stupid. Please, uncles and aunts, brothers and sisters, be my teachers. I want to learn from you." '

Arts faculties in particular needed to be reformed, and Mao singled out Wu Han's play, conceding the analogy.

As an aside, Mao noted in his headmasterly way an improvement in Bertrand Russell. 'He recently sent me a pamphlet which should be translated and read. Russell is now a bit better politically. He is anti-revisionist and anti-American and he supports Vietnam. This idealist has acquired a little materialism. I am talking about his actions.'

This in turn prompted an unusual defence of social eclecticism: 'A man should work in many fields, have contact with all sorts of people. Leftists should not only meet Leftists, but also Rightists. They should not be afraid of this and that. I myself have met all sorts of people. . . .'

There followed a characteristically sycophantic interjection from one of Mao's radical circle. Mao was saying that people should use a more popular style of writing.

'We all talk like students,' he complained.

'The Chairman excepted,' Chen Po-ta interrupted.

This time Mao accepted the flattery, which on other occasions he was often quick to rebuff.

'I', he immodestly agreed, 'have been involved in the peasant movement, the workers' movement, the student movement, the Kuomintang movement, and I have done military work for over twenty years, so I am somewhat better.'

But Mao was still left on the sidelines on the issue of a Party purge. 'At that time,' he later recalled, 'the majority did not agree with my view, and I was left alone. . . . They said that my views were outmoded. . . .'

The year ended with a family occasion. Mao's son, An-ching, and his wife visited the old man, who 'happily wielded a brush', the young couple recalled, 'to write out a poem for them.

Mao's daughter by Chiang Ching, Li Na, was also growing up. In 1966 he wrote her a dedication on finishing school, in the form of four pieces of advice:

(1) Heaven will entrust you with a great duty, but first you must steel your own will with pain, work with your own hands, go hungry and be worn out and throw off your undisciplined behaviour in order to exercise forbearance and learn from your mistakes. (2) Total materialists are afraid of nothing. (3) The road is hard, but the future is always radiant. (4) In the future, which holds your destiny in readiness, sorrows will plague you and you will suffer many reverses, but never turn back.

At the beginning of 1966 the girl's mother, Chiang Ching, made her decisive entry into politics on the back of Mao's ideas. She struck a bargain with Lin Piao, offering to share with the Defence Minister her cultural skills and the political advantages of being the Chairman's wife, in return for a position in the top echelon of the army. Lin entrusted her with the task of leading a forum on literature and art for the armed forces in Shanghai.

'Comrade Chiang Ching', he told his men before she arrived, 'talked with me yesterday. She is very sharp politically on questions of literature and art, and she really knows art. . . .'

This heralded a new phase in the career of Mao's wife in which she began to be described as 'the moon reflecting the light of the sun'. Up to now she had, in her own words, 'worked as secretary to the Chairman, my main task being to investigate into international questions. In the realms of culture and education, I am counted as a mobile sentinel. That is to say, I place orders for certain periodicals and newspapers, scrutinize them, and then present to the Chairman all those which I consider to be worthy of attention. . . . This has been the main body of my work for many years.' After 1966 she combined these duties with that of being secretary to the members of the Standing Committee of the Central Committee.

Lin was piling flattery upon flattery in his public statements about Mao. 'The thought of Mao Tse-tung', he wrote, 'is the zenith of Marxism-Leninism in the contemporary era. . . . Everything he says is truth, and every phrase he utters is worth ten thousand phrases.'

Mao had to put up with it, against his better judgement, because Lin was virtually his only ally within the senior ranks of the Party. He himself was meanwhile preaching the concept of rebellion, particularly against the rightists in the Ministry of Propaganda who were 'confiscating and suppressing' the works of the leftists. 'The central Ministry of Propaganda', he complained in February, 'is the Palace of the Prince of Hell. It is necessary to overthrow it. . . . I have always advocated that whenever the central organs do something wrong, it is necessary to call upon the local authorities to rebel and attack the central government.' In the same month he had commented: 'It is to the advantage of despots to keep people ignorant; it is to our advantage to make them intelligent.'

But the Politburo, in Mao's absence, accepted Peng Chen's resolution effectively blunting the work to reform culture. Mao expressed his strong dissatisfaction. In March the Politburo came to Hangchow, and Mao lectured it on the sins of the Peking Committee and talked for the first time about the need for a Cultural Revolution.

From Hangchow Mao went on to the Tsunghua hot springs resort outside Canton, where he experienced, a week later, the final frustration that caused him to launch the Cultural Revolution. He was visited by a delegation of Japanese Communists sympathetic to Moscow. He told them that war between China and America was 'inevitable' and would occur 'within two years at the latest'. He predicted that Russia would use the American attack on China as a pretext to occupy the north-eastern part of China: 'The result will be a confrontation across the Yangtze of the Chinese Liberation Army and the Russian Army.' (His predictions were not as good now as they were in the 1940s.)

The Japanese Communists pleaded with Mao to expedite the trans-shipment of Soviet aid material to North Vietnam, then undergoing American bombing. Mao was astonished. He would never have agreed to facilitate help, even to a third country, from the revisionist Russians. (Chinese aid to Vietnam continued, and after the war had ended the Chinese claimed they had given more to Vietnam than the Russians had.) One of Mao's aides broke it to him that Russia had been sending military equipment to North Vietnam via Chinese railways, adding lamely that 'we are sabotaging some of their equipment in an effort to discredit Soviet assistance in the eyes of the North Vietnamese.'

Mao was angry at being bypassed on such a critical issue, and shouted to his own aides, in front of the Japanese: 'You weak-kneed people in Peking!' The joint communiqué which Chou En-lai had signed with the Japanese delegation referring to joint action by China and Russia in support of Vietnam was scrapped because of Mao's anger. The Japanese attempt to mediate between the two Communist giants on this single issue of helping the Vietnamese Communists thus came to nothing, and the conspiracy of silence by which the rest of the Chinese Politburo had hoped to override Mao was exposed.

After brooding briefly on this scene in front of the Japanese, Mao issued an order later in the day to dissolve the Party's Central Propaganda Department, its Peking Committee and the group in charge of cultural reform. He was committed to a full-scale confrontation with Peng Chen.

The Great Proletarian Cultural Revolution now formally opened, to provide the most astonishing episode in Mao's long and fruitful career. He himself described it as 'a politics course not given in the classroom', which led China 'to the brink of chaos' (most of his colleagues would have said, over the brink). But there was also an element of revenge in the way it worked out.

Chiang Ching put this at its broadest when she said: 'We must take into account not only the fifty days' (in the summer of 1966 when Mao had been forced out of Liu Shao-chi's Peking kingdom) 'and the seventeen years' (from 1949 to 1965, when Mao was not obeyed), 'but also the nineteen-thirties.' It was, perhaps, a last desperate effort in one single throw at the end of a long career to achieve all the changes and reforms that had so far eluded him.

Having decided that the Communist Party itself had become bureaucratic and counter-revolutionary, part of the vested interests against which the ordinary man in the street had to struggle, Mao took two allies – the army and the students – to overthrow the Party by force. He could rely on the army because of its loyalty to him and to Lin Piao, his disciple who had been defence minister for the past seven years. He could rely on the the students because the younger generation was always radical and ready to unseat old fogies in office whatever their political colour.

The Cultural Revolution operated at three levels. At one level it was a power struggle 'within the palace' between Mao and his Politburo rivals headed by Liu Shao-chi. At another level it was a crusade across the country to attain higher levels of democracy, socialism and collective spirit. At the lowest level it was a lifting of the constraints of law and order for a short period during which local scores could be settled and leadership rivalries fought out – individually as well as factionally.

Those who knew Mao's sternness of purpose knew what to do. On 14 April Kuo Mo-jo, Mao's fellow poet and President of the Academy of Sciences, confessed: 'In the past decade, a pen has always been in my hand, writing and translating works amounting to many millions of words. However, in the light of present-day standards, what I have written, strictly speaking, should all be burned. It has no value, none whatsoever. What is the main reason for this? It is the inadequate study of Chairman Mao's thinking. . . .'

In May Mao summoned an enlarged Politburo meeting in Hangchow which, packed by his own supporters, carried through the purge of Peng Chen and a handful of other 'rightists'. A new radical Cultural Revolution group to run the campaign was appointed, including Chen Po-ta, Chiang Ching,

Chang Chun-chiao, Yao Wen-yuan and Kang Sheng. But it took twelve days to persuade Peng Chen to confess his mistakes, and Mao's circular which the Politburo approved, advising Party committees about the new situation, was not published until a year afterwards because Mao did not yet control the press.

Mao dropped a hint as to whose head he was really after. 'Those representatives of the bourgeoisie', he told the Politburo sternly, 'who have sneaked into the party, the government, the army, and various cultural circles are a bunch of counter-revolutionary revisionists. . . . Some of them we have already seen through, others we have not. Some are still trusted by us and are being trained as our successors, persons like Khrushchev, for example, who are still nestling beside us. . . .'

Mao's supporters said that the men 'still nestling beside us', as disloyal as Khrushchev proved to be to Stalin, were headed by Liu Shao-chi.

Mao's demands were backed by big battalions. During these opening weeks of the Cultural Revolution Lin Piao moved the 38th Army, fully loyal to himself, into Peking to ensure that things went the way of himself and his master. But on 18 May, at a Central Committee meeting in Hangchow, Lin began to show his true colours in an extraordinary speech warning against rightist *coups d'état,* which, he claimed, 'have today become a fad'. There had been over sixty of them in the capitalist countries of the Third World since 1960, while in Chinese history, 'there are many examples in which we see that political power was lost through *coups d'état* before a dynasty had been going for ten, twenty, thirty or fifty years.'

Today in China,

There is a likelihood of counter-revolutionary *coups d'état,* killings, seizure of political power, capitalist restoration. . . . You may have smelled it – the smell of gunpowder. . . . Seizure of political power depends on gunbarrels and inkwells. . . . Now Chairman Mao still lives, so we can enjoy the shade under so big a tree. . . .

No matter how long Chairman Mao will live – ninety or over one hundred years, he is forever the supreme leader of our Party and his words will be the guideline of our actions. Whoever is against him shall be punished by the Party and the whole country. Whoever makes a secret report after his death as Khrushchev did must be an ambitious conspirator and a big bad fellow and shall be punished by the entire Party and the whole country.

Mao Tse-tung's Thought is an everlasting universal truth. . . . Every sentence of Chairman Mao's works is a truth, one single sentence of his surpasses ten thousand of ours.

At two o'clock in the afternoon of 25 May the first big-character poster was put up at Peking University by a radical young lecturer in response to Mao's new call for criticism of rightists. It was like the Hundred Flowers again. Mao telephoned Kang Sheng from Hangchow and told him to publish this poster in the *People's Daily* and also over the radio, thus rescuing the incident from obscurity.

The deification of Mao was growing. On 10 June *Red Flag* published an editorial in which it was said that 'The theory and practice of Comrade Mao Tse-tung may be likened to the ceaseless movement in the skies of the sun and moon and the endless flow of the rivers and streams on earth.' Another Chinese press report on 2 June declared: 'We have the invincible moral atom bomb of Mao Tse-tung's Thought. . . .'

On 8 July Mao wrote a letter to his wife in which he commented on this disturbing trend, especially in Lin Piao's extraordinary speech to the Politburo three weeks earlier.

I was quite uneasy at some of his thinking. I have never believed that the several booklets I wrote would have so much supernatural power. Now, after he exaggerated them, the whole nation has exaggerated them. . . . It seems that I have to concur with them. It is the first time in my life that I unwillingly concur with others on major questions. I have to do things against my own will!

His comrades, Mao lamented, often did not believe that he made mistakes and had to correct himself.

I have self-confidence, but also some doubt. I once said when I was in my teens: I believed I could live two hundred years and sweep a thousand miles. I was haughty in appearance and attitude. But I also doubt myself a little, and have always felt that when the tigers are absent from the mountain, the monkey will call himself King. I have become a king in this way, although I am just a monkey. This is not vague eclecticism, for in fact I have a nature which is primarily tiger-like [self-assured, all-powerful] and secondarily monkey-like [impish, spontaneous and changeable].

Mao here quoted a maxim from the Han Dynasty: 'A tall thing is easy to break; a white thing is easy to stain. The white snow in spring can hardly find its match; a high reputation is difficult to live up to.' The last two sentences, he wrote now to Chiang Ching, 'refer exactly to me' – and he had read them out at a Politburo meeting.

Mao guessed that the intention of the deifiers was to use him in the way that previous generations had used pictures of Chung

Kuei to post on their doors at the New Year to protect their houses against ghosts. 'I became the Chung Kuei of the Communist Party', Mao wrote, 'as early as in the 1960s.' But the higher you fly, the harder the fall. 'I am now prepared to be broken to pieces. This does not bother me. For the matter can never be destroyed; I may become pieces, that's all.'

Most of the one hundred Communist parties around the world no longer believed in Marxism. 'I suggest that you should also pay attention to this problem and should not become dizzy with success.' His wife's current triumphs in the Cultural Revolution should not go to her head. 'You should remind yourself often of your weak points, shortcomings and mistakes. On this I have talked with you numerous times. . . .'

What he was writing in this letter to Chiang should not be published, Mao added. 'The above seem to be black words. . . . Maybe we should wait until I die when the rightists come to power, and let them do the publication.' Mao's final sentence was: 'Our future is bright, but the road before us is twisted.'

During all this time, while he had been sojourning in southern China, there were frequent reports of Mao's bad health. Once it was said, in the spring of 1966, that he had lost consciousness because of tuberculosis, jaundice and hypertension. Arterial sclerosis was diagnosed in one newspaper, and another report in May had Mao resting in the summer resort of Kuling, 'under strict doctors' supervision', on a rigid diet, recuperating from a heart condition and high blood pressure. A Hong Kong story later in the year said that Mao had cancer of the throat, and for that reason did not speak in public.

The world, not to mention China, was therefore astonished to learn that on 16 July 1966 Mao, at the age of seventy-two, had again swum across the Yangtze river. The *People's Daily* waited nine days before informing the Chinese population. Mao covered the nine miles in 65 minutes, going with the currents, at the head of 5000 young swimmers of Wuhan in their annual contest along the course first charted by Mao a decade before.

Two days after this telling swim, Mao returned to Peking. Politically it should have been in triumph, but he himself said that, 'After my return to Peking . . . I felt very unhappy and desolate.'

Almost his first action on arriving at the capital was to telephone encouragement to the Tsinghua University rebels (who had started putting big-character posters up at the end of May denouncing rightists) and stake out his own personal position at this moment of truth.

'It seems to me', he told them, 'that I must personally think about the end of the revolution. Am I on the right side? No! Will China be no longer proletariat, but bourgeois, at the end of the movement? Absolutely not! Why am I afraid? Haven't we seen what they want after the first period? Reviling, intimidation, threats, black-mailing – posting of "labels" everywhere, striking with sticks and pourings of reproaches of a certain "big general" into one's ear.'

The big general was, of course, Liu Shao-chi.

Mao did not, perhaps, know at that time that the student leader at Tsinghua had criticized him in a poster commenting on a 1961 scandal about 'volunteers' being exposed to uranium isotopes in a university experiment.

Mao threw himself into a series of work conferences to guide the development of his Cultural Revolution. 'It is anti-Marxist', he declared at the first one, 'for the Communist Party to fear the student movement.' But he had not at this stage decided on the necessity of purging the senior leadership. 'Four days after my arrival in Peking, I was still inclined to preserve the existing order of things.' Predictably he had good things to say about the big-character posters, singling out for particular praise the one which had launched the entire movement.

Some of the schoolboy revolutionaries, the Young Pioneers, had stuck up big-character posters about their fathers, complaining that they neglected to explain Mao Tse-tung's thought to them and only asked about their marks at school, giving prizes for good marks. Mao asked the message to be passed on to them: 'You have done well to put up those big-character posters.'

But he cursed his colleagues for not taking the trouble to see things with their own eyes, or deal properly with people who needed their help.

When good people come, you refuse to see them. All right, I will see them. You send small fry to see them instead of yourselves. But I will see them. In one word, scared. Scared of revolution, of use of arms. Nobody is willing to go to the lower levels, to go to the trouble spots, to use his own eyes.

You will not go and see; you are preoccupied every day by routine business. You have no real understanding. How can you guide anything? . . . All those who are here at this conference should go to the trouble spots.

Some people are afraid of opening their mouths. When you are asked to speak, say something like this: 'We come to learn, to support your revolution.' Go at once when you are asked to go, and go again.

He spoke of the cruel logic of revolution.

We must be prepared for the revolution to be turned against us. . . . If you now want to carry the revolution through to the end, you must discipline yourself, reform yourself in order to keep up with it. . . .

There are some comrades who struggle fiercely against others, but cannot struggle with themselves. In this way, they will never be able to cross the pass.

It is up to you to lead the fire towards your own bodies, to fan the flames to make them burn. Do you dare to do this? Because it will burn your own heads.

'We are prepared,' his listeners were recorded as responding. 'If we're not up to it, we will resign our jobs. We live as Communist Party members and shall die as Communist Party members. It doesn't do to live a life of sofas and electric fans.'

A few days later Mao convened a meeting of the senior leadership which decided to withdraw the work teams sent out earlier under Liu Shao-chi to carry out the rectification campaign. Liu now realized that he was the unmistakeable target of Mao's hostility. Pacing up and down his drawing room in a state of inner turmoil, he told his daughter:

'They want me to make a self-examination, don't they? If they want me to come to your school to make a self-examination, I will do so for there is nothing to be feared. . . . You should do some labour and help write wall posters and sweep the floor. In this way, your schoolmates will not accuse you of behaving like officials and lords.'

The daughter, however, was on the side of her fellow student rebels, and therefore of Mao, rather than of her own father. When she suggested that his mistake was not 'fortuitous', her mother burst out:

'Your father serves on the Central Committee, and there are things he cannot tell you. But you always exert pressure on him.'

'If you feel', Liu told his daughter, 'this family hampers you, you may renounce it, and if you are not financially independent, I can give you money.'

A few days later he admitted to his daughter that he had 'made errors in orientation and in line, and indicated that he was willing to remould himself.'

Meanwhile Mao was encouraging the Red Guards. On 1 August he wrote a letter to the Red Guards of the Tsinghua

University Middle School acknowledging the big-character posters which they had sent him.

You say it is right to rebel against reactionaries; I enthusiastically support you.... No matter where they are, in Peking or in China, I will give enthusiastic support to all who take an attitude similar to yours in the Cultural Revolution movement.

Then came the sting in the tail.

Another thing, while supporting you, at the same time we ask you to pay attention to uniting with all who can be united with. As for those who have committed serious mistakes, after their mistakes have been pointed out you should offer them a way out of their difficulties by giving them work to do, and enabling them to correct their mistakes and become new men.

In the first half of August Mao chaired a Central Committee meeting which approved his Cultural Revolution by a small majority. 'Only after some debate', he told some Albanian visitors a year later, 'could I gain the endorsement of a little over half of the comrades. There were still many people who did not agree with me....' The Russians claimed that only forty-six of the ninety-one full members of the Central Committee were present, together with thirty-three of the eighty-nine alternates, and that the galleries were packed with young Red Guards.

On the first day Lin set the tone of obsequiousness. 'My heart', he told his comrades, 'has been quite heavy recently. My ability does not measure up to my work. I expect to make mistakes, but I will do my best to keep them to a minimum. I will rely on the Chairman.... Chairman Mao is the axle; we are the wheel.... He ... has ideas, many of which we do not understand.... I have no talent; I rely on the wisdom of the masses and do everything according to the Chairman's directives.'

On the fourth day Mao roundly denounced his opponents.

I sense danger. They themselves ordered the students to make revolution, but when everybody rose up, they wanted to suppress them. The so-called orientation and line, the so-called trust in the masses, and the so-called Marxism are all false and have been for many years already....

Even under a proletarian dictatorship, the masses should be allowed to petition, demonstrate and litigate. Moreover, freedom of speech, assembly and publication have been inscribed in the constitution. Judging from this act of suppressing the great cultural revolution of the students, I don't believe there is genuine democracy and genuine Marxism.

On the next day Mao strode vigorously into the arena to write his own big-character poster, bluntly entitled: 'Bombard the Headquarters':

China's first Marxist-Leninist big-character poster and Commentator's article on it in the *People's Daily* are indeed superbly written! Comrades, please read them again. But in the last fifty days or so some leading comrades from the central down to the local levels have acted in a diametrically opposite way. Adopting the reactionary stand of the bourgeoisie, they have enforced a bourgeois dictatorship and struck down the surging movement of the great Cultural Revolution of the proletariat. They have stood facts on their head and juggled black and white, encircled and suppressed revolutionaries, stifled opinions differing from their own, imposed a white terror, and felt very pleased with themselves. They have puffed up the arrogance of the bourgeoisie and deflated the morale of the proletariat. How poisonous! Viewed in connection with the Right deviation in 1962 and the wrong tendency of 1964 ... shouldn't this make one wide awake?

'I began to understand this mistake I myself had made,' Liu confessed subsequently, 'only after Chairman Mao's big-character poster.... Before that I did not know that I had committed such a grave error.'

On 8 August the Central Committee accepted Mao's sixteen articles on the conduct of the Cultural Revolution, the charter of the campaign. They began:

The Great Proletarian Cultural Revolution now unfolding is a great revolution that touches people to their very souls and constitutes a new stage in the development of the socialist revolution in our country....

Large numbers of revolutionary young people, previously unknown, have become courageous and daring path-breakers. They are vigorous in action and intelligence. Through the media of big-character posters and great debates, they argue things out, expose and criticize thoroughly and launch resolute attacks on the open and hidden representatives of the bourgeoisie....

Let the masses educate themselves in this great revolutionary movement and learn to distinguish between right and wrong and correct and incorrect ways of doing things....

The method to be used in debates is to present the facts, reason things out, and persuade through reasoning. Any method of forcing a minority holding different views to submit is impermissible. The minority should be protected because sometimes the truth is with the minority....

It is necessary to institute a system of general elections, like that of the Paris Commune, for electing members to the Cultural Revolutionary groups and committees and delegates to the Cultural Revolutionary congresses. The lists of candidates should be put forward by the revolutionary masses after full discussion, and the election should be held after the masses have discussed the lists over and over again. . . .

The Great Proletarian Cultural Revolution is a powerful motive force for the development of the social productive forces in our country. Any idea of counterposting the Great Cultural Revolution against the development of production is incorrect.

According to one of the provincial first secretaries present, Mao himself added the words, 'Wage peaceful not violent struggle', to the original draft of the sixteen articles.

Mao celebrated his success in the Central Committee by going out on to the streets of Peking to urge the passers-by to carry out the Cultural Revolution to the end.

'It would be impossible to say', reported one of the Communist newspapers of this scene, 'how many hands were stretched out to him. Many eyes were filled with tears of joy . . . many who had shaken hands with Chairman Mao told everyone they met: "Come and shake hands with me! My hands have just touched those of the great Chairman Mao!"'.

On 18 August Mao took the salute at the first of eight unprecedented march-pasts of a million Red Guards in Tienanmen Square. The press commented: 'We will smash the old world to smithereens and create a new world. . . . Sailing the sea depends on Mao Tse-tung's thought. . . . Chairman Mao is the reddest sun of our hearts.' Some of the Red Guard leaders adopted the new personal name Wei-tung, meaning Protect Mao.

Mao urged Red Guards all over the country to make journeys to exchange their experiences. 'After all,' he argued, 'the trains are free now, are they not?'

But it was quickly apparent that all was not in fact going well. Chou En-lai told the students at Tsinghua that Mao had found that 'almost ninety per cent of the work teams throughout the whole country had committed general mistakes in their orientation.' The Rector of Wuhan University, one of the founders of the Communist Party, had to ask for Mao's help against Red Guard persecution. But the official prohibition of physical attacks on this old scholar was ignored by the young rebels, and within days he was dead.

Mao was initially tolerant of his enthusiastic young revolutionaries' excesses. 'Young people', he declared, 'should be permitted to make mistakes.' He was even indulgent about their tendency to form factions and fight among themselves. 'Young people can look at problems this way and that way. The like-minded among them often club together; this is nothing unusual.' He defended the 'so-called chaos at various places', and told a work conference in late August:

> In my opinion we should let the chaos go on for a few months and just firmly believe that the majority is good and only the minority is bad. It does not matter if there are no provincial Party committees. There are still district and county Party committees! . . . In my view, Peking is not all that chaotic. The students held a meeting of 100,000 and then captured the murderers. This caused some panic. Peking is too gentle. . . .

But where his own friends were threatened with an unjust death at the hands of the Red Guards, such as the veteran General Hsu Hsiang-chien, Mao's response was to invite them to stay in his house at Chungnanhai until it was all over.

By now Lin Piao was virtually out of control, carrying the cult of Mao to patently absurd lengths. Chiang Ching afterwards said that his flagrant disloyalty began to dawn on Mao during the middle of 1966. On 18 September Lin, in a speech about intensifying the study of Mao's writings, said:

> Chairman Mao stands much higher than Marx, Engels, Lenin or Stalin. There is no one in the world today who has reached the levels of Chairman Mao. . . . We must destroy the racial inferiority complex which holds that foreigners are better than Chinese. . . . Among foreigners or the ancients is there one higher than Chairman Mao? Is there anybody with such mature thinking? A genius like Chairman Mao emerges only once in several hundred years in the world and in several thousand years in China. Chairman Mao is the greatest genius in the world. . .

Mao was in the unenviable position of having to rely on a disloyal ally in order to overcome his substantive opponents in the Party. Many intellectuals took a very different view of Mao. Lao She, the poet who took his own life in September, reportedly left a suicide note accusing Mao of betraying world socialism, while a Red Guard group in Wuchang accused him of having the wrong credentials: 'Chairman Mao comes from a rich family of farmers.'

At a work conference in October Liu Shao-chi and Teng Hsiao-ping confessed their errors in connection with sending out the work teams. Liu also acknowledged a number of earlier mistakes – insufficiently holding back the 'left' tendencies in land reform in the 1940s, being insufficiently enthusiastic about co-operativization in the 1950s, and right opportunism in 1962.

Mao responded to these confessions with his own list of grievances against Liu and the government which he had headed, not only for their mistakes as such, but also for their failure to consult him. Summing up, Mao said:

'The Cultural Revolution has been carried on for only five months. It will take at least five years to get some experience. One big-character poster, the Red guards, the great exchange of revolutionary experience, and nobody – not even I – expected that all the provinces and cities would be thrown into confusion. The students also made some mistakes, but the mistakes were made mainly by us big shots. . . .

'What I'm responsible for', Mao went on, 'is the division into first and second lines of leadership. . . . I wanted to establish their prestige before I die; I never imagined that things might move in the opposite direction.'

'Supreme power', Tao Chu, the Canton Party boss, observed, 'has slipped from your hands.'

'This is because I deliberately relinquished it. Now, however, they have set up independent kingdoms. . . . Teng Hsiao-ping never came to consult me: from 1959 to the present he has never consulted me over anything at all. . . .'

'Teng Hsiao-ping', he went on, 'is deaf. Whenever we are at a meeting together, he sits far away from me. For six years . . . he has not made a general report of work to me. He always gets Peng Chen to do the work of the secretariat for him. Do you say that he is able? Nieh Jung-chen says: "That bloke is lazy." '

As Teng himself subsequently confessed, 'The more contacts I had with Liu Shao-chi, the less instruction I requested from Chairman Mao.'

But Mao recalled that Liu Shao-chi had stood by him in earlier Party battles.

'We shouldn't condemn Liu Shao-chi out of hand. If they have made mistakes, they can change, can't they? When they have changed it will be all right. Let them pull themselves together, and throw themselves courageously into their work. . . .'

Mao closed the conference with a speech bewailing his earlier retirement from the front line of leadership. He also tried to overcome the confusion and uncertainty which the suddenness of the Cultural Revolution had caused.

It all happened within a very short period. . . . The time was so short and the events so violent. . . . Even before the letter to the Red Guards had gone out, the Red Guards had mobilized throughout the country, and in one rush they swept you off your feet.

Since it was I who caused the havoc, it is understandable if you have some bitter words for me. Last time we met I lacked confidence and I said that our decisions would not necessarily be carried out. Indeed all that time quite a few comrades still did not understand things fully. . . .

I think that there are advantages in being assailed. For so many years you have not thought about such things, but as soon as they burst upon you, you began to think. Undoubtedly you have made some mistakes, some mistakes of line, but they can be corrected and that will be that!

Whoever wants to overthrow you? I don't, and I don't think the Red Guards do either. . . .

You find it difficult to cross this pass and I don't find it easy either. You are anxious and so am I. I cannot blame you, comrades, time has been so short.

At the seventh mass rally of Red Guards a few days later, Mao seized the microphone and shouted: 'Long live comrades! You must let politics take command, go to the masses, and be with the masses. You must conduct the great Proletarian Cultural Revolution even better.' They were the only words which he was to address directly to the Chinese people, face to face, in the entire Cultural Revolution.

The last of the rallies was on 25 November. They had brought China's railway system almost to collapse, and they had put the fear of God into the people of Peking, but they had certainly made the younger generation in the various provinces feel that they were participating in China's modernization in a way they never had before. But Mao was dissatisfied with the implementation of his instructions.

'You have let me down,' he told the Red Guard leaders, 'and what is more, you have disappointed the workers, peasants and army men of China.'

On the day following the last mass rally, Mao headed south and went incommunicado for two months (the coldest months in Peking). He left Chen Po-ta and Chiang Ching in Peking to keep the good work going. Chiang Ching's style of address may be judged from the following passage in a speech just after Mao's departure:

Imperialism is moribund capitalism, parisitic and rotten. Modern revisionism is a product of imperialist policies and a variant of capitalism. They cannot produce any works that are good. Capitalism has a history of several centuries, but it has only a pitiful number of classics. . . . On the other hand, there are some things that really flood the market, such as rock-and-roll, jazz, strip-tease, impressionism, symbolism, abstractionism, Fauvism, modernism – there's no end to them. . . . In a word, there is decadence and obscenity to poison and corrupt the minds of the people. . . . Don't hit others and beat them. Struggle by force can only touch the skin and flesh, while struggle by reasoning things out can touch them to their very souls.

Most of all Chiang Ching revelled in her new role as the publicly acclaimed messenger of Mao. 'Chairman Mao sends you his best regards,' she would announce to the rows of delighted faces before her. 'You must all want to know how Chairman Mao is. Let me tell you, he's in robust health.'

But Lin Piao continued to misrepresent the aim of Mao's teaching. In December, in a foreword to the second edition of the 'Little Red Book' of *Quotations*, he wrote:

'In order really to master Mao Tse-tung's thought, it is necessary to study many of Chairman Mao's basic concepts over and over again, and it is best to memorize some of his important passages and study and apply them repeatedly. . . .'

27
THE BLACK HAND*

At the end of 1966 Mao was seen on television screens with a young nurse at each arm helping him to walk, and a Western report said that he had to be taken to hospital for examination. At this critical stage of the Cultural Revolution he celebrated his seventy-third birthday. He had told Montgomery that seventy-three and eighty-four were the difficult ages. He never lived to reach eighty-four, but his seventy-third year was arguably the most difficult in his many years of power. In it he had to decide how far to go in backing the forces of youth and change against those of experience and wisdom.

The main victim of his invervention was his old colleague Liu Shao-chi, the man without whose collaboration Mao might well have failed to win the chairmanship of the Party in the 1940s. Chiang Ching and the Red Guards, ready to go far beyond Mao himself, used Liu's daughter to bring her father down.

'I am of the opinion', the girl announced in late December, 'that my father is really the number one Party person in authority taking the capitalist road. For more than twenty years he has all the time opposed and resisted Chairman Mao and Mao's Thought, carrying out not socialism, but capitalism.'

This had been helped by Chiang Ching's arranging a meeting between Liu's daughter and her real mother, Liu's former wife whom Liu had not allowed her to see before: this lady retailed her own complaints against Liu. The Red Guards also decoyed Liu's present wife, Wang Kuang-mei, to the hospital by getting her daughter to pretend that one of her children had broken a leg, and were then able to examine her in person.

In the early part of January Mao welcomed the Red Guards' takeover of newspapers in progressive Shanghai, and the rebel-

*Black hand is a Chinese underworld phrase for the unknown perpetrator of some sabotage or betrayal.

lion of workers in Shanghai factories. He thoroughly approved of
these power seizures. 'This is one class overthrowing another,' he
said enthusiastically. 'It is a great revolution.'

In Peking Chou En-lai struggled to keep the Cultural Revolution on an even keel. He turned his back on one Red Guard
audience when they shouted 'Down with Liu Shao-chi and Teng
Hsiao-ping' and only turned to face them again when they called
to overthrow the reactionary *line* of Liu and Teng. He told them:

Liu and Teng are still members of the Standing Committee of the
Politburo, and your calling for the overthrow of these two makes my
position very difficult. The task Chairman Mao assigned me is to persuade you not to do that. You can thoroughly criticize the bourgeois
reactionary line which these two persons represent, but you cannot
drag them out and struggle against them. . . .

As, regards your plan to drag them out by besieging Chungnanhai,
we in the Party Central and Chairman Mao recommend you do not
take such action. . . . As you are besieging Chungnanhai from early
morning to late at night and speaking angrily over the microphones,
our great leader and comrades who are working under his guidance
cannot devote themselves to work calmly.

Chiang Ching and Chen Po-ta, at another Red Guard meeting, called for a people's government in Peking along the lines of
the Paris Commune. Mao approved the idea, and early in February Shanghai took the lead by forming itself into such a commune, but then he had second thoughts.

Back in Peking after his two-month absence, he summoned the
two Shanghai leaders, Chang Chun-chiao and Yao Wen-yuan,
for a series of discussions which proved crucial in Mao's thinking
about the Cultural Revolution. These two men represented in
their actions in Shanghai a more radical approach than Mao was
willing to authorize.

For one thing, Mao disapproved the Shanghai People's Committee's demand that the Premier of the State Council should do
away with all Heads.

'This is extreme anarchism,' he commented. 'It is most reactionary. If instead of calling someone the "head" of something
we call him "orderly" or "assistant", this would only be a formal
change. In reality there will still always be "heads". It is the
content which matters.'

Mao came down against the changing of names generally.
'This is like our Red Guards who have changed almost all the
street names of Peking, making it impossible for us to remember
them. We still remember their former names. . . . I think we

should be more stable and not change all the names.'

The same went for the idea of changing the People's Republic of China to something like the Chinese People's Commune.

This would give rise to the question of changing the political system, to the question of the State system, and to the question of the name of the country. . . . If there is a change, it will be followed by the question of recognition or non-recognition by foreign countries. . . . I surmise that the Soviet Union would not extend recognition. . . . She would not dare to recognize, since recognition might cause troubles for the Russians. How could there be a Chinese People's Commune? It might be rather embarrassing for them, but the bourgeois nations might recognize it. If everything were changed into Commune, then what about the party? Where would we place the party? . . . Where would we place the Party Committee? There must be a Party somehow! There must be a nucleus, no matter what we call it.

During these interviews Mao passed judgement on a number of slogans. 'Doubt everything and overthrow everything' was, he said, 'a reactionary slogan'. He also prohibited further use of a quotation of his from 1919, 'The world is ours', which the Red Guards were using with great éclat. Mao declared that he could not 'altogether remember it himself'. He was beginning to retreat.

Mao was particularly disappointed that his clear explanations and instructions to the Red Guards had been ignored.

In February, he wrote to Chou En-lai:

Recently many revolutionary teachers, students and masses have written to me asking whether it is considered armed struggle to make those Party persons in authority taking the capitalist road and freaks and monsters wear dunce caps, to paint their faces, and to parade them in the streets. I think it a form of armed struggle. . . . [But, he added,] I want to stress here that, when engaging in struggle, we definitely must hold to struggle by reason, bring out the facts, emphasize rationality and use persuasion. . . . Anyone involved in beating others should be dealt with in accordance with the law.

He opened his mind about the excesses of the young radicals to an Albanian delegation which came to Peking early in February.

The Red Guards are helping us, but there are some among them who are unreliable. Some wear dark glasses and mouth-masks, hold clubs and knives in their hands and go around causing trouble, attacking, killing and injuring people. Most of these people are the children of top cadres, like the daughters of Ho Lung and Lu Ting-yi.

Mao then complained about the past neglect which had brought about the present situation.

A number of years ago I said that I wanted to clean out several millions . . . they didn't heed my words. There was nothing I could do. . . . It looks as if my way of doing things no longer has any efficacy in China. Because the principals of the colleges and high schools have been in the hands of Liu, Teng and Lu for a long time, we can't get in. There is nothing we can do. . . .

In the past we only grasped individual problems, individual personalities – from the winter of 1953 to 1954 we struggled against Kao and Jao, in 1959 we purged Peng Teh-huai. . . . In addition we also did some struggling in the cultural circles and in the villages and factories. That was the Socialist Education Movement. . . . None of these solved the problems – we couldn't find a form, a way publicly and totally to expose our dark side from the bottom right up to the top. Thus we are now engaging in a great Cultural Revolution.

In an interesting digression, he added:

I don't believe in elections. There are over two thousand counties in China, and if each county elects two people then there will be more than four thousand people; and if they elect four people then there will be ten thousand – where is there a big enough place to hold a meeting for that many people? How could one know that many people? I was elected by Peking but aren't there quite a few people who have never seen me? But if they haven't even seen me how can they elect me?

By the middle of February the Cultural Revolution was almost getting out of Mao's control, with Red Guards attacking the older generation indiscriminately. He agreed with Chou En-lai that the remaining senior members of the government should be protected from attack. It was only after this decision that Chou came out with his first public denunciation of Liu Shao-chi. But some of them refused to be diplomatic and continued to speak their minds honestly.

Chen Yi, the Foreign Minister, told a Red Guard rally in February:

In my opinion, the wall poster criticizing Chairman Mao may also be justified. Chairman Mao is also a cog. . . . Chairman Mao became a dictator in directing the Great Proletarian Cultural Revolution. Lin Piao is also of no importance. He used to be under my command. . . . You should study well Chairman Liu's Thought. Lui Shao-chi is my teacher, my master, my king. His level is quite high. . . . There is a rumour running that Liu Shao-chi has been deprived of his post, isn't there? That needs to be decided by the National People's Congress. . . . Some people hide behind the curtains, simply ordering some 'children' to write big-character posters. What poor taste they have!

Chen Yi also declared during the Cultural Revolution:

We have cherished no blind faith in any individual person. We have blind faith neither in Stalin, nor in Khrushchev, nor in Chairman Mao. Chairman Mao is just one of the people. How few are the people who have never opposed him? Few indeed. (Vice-Chairman Lin Piao has not, and so he is a great man.) I think it would be a good record if twenty per cent of our Party members have genuinely supported Chairman Mao.

They were all bubbling over with anger at the behaviour of Lin Piao. Teng Hsiao-ping went to see Mao, his former master, before going out to do his rural penance in Kiangsi province. Mao said that Teng had been competent but haphazard in work, failing to keep in mind the concept of class struggle.

'I was defiant at that time,' Teng afterwards recalled, 'so I replied that I had better follow Lin Piao's example, learning how to make meritorious achievements out of nothing and learning how to suspect everything and assail everything – such a course of action might be called not doing things haphazardly and having a strong sense of class struggle.'

'History will judge', Mao replied, smiling and with a touch of ambivalence, 'whether Lin Piao is correct or not; you don't have to be defiant.'

The 'February Adverse Current', as it became known, involved the virtually open rebellion of nine prominent leaders who burst out against Mao and his new lieutenants – especially Chang Chun-chiao, but also Chiang Ching and Kang Sheng – over their handling of the Cultural Revolution. The nine included Chu Teh, Chen Yun, Chen Yi, Li Hsien-nien, Teng Tzu-hui, Yeh Chien-ying and Tan Chen-lin – all old-timers of considerable seniority.

Their outburst erupted during a meeting on 16 February when Tan Chen-lin cried out:

'I have made no mistakes. I need no protection from others. . . . I should not have lived for sixty-five years, should not have joined the revolution, should not have joined the Party and should not have followed Chairman Mao in making revolution for forty years.'

The resentment of these nine veteran leaders was deep-rooted. General Hsu Hsiang-chien had 'pounded the table twenty times within one hour', and Yeh Chien-ying had even broken his fingers as a result of pounding (his son-in-law, a pianist, had his fingers bruised by Red Guards). Another general, Nieh Jung-chen, alleged that: 'The policy towards the children of high-ranking cadres is one of killing without teaching.'

If such leaders did make self-criticism, it was usually not accepted. 'Chu Teh,' said Lin Piao during the Cultural Revolution, 'you are very ambitious. Your self-criticism is extremely inadequate. Some people think that he made self-criticism voluntarily. That is not so. It was because the Party Centre decided that he should "strip himself naked". . . . Chu Teh is not obeying Chairman Mao. He tried to become the leader himself. At the time of the Kao Kang incident, he advocated the idea of becoming Chairman in turn. . . .'

Mao's solution to the excesses of the Red Guards was to put them into the hands of the soldiers. On 7 March he issued a directive for the army to extend its role.

'The army', he wrote, 'should give military and political training in the universities, middle schools and the higher classes of primary schools, stage by stage and group by group. It should help in re-opening school classes. . . .' Mao also put out a new instruction on 10 March urging that revolutionary committees should now be formed on the basis of a three-way alliance between the rebel youth, the experienced cadres and the armed forces.

Mao had all this time been operating on the narrowest margin of legality. When the Politburo Standing Committee convened in March 1967 he could muster only five supporters (Lin Piao, Chou En-lai, Chen Po-ta, Kang Sheng and Li Fu-chun), against five opponents (Liu Shao-chi, Teng Hsiao-ping, Tao Chu, Chu Teh and Chen Yun). Only by his own casting vote as Chairman could he give himself a majority.

But Mao could not let the Red Guards be sent back to their schools before they had completed their task of rooting out his opponents within the Party. 'Have no fear of chaos,' he reassured them on 6 April. 'The more chaos you dish up and the longer it goes on, the better. Disorder and chaos are always a good thing. They clarify things. . . . But never use weapons. It is never a good thing to open fire. . . .'

As if reading his mind, a gang of thirty Red Guards broke into Liu Shao-chi's bedroom three days later and forced his wife to accompany them to Tsinghua University, where, dressed in a tight-fitting gown, spike-heeled shoes, a straw hat and a necklace of gilded ping-pong balls decorated with skulls, she was denounced before a rally of 300,000 youngsters. This was a caricature of the dress which she had worn on some of her public appearances with Liu during his visits to Indonesia and other Asian countries. Chiang Ching, who had never made public appearances with Mao during the time that he was head of state, was thus accorded a revenge of a sort.

The world heard no more of Liu Shao-chi. Liu could have chosen to fight against Mao, with a good chance of a numerical majority in the Central Committee. But the civil war which this would have opened up would have been ruinous for China, and in rejecting this course and thus placing the national interest above his own, Lui showed dignity and courage. He also doubtless accepted Mao's superiority in political manoeuvre.

Speaking to visiting dignitaries from the Albanian armed forces on 1 May 1967, Mao ruminated about the succession problem.

I had originally intended to train some successors from among the intellectuals, but this would now appear to be impractical. It seems to me that the world outlook of intellectuals, including those young intellectuals who are still receiving education in schools, and those both within and outside the Party, is still basically bourgeois. This is because in the more than ten years since liberation the cultural and educational circles have been dominated by revisionism, and so bourgeois ideology has seeped into their blood.

But did Mao really know what he was striving for? At the beginning of June he disowned Red Guard anarchism, yet three weeks later he was being quoted in the *People's Daily* to the effect that: 'We, the Communists, do not want official positions; we want revolution.' And Mao knew only too well the genuine bitterness of the young radicals, colourfully expressed in a July pamphlet by the Red Guards of one of the schools:

For seventeen years our school has been ruled by the bourgeois class. We shall not tolerate this any longer! . . . Old and young gentlemen, we tell you frankly, you all stink and you are nothing but rotten trash. . . . Formerly you were in a privileged position, sat on our heads and shat on us to show that you were superior. . . . You thought you could make use of the temporary existing bourgeois education to climb higher up the ladder to become white experts, get into the university, join up with the 'professors, experts'. Your heart was set on a small car, a little modern house, a white coat, a laboratory . . . on enjoying comfort, affluence, a good reputation, a good salary. . . . Really wicked eggs! We tell you: if you do not wish to change, if you remain reactionary, we will not spare you! . . . Your class hatred will stick to the points of our bayonets. Your guts will be dug out. . . .

Mao nursed his dilemma in his old, old way: he went touring, first of all in the south but later in the north and east. What he saw during his three-month journey dismayed him.

'I think this is a civil war,' he told Chou En-lai, 'the country is divided into "800 princely states".' In Kiangsi, he observed, 'So many cadres have collapsed. Is this good or bad? Have you ever studied this problem? . . . We should criticize the idea of over-throwing everything.'

'There is no fundamental clash of interests', he said on another occasion, 'within the working class. Why should they be split into two big irreconcilable organizations? I don't understand it.'

While Mao was travelling, the military commander in Wuhan rebelled against central authority and held two senior envoys sent from Peking to bring him back to order. Chou En-lai's diplomacy was needed to get the regime out of a very awkward crisis, a crisis of authority provoked by the long challenge which the Red Guards had presented.

In August Mao prepared to accept a return to normality. He wrote in the *People's Daily* that 'The present Great Proletarian Cultural Revolution is only the first; there will inevitably be many more in the future. The issue of who will win in the revolution can only be settled over a long historical period.'

In this context, China's international importance became greater. 'China', Mao declared in September, 'is not only the political centre of world revolution but should become the military and technical centre, supplying weapons to the world's revolutionaries. By now China should be able openly to supply weapons marked in Chinese characters to the world revolutionaries . . . and become the arsenal of the world revolution.'

Brezhnev, the new spokesman for the Russian Communist Party, was by now able to deliver a formidable indictment of the Cultural Revolution:

The latest events in China show that Mao Tse-tung and his followers are jeopardizing the Chinese people's revolutionary gains. . . . The established bodies of the Party and the constitutional bodies of State power have actually ceased their activities. The trade unions, the Youth League, and public organizations have been dissolved. Many prominent and esteemed Party and Government leaders, well-known participants in the Chinese revolution, outstanding military commanders, major representatives of culture and science are being defamed and subjected to inhuman repression.

(Yet Brezhnev and Kosygin maintained up to 1969 at least a 'hot line' to Mao and Chou for use in crises.)

Late in September Mao returned to Peking from his inspection tour of the provinces. He criticized the conduct of affairs during his absence by his wife, Chiang Ching, and Chen Po-ta, and demanded their self-criticisms. No one was exempt from the process of self-criticism: even Mao himself had undergone this in 1959. Chiang found it necessary to take a seven-week rest.

'I am an ordinary Communist,' she told a meeting just before Mao's return, 'a little pupil of Chairman Mao, and a little pupil of the broad masses. I have to learn from my dear comrades. Comrades, to do some good for the people is the duty of a Communist. . . . I am only a small screw.'

Mao's two daughters were also 'small screws' in the Cultural Revolution. Li Min, the elder, was made a leader of the Science and Technology Commission (responsible for nuclear developments, among other things) of the Ministry of Defence, and later mounted a poster against Nieh Jung-chen, the man in charge of it. Li Na became acting chief editor of *Liberation Army Daily*, at this time the principal organ of the pro-Mao group in the Central Committee.

But Mao's house at Chungnanhai was surrounded and rendered inaccessible by rebels during his absence. Even his own home was not sacred to some of the young radicals whose anger he had unleashed.

Meanwhile Lin Piao was still plodding along his cul-de-sac of saying that all that mattered was to follow Mao's instructions unquestioningly. On one occasion he laid down that 'Mao Tse-tung Thought must be implemented both when we understand it and when we temporarily may not understand it.' 'Mao Tse-tung Thought', he had written in August, 'must be taken as the yard-stick for everything. In Chairman Mao's Thought and instructions, we must have strong faith without any doubt whatsoever at all times and on all questions.'

A collection of Mao's informal speeches and conversations was published by Lin, without his permission, under the title *Long Live Mao Tse-tung Thought*. Mao saw one through the good offices of Chou En-lai and Chiang Ching, and reportedly passed judgement that 'two-thirds of it was Lin Piao's thought'. He was almost the last to see the book, although it was selling all over the country for only 60 cents.

Mao wrote to Lin and Chou in December asking them to

reduce the cult of personality. But at the end of the year, just after his seventy-fourth birthday, a huge statue of Mao, three times lifesize, was unveiled at Shaoshan – 'the place where the red sun rose'.

At one high-level meeting early in 1968, Mao's colleagues found themselves dealing with an unusual problem.

'The traffic police,' one of the comrades reported, 'use *Quotations from Mao Tse-tung* for a baton. How could this be allowed? It cannot be taken as words of command. . . .'

'They use *Quotations from Mao Tse-tung*,' Lin Piao asked disbelievingly, 'as a baton? How could the precious book be used as a baton?'

'*Quotations from Mao Tse-tung*,' Chiang Ching ruled authoritatively, 'should not be used as a baton, or as words of command standing for 'one, two, three, four'. Since the papers have reported it, we must have this matter investigated.'

'I heard,' Kang Sheng broke in, 'that you would study *Quotations from Mao Tse-tung* while you were eating. . . .'

The trouble with the Cultural Revolution, as Mao was now discovering, was that so many people lacked the capacity to make good judgements. 'Our people do not have good eye-sight: they are unable to differentiate the upright from the crooked. They may be able to tell the good from the bad in the light of their activities under normal conditions. Nevertheless, we are rather inept at singling out certain people in the light of their activities under special conditions.'

In the spring Mao sought desperately to resolve the factionalism which plagued the Red Guards and to improve their relations with the army. But at the end of July he had regretfully to send the army and contingents of factory workers into Peking University to put an end to the fighting between the Red Guards there. On the following day he called the Red Guard leaders for a difficult, painful meeting with himself and his colleagues. Mao shook hands with the first four rebels who walked into the room, observing: 'All are young!'

Shaking hands with a fifth, he went on, 'Are you Huang Tso-chen? I haven't met you before. You were not killed?'

'Haven't seen you for a long time,' Chiang Ching added.

'We met last time at Tienanmen,' Mao went on, 'but there was no chance to talk with you at that time. That was bad! You people don't come to see me unless you have important business. But I have read all your reports. I understand your situation very well. Kuai Ta-fu [the outspoken Tsinghua University student leader, of whom Liu Shao-chi had once said that he should be 'shot at as a living target'] did not come. Is it because he is unable to come or unwilling to come?'

One of the older leaders said that he was unwilling to come.

'No,' one of the Red Guards, a girl, broke in. 'At this moment, if he knew that there was a meeting with the Central Committee Cultural Revolution Group, he would cry because he missed the chance to meet the Chairman. I am sure that he is unable to come.'

'Kuai Ta-fu should capture the black hand,' said Mao, cleverly introducing the theme he meant to pursue. 'So many workers were sent to schools to "suppress" and "oppress" the Red Guards. Who is the black hand? The black hand is still not captured. The black hand is nobody else but me. Kuai did not come. He should have come to grab me. . . .

'If you cannot handle the problem, we may resort to military control, and ask Lin Piao to take command. . . . The problem has to be solved one way or the other. You people have engaged in the Great Cultural Revolution . . . for two years. Now . . . you are struggling, but it is armed struggle. The people are not happy. The workers are not happy. The peasants are not happy. Peking residents are not happy. The students in most of the schools are not happy. Most students in your school are also not happy. Even within the faction that supports you there are people who are unhappy. Can you unite the whole country this way?'

'Nobody foresaw this kind of fighting,' Mao went on. 'Suspension of classes for half a year was originally planned. It was so announced in the newspapers. Later, the suspension was extended to one year. As one year was not enough, it was extended to two years and then to three years. I say, if three years is still not enough, give them as many years as necessary.'

The conversation went off at a tangent, but eventually Mao brought it back. 'I invited you to come over today to talk about this matter so that you will be prepared. I have never made any tape recordings before, but I'm doing it today. Otherwise, you will interpret what I said today in the way you wish after you go home. If you do so, I will play this tape back. You had better discuss this. Once I play this recording, many people will be put in a defensive position.'

Mao went on, 'The masses just don't like civil wars. . . . Now, I am issuing a nationwide notice. If anyone continues to oppose or fight the Army, destroy means of transportation, kill people or set fires, he is committing crimes.'

There was a discussion about who had interceded to save the day for one of the Red Guard groups. Somebody said that it was Mao's wife, Chiang Ching.

'I don't particularly like the army corps of Normal University,' Chiang Ching explained. 'But the weather is so hot; you cut their water, electricity and food supply. They were not allowed to see daylight for three months during the summer. How could you have done this? As I heard this, I could not help crying. There were hundreds, at least scores of them. After all, they are the masses.... Proletarians should observe proletarian humanitarianism. These several tens of counter-revolutionaries are, after all, youths. They want to strangle me to death. I'm not afraid of being fried in oil. I heard that the Chingkangshan Red Guard organization of Peking University wants to fry Chiang Ching.'

'Frying', Yao Wen-yuan observed helpfully, 'is only a way of speech.'

Mao mentioned another young Red Guard leader who was hostile to Chou En-lai, who nevertheless protected him.

'People said the Premier was magnanimous,' Mao said. 'I agree with the Premier. These people should not have been arrested in the first place. Too many were arrested, because I nodded my head.'

'This has nothing to do with the Chairman,' insisted Hsieh Fu-chih, the security chief. 'It was I who did the arresting.'

'Don't try to free me from my mistakes,' Mao chided, 'or to cover up for me. I ordered the arrests; I also agreed to their release.'

'You did not ask me to arrest so many,' Hsieh demurred.

Later Mao said that children were collecting big-character posters as waste paper for sale.

'How many cents a pound?' he asked.

'Six cents,' Hsieh replied. 'The children are making a fortune.'

At this point the missing Kuai arrived, and Mao stood up and went forward to shake his hands. Kuai explained his case through his tears – Tsinghua University was in danger, because workers under the control of black hand were coming into the campus to suppress the students.

Mao conceded his position, as he had to the others:

'I have become the black hand,' he revealed dramatically. 'Take me to the garrison headquarters.'

Then there was a little exchange which brought out the

sycophancy surrounding Mao. Chen Po-ta, his former secretary, suddenly exclaimed:

'Follow the Chairman's teaching closely; resolutely carry it out.'

'Don't talk about teaching,' Mao put in sharply, only to be followed by Yao Wen-yuan, his wife's confidant, saying:

'The Chairman's words today have profound meaning.'

But then they focused on the notorious Kuai.

'Let Kuai Ta-fu wake up,' Mao declared.

'Kuai Ta-fu,' Chen Po-ta repeated, 'you should wake up. Stop the horses at the edge of the precipitous cliff. You are on a dangerous course.'

'Stop the horses', added Lin Piao, ever open to a rhetorical repetition, 'at the edge of the precipitous cliff. Admit your mistakes!'

'Don't use the words "admit mistakes",' Mao rebuked.

But it was left to Lin to put his dilemma most clearly to Kuai.

'Today', he said, 'Chairman Mao shows his personal concern about you, and has made the most important, the most correct, the clearest and the most timely teaching. If you turn a deaf ear to this again, you will be committing a grave mistake. You Red Guards have played an important role during the great Cultural Revolution. Now, a great revolutionary unity has been achieved in many schools throughout the nation. As far as great unity is concerned, some of the schools are still lagging behind. You should catch up. You have failed to see what is needed at different stages of the movement.'

One of the girl Red Guards spoke up for Kuai.

'I love Kuai Ta-fu very much. I am also aware of the fact that as long as I am with him, I will be involved in many things. But I feel that I must do my best to protect him lest he collapse. His fate is linked with that of the Red Guards throughout the country.'

She was immediately attacked for her unwillingness to make self-criticism.

'I criticized you several times,' Chiang Ching told her. 'You have never expressed yourself.'

'Don't criticize her,' Mao snapped, in a rare public rebuke of his wife. 'You always blame others; never blame yourself.'

'I was saying that she lacked so much in self-criticism spirit,' Chiang Ching defended herself.

'Young people cannot stand criticism,' Mao said. 'Her character is somewhat like mine when I was young. Kids are strong in subjectivism, very strong. They only criticize others.'

'Kuai Ta-fu is smiling now,' Chiang Ching noticed. 'Relax a little, don't be so tense.'

'If you want to arrest the "black hand",' Mao told Kuai, 'the "black hand" is me. What can you do to me? We are sympathetic with your side.'

Mao began to wind up the discussion.

'None of you has slept yet,' he observed. 'Kuai Ta-fu, if you don't have a place to sleep tonight, go with Han Ai-ching [the girl who had spoken up for him] and sleep at her place. Han Ai-ching, you should take good care of him. When you people get together, go to Han Ai-ching's place to take a little rest, then hold a meeting. . . . Kuai Ta-fu, is your action against the Central Committee? . . . Even a meeting at the Municipal Revolutionary Committee did not stop you. I cannot but extend my single "black hand". I mobilized the workers to stop your fighting. The fighting went on for so many days. As the workers marched in with drums and gongs, you still did not pay any attention. You are isolated from the masses, the workers, the peasants, the soldiers, the majority of the students, and your own people. Many people are saying uncomplimentary words about you.'

The elders pressed Kuai hard to compromise with the other factions and with the Party leadership.

'Unity is needed,' Mao insisted. 'We need Kuai Ta-fu. Without Kuai Ta-fu unity cannot be achieved.' The rest of the conversation petered out without any conclusion, or any commitment by the stubborn Kuai to mend his ways.

Mao began to say things now which lent his authority to the restoration of certain basic institutions of the kind which had been discredited during the Cultural Revolution. 'It is still necessary', he wrote at the end of July, 'to have universities' – though he added: 'Here I refer mainly to the need for colleges of science and engineering.'

In August Mao ended his honeymoon with the Red Guards, declaring that their leading role in the Cultural Revolution was now over. He convened the Central Committee which approved the dismissal of Liu Shao-chi from all his posts in the Party and accepted a new draft Party constitution prepared by Mao's group. It put his Thought back into first place, and even named Lin Piao as his successor.

The Chinese Communist Party takes Marxism, Leninism and Mao Tse-tung Thought as the theoretical basis guiding its thinking. Mao

Tse-tung Thought is the Marxism-Leninism of the era when imperialism is heading for total collapse and socialism is advancing towards world-wide victory. . . .

Comrade Lin Piao has consistently held high the great red banner of Mao Tse-tung Thought, and has most loyally and resolutely implemented and defended the proletarian revolutionary line of Comrade Mao Tse-tung. Comrade Lin Piao is the close comrade-in-arms and successor of Comrade Mao Tse-tung.

Mao justified the Cultural Revolution, which he described as 'a great political revolution under the conditions of socialism made by the proletariat against the bourgeoisie and all other exploiting classes'.

He also reiterated that there was no final victory in the Cultural Revolution, and that it would have to be repeated in the future.

A human being has arteries and veins through which the heart makes the blood circulate, and he breathes with his lungs, exhaling carbon dioxide and inhaling fresh oxygen, that is, getting rid of the stale and taking in the fresh. A proletarian party must also get rid of the stale and take in the fresh, for only thus can it be full of vitality. Without eliminating waste matter and absorbing fresh blood the Party has no vigour.

At the end of 1968 Mao told the radical youngsters who had helped him to expel his main rival in the Party to go home. 'Young rebels must go to the villages and accept re-education by the poor and lower middle peasantry. This is a necessity.' Cadres and other city-dwellers 'should be persuaded to send their sons and daughters who have finished junior or senior middle school, college or university, to the countryside.'

The Ninth Congress of the Chinese Communist Party in April 1969 was a congress of victory over Liu Shao-chi and other rightists. But the seeds of further dissension were already there, particularly in the new Party constitution where Lin Piao was named as Mao's successor in order to furnish, in the words of a Party document, 'the fundamental guarantee that our Party and State will never change their colour, and that Mao Tse-tung Thought will be faithfully adhered to. . . .' There could hardly have been a cruder insult to man's reason or to the ideas of democracy and socialism. Mao was obviously unhappy with the situation. His own address showed signs of loss of direction and of a new kind of tired defensiveness.

'What I'm going to say', he began, 'is old stuff with which you are all familiar. There is nothing new. I am simply going to talk about unity. . . .'

He referred to China's external vulnerability during the Cutural Revolution, which had been a source of such concern, particularly to the military: this was when tension on the Russian border was building up to a climax.

Others may come and attack us [he commented], but we shall not fight outside our borders. We do not fight outside our borders. I say we will not be provoked. Even if you invite us to come out we will not come out, but if you should come and attack us we will deal with you. It depends on whether you attack on a small scale or a large scale. If it is on a small scale we will fight on the border. If it is on a large scale then I am in favour of yielding some ground. China is no small country. . . .

But the main problem remained the internal political one.

Haven't I said these two sentences before: the answer to the problem of the localities lies in the army; the answer to the problem of the army lies in political work?

But Mao was reliving old problems and old dreams.

For years we did not have any such things as salaries. We had no eight-tier wage system. We had only a fixed amount of food, half an ounce of oil and half an ounce of salt. If we got a couple of pounds of millet, that was great. As for vegetables, how could we get vegetables everywhere the army went?

Now we have entered the cities. This is a good thing. If we hadn't entered the cities Chiang Kai-shek would be occupying them. But it is also a bad thing because it caused our Party to deteriorate.

But it was now twenty years since the Party had entered the cities. How could China fail to think of Mao as a man living in the past?

Lin Piao had no qualms at all in delivering a long and boring psalm to Mao's Thought. Every revolutionary committee, he insisted, in a paragraph which mentioned Mao's name fourteen times,

. . . must put the living study and application of Mao Tse-tung Thought above all work. . . . The Communist Party of China owes all its achievements to the wise leadership of Chairman Mao. . . .

And yet some part of Mao enjoyed it all. A film made of the Congress approving the new constitution showed Mao as the Chairman calling for the votes, looking round with apparent delight to see all the Little Red Books held up high in the air to convey unanimity, and announcing gleefully: 'Passed'. On either side of him Lin and Chou flashed quick, almost furtive glances at him from time to time to see how he was reacting.

After the Ninth Congress the Chinese press dropped the hyphen in Mao's name, apparently as a stylistic simplification enabling his name to be placed more easily on a par with those European saints in the Communist hierarchy, Marx and Lenin. But this was done with no other names, only Mao's.

During all this time, Mao's wife later alleged, the Mao household were being slowly poisoned by men of Lin Piao placed in their residence. According to Chiang Ching, the poison affected her neurologically, attacking her brain and memory, and she did not fully recover until two or three years later. Mao had also been made ill by the poison.

By the following summer Mao Tse-tung Thought had itself become 'the Red Sun' in the official propaganda, not merely Mao himself, thus opening up the possibility of a successor inheriting its stewardship, and Lin was already projecting himself as a better interpreter of Mao Tse-tung Thought than Mao himself! Lin, a provincial radio broadcast claimed in October,

... listens best to the voice of Chairman Mao. Vice-Chairman Lin is the best, the best, in learning the Thoughts of Mao Tse-tung. His understanding is the deepest, the deepest. He penetrates into them most thoroughly, most thoroughly, he applies them most fully, most fully. . . .

Every single word of Vice-Chairman Lin contains an infinitely deep proletarian feeling towards Chairman Mao. . . . It may happen that when we first hear the instructions of Chairman Mao we do not understand them fully. But when Vice-Chairman Lin explains them, then they are easy to understand, and one understands them more deeply.

Mao's wife went out to visit a temple in the Sun Yat-sen park in Peking during this period and found a portrait bust of the Chairman inserted among the Buddhas and relics of Sun. She ordered it to be removed. A little while later she went to the White Cloud Palace, one of the buildings in the Summer Palace, and found giant characters more than six feet high and designed in Lin Piao's style of calligraphy put there, saying: 'Read Chairman Mao's books; listen to his instructions.' Lin was blatantly building up Mao's cult in order to be able to exploit it for himself. Mao's last battle lay ahead.

28
A LEAKY UMBRELLA

In August 1970 Lin Piao and Chen Po-ta, Mao's leading collaborators in the Cultural Revolution, attempted a political
takeover, apparently in the belief that Mao had become an
impossible leader and that Lin's control over the armed forces
would persuade other politicians to go along with their own
radical policies. The idea was to install Lin as Head of State and
for the Central Committee to pass a resolution by Chen on the
significance of genius in the process of historical development.
Chen, who would have become Lin's *de facto* prime minister, had
evidently decided that Lin Piao was more determined to implement Maoist mobilizatory policies than Mao himself – and had
more muscle for the job.

But the idea of Lin going behind his back and during his
lifetime to become Head of State made Mao so angry that Chou
En-lai and the generals who detested Lin Piao were able to
persuade him to abandon these two disciples. Lin, faced by this
setback, presumably decided to sacrifice Chen Po-ta in order to
save his own skin, since it was only Chen who was drummed out
of the leadership on this occasion. The Central Committee
inserted in the new draft constitution of China Mao's nomination for life as 'Head of State of the proletarian dictatorship in
our Country and Commander-in-Chief of the whole country and
the armed forces.'

Mao's account of this Central Committee meeting was that his
enemies

... engaged in surprise attacks and underground activities. Why
weren't they brave enough to come out in the open? It was obvious they
were up to no good. First they concealed things, then they launched a
surprise attack. They deceived three of the five standing members
[Mao, Chou and Kang Sheng] and the majority of comrades in the
Politburo.... Their coup ... went on for two-and-a-half days.... A
certain person was very anxious to become state chairman, to split the
Party, and to seize power.

Mao commented:

They said ... that opposition to genius was opposition to me. I am not a genius. ... Genius just means someone who is a little more intelligent. Genius does not depend on one person or a few people; it depends on a party. ... Genius depends on ... collective wisdom.

Mao told Lin that some of his statements were incorrect.

For example, he said that the whole world produces only one genius every few hundred years, and China every few thousand years. That just doesn't square with the facts! Marx and Engels lived in the same era, and it wasn't even a hundred years until Lenin and Stalin; so how can you say it takes a few hundred years to produce one? China has had Chen Sheng and Wu Kuang [leaders of the first peasant rising in the third century BC], Hung Hsiu-chuan [the Taiping Rebellion leader] and Sun Yat-sen. How can you say it takes a few thousand years to produce one?

Mao criticized Chen Po-ta's attitude as 'idealistic *a priori*-ism' and Chen was never seen again in public after this meeting.

It might seem strange that Mao should so savagely turn on a colleague who had been close to him in the past and had contributed much to Mao's own legend. Mao may have calculated that a scapegoat was needed to take the blame for the excesses of the Cultural Revolution, and that by sacrificing Chen Po-ta the basic tenets of Maoism could be preserved for implementation at a later period.

But Mao may in any case have had so little influence by this time in the Central Committee that he could not prevent Chou En-lai and the generals, together with those leftists hoping to survive by dissociating themselves from the extremists, from taking whatever decision they wished. One thing is sure, that Chen's fall must have been taken by many cadres in the Party as an indication that Mao's radical policies, which Chen had been so involved in helping to draft, were now being dropped by the Party.

Three years later, the Tenth Party Congress formally expelled Chen Po-ta and condemned him as a 'principal member of the Lin Piao anti-Party clique, anti-Communist Kuomintang element, Trotskyite renegade, enemy agent and revisionist'. All of this must have discredited in the eyes of many Chinese Communists Mao's judgement of human nature, since the Chairman had worked so intimately with a man who turned out all along to be of a different colour.

These thoughts must have occurred to Mao himself, because

immediately after the Lushan meeting he sent an open letter to the whole Party explaining his position.

Chen Po-ta is a sham Marxist-Leninist. For a long time Chen Po-ta has been arguing with me on the question of genius, holding that a genius is born with natural talents rather than deriving his talents from practice or from among the masses. He wants me to recognize him as a genius, and in so doing he covets nothing less than the chairmanship of the state. In my opinion, he is a careerist. . . .

On 1 October, Edgar Snow and his wife attended the annual celebrations of the National Day, and Mao led them to stand on either side of him on the huge balcony overlooking Tienanmen Square, facing the million Chinese citizens parading below. It was the first time that Americans had been so honoured, and it was widely seen as a gesture of reconciliation. Mao's ideological line about the United States had not, of course, changed. Earlier in the year he had spoken, in the course of a statement about Indo-China, of 'Nixon's fascist atrocities'.

In November 1970 the breakthrough in Mao's long wait for American recognition came as a by-product of a state visit by President Yahya Khan of Pakistan. The Pakistani had conferred with President Nixon in the White House a few weeks earlier, and he gave Chou En-lai a personal letter from Nixon suggesting a high-level American visit to China. Chou was not encouraging, but promised to discuss the matter with Mao that night.

To Yahya Khan's surprise Chou told him next day that China welcomed the proposal and would be glad to receive a 'high-level person' for face-to-face discussions, adding that Mao himself had commented, 'This is the first time that a message from a head of state was sent to a head of state through another head of state.'

The American behaviour during the sabre-rattling on the Amur and Ussuri Rivers at the northern end of the Sino-Soviet border in 1969 was no doubt the most compelling consideration in Mao's change of mind about inviting Nixon. The details are still obscure, but at least Nixon refused to give moral backing to a Russian attack on China.

Edgar Snow had been touring China during these dramatic exchanges. On 10 December he was woken up early in the morning in his Peking hotel and summoned for breakfast with Mao at his residence in the Imperial City. They talked until one in the afternoon.

'He was slightly indisposed', Snow noted, 'with a cold and he wondered out loud what doctors were good for; they could not even prevent a simple disease like colds, which cost so much lost time.' He agreed to try doses of ascorbic acid as recommended by Dr Linus Pauling, which Snow suggested.

They discussed Snow's articles about their last talk, six years earlier, where Mao had acknowledged that there was 'a cult of personality' in China and for a reason. The cult had doubtless been overdone, but it was hard, Mao said, for people to overcome the habits of 3000 years of emperor-worshipping tradition. He listed the 'Four Greats' which had been applied to him – 'Great Teacher, Great Leader, Great Supreme Commander, Great Helmsman'.

What a nuisance, was his comment. They would all be dropped eventually, and only the word 'teacher' would be retained. He had always been a schoolteacher since his youth in Changsha and still remained one: all the rest of the titles would be declined, thank you. And Mao said again that he would 'soon be going to see God'.

Snow made a complimentary remark about China's recent progress in birth control. No, the Chairman said, Snow had been taken in. Women in the countryside still wanted to have boys, and would go on trying to have boys if the first children were girls. Snow talked of the women's liberation movement in the US and Mao spoke of his high hopes for the peoples of China and America: if the Soviet Union would not point the right way, then Mao would place his hopes on the American people. The US had a higher industrial production than any other country, and universal education. He would be happy to see a revolutionary party emerge there, though he did not expect it in the near future.

Meanwhile, he went on, China was studying the matter of admitting Americans from the left, middle and right to visit China. Should a rightist like Nixon, representing monopoly capitalism, be permitted to come? Yes, Mao answered himself, Nixon should be welcomed because the problems between China and the US would have to be solved with Nixon. Mao would be happy to talk with him, whether he came as a tourist or as President of the US.

China should also learn from the way the US had developed through decentralization, spreading responsibility and wealth among the fifty states. A central government could not do everything and China's future would depend on regional and local initiatives.

Snow asked whether the Russians feared China. It was said that they did, Mao answered. A person could become frightened even by a few mice in his room, he might fear that they would eat up his sweets. The polemics would have to go on for ten thousand years if necessary. When Kosygin himself had come, Mao told him after their talk that the Russians might be let off one thousand years but no more.

The Russians looked down on the Chinese and on many other peoples, thinking that they had only to give an order and everyone else would obey. They did not realize that there were people who would not do this, and that one of them was his humble self. China's ideological differences with Russia were now irreconcilable, but they would eventually be able to settle their problems as between states.

When Mao finally escorted Snow to the door at the end of the morning, he described himself as a lone monk walking the world with a leaky umbrella. Sinologists pointed to a *double entendre* in the Chinese phrase for 'monk under an umbrella' which, through a pun, can also mean, 'I know no law, I hold nothing sacred.'

At the beginning of 1971 Mao countered Lin Piao by dismissing the military leadership in North China and Peking itself, relieving the 38th Army of its commanders sympathetic to Lin and moving it out of the capital, thus removing the cornerstone of his former lieutenant's power. Meanwhile Mao and his personal entourage quietly evacuated their home at Chungnanhai, where their enemies had infiltrated and where afterwards they claimed they could neither eat nor sleep safely, moving for their security first to the Chinhai Hotel and then to the Great Hall of the People in Tienanmen Square.

Lin Piao, with his wife (Yeh Chun, herself holding general's rank) and son, planned from the distance of Shanghai and other central Chinese cities a desperate last *coup d'état* against Mao. The son, as deputy director of operations of the air force, had key contacts with the air force.

On 18 March the younger Lin said to two senior air force officers: 'We have to work out a plan for a coup.' He added that 'the viscount' (his mother) 'had said that attention should be paid to security.'

Two days later a third high-ranking air force officer arrived in Shanghai to join the discussions. Finally, between 22 and 24 March the famous '571 Engineering' plan was concocted. The sounds of the Chinese words for five, seven and one – *wu*, *chi* and *i* – can also mean 'armed uprising'.

The 571 plan outlined the intolerable situation which China was in.

B52 [their code name for Mao] has not much time to go. He is anxious to make arrangements within the next few years. He does not trust us. We had better act boldly rather than be captured defenceless. . . . Of course, we do not deny his historic role in unifying China; it was precisely because of this that during the revolution we gave him the status and support he deserved. Now, however, he abuses the trust and status given him by the Chinese people. . . . He is not a true Marxist-Leninist, but rather one who follows the way of Confucius and Mencius, one who dons Marxist-Leninist clothes but implements the laws of Chin Shih-huang. He is the biggest feudal despot in Chinese history. . . .

The present conditions are: sharp political contradictions within the country; signs of danger all around; the dictator losing ever more of the people's support; the internal situation in the ruling group uncertain, and power struggles, intrigues and inner fights almost at boiling point; army troops suffering oppression; the middle and higher cadres not obeying orders, and discontented. A clique of scholars is acting tyrannically; they have military power, but they have enemies on all sides. They are over-inflated and are over-estimating their power.

The cadres, who have had a long history of Party struggles, and were discarded and badly hit during the Cultural Revolution, are angry but dare not talk. The peasants have not enough food or clothing. The sending of young students up to the mountains and down to the villages is a camouflaged Labour reform. The Red Guards were first deceived and then made use of, turned into cannon fodder, to become scapegoats in the later period. . . . The freezing of workers' wages (particularly young workers) was a form of exploitation.

The Soviet Union is being opposed and attacked. Our action will be supported by the Soviet Union.

Our difficulties are: our forces are not yet well prepared: the masses still have a deep, blind faith in B52; on account of B52's divide-and-rule tactic there are complex contradictions within the army and it is difficult for us to create a united force; B52 rarely appears; his movements are hidden and treacherous and tight security measures surround him, which makes our action quite difficult.

Both we and the enemy are in a dilemma. The present apparent equilibrium cannot last long. . . . This is a struggle of life and death. . . . Either we get ready and devour him or the enemy opens his mouth to devour us. In such immediate danger, whether we are ready or not, we must act.

Tactical timing and ways of acting: if B52 falls into our hands the enemy battleship will also be in our hands; they will fall into the trap on their own. Use a high-level meeting to catch them; or cut off his right-hand men – this would do it – or force B52 to give in; or do it in the form of a palace revolution; or use special methods such as gas or germ warfare, bombing, 543 [a secret weapon], an arranged car accident, assassination, kidnapping or city guerrilla troops. . . .

Today he uses this force to attack that force; tomorrow he uses that force to attack this force. Today he uses sweet words and honeyed talk to those whom he entices, and tomorrow he puts them to death for some fabricated crimes. Those who are his guests today will be his prisoners tomorrow.

Looking back at the history of the past few decades, do you see anyone whom he had supported initially who has not finally been handed a political death sentence?

Is there a single political force which has been able to work with him from beginning to end? His former secretaries have either committed suicide or been arrested. His few close comrades-in-arms or trusted aides have also been sent to prison by him. Even his own son has been driven mad by him.

He is a paranoid and sadist. . . . Once he hurts you he will hurt you all the way and he puts the blame for all bad things on others.

The various ways by which Lin could succeed to Mao's throne were discussed in detail by his followers. According to the confession of one of them, it was felt that a peaceful transition would be the ideal, except that it would take five or six years, during which time much could change, 'and nobody can predict that the chief' (Lin Piao) 'will retain his present status that long.'

Lin might, after all, be ousted by others. 'Nothing is predictable. The Chairman commands such high prestige that he need only utter one sentence to remove anybody he chooses.' To which another aide objected: 'The chief has been chosen by the Chairman himself.' But the first aide capped this with the comment: 'Liu Shao-chi was also his own choice.' Therefore it came down to the preferred option of taking power ahead of time.

One way was to get rid of Chang Chun-chiao (considered Lin's most prominent rival), while preserving Lin's status and thus assuring his succession to Mao. The other possibility was to 'endanger the life of the Chairman himself', although this would create a political situation which would be difficult to handle.

In April, Mao put into action his favourite tactic of attacking the enemy at the side rather than the front. He arranged a conference of ninety-nine senior cadres which carried further the criticism of Chen Po-ta but which also called on five generals loyal to Lin (including his wife) to make self-criticisms. Chou En-lai was in the chair. Lin's wife was so nervous that she wanted to put plan 571 into operation immediately, but Lin decided to wait.

He allegedly attempted a revenge on Chou En-lai by trying to have his aircraft shot down on returning from a visit to Vietnam. Lin Piao, with Chiang Ching, allegedly cabled a general in Yunnan on the Vietnamese border to shoot down an 'enemy' plane which was about to intrude in Chinese airspace. When the general saw that it was a passenger plane and not a military aircraft he forced it down before shooting. Chou En-lai stepped out, took Lin's telegram from the general's hands and carried it on to Peking with him. He did not, however, take it to Mao, but kept it until his deathbed, giving it then to his wife to show to Mao.

In the middle of August, Mao left on a secret tour of the provinces to elicit opinion about Lin Piao's activities and role. He attacked Lin's political use of his wife, in terms which many of his listeners must have applied in their own minds also to Chiang Ching.

I never approved of one's wife becoming the office manager in one's own work unit. Over at Lin Piao's it is Yeh Chun who manages his office. When the four of them want to ask Lin Piao about anything they have to go through her. In doing any work one should do it oneself and read and endorse papers oneself. One should not rely on one's secretary. One shouldn't let one's secretary wield so much power.

My secretary is only responsible for receiving and despatching papers. I select the documents myself, read them myself, and when something has to be done I do my own writing so that no mistakes are made.

This was doubtless to dispel the damage to Mao's own reputation arising from the fact that Chen Po-ta had been for such a long time his own personal secretary, but it equally distanced him from his own wife who was now going to take the centre of the stage in Mao's final political struggle.

Mao then listed the 'ten big struggles over line', in which his leadership (actual or potential) of the Party had been threatened – by Chen Tu-hsiu in 1927, Chu Chiu-pai in 1928, Li Li-san in 1930, Lo Chang-lung in 1931, Wang Ming from 1931 to 1934, Chang Kuo-tao in 1935, Kao Kang in 1953, Peng Teh-huai in 1959, Liu Shao-chi in 1967 and now Lin Piao in 1970.

While Mao was making some of these remarks, Lin's men were allegedly planning to bomb his train on his way from Hangchow to Shanghai. But Lin's daughter Tou-tou, overcome by conscience, rushed to tell Chou En-lai about the plot just in time to warn Mao, whose life was thus saved. When Mao did return to Peking unharmed on 12 September, Lin fled, taking an air force Trident jet from Peitaiho and flying it north-westwards, presumably to Russia. But the plane crashed over Mongolia at two-thirty in the morning and all nine passengers were reported killed. The rebellion was over.

Mao had always harboured a certain contempt for Lin, possibly for his intellectual limitations. This thin, stooping, hesitant man totally lacked charisma and what is surprising is that he ever came so far in the Chinese leadership. Only a driving ambition propelled him. In a remark which Shakespearians would savour, Mao once observed: 'Lin ... eats over a pound of meat a day, and he's still not fat, even after ten years of it.' The world still waits for the true story of Lin's fall, of which only the Maoist side is known, but the least that can be said is that he was incapable of organizing a successful assassination.

Within days, Lin's memory was execrated in China. A provincial radio station dismissed him as 'dogshit, indigestible to human society'.

On 21 February 1972 the almost unbelievable happened. Richard Nixon flew into Peking to see Mao. Vassal kings had brought tribute to the Forbidden City back through the centuries, but never before had the head of the world's most powerful nation come in person to greet the leader of China.

Within three and a half hours of his touch-down Nixon was in Mao's office under the glare of Chinese television cameras. Mao had to be helped to his feet by one of his secretaries.

'I can't talk very well,' was his first remark to the American president as he shook his hand. Chou En-lai told Nixon later that the Chairman had been down with 'bronchitis' for about a month. This was not their only handshake. Later in the conversation came what Nixon described in his diary as 'the most moving moment' when Mao reached out his hand, 'and I reached out mine, and he held it for about a minute.'

Kissinger, who was present, observed that he had told his students at Harvard to read Mao's works. Mao made a self-deprecatory remark, whereupon Nixon commented: 'The Chairman's writings moved a nation and have changed the world.'

'I haven't been able to change it,' Mao insisted. 'I have only been able to change a few places within the vicinity of Peking.'

They bantered about the names which Mao and Chiang Kai-shek called each other, and about Kissinger's skill in using pretty girls as a cover for his secret visits to Paris and Peking.

'I voted for you', Mao told Nixon with a broad smile, 'during your last election. I like rightists,' he went on, warming to his theme and mentioning Edward Heath and the Christian Democrats in Germany. 'I am comparatively happy', he confided, 'when these people on the right come into power.'

Nixon had been well enough briefed to quote a phrase to

Mao's face from one of his poems, and Mao beamed with pleasure. In the final exchange of banter Mao suggested that Nixon and Kissinger were not among those who would be personally overthrown when capitalism was defeated.

'If all of you are overthrown,' he explained, 'we wouldn't have any more friends left.'

Henry Kissinger found Mao

... grossly overweight, but he had a remarkable capacity to dominate things around him. Physically he exuded will power. Mao dominated ... by this feeling of will.

We only talked for little over an hour and I have no way of knowing if Mao has more than an hour or two of effective mental force during a day. But he did convey this impressive atmosphere of tremendous power. Very recently I reviewed the transcript of our conversation and I found it like the overture of a Wagnerian opera. Every single thing we discussed in the subsequent conversations with Chou En-lai was previously mentioned in that single talk with Mao.

The visit brought prestige to Mao, and this may have been in his mind when he agreed to it. It would certainly be difficult for his colleagues to push him aside again after such a success. But by the same token he also lost face with the radicals in his Party, the outlook of whom can be guessed from the remark reportedly made by the then Chinese Foreign Minister, Chiao Kuan-hua, in an internal speech a few years later about the visit of Imelda Marcos, First Lady of the Philippines. She had, Chiao explained, been 'selected through a beauty contest'.

She is the product of a corrupt capitalist system, under which capitalists toy with women. From this you can understand what class the President of the Philippines and his wife represent. Nevertheless, in the present international situation, we have to talk with them, as we had to invite Nixon and talk with him. The brilliance of Chairman Mao consists in this, that he can discriminate between what is important and what is not.

Nixon was followed by the Japanese Prime Minister, Kakuei Tanaka, who had come to negotiate the establishment of diplomatic relations wth Premier Chou En-lai. The two premiers came to see Mao afterwards.

'Did you finish your quarrel yet?' he asked them. 'Quarrels are good for you.'

'We have had amiable talks,' Tanaka replied cautiously.

'Truly good friends', Mao went on, 'are made only by quarrels.'

Mao then went on to make small talk about food and drink. 'Do not drink too much *maotai*, it will hurt you.'

'I hear *maotai* is 65° proof,' Tanaka responded, 'but I really enjoy it.'

'Oh no, it's 70° proof, not 65°,' Mao said. 'Who gave you the wrong information? Incidentally, there are too many old things in China. It is not good to get tied up by them. When I was small, my father was very hard on me and so I rebelled against him. . . . Be that as it may, you seem to have a rough time in elections in Japan, don't you?'

Tanaka talked about the eleven general elections he had contested, and in which he had spoken a lot on the street.

'Speaking on the street', Mao observed, 'is a tough job. Please take good care of your health.'

The Japanese leader explained that nobody could be elected in Japan without making street speeches.

'How is your parliamentary system?' Mao inquired.

'It has its problems, too.'

'In Japan, too, there seem to be a lot of problems, don't there? If you have to go so far as to speak in the street, that must really give you a hard time.'

Mao presented some books to the Japanese, commenting: 'I am fond of reading books. I think it is not good for my health, but I can't go to sleep without reading a book.'

Mao's wife did not fare so well with her American encounter. She received a young Chinese-speaking American professor who had come to do research on the Chinese women's movement, Roxane Witke. Chiang Ching decided to give Witke a series of interviews about her own life story and her contributions to the Chinese revolution, perhaps thinking that she had at last found her Edgar Snow. During August 1972 she spent about sixty hours with the young American visitor, revealing such things as her worship of Greta Garbo and appetite for Hollywood movies, and this material was later published in Witke's book, *Comrade Chiang Ching*.

Although Chiang Ching had Chou En-lai's agreement as well as the help of Wang Tung-hsing, Mao's bodyguard, in this venture, Mao himself had apparently not been consulted. According to Chiang's enemies, Mao was angered by the incident, presuming that its purpose was merely to build up his wife's reputation, and felt that Party and state secrets as well as personal confidences had been betrayed. It was said from the anti-Chiang side that the Witke interviews worsened Mao's physical condition and health from the autumn of 1975 on, and that soon afterwards Mao stopped living with his wife.

From this time on, there were also rumours in China that Chiang Ching sometimes asked Mao for money, and that he paid over to her some of his book royalties – to the amount of $15,000 on one occasion, it was alleged. After 1973 Chiang Ching apparently moved her residence to the Tiaoyutai (Fishing Terrace) guesthouse near the Pool of the Jade Abyss, where Nixon and other foreign dignitaries had stayed, and it was said that she had to write a note to Mao if she wanted to see him.

She had by now become remarkably unpopular in China. Gossip said in her final days of power that she had taken as her lover the world table tennis champion, Chuang Tse-tung.

In August 1973 Mao chaired his last Party Congress, the Tenth. Organized by Chou En-lai, it issued a communiqué condemning Lin Piao as a 'bourgeois careerist, conspirator, counter-revolutionary, double-dealer, renegade and traitor'. Chou, however, was already ill with incurable cancer, so Mao's new succession problem was intractable.

President Pompidou came in September. 'Well, for my part, I am shattered,' was Mao's first remark to his French visitor. 'I am weighed down with illness.' He noted that de Gaulle had criticized China in his memoirs. 'But at that time', Mao explained, 'everyone was against us, and under those circumstances we were forced to appear aloof. . . . The Americans said we were worse than Hitler. As for Khrushchev. . ., in 1955 he said to Adenauer: "Help me to oppose China." '

Pompidou said that he had met the Russian and American leaders, that both claimed to be peaceful, and had reason to be peaceful.

'I don't agree at all,' Mao exclaimed, waving his hands in disagreement. 'Sooner or later there will be war. The best plan would be to assume the eventuality of this war. Only after that should you look towards the possibility of peace. Otherwise we would let our guard drop.'

Mao had comments to make on Kissinger and Napoleon: 'Kissinger likes giving briefings, and quite often his proposals are not very intelligent. . . . Napoleon's methods were the best. He dissolved all the assemblies, and he himself chose the people to govern with.'

Pompidou asked about the Chinese population.

'Well,' Mao replied, 'even I don't know the exact figures. I am not sure that we are eight hundred million. I doubt even if we have reached seven hundred million. The censuses make it look as if the Chinese are always growing. On the other hand, they always show the harvest diminishing.'

After that the conversation strayed superficially through Napoleon's campaigns, Nelson and Wellington, and even Alexander. Mao's knowledge of these matters was creditable, and he slipped up only on one minor question. 'The French Ambassador', he said, 'speaks French with an accent like Robespierre and Napoleon.'

'Napoleon', Pompidou pointed out, 'had an Italian accent.'

'Yes,' said Mao, thinking perhaps of himself, 'and people laughed at him.'

During these final years Mao received dozens of the world's statesmen, including Ceausescu of Romania, Emperor Haile Selassie of Ethiopia, Mobutu of Zaire, Trudeau of Canada, Whitlam of Australia, King Mahendra of Nepal, Kaunda of Zambia, Nyerere of Tanzania, Boumedienne of Algeria, Bhutto of Pakistan, Senghor of Senegal and Gowon of Nigeria.

In 1974 Mao called for a new campaign to discredit Lin Piao and root out his ideas, to be combined with criticism of Confucius. The radicals among his group, including his wife, tried to turn the latter part of the campaign against the moderate-centrist-realists, Chou En-lai and Yeh Chien-ying. Mao's last challenge before his death was to contain his wife's ambition.

In March 1974 he wrote to her saying: 'Nothing will be gained by seeing me. The books by Marx and Lenin, and my books too, are all there. You do not read books by Marx and Lenin, and you do not read my books. There is no point in seeing me. You have made too many enemies. It is lucky that I'm still around. What will you be after I am dead? I'm already eighty and in poor health. You are still troubling me with trifles. Why can't you be more considerate of me? I do envy the Chou En-lai marriage.'

But she kept writing, and Mao replied again: 'Even if you see me, we have nothing to say to each other. We have seen each other several times, but you never implement my instructions. You always talk about trifles; you never discuss major issues with me. There are over two hundred members in the Party Central Committee; you must talk with them and take action. You must know your own ability. People are dissatisfied with you, don't you know that?'

The government over which Mao loosely presided now consisted of an alliance of convenience between two almost equally balanced groups, the realists under Chou En-lai and the radicals under the so-called Gang of Four – Chiang Ching, Chang Chun-chiao, Yao Wen-yuan and Wang Hung-wen (the textile worker who had risen to the leadership of the younger generation during the Cultural Revolution in Shanghai, and was then suddenly promoted to be Vice-Chairman of the Party).

The radicals' chances of ensuring their succession to Mao were greatly enhanced in April when Chou En-lai went into hospital with cancer. Without his firm hand at the helm, it was easier for the radicals, who had better access to Mao, to get things done their way. A few weeks later Chiang Ching began to receive foreign dignitaries.

She began to be built up as a political power in her own right. In July she was hailed as an 'Expounder of Mao Tse-tung Thought', an honour accorded till then only to Chou En-lai and Lin Piao. The media began a vigorous praise of the Empress Wu Tse-tien, a famous seventh-century ruler and founder of a brief dynasty. Born a commoner, the Empress Wu entered the palace as a lowly concubine who acquired the first place in the Emperor's affections. When he died, his son married Wu, who helped the new emperor to rationalize state affairs. She was called the Sage Queen and ascended the throne herself after her husband's death. For half a century she initiated numerous reforms, including the better status of women. The new discussion in 1974 of the good side of her character and the benefits of her reign were of obvious relevance to the political future of Chiang Ching.

At a Politburo meeting that summer Mao criticized his wife before his comrades. 'Stop slapping big hats on others at will. . .,' he told her. 'It is hard to you to mend your ways.' To his comrades he said: 'She doesn't speak for me, she speaks only for herself.' And to her and her three radical colleagues he said that they should not cluster into a 'gang of four'.

When the warm weather ended, Mao journeyed south, this time to his home city of Changsha, where his aides recalled afterwards that, 'The pair of slippers he wore, which had been repatched many times, were again broken. He still could not discard the slippers and had his aides again repatch them.'

But he was not left for long in peace. The young Wang Hung-wen arrived in mid-October with a series of excited allegations against Chou En-lai. 'It seems', the young man reported, 'that a second Lushan conference is in the making in Peking. I did not tell Premier Chou . . . that I would come to Hunan. The four of us held a meeting all night and it is with their consent that

I come here to report to you. I should leave when Premier Chou is taking a rest. In coming here I run a great risk. . . . Although Premier Chou is seriously sick, he is "busy" finding people to talk. Those who often visit the Premier's residence include comrades Teng [Hsiao-ping], Yeh [Chien-ying] and Li [Hsien-nien].' But Mao was unmoved, and merely said that all this should be discussed face to face.

He again commented in his own hand, in November, on the margin of a letter sent to him by Chiang Ching: 'Don't flaunt yourself in public. Don't write instructions on documents. Don't take it upon yourself to form a cabinet. You have offended too many people. . . .'

But a week later Chiang Ching is said to have written again to her husband an extraordinary letter combining further demands with abject apology and fierce complaint.

'I did not live up to the Chairman's expectation,' she is supposed to have written to Mao. 'Because I did not have a correct self-assessment, I indulged in the joy of over-valuing myself. I have been muddle-headed. . . . Some of the strange things are really frightening. I awakened with fear. . . . I have had almost nothing to do since the Ninth Congress. I have been neglected and given almost no work. . . .' She also demanded money and official posts, her enemies later charged.

Mao's response was to deny that she was idle. 'Your work', he wrote, 'is to make a research of the current affairs both within the country and in other countries. This is already a great task. . . . Don't say that you have nothing to do. . . .'

The next visitor to Mao was his young cousin Wang Hai-jung, relaying a request from Chiang Ching about the promotion of Wang Hung-wen as part of the personnel arrangements being discussed by the Central Committee for the Fourth National People's Congress which was about to meet in the New Year. Mao listened to his 'niece' with irritation. 'Chiang Ching', he told some comrades, 'has wild ambitions, hasn't she?'

The end was now approaching. Mao did not attend important meetings of the Central Committee and National People's Congress in Peking at the beginning of 1975, although he was well enough to receive Franz Josef Strauss, the conservative West German leader, in his southern resort at a time when the Congress was in session in Peking. Everything now hinged upon appointments to state and Party posts, and how far those criticized in the Cultural Revolution were to be rehabilitated.

Mao left these matters broadly to Chou En-lai, but he did

propose that Teng Hsiao-ping, having worked off his sins during the Cultural Revolution, be restored to the vice-premiership and other posts and be made responsible for the daily work of the Central Committee during Chou En-lai's illness – contrary to the desire of the four radicals.

Afterwards Wang Hai-jung again reported to Mao on Chiang Ching's behalf, to say that his wife was displeased with almost all of the Politburo members, following Mao's nomination of Teng Hsiao-ping. Mao's response was terse.

'Few people', he told her, 'are suitable to her taste. Only one. She herself.'

'What about you?' Miss Wang asked.

'She has no respect for me. She'll have disputes with all people in the future. Today, although people get along with her, their relations are not sincere. After I die, she will make trouble' – a prophecy which was amply fulfilled.

Chiang Ching attempted a self-criticism at a Politburo meeting, but confessed afterwards that

I did not make a thorough self-examination. . . . I failed to reform my ideology. . . . The understanding that there is a gang of four helps me to realize that this reality might give rise to sectarianism, which may cause splits in the Party Central Committee, and helps me understand why the Chairman has talked about this three or four times in the last year. I did not imagine this to be an important question concerning principles. The Chairman seldom makes concessions on issues concerning principles.

On 3 May at a Politburo meeting Mao again criticized them with the warning:

Practise Marxism-Leninism, and not revisionism; unite, and don't split; be open and above-board, and don't intrigue and conspire. Don't function as a gang of four. Stop doing that any more. Why do you keep on doing so? Why don't you unite with the more than two hundred members of the Central Committee of the Party? A few banding together is no good, never any good.

At this stage of Mao's career much was done through inter-mediaries, and it was clear that the people best able to gain Mao's ear on a personal visit were the youngsters. The Gang of Four chose Wang Hung-wen or Wang Hai-jung to speak for them rather than Mao's own wife, and now Chiang Ching arranged for another young person to take up residence with Mao, namely his nephew Yuan-hsin. The boy was very much under Chiang Ching's influence, and it was generally said that his being stationed so near the Chairman made it easier for the four radicals to take advantage of Mao's physically weakened condition in order to feed in radical information, and worm out instructions in his name beneficial to their cause.

In September Chiang Ching insisted that the tape recording of her talk at a conference be relayed over the radio, and the text printed and distributed. Mao's reaction was short and to the point, according to his successor Chairman Hua, speaking after his death.

'Shit,' Mao exploded, in this account. 'Wide of the mark. Don't distribute the text, don't play the recording, don't print the text.'

According to his own staff, Mao warned them against his wife. 'Chiang Ching', he once told them, 'is a paper tiger, which can be punctured with a mere stroke. She bullies soft types but fears tough ones. She fears the masses too. You must fight her and don't budge an inch on matters of principle. What's there to be afraid of? I am here with you.'

In July 1975, Mao received Premier Kukrit Pramoj of Thailand. He told the Thai that the Watergate scandal was the result of 'too much freedom of political expression in the United States. . . . What's wrong with taping a conversation when you happen to have a tape recorder with you? Most people in America love playing with tape recorders.'

Mao complained of pains in his legs and failing eyesight, and his lips trembled when he talked. He told Kukrit how to fight against his Communist insurgents in Thailand. 'You don't need to worry about the Communist Party of Thailand,' Mao disingenuously assured him. 'It has existed for more than a decade but not a single Thai Communist has come to see me here.'

The next visiting statesman was Helmuth Schmidt, the West German Chancellor, who described Mao as needing help whenever he sat down or stood up.

His mouth stays open, his jaw hangs down, his face is stiff like a mask. . . . Mao has little voice left and can only articulate in a croak with difficulty. Three women . . . read his lips, confer with each other when in doubt as to what he has said, and then confirm through him that they have understood correctly. When confusion remains, he writes what he means with a soft pencil on notepaper, briskly and confidently. . . .

'Nobody listens to me,' Mao complained to the Chancellor.

Schmidt quoted the German proverb, 'Constant dripping wears the stone'.

'I myself', Mao replied sadly, 'do not have enough water left.'

At the end of the year David and Julie Eisenhower visited Mao and found him concerned with the problem of the younger generation. 'He actually sounded sceptical', Julie Eisenhower wrote, 'and disappointed in his people, especially the young, untested generation.' He did not rate the chances of permanent success of his revolution over 50 per cent.

'Young people', Mao told the American couple, 'are soft. They have to be reminded of the need for struggle. . . . There will be struggle in the Party, there will be struggle between the classes, nothing is certain except struggle. . . . It is quite possible the struggle will last for two or three hundred years.'

But when he spoke, the sounds came out as grunts – 'harsh, primitive, laboured' – and when the interview was over, Julie Eisenhower's last glimpse was 'of a weary man turning, attempting words with his nurses, then being led away to be alone again.' Other visitors found him pale, wasted and drooling at the mouth.

At the beginning of 1976 Chou En-lai died. Mao paid several visits to the deathbed of the comrade he had only recently come to trust, and yet who had proved more loyal and steadfast than any of the others. The expected bridging function which Chou would have played in the succession question had he outlived Mao was now impossible. The radicals, led by Chiang Ching, hoped to be able to take over cleanly. As the next senior man on the Central Committee, the young Wang Hung-wen – who ten years earlier had been a mere security guard in a textile mill – now took over that part of Chou's work. Mao is alleged to have sighed despairingly: 'If we let Wang Hung-wen continue like this, we will soon starve.'

To the general surprise, Mao appointed Hua Kuo-feng to be acting Premier of the State Council in place of Chou. It was said that Hua declined the offer at first, giving among other reasons the fact that his Marxist-Leninist theoretical level was not high.

'I have appointed you', Mao is then supposed to have told him, 'precisely because you know your level is not high enough. A man who has shortcomings will not be proud and will continue to improve himself.'

When Wang Tung-hsing, his chief bodyguard, congratulated Mao on the appointment, Mao explained his reasons for choosing Hua: 'Firstly, he has had experience in work at the prefectural and provincial levels, and his performance as Minister of Public Security over the past several years is not bad. Secondly, he is loyal and honest. Thirdly, he is not stupid.'

Hua was not objectionable by his personality, record or known views, either to the radical group on the one hand, or to the realists and rightists on the other.

This is presuming that Mao did in fact make a conscious choice, that he did indeed personally propose to the Politburo on 21 January and again on 28 January the appointment of Hua. He did sign a Central Committee document appointing Hua as acting Premier on 2 February. But we have no other person's word for Mao's role in all this except that of the man who became the principal beneficiary of that account, Chairman Hua himself.

The Gang of Four were furious about the failure of one of their own group to win the acting premiership, and they turned their guns on their opponents.

Mao is said to have stated his position about Teng Hsiao-ping in a memorandum sent out to the Party in February, that he was 'a very clever man and material which should be sought' – like cotton outside but 'like a steel needle' inside. His shortcomings were exaggerated self-confidence and refusal to accept criticism.

Chiang Ching's response was very clear. She told a meeting that 'In China there is an international capitalist agent named Teng Hsiao-ping. It might be correct to call him a traitor. Nevertheless, our Chairman has been protecting him. What I have said is my personal opinion.'

But Mao had obviously retained his liking for Teng in spite of Teng's opposition to his Cultural Revolution policies. Khrushchev recalled Mao's pointing Teng out to him once and saying: 'See that little man there? He's highly intelligent and has a great future ahead of him.' At least Teng was straightforward and not devious in his disagreements with Mao.

But on 5 April the so-called Ching Ming riots broke out in Tienanmen Square, where supporters of Chou En-lai attempting to pay respects to his memory were harassed by rowdies of the radical faction. It seems likely that Mao's nephew told him a pack of lies about the events leading up to the trouble and persuaded him to dismiss Teng Hsiao-ping as responsible for it. Hua was then appointed as the senior Vice-Chairman of the Party and confirmed as Premier – all, according to Hua himself, 'upon the personal proposal of Chairman Mao.'

Yeh Chien-ying spirited Teng away from Peking to save his skin, although he later attended a Politburo meeting packed by radical students. It has become a famous story now in China how Teng listened with his eyes lowered to the attacks on him from all quarters for some time, but then, as they reached a crescendo, got up from his armchair and slowly walked out to the toilet. There he stayed for two hours, long enough for the enthusiasm of the students to die away and for the purpose of the meeting to be frustrated.

At the end of April Mao received Premier Muldoon of New Zealand, and afterwards Hua stayed on to confer with him. He brought away a three-point directive by Mao saying: '(1) Carry out the work slowly, not in haste; (2) Act according to past principles; (3) With you in charge I am at ease.'

Early in June, Mao had his last known major collective meeting with his surviving colleagues, from all factions in the Party – Hua Kuo-feng, Wang Hung-wen, Yeh Chien-ying, Chang Chun-chiao, Yao Wen-yuan, Li Hsien-nien and Chen Yung-kuei – but not his wife.

He is supposed to have said,

I sent for you, not because I plan to leave a will. I've never had any faith in such formality. Chin Shih-huang left a will. It was later falsified by Prime Minister Chao Kao, wasn't it? . . . Isn't it true that some of you are expecting me to meet Marx as soon as possible?

At this point, Hua interrupted Mao with a 'No'.

No? None of you is looking forward to my death? I don't think so. I was called a dictator and a Chin Shih-huang even before the Lushan Conference. First there was Peng Teh-huai. Then came Liu Shao-chi, Lin Piao and Teng Hsiao-ping. They rebelled against me and opposed me. There are even people who attacked me' (here Mao referred to himself by his nickname B52) 'in the name of Premier Chou. So I am the target of everybody, standing alone. I said before I don't care about being alone. The truth is always on the side of the minority. Even if the entire Politburo and the Central Committee are against me, the earth will go on rotating. . . .

I have predicted that full-scale capitalist restoration may appear in China. I think it will be bad then. . . .

Some people say my brain is made of granite and therefore cannot change. I agree with them. Can I remain a good Communist if I have changed? Marxist principles and the basic line of the Party are not subject to change.

It is my idea that there shall be no presidency for the country. The best solution is for the Politburo to produce a tripartite leadership of old, middle-aged and young cadres. It is up to the Politburo to decide whether Chiang Ching shall be included.

Don't settle old accounts. Even if past purges were directed against the wrong targets, there should be no redress. Trying to change what has been done ... will result in thousands and tens of thousands of heads rolling.

From now on you should help Chiang Ching carry the Red Banner. Don't let it fall. You should alert her against committing the errors she has committed.

The fight against the two super-Powers must be continued. The two hands [i.e. the strategy of alternating the use of war and peace] must be kept busy. You must stick it out. ...

After I die, send my remains to Hsiangtan, Hunan. I don't believe in ghosts, and I'm not afraid of my body being whipped. Even if someone does whip my corpse, it's nothing.

You too should be brave. Get rid of that scholarly air. In this world revolution is still the main stream. Will it do without struggle?

The portents were already apparent that a dynasty was ending. In March a shower of meteorites had hit Kirin province, and the *People's Daily* recalled that in the third century BC the landing of a meteorite had been the start of a rumour about dividing the land after the death of the first emperor, Chin Shih-huang. In July came the devastating earthquake at Tangshan, which convinced many superstitious Chinese that a great death was at hand.

In September Mao began to fail, and Chiang Ching was summoned from Tachai, where she had been visiting, to be with him. She rubbed his back, exercised his limbs and sprinkled talcum powder on his body to comfort him. She had already been circulating a poem by Mao which she claimed he had sent her as a kind of last testament.

You have been wronged. Today we are separating into two worlds. May each keep his peace. These few words may be my last message to you. Human life is limited, but revolution knows no bounds. In the struggle of the past ten years I have tried to reach the peak of revolution, but I was not successful. But you could reach the top. If you fall you will plunge into a fathomless abyss. Your body will shatter. Your bones will break.

To this day Mao's true feelings about his wife remain a mystery. His condition worsened. The old man was now on his last journey, and at ten past midnight on 9 September 1976 he died.

There was an immediate crisis about what to do with his body. The Vietnamese were asked how they had handled the remains of Ho Chi Minh, and in the end, after much hesitation and in-fighting, an autopsy was performed and chemicals supplied to allow the body to be displayed in a mausoleum – the last thing

Mao would have wanted for himself.

Hua took firm charge of events, but the bickering intensified. Chiang Ching was discovered taking documents from Mao's office without authorization and allegedly tampering with them. On being rebuked by Hua, Chiang Ching complained: 'You want to throw me out when Chairman Mao's body has not yet turned cold. Is this the way to show your gratitude for the kindness rendered to you by Chairman Mao who promoted you?'

'I will never forget Chairman Mao's kindness,' Hua replied. 'I ask you to return Chairman Mao's documents precisely because I want to repay Chairman Mao's kindness, to enable everybody to unite together and forever implement Chairman Mao's behests. As for throwing you out, I have no such intentions. You live peacefully in your own house, so no one will dare to drive you out.'

At the State funeral in Peking, Mao's body was encased in a crystal sarcophagus. His widow, in a black headscarf, presented a wreath of sunflowers, green corn, ears of wheat, maize and the fruit of yellow corn inscribed, 'From your student and comrade-in-arms. . . .' Three weeks later, Chiang Ching with her three radical colleagues was arrested by Hua and her hopes of exerting influence after her husband's death were destroyed.

China was stunned by the loss of the man who had represented complete political authority for more than a generation. As the citizens stumbled past his coffin, their eyes streaming with tears, the largest nation on earth tried to come to terms with a void that could never be filled.

CONCLUSION

Despite the five volumes of *Selected Works* and the trappings of scholarship, Mao Tse-tung was essentially a man of action. He was interested in the results of social change, more than the theories behind it. A sentimental scholar once told him that Communism was love. 'No, comrade,' Mao replied, 'Communism is not love; Communism is a hammer which we use to destroy the enemy.'

It is not Marxism which attracted him into public life. 'Society', he observed in his old age, 'pushed men like us onto the political stage. Who would have thought of promoting Marxism? We had never heard of it. What we had heard and read about was Confucius, Napoleon, Washington, Peter the Great and the Meiji reformation, the three heroes of Italy, all of whom were part and parcel of capitalism.' What propelled him was a concern for the dignity and equality of human beings caught in an outmoded social structure which had to be destroyed.

In intellectual terms Mao was a barrack-room philosopher, fascinated by intellectual constructions but not able truly to compete with the great thinkers. Milovan Djilas, the Yugoslav Marxist, said of Mao: 'He uses Marxism as a religion. He is even more convinced by his own theories than Lenin or Stalin. But his ideas are very simplified; even his Marxism is simplified.' What Mao did with Communism was to express it in a way that ordinary people could understand as well as professors, and to localize it so that the people of China could understand it as much as the people of Europe.

Indeed, one of Mao's lasting achievements was to detach Communism from its European proletarian beginnings and apply its essential tenets to the situation of other continents, other centuries, other social mixes. He tried to restate its fundamentals in universal categories that were applicable for all stages of human history and usable for all kinds of revolutionary change. In particular, he put the peasants on the Marxist map, previously reserved for the élite of factory-workers. 'You must realize', Mao told Malraux, 'that before us, among the masses, no one had addressed themselves to the women or to the young. Nor, of course, to the peasants. For the first time in their lives, every one of them felt involved.' In this respect Mao spoke and acted for the entire Third World of Africa, Asia and Latin America.

The energy that drove him was hatred of the fiercest kind, derived from his personal sense of rejection. His own father refused to treat him as a theoretically equal, if practically limited, individual, and his quarrels with his father have become famous. He set out from Shaoshan, his native village, more determined to prove his father wrong, and prove his own judgement better than his father's, than to improve his own knowledge and personality. He had a chip on his shoulder from the first time he tried to escape from his ancestral home at the age of ten.

Once out in the world, he experienced rejection from all kinds of father figures – from classmates of better social standing, teachers of intellectual condescension, fellow Communists superior in Marxist training and foreigners with all sorts of skills and superiorities lacked by the Chinese.

To the Chinese establishment of the 1920s and 1930s Mao appeared as an amusing but lightweight figure desperately trying to make up for his inadequate education. Nobody of stature in Peking, as Mao himself ruefully recalled, had any time for a young library assistant 'speaking southern dialect'. (It is striking that the other great lonely dictators of modern times – Napoleon, Stalin and Hitler – all suffered from the same disadvantage.)

But in his case Mao was not merely angry because he felt himself unloved: he identified with the peasantry in their rejection by the Chinese élite, by the Chinese tradition, by the Chinese system. As long as he himself was accepted as a leader the peasants had a chance to become modern emancipated men and women, but whenever his leadership was spurned their interests were also set back. Hence his vitriolic rage at the numerous rebuffs given to him by the Communist Party. 'I am a fellow', he observed at a meeting during the Cultural Revolution, 'who has been expelled by others five times, and then invited back. Thus, the leader of the masses is not self-appointed. He attains his stature in mass struggles.' This explicit identification with the people is one that earned him immense devotion by his followers in earlier years.

'Chairman Mao', said Chen Yi, the Foreign Minister, 'is a man ... who has been most humiliated, wronged and maltreated. ... He has been dismissed from his post, retained in the Party for observation, pronounced an opportunist, disgraced, and sent to the rear for rest and visited by nobody, because nobody dared to get close to him.'

Whereas other potential leaders in the Chinese Communist Party appeared to be more interested in pleasing their teachers in Moscow while following a more or less traditional Chinese mode of public life, Mao owed nothing to the Russians and carved out an entirely new and daring style of leadership inspired as much by the romantic egalitarianism of the Robin-Hood-like heroes of *Water Margin* as by the theoretical works of European Marxists. He taught that men were equal even if they were completely uneducated – a totally new concept in China. One of his finest statements was the one he made in the early throes of the Cultural Revolution, that, 'It is to the advantage of despots to keep people ignorant; it is to our advantage to make them intelligent.' He campaigned for the rights of women, and for the rights of students to have some say in their education.

All this was part of an insight that Communism ought to be constructed on the base of a society of individuals already emancipated. During the late 1940s Mao set out in some detail the programme which the Communist Party would follow during the capitalist phase – the so-called New Democracy – which would have to precede socialism. Even after the Communists captured power he envisaged that national capitalism would have to be developed and individual emancipation achieved to prepare people for modern life. Communism, in effect, was premature in the China of 1945 or even 1949.

To some extent Mao was playing to the American gallery in these writings; and also seeking to disarm potential opponents within the Chinese right wing. But there was an element of sincerity in them, and when after 1949 the momentum for introducing socialism built up, he no doubt reconciled his earlier position by arguing that socialism and individualization – collective and personal modernization, if you like – would have to run simultaneously as two parallel revolutions in Chinese life. But the weaknesses of this rationalization he never fully acknowledged or explored.

The trouble was that the Chinese clung obstinately to their old ways of doing things, and much of Mao's energy had to be expended on efforts to change irrational traditions before new rational substitutes could be implanted. The Samuel Smiles element in his Little Red Book is an example of this: one of the sayings which readers found blazoned across the top of one issue of the *People's Daily* during the Cultural Revolution was 'Think Hard'. Mao's voice was so often the voice of sanity and reasonableness, while his revolutions were waged on the ground by individuals formed in the old society.

'We should teach our comrades', he said, for instance, in 1956, 'who are sent to foreign countries to be honest, sincere, and call a spade a spade; and we must let everyone see what is good, bad or mediocre in us. . . . If our ·country has small feet, and others want to photograph them, let them do it. If our clothes are not good, let us not be afraid they will look unsightly. If we tell lies in front of foreigners, some day those lies will surely be exposed.' Anyone who has visited China will know how much those words needed to be said, and how much they still need to be repeated.

But Mao forgot to be equal himself. It was not because of any corruptibility in him: in material matters he was more modest and undemanding than any of his peers, and indeed he became famous as the world leader liable to appear in patched clothes, frayed cuffs or sagging socks. No, what made it difficult was his remoteness. He never really had any friends, and he never allowed others to get close to him – not even Chiang Ching, who became his political collaborator as well as his wife and yet confessed in the end that she neither understood him nor knew him. Emi Siao, who knew Mao as well as anyone in his schooldays and then went on to share some of his life in Communist opposition, confessed, 'Mao is the most complex person we have. . . . None of us have really understood him. I have known him longer than anyone else, but I have never got to the root of him.'

Chen Yi has explained that, 'When he assumed power, all comrades patched up their differences with him, yet he didn't allow others to apologize to him.' This was taken to illustrate Mao's humility, but in fact it shows the opposite. He was not ready to open up to these men, having been wounded by them in the past and fearing their wounds again in the future.

By not allowing his colleagues to differ with him on a reasoning and principled basis, Mao constructed willy-nilly a dictatorial system anchored in his own infallibility. 'My conviction', he told Malraux, 'did not take shape. I always felt it.' Mao enjoyed the cut and thrust of dialectical debate, and preferred a direct engagement with an opponent, with no fudging or holding back.

'There must be a confrontation of ideas,' he once said. 'As in fighting, you thrust your sword at me and I thrust mine back and the two swords must cross – this is confrontation. Without a confrontation of ideas no clarity or thoroughness can be attained.' But Mao could never endure defeat: he was a bad loser.

Instead of heading a team of Communist talents to fight the revolution before 1949 and govern the country thereafter, Mao spent his fifty-six years in the Chinese Communist Party in ten debilitating 'two-line' struggles against his own comrades. No sooner had he defeated one rival than another, often the one who had helped him most in the previous campaign, appeared to threaten him. As one of his critics, General Hsu Shih-yu, is supposed to have said shortly after his death, 'During his lifetime, Chairman Mao libelled as "class enemies" all those in the Party who dared to make suggestions to him. He indiscriminately described as "class struggle" all the disputes arising from opinions different from his own.'

In the cases before 1949, and even in the case of Kao Kang in the early 1950s, Mao's actions against his rivals can possibly be justified on nationalistic grounds, by the need to preserve the independence of the Party from Russian control. But he began to go badly wrong in 1959 when he turned against Marshal Peng Teh-huai, whose criticisms of the economic policies of the Great Leap Forward were very much to the point and expressed feelings widely held in the Party. Mao insisted on labelling him as a traitor, and Peng's unwise dealings with Khrushchev made him more vulnerable than he need have been. Again, the Maoist accusations against Liu Shao-chi were far-fetched. He was a loyal and sincere, if unimaginative colleague who had taken a great deal of arrogance from Mao in the past without seeking an upheaval in the Party over it.

After that, and after the failure of both the Great Leap Forward and the Cultural Revolution, Mao's two biggest experiments, he was left, with one exception, only with second-raters – Lin Piao, Chen Po-ta and Chiang Ching. It was perhaps predictable that he should seek either to bring them down or to curb their activities.

The exception was Chou En-lai, with whom his relationship was richly subtle. He never fully trusted Chou any more than he did the others – until it was too late. Khrushchev has testified how Mao would run Chou down in conversation, and there have been several suggestions of Chou's being less than enamoured of

Mao's leadership. But there was a quality in Chou's personality which made him an implementer of other men's ideas, a minister rather than a monarch. Precisely because of his mandarin background Chou may have preferred to do what he was told, and avoid final responsibility for the high policy line. Perhaps Chou's personal Communism found expression in accepting Mao's leadership: for him too, Mao was identified with the peasant masses. After handing the baton to Mao at the Tsunyi conference in 1935, Chou avoided taking big decisions and offered himself instead as Mao's best diplomat, the servant of the king.

Vindictive he may have been, but cruel to his opponents Mao was not, at least by the yardstick of what other Chinese and Communist rulers had done. Purges were not as large in scale, nor did they lead to death or physical violence to the same degree as in Soviet Russia. Mao hoped that opponents would learn their lessons from experience, would alter their attitudes and viewpoints, and even come back from their exile of rural re-education, purged of their wrong ideas. Cure the sickness, save the patient.

His defect was his inability to work for long with anybody who had genuine self-confidence in his own judgement and would not change his ideas merely because Mao told him to. He became disenchanted with such colleagues and sometimes vindictive in his personal attitudes towards them. As Chairman he must have ultimate responsibility for the millions of deaths in China's class war, but he always conceded that revolution was no tea party. Mao's tyranny lay not in excessive personal cruelty leading to deaths or imprisonment of colleagues but in his incapacity to collaborate with men of real talent.

Although Mao had shining ideals, and a genuine sense of identification with the peasant masses of China which enabled him to be highly self-confident and determined about implementing those ideals, he lacked the practical political and administrative skills to see them put into effect. Nor did he acquire the capacity loosely to guide a team of such politicians and administrators as they proceeded with the job of implementing his ideals. The personality problems which had given him the energy to drive himself to the top, to seize the dragon's throne, tragically prevented him from trusting the colleagues who shared those ideals and could have worked with him gradually to implement them.

But Mao's political career can only be called a failure against his own impossibly high criteria of ambition. He did preside over the creation of a completely new state in China, the People's Republic, in which 900 million people enjoy a very much better life than previous generations going back for several centuries. Thanks to the positive achievements of the Cultural Revolution, there is now a generation emerging in China which is not waiting meekly to be told what to do, but will insist on its own demands being met. This may not bode well for Communism but it is good for China.

Ironically future generations may blame Mao for not taking sufficient advantage of the country's political docility during the first quarter-century of Communist rule. On a Stalinist model, so much more could have been done in that time to build up the economy before distracting political lobbies became vocal. It might be argued by later historians that Mao was too kind-hearted in insisting on the element of human dignity at a time when not many others were complaining about it – but when the building of an economic infrastructure was urgently needed. Mao tried to do too much in the economy in the Great Leap Forward, but at other times he perhaps did too little.

If Mao had been able to combine such experiments as the Cultural Revolution and the Great Leap Forward, both of which had exciting positive elements, with a better understanding of his colleagues and willingness to work with them, China would be in a happier state today. But one cannot have everything, and with a hero of this size one cannot carp too much. Many Chinese were obviously happy to have such a hero, blissfully blaming his lieutenants for any aspect of his rule which they did not like.

Like Mahatma Gandhi, the only other contemporary Asian or Third World figure to match him in stature, Mao's instinctive vocation was that of teacher. Like Gandhi, but even more so, he carried his desire to change the world from the classroom into the political arena. Here he was brilliant in manipulating men and women at first hand, but was less successful at managing the complexities of public affairs. Unlike Gandhi, he would not give up authority in spite of these political misadventures after 1958: he clung to power and to his own ideas with the same dogged obstinacy with which he had wrongly defended *Romance of the Three Kingdoms* before his teachers when he was at school.

But in the end who can deny that this was an inspiring career, from Shaoshan to Peking? Who would be churlish enough to rate the faults higher than the achievements? Who would begrudge Mao his fame and his legend? He came from the 'wrong side' of China, was denied the normal processes of education, and therefore came late to an appreciation of intellectual matters. What he did know was poverty, degradation, exploitation and injustice – and he spent his entire life combating these by his best lights. He did this, not on the scale of a nation of twenty or thirty or forty million, as European reformers did, but across the entire civilization of China, which is as big a canvas as the whole of Europe.

He chose Marxism as his weapon, because that happened to come into fashion at the time when he needed a weapon. He proceeded to guide his own Party towards a realistic perception of the role of the peasants who constituted the vast majority of the Chinese population, and then showed it how to fight battles.

He was able to take the Party into power because of the corruption of its rival and the unwitting intervention of Japanese imperialism. Once in power he rapidly transformed the structure of the Chinese economy into a socialist one which rejected the Euro-American model of industrialization and insisted on preserving the human element, even at the cost of speed and economies of scale.

Having defeated Japan and Chiang Kai-shek in the 1940s, he went on to declare war against the earth in the 1950s and against human nature in the 1960s. He tried for the extremes – of thorough-going free speech in the Hundred Flowers, of personal collectivism in the Great Leap Forward, of integral equality between leaders and led in the Cultural Revolution. In each case he failed, because his Party would not support him, but in each case there was some residue of the experiment which survived in China and made its Communism, its national life, distinctive. The modified people's commune is now entrenched as a vehicle for China's agrarian development in all its aspects – political, social and economic.

The person behind this achievement, however, remains inscrutable. A man of enormous energy and drive, fuelled by a consuming hatred of authority and resentment of being rejected on grounds of breeding or education, he stormed through life detached and seemingly invulnerable to its blows. He persuaded many of his closest kinfolk and friends to join his revolutionary cause, only to see them die in the cruel fight for its success. From his succession of marriages only an occasional glimpse of affection is revealed. He was loving with his children while they were infants, but cavalier and insensitive once they were adult. In the end no one gained his heart: the human emotions were for him subordinated to the lonely quest for power.

NOTES ON SOURCES

Mao Tse-tung is almost as difficult a subject for the biographer as William Shakespeare. The amount of established and undisputed factual information about his life and activities is remarkably small. A scholarly narrative of Mao's life would be either short and unsatisfying, or else filled with tedious discussion of the authenticity of whichever 'facts' are selected. There are, however, a number of sources of quite different origin which between them almost span his life and also cover the full range of biases and points of view. Mao himself dictated to Edgar Snow his own brief autobiography up to the age of forty-three, and this was published in *Red Star*. Two of his student friends left their own memoirs of his early days, namely *Emi* Siao and *Siao* Yu, while a Chinese biographer, *Li Jui*, published in the 1950s under the People's Republic (and therefore with the inferred approval, if not of Mao at least of his aides) an account of his early years as a student and young political activist.

Other friends and colleagues of Mao wrote memoirs, including recollections of their dealings with him, notably *Chang* Kuo-tao, *Kung Chu*, *Wang* Ming and his orderly, Chen Chang-feng. Other colleagues, like Lin Piao and Peng Teh-huai, spoke about Mao to comrades who recorded what they had said. Much of this material must be taken with several grains of salt, in the knowledge that an ulterior motive may lie behind the version of events offered (the same is, of course, true of Mao's own account, and that of his schoolfriends and of Li Jui). The account which is given least credence by Sinological scholars is that by Wang Ming, who wrote from Moscow and was published there after the break in political relations between the two countries. A similar remark applies to the memoirs of Otto Braun, who accompanied Mao on the Long March and then wrote his memoirs in East Germany. But even these accounts have material which sheds some light on a part of Mao's life without necessarily consistently falsifying it in every particular. I have therefore utilized some conversations, descriptions and observations by these contemporaries out of a conviction that although their precise exactitude cannot be guaranteed, they do seem to convey at least some of the flavour of the events described and are therefore useful, provided the possible motives of either character assassination or hagiography are first searched out and discounted. Some Russians, like Khrushchev and Vladimirov, also left what are alleged to be memoirs: the former are believed by many Sovietologists to be authentic, the latter probably not.

Later in his life Mao began to meet numerous Westerners, especially journalists like Edgar Snow, and these have left eye-witness accounts of him in his Yenan days and afterwards.

But even the authenticity of what Mao himself said or wrote during his lifetime has come under challenge. What he wrote was sometimes published in newspapers or periodicals which have survived, and as to those there is little question. But others did not survive in a contemporaneous form, and for many of his important speeches and articles we are dependent on the *Selected Works (SW)* which were heavily edited by him and his aides years or even decades after the event in order to make them politically more appropriate for the 1950s. For his political writings after 1949 we depend mainly on the informal records which were collated by Red Guards and others during the chaotic conditions of the Cultural Revolution period, notably in the collection referred to here as *Wan Sui*. The most interesting selections of these in English translation are to be found in Stuart Schram's *Unrehearsed* and *Thought*, and Jerome Chen's *Papers*. But even these have to be treated with caution, because they were not, as far as we know, vetted by Mao before being published or circulated by his youthful followers and then 'leaked' to the West. Some of them are now gradually being republished in the official Chinese press which lends some authenticity to their texts. But then the successor government after Mao's death had its own motives in presenting Mao's policy directions in a certain way, and so these must in turn be suspect.

It is understandable from all this that many books have been published which go into the pros and cons of believing or disbelieving all these varying and sometimes conflicting pieces of evidence about Mao's life. But this book is not intended to contribute to that scholarly debate, but rather to offer the lay reader the broad results of the scholarship, together with the maximum of colourful detail and contemporaneous comment consistent with the rather broad criterion of whether they are useful to a reader who wants to capture Mao's life, including its smell and flavour, as much as possible as it was. There is no fiction of mine in this book, and if there is a little fiction from Mao's contemporaries quoted by me, it is fiction which I honestly believe will help people understand the life of this man for whom secrecy was a condition of revolutionary work, and who carried the habit of spurning publicity about his private life into his period of power after 1949.

A word on previous biographies. Apart from the three early accounts by Chinese contemporaries (Emi Siao, Siao Yu and Li Jui), the four Western biographies of importance are by Stuart *Schram*, Jerome *Chen* (up to 1949 only), Robert *Payne* and *Han* Suyin. There are also now several interpretative books on Mao of which *Pye* is the outstanding in psychological terms, while *Scales* is useful in giving a range of specialist assessments by economists, historians, political scientists and others.

Books and periodicals cited more than once are abbreviated in the notes as follows:

Bands   Claire and William Band, *Dragon Fangs, Two Years with the Chinese Guerrillas* (London 1947)

Braun   Otto Braun, *Chinesische Aufzeichnungen 1932–9* (Berlin 1973)

CB   Current Background (Hong Kong)

Challenge   Gunther Stein, *The Challenge of Red China* (New York 1945)

Chang   Chang Kuo-tao, *The Rise of the Chinese Communist Party* (I) 1921–7 (II) 1928–38 (University Press of Kansas 1971 and 1972)

Chen   Jerome Ch'en, *Mao and the Chinese Revolution* (London 1965)

Chow   Chow Ching-wen, *Ten Years of Storm* (New York 1960).

CNA   China News Analysis (Hong Kong)

Compton   Boyd Compton, *Mao's China: Party Reform Documents 1942–44* (Seattle 1952)

CQ   The China Quarterly (London)

Cressy   Violet Cressy-Marcks, *Journey Into China* (London 1940)

Day   Henri Day, *Mao Zedong 1917–1927 Documents* (Stockholm 1975)

Dittmer   Lowell Dittmer, *Liu Shao-chi and the Chinese Cultural Revolution* (Berkeley 1974)

Domes   Jurgen Domes, *China After the Cultural Revolution* (London 1976)

Dragon   Eric Chou, *The Dragon and The Phoenix* (London 1971)

Emi   Emi Siao, *Mao Tse-tung: His Childhood and Youth* (Bombay 1953)

Fan   K. Fan (ed.), *Mao Tse-tung and Lin Piao* (New York 1972)

Han I   Han Suyin, *The Morning Deluge, Mao Tse-tung and the Chinese Revolution 1893–1953* (London 1972)

Han II Han Suyin, *Wind in the Tower, Mao Tse-tung and the Chinese Revolution 1949–1975* (London 1976)
Hymn Agnes Smedley, *Battle Hymn of China* (London 1944)
IHT *International Herald Tribune*
Inside Helen Foster Snow, *Inside Red China* (New York 1939)
Issues *Issues and Studies* (Taipei)
Journey Edgar Snow, *Journey to the Beginning* (New York 1958)
JPRS Joint Publication Research Service: Translations on Communist China (Washington)
Kämpfte Anna Wang, *Ich kämpfte für Mao* (Hamburg 1973)
Kau Michael Y. M. Kau, *The Lin Piao Affair: Power Politics and Military Coup* (White Plains, New York 1975)
Karnow Stanley Karnow, *Mao and China* (New York 1972)
Kung Chu Kung Ch'u, *Wo yo Hung Chun (The Red Army and I)* (Hong Kong 1954)
Kuo Warren Kuo, *Analytical History of the Chinese Communist Party* Vols I to IV (Taipei 1966 *et seq.*)
Li Ang Li Ang, *Hung-se Wu-t'ai (The Red Stage)* (Chungking 1942)
Li Jui *The Early Revolutionary Activities of Comrade Mao Tse-tung* (White Plains 1977)
Loh Robert Loh and Humphrey Evans, *Escape from Red China* (London 1963)
Long Edgar Snow, *The Long Revolution* (London 1973)
MacFarquhar Roderick MacFarquhar, *The Origins of the Cultural Revolution I* (London 1974)
Malraux André Malraux, *Antimemoirs* (New York 1968)
Mao Jerome Ch'en (ed.), *Mao* (Englewood Cliffs 1969)
March Chen Chang-feng, *On The Long March with Chairman Mao* (Peking 1959)
Nakajima Mineo Nakajima, 'The Kao Kang Affair and Sino-Soviet Relations' in *Review*, Japan Institute of International Affairs, Tokyo 1977
NCNA *New China News Agency* (Peking)
Nixon Richard Nixon, *Memoirs* (London & New York 1978)
NYHT *New York Herald Tribune*
NYT *New York Times*
OFNS *Observer Foreign News Service* (London)
Papers Jerome Ch'en, *Mao Papers – Anthology and Bibliography* (London 1970)
Parris Parris H. Chang, *Power and Policy in China* (University Park 1975)
Payne Robert Payne, *Mao Tse-tung* (New York 1950)
PD *People's Daily* (Peking)
Poems Mao Tse-tung, *Poems* (Peking 1976)
PR *Peking Review*
Pye Lucien Pye, *Mao Tse-tung, The Man in the Leader* (New York 1976)

Red Star   Edgar Snow, *Red Star Over China* I (London 1937); II (London 1968)

Rue   John E. Rue, *Mao Tse-tung in Opposition (1927–35)* (Stanford 1966)

Scales   Dick Wilson (ed.), *Mao Tse-tung in the Scales of History* (Cambridge 1977)

Scharping   Thomas Scharping, *Mao Chronik* (Munich 1976)

Schram   Stuart Schram, *Mao Tse-tung* (London 1967)

SCMM   *Selections from Chinese Mainland Magazines* (Hong Kong)

SCMP   *Survey of the Chinese Mainland Press* (Hong Kong)

Service   John S. Service, *Lost Chance in China* (New York 1974)

Siao   Siao Yu, *Mao Tse-tung and I were Beggars* (London 1961)

Smedley   Agnes Smedley, *The Great Road* (New York 1956)

Solomon   Richard H. Solomon, *Mao's Revolution and the Chinese Political Culture* (Berkeley 1971)

SR   *Selected Readings from the Works of Mao Tse-tung* (Peking 1971)

Sulzberger   C. L. Sulzberger *An Age of Mediocrity, Memoirs and Diaries 1963 – 1974* (New York 1973)

SW   *Selected Works of Mao Tse-tung* (Peking) Vols I (1965); II (1965); III (1965); IV (1961) and V (1977)

SWB/FE   BBC Summary of the World Broadcasts, Far East (London)

Talbott   Strobe Talbott (trans.), *Khrushchev Remembers* (I); *The Last Testament* (II) (London 1971 and 1974)

Thought   Stuart R. Schram, *The Political Thought of Mao Tse-tung* (New York 1969)

Thunder   Theodore White and Annalee Jacoby, *Thunder out of China* (New York 1946)

Turning   *The Great Turning Point* (Peking 1962) (no editor)

Unrehearsed   Stuart Schram (ed.), *Mao Tse-tung Unrehearsed* (London 1974)

Wakeman   Frederic Wakeman Jr., *History and Will, Philosophical Perspectives of Mao Tse-tung's Thought* (Berkeley 1973)

Wales   Helen Foster Snow (Nym Wales), *The Chinese Communists: Sketches and Autobiographies of the Old Guard* (Westport 1972)

Wang   Wang Ming, *Polbeka Kuk i Predatelstvo Mao Tse-tung* (Moscow 1975)

Wan Sui   *Miscellany of Mao Tse-tung Thought (1949–68)* Parts I and II, JPRS 61269

Wilson   Dick Wilson, *The Long March 1935* (London 1971)

Witke   Roxane Witke, *Comrade Chiang Ching* (London 1977)

Women   Helen Foster Snow, *Women in Modern China* (The Hague 1967)

INTRODUCTION

For an intriguing verdict on Mao by young intellectual refugees in
Hong Kong see *Huang Ho* Oct '76, trans. into English in *Freedom at
Issue* Mar '77. 50 million deaths R. L. Walker, *The Human Cost of
Communism in China* (US Senate 1971); Lins on Mao *Kau* 84; Stalin
Talbott I 462; Khrushchev *Talbott II* 463; East Germans *China Daily
News* 24 Mar '54; Castro *Daily Telegraph* 28 Jul '78; Neruda *CQ* 31,
135; Sukarno from interview with Indonesian official; Bhutto *Karachi
Radio* 11 Sep '76 and *SWB/FE/*5309; Montgomery in *Sunday Times* 15
Oct '61.

Chapter *1*: CHILD OF THE SNAKE (1893–1910)

Passim: *Red Star, Siao, Li Jui, Pye* and *Emi*, also *Issues* Nov '73 and *CB*
900. Mao on his father, *Wan Sui II* 389 and 496. Mao's words on
Hunan from *Day* 82 and 142; on China from *Thought* 164 and 375,
Day 93–4 and *SW V* 313. Mao's jealousy of brothers *NCNA* 10 Sep
'77; the burglary *Wan Sui II* 389.

Chapter *2*: A STUDENT OF ETHICS (1911–15)

Passim: *Red Star, Li Jui, Schram* and *Siao*. Mao on getting steamed up
Unrehearsed 137; the teacher on Mao's army experience was Hsu
Te-li in *Bands* 249; on eating honeydew *Wan Sui II* 442; Hsu on
Mao's talent for leadership *Bands* 250; Mao's textbook and notes in
Li Jui; on Prof. Wang see *Wakeman* 157–65; Mao at Pantsang *NCNA*
16 Sep '77; on Siao's alleged theft see *Day* 32.

Chapter *3*: THE DRAGON IN HIS DEPTHS (1915–18)

Passim: Red Star, Li Jui, Schram and *Red Star*. Toten letter *Day* 18; Mao
on physical education *Thought* 155–60; the East is backward *CB* 900,
14; New People's Study Society *Kuang-ming Daily* 4 Jul '78; Green
Forest University *Wan Sui II* 385.

Chapter *4*: CONVERSION (1918–21)

Passim: *Siao Yu, Red Star, Li Jui, Schram* and *Chen*. Mao on risk of
deculturization by going abroad *Day* 294. Mao and Tsai Chang
Dragon 282, *Women* 236 and *Witke* in *CQ* 31, 132. Mao's bad health
and cabbage-cooking in Peking, information from Tchen Ni-kia now
retired in Brussels; reasons for not going to France *Bands* 249; Hu
Shih *CQ* 10, 163 and *Schram* 42; Mao's anarchist friends in Peking
Rue 28; his reading Chang *CQ* 13, 62; Li Ta-chao on peasants
Thought 32. Changsha again: Mao on teachers *CQ* 49, 81–2; mother's

death *CB* 900; Mao's ode *Li Jui* 320; Great Union *CQ* 49, 76ff. Mao's writings on women *Witke CQ* 31, 128ff and *Thought* 334–7. In Peking, Mao and *Communist Manifesto* Cheng *Issues* Dec '73, 79. Mao on parents' deaths *Chinese Studies in Philosophy* vol. v, 3 '74 14–15; laundering in Shanghai *Hsin Hunan Pao* 1 Jul '50, in *Issues* Dec '73, 79; Yang finance for Book Society, Weigelin in *Eastern Horizon* Mar '77, 13; Mao on Hunan separatism Macdonald *CQ* 68, 751–77. Russell and Dewey, Bertrand Russell, *The Problem of China* (London 1922), 224; Yang Kai-hui, Weigelin in *Eastern Horizon op. cit.*

Chapter 5: WE MASONS (1921–4)

Passim: Siao, Kuo I, Red Star, Li Jui and *Schram*. 1st Party Congress: Chen Pantsu in *Communist International* Oct '36, 1361–4 and *New Observer* (Peking) 1 Jul '57. Chang's description in *Chang I* 140–1; following description and drinking anecdote *Li Ang* § 8; Mao threatens brother *Wan Sui II* 359. 2nd Congress *Kuo I* 50–9, *Rue* 35–6. Anyuan strike *Hungchi Piao-piao* May '59, 148–56. 3rd Congress *Chang I*, 296ff, *Day* 154–5. Shanghai articles Jul–Aug '23 *Day* 158–69 and *Thought* 206, 210. KMT Congress *Chang I* 316ff, Mao on Sun *Wan Sui II* 408, KMT delegate memoir Huang Chi-lu in *Kuo I* 1972. See also Koo on Mao *New Yorker* 18 Apr '77. May '24 Central Committee *Day* 152.

Chapter 6: THREE POTATO RICE (1925–7)

Passim: Red Star, Schram, Li Jui and *Rue*. 4th Congress *Han I* 137, *Day* 180–1; Mao on investigating peasants *Wan Sui II* 389; on Hong Kong and foreigners *Day* 208ff; on class analysis *SW I* 13, but see *Thought* 213–14, *Day* 299, *Kuo I* 247 and *Rue* 48–9; on missionaries *Day* 231. Confucian tablet episode *Li Ang* § 8. PMTI *CQ* 8, 182 and *Rue* 51. *Chang* 1, 656–658. Kuo Mo-jo *Day* 5–6. Mao on peasant question Sep '26 *Day* 303; back in Changsha *Hunan Radio* 7 Sep '77, *SWB/FE/* 5617. Mao's Report on Hunan *SW I* 23–56, *Day* 340ff; Comintern comments Wittfogel in *CQ* 1, 21; Pantsang visit Yang Kai-chih in *NCNA* 10 Sep '77. Mao on Horse Day *Kuo I* 329, his latest directives *Day* 373–4.

Chapter 7: A MOUNTAIN KINGDOM (1927–8)

Passim: Red Star, Chen, Schram, Rue, Kuo. Nanchang Uprising: Chu Teh (per *Smedley*) says Mao participated in planning but I prefer Wales aliter. Kiukang conference *Rue I* 355. Changsha Uprising Hofheinz in *CQ* 32, 37–87 and *NCNA* 30 Jul '77. Mao's capture *Kuo II* 18–19, Liu Hsing in *CNA* 907. Sanwan regrouping *NCNA* 30 Jul '77; Mao's volte-face Aug-Sep '77, Hofheinz in *CQ* 32, 61; exaggerated numbers *Li Ang* 24; CC blames Mao *CQ* 2, 25 and 33; Mao's defence *Unrehearsed* 290–1. Chingkangshan described by Mao *SW I* 86–87; bandit leaders murder allegation in *Issues* May '75, 105. Ho Tzu-chen *Schram* 191, *Witke* 503, Helen Snow *Inside* 178; Chu on marriage in *Smedley 223;* meeting Mao *ibid* 226. Historian on meeting *Kuo I* 412; Lin Piao's history *Kau* 19; Mao on him *ibid* 21; visitor on Mao *Kung Chu*; Braun on Chu and Mao *Braun* 84; Why is it? *SW I*, 63.

Chapter 8: MUTINY (1928–30)

Passim: Red Star, Rue, Schram, Kuo and 'The Struggle' *SW I* 73–104. Tract on wrong thinking *SW I* 105; Kutien conference *Lau* 22; 'A Single Spark' *SW I* 117; Li Li-san on dispersion in *Kuo II* 11; batman's memoirs *March* 5–6; Mao's obituary *Inprecorr* X, 14; 'Oppose Bookism' *Rue* 305; Yang's execution Weigelin in *Eastern Horizon* Mar '77, 14; Chou and Sec-gen on Mao *Kuo II* 136. Futien Mutiny: alleged torture *Radio Moscow*; 'You Know Who' *Kung Chu* 266 (see *CNA* 759); Ho's relative Chou I-chun, per Li Ang (see *CQ*, 18, 5).

Chapter 9: IN DISGRACE (1931–4)

Passim: Red Star, Kuo, Schram, Rue. 1st encirclement *SW I* 219 and 227; 'no voice in centre' *Unrehearsed* 291; marriage law *Thought* 337; 2nd encirclement *SW I* 228; 3rd encirclement *SW I* 217 and 229–30; Tsai's death *Li Jui* 68; Mao's open letter to KMT *Thought* 218–19; Chou conciliates Mao with foes per Tsai Hsiao-chien, see *CNA* 883; Liu on timepieces *Kuo II* 439; Mao on Ningtu conference *Wan Sui II* 24 Oct '66 (NB Kuo argues Mao must have meant Hsiang Ying because Lo Fu not then in Juichin); Lin's promotion *Kau* 23–4; Mao on economic work *SW I* 129; on League of Nations *Thought* 390 Fukien rebellion, Dorrill in *CQ* 37, 31; Braun on CC session *Braun* 69–70; Mao on Lo Fu *Wan Sui II* 344; Braun on Mao *Braun* 78–81; Mao's speech Jan '34 *Thought* 221; Liu Shao-chi *Dittmer* 21; malaria, Fu Lien-chang, 'Mao chu-hsi tsai Yutu,' in *Hung-chi Piao-piao*, Jan 59, 6–7; Kung Chu's chicken *Rue* title pages.

Chapter 10: THE LONG MARCH (1934–5)

Passim: March, Wilson, Red Star, Rue. Mao on worst period *Wan Sui I* 100; 'unnecessary' *Payne* 164; 'exact plans' *Payne* 148; Mao might have been left behind *Kau* 25; Mao's resolution in Chen, *CQ*, 40, 1. Mao's promotion at Tsunyi is extremely controversial: *Braun* 144 (revising his earlier opinion) insists it was only to Politburo Standing Committee but see Jerome Chen, Heinzig, Kuo and other sources cited in *Wilson* § 10–11. Mao on Lo Fu *Unrehearsed* 268; Mao on crossing Yangtze *Wan Sui I* 56; Lin at Huili per Hsiao Hua in *People's Daily* 9 Sep '77 and *SWB/FE*/5615; Mao talks to Braun re Sikang

Braun 159–60 and 167–9; Mao on crossing Tatu *Wan Sui I* 55; on fish *Payne* 86; Lu Hsun cable *CQ* 4, 22; Mao on Long March *SW I* 160.

Chapter 11: YENAN (1935–7)

Passim: *Red Star, Schram, Kuo III*. Mao's bowels *Journey* 165; his dental fillings information from Dr Magdalena Robitsche-Hahn in *Das Neue China*, Düsseldorf, 15 Nov '76 (speech of 18 Sep '76); on Kao *Naka-jima* 10; parodies critics *SW II* 164–7; poem *Snow* is dated 1944–5 in *Chen* 341; on Ko Lao Hui *CQ* 27, 11–13; on Russians *Journey* 169; Braun on Sian Incident and caves *Braun* 251 and 300; Ho 'stubborn' per Chiang Ching in *Witke* 503; Braun on dancing *Braun* 342; 'Please dance' David Barrett, *Dixie Mission* (Berkeley 1970) 51; co-ed Harrison Forman, *Report from Red China* (New York 1945) 97; Mao's enthusiasm for women *Li Ang* 75; Mao on Anna Wang's child *Kämpfte* 128; Mao meets Smedley *Hymn* 121–3; permanent wave per Anna Wang in interview; Mao and Lily Wu in *Wales* 252, *Braun* 343 and *Witke* 162; alleged torture by Chang's men *Kuo III* 241–3; Snow on Mao's individualism *Journey*; letter to Spain *Thought* 424; *Cressy* 163–4.

Chapter 12: BLUE APPLE (1937–8)

Passim: *Witke, Kuo* and *Wang*. Mao's *Problems of Strategy SW II* 79–112. Mao's *Dialectical Materialism*: *Thought* 180–90 and 86–7; *CQ* 19, 11; *Long* 206. Mao's *On Practice* and *On Contradiction*: Western comment *Thought* 88, Politburo criticism by Teng Fa per Sheng Shih-tsai in Allen Whiting *Sinkiang – Pawn or Pivot?* (East Lansing 1958) 229–31. *On Practice* in *SW I* 295–310; *On Contradiction* in *SW I* 331–47. Mao advises Smedley *Hymn* 121; thanks Japanese *Long* 199 and *Solomon* 205. A comrade on Lan Ping, Liu Chun-hsien per Yang Tzu-lieh, see *Witke* 162; Po Ku on Chiang *Braun* 323. The divorce: arguments *Kämpfte* 112–13; Mao on marriage *SW V* 346; Mrs Chang on Ho in *Witke* 162–3; Kang Sheng *Issues* Sep '77, 21. The condition first claimed in *New Statesman*, London, 20 January 1967. War: Mao on 10% against Japan *Chow* 80 and *Kuo IV* 14. Wang's return *Kuo IV*. *Problems of Strategy SW II* 79–112; *On Protracted War SW II* 113–94 and *Thought* 392–3. Mao as orator *Cressy* 188 and *Hymn* 122. Mao on collectivism *Cressy* 165–6; his letter to Chiang Kai-shek *Kuo III* 507–8; on Chamberlain *SW II* 264; Oct '38 speech *SW II* 195 and *Thought* 228–9; Mao on military challenge *SW II* 224–5.

Chapter 13: FIGHT OF MAD DOGS (1938–41)

Passim: *Witke, Kuo* and *Wang*. Mao on bourgeois-democratic revolution *SW II* 238 and 242–3; on youth *Thought* 355 and 353; Roman Karmen, *God v Kitae* (Moscow 1941) 108; Mao on Molotov Pact *Kuo*

IV 111 and *Time* 20 Sep '76; on mad dogs *Kuo IV* 112–13; on England
and Europeans *Thought* 399 and *SW II* 297; Snow's second visit
Edgar Snow *Scorched Earth* (London 1941) 260, 269–74. Mao on Lu
Hsun *Papers* 14–15; on capitalism and missionaries *SW II* 329 and
312; on Stalin *SW II* 335–6 and *Thought* 427; Mao on Bethune *SW II*
337–8; On New-Democracy *SW II* 339–84; on fighting England
Wang 191–3, *Radio Moscow* 10 May '70 and *Kuo IV* 519–22; reported
death *NYT* 24 May '40; on 100 regiments *Wan Sui II* 345; Russians
on Mao in *Kuo IV* 18–23 and 510–11; Mao on Anhwei incident *SW II*
15; on blockade *SW III* 112; Preface *SW III* 11; Reform our Study *SW*
III 17; on invasion of USSR *Kuo IV* 514 and 549–50; on whom cadres
love *Wang* 63–4; alleged poisoning *Wang* 38–54.

Chapter 14: LOVE IN THE ABSTRACT (1942–5)

Passim: *Witke, Compton, Kuo, Service* and *Chen.* Wild Lily *Witke* 184 and
507, *Unrehearsed* 185; 'Rectify' *SW III* 35–51 and *Thought* 174–9;
'Oppose Stereotyped' *Thought* 344; Russian on Chang is Vladimirov;
Yenan Forum Hsia in *CQ* 13, 226 and 239–46; Mao's 1st talk *SW III*
69–74; 2nd talk *SW III* 74–98; Mao on mass line *SW III* 119; Liu on
chairman *SCMP* (S) 201; cult *Chen* 20–1; Ai Ching's poem *Ai Ching*
Hsuan-chi (Peking 1951); Mao Tse-tungism in *Wang* 15–17; Liu on
Mao, Schram in *Asian Survey* Apr '72, 279–80 and *Dittmer* 22; Tse-
min's death *Li Jui* 341 and *Issues* Nov '73, 64; Harrison Forman *op.*
cit. 178–9; Gunther Stein *Challenge* 107–20; Votaw in *Service* 256–8;
Stein on Americans, *Challenge* 350–1; Mao talks to *Service* 295–307;
Hurley's arrival *Thunder* 253–4; Roosevelt telegram *Wang* 198–200;
Cromley cable *Foreign Affairs* Oct '72, 44 and 55; Mao's sons *Witke*
504, *Pye* 218–21, *Schram* 245 and *Unrehearsed* 319; 'one went mad'
Unrehearsed 143; An-ying and Wu Men-yu *Wang* 106; Wu himself
Challenge 16 and Burchett in *Neue Zürcher Zeitung* 7 Mar '47; pistol gift
SWB/FE/5955 Mao Chu-hsiung *Witke* 164; Mao's 13 Mar talk with
Service 373–7; Service's return to USA *Service* 380–90; panther ban-
quet and carding Amelia Hinsdell in *New China* Spring '77; Mao on
American neighbours *Thought* 172; *Resolution on Certain Questions* in
SW III 177–220; Liu on 'guides' *Collected Works of Liu Shao-chi* 96; Liu
and Mao's prestige Omori in *New Republic* 18 Jan '67; Liu's brother
on Mao *SCMP* 3916; Liu's praise of Mao *Thought* 111 and Strong in
Amerasia Jun '47; Mao on Chou *Wang* 171; Mao with praesidium
Wang 170; Mao on New Democracy *SW III* 279–81; Mao on cesspool
Thought 403; on atom bomb *SW IV* 21; 'my humble self' *NYT* 27 Aug
'45.

Chapter 15: SUP WITH THE DEVIL (1945–8)

Passim: *Witke, Chen, Schram, Turning.* 'Only touched the cup' Theodore White in *Thunder* 123; Mao in Chungking *Daily Telegraph* 3 Sep

'45 and *NCNA* 18 Sep '77; Chou as taster *Daily Telegraph* 11 Jan '76;
Mao on Chiang's 'underhand orders' *Unrehearsed* 197: on 'The
people want peace' *Guardian* 14 Sep '45; Hinton, Tannebaum, Bell
and Hyman memoirs in *New China* Spring '77; Mao's nerves *Wang*
201; on the KMT agreement *SW IV* 53–7; Shanhaikwan *CQ* 18, 217;
Chang Ju-hsin on Mao *Papers* 130; Mao on Stalin *SW V* 304; Payne
Journey 84–5; Mao to Strong *SW IV* 101; Li to Steele *NYHT* 8 Sep '46;
Welles on Li *NYT* 11 Oct '46; Steele on Mao *NYHT* 2 Oct '46; Mao
on casualties *SW V* 115; Mao recovered *NYT* 13 Dec '46; melon seeds
Hailey in *NYT* 22 Dec '46; Samson *News Chronicle* 27 Jan '47; Tang
poem *Chow*, 74; Mao's 9 Apr circular *SW IV* 131; Mao offered
stretcher *Turning* 76; orders to Peng *SW IV* 133–4; the radio *Turning*
69; Liu on leeks *SCMM* 651; 'The Present Situation' *SW IV* 165–73;
Jan '48 directive *SW IV* 185–6.

Chapter 16: LAST LAP TO PEKING (1948–9)

Passim: Witke. Mao on journalism *SW IV*; on Lin *Wang* 221 and *Issues*
May '75, 108; arguing with *Wang* 73–81; New Year message *SW IV*
302; call to south *SW IV* 349; Mar '49 speech *SW IV* 363–74; Wang
on Mao's 'plot' *Wang* 166–7; Mao as emperor *Wang* 250; Chiang
Ching ill *Witke* 225–6; she grows rice *Witke* 30; Mao's eating habits
Witke 274–5; Mao on steam heat *Wan Sui II* 416; salary Hughes in
Sunday Times 25 Aug '57 and *Long* 168; bodyguard memoirs *NCNA* 7
and 14 Sep '76; smoking Rhodes *OFNS* 17 Oct '61; barber's shop
Hughes in *NYT* 2 Feb '64; table-tennis Zorza in *Guardian* 26 Mar '59;
wooden bed *Red Flag* 7 of '77; talking back *Witke* 341; Mao's sons *Pye*
221 and *Witke* 164, 232, 504n: *Han II* 86 says An-ching worked as
commune accountant. Cable about sons *NCNA* 11 Sep '77;
Amethyst *SW IV* 401; Mao's Jun '49 speech *SW IV* 414–23; Mao on
Americans *SW IV* 437–8; 'people are precious' *Thought* 350; Sep '49
address *SW V* 16–18; Ching Ping Mei *Chow* 81.

Chapter 17: MEAT FROM THE TIGER'S MOUTH (1949–51)

Passim: Talbott I, Nakajima, Witke. Stalin on Mao as second Tito
Unrehearsed 191; Kao in *Nakajima*; Stalin betrays Kao *Talbott I* 243–4;
Stalin asks Mao about Shanghai *Talbott I* 239; 'I argued with Stalin'
Unrehearsed 101; tiger's mouth *Wan Sui I* 58; Khrushchev on Korea
Talbott I 368; the bed *NCNA* 6 Sep '77; Jun '50 declaration *SW V*
30–5; Mao's misgivings about Korea per Liu Shao-chi *Wang* 206–7.
An-ying's death *Talbott I* 372: other dates are 25 Oct *Red Star II* 486
and 25 Nov *SWB/FE*/5955; 'unsettling' *Witke* 232; Peng blamed *CQ*
61, 72 and *MacFarquhar* 360. Wu Hsun *Witke* 238–44 and *SW V* 58;
Chiang's resignation *Witke* 255; mattress *Talbott I* 282; revision of
Works *Thought* 177 and 184, *Papers* and Wittfogel in *CQ* 2, 17–19;
Mao on need for doctrine *Wan Sui II* 305; citations analysed *CQ* 19,

17; on Mao's reading Vladimirov (see *Witke* 172); Mao on books
Wan Sui II 152 and *Unrehearsed* 232; his philosophical mistakes *Wang*
121; Mao on 'modicum' *Wan Sui II* 400; on his own Marxism *SR*
455–6; on negotiations with KMT *SW IV* 373–3; on wind *PD* 2 Jun
'66; on tidal waves *PD* 26 Jul '66; on balance *Wan Sui I* 220; on seeds
SW IV 58; masses fair *SW V* 438; on class standing *Wan Sui II* 433; on
Peng *Wan Sui II* 383; on intellectuals *Wan Sui II* 479; Confucius
Thought 25; spontaneity *Wan Sui II* 275; on role of subjective *Thought*
284; Mao Thought as precious asset *PD* 10 Sep '77; verse on Mao's
works *CQ* 23, 190; work of blood *Wan Sui II* 340, *The Times* 24 Dec
'63; Zanzibari compliment on readability *Wan Sui II* 371.

Chapter 18: WIELDING THE WHIP (1952–4)

Mao on Stalin *Thought* 429; Mao to Indian Communists *Thought* 379;
on Korean War *SW V* 78–9; on bureaucracy *Fan* 102; Liu on collectivization Schram in *Asian Survey* Apr '72, 283; Mao rebukes Liu *SW*
V 92; his Politburo address on collectivization *SW V* 121–9; Mao's
son *Witke* 164–5; *Dream* in *Witke* 278–81; Mao thereon *Wan Sui II* 391;
Kao *Wan Sui I* 31, but see *Nakajima* 17 and *SW V* 162; Mao's fifty-
year projection *SW V* 140; on alphabets *Issues* May '74, 97; on music
Unrehearsed 85–9; meets Dalai Lama, *My Land and My People* (London
1962) 99–106; meets Khrushchev *Talbott I* 469 and *Talbott II* 249–50;
takes Chiang aside *Witke* 262.

Chapter 19: CATCHING THE HIGH TIDE (1955–6)

Passim: Parris and *Solomon*. Kao *Nakajima* 8; Khrushchev on Kao
Talbott II 244; Mao on distance *SW V* 165; Mao's bodyguards on
their work *NCNA* 7 Sep '77: Mao on new upsurge *SR* 402–11; Liu's
confession *MacFarquhar* 19; Mao on 'great debate' *SW V* 213–31 and
Wan Sui I 15–17; travels the kingdoms *SW V* 222; *Socialist Upsurge SW*
V 244–50; Mao's 'explanation' *SW V* 243–5; talks to Shanghai
businessmen *Loh* 135–7; cat and pepper Karl Eskelund *The Red Mandarins* (London 1959) 150–1; Mao on handicrafts *SW V* 282; on
industry and technology OECD, *Science and Technology in China* (Paris
1977) 210; Sukarno's invitations *CQ* 62, 188 and *NCNA* 25 Jan '65;
Mao to Sukarno *Wan Sui I* 56; to Latins *SW V* 325–6.

Chapter 20: THE NIGHT OWL (1956)

Passim: *MacFarquhar*. Khrushchev on Mao's reaction *Talbott I* 462;
Mao on Stalin *Unrehearsed* 101; 'stand up and clap' and Chou's
contrary advice *Chow* 84; Mao on Stalin again *Thought* 432–4 and
303; *Ten Major Relationships SW V* 303–6 or *CQ* 69, 221 and 126; Mao
on gentlemen's agreement *Wan Sui I* 118; talks to Edgar Faure *The*
Serpent and the Tortoise (London 1958) 29–32; swims *NCNA* 17 May

'57 and *NYT* 24 Aug '57; opens bridge Hughes in *Sunday Times* 13 Oct '57; refuses to read editorial *Wan Sui I* 83 – and see 118; Chou confesses *MacFarquhar* 87; Mao's Aug '56 speech *SW V* 315–17; Peng and Lin on new constitution and Lin on collective leadership *MacFarquhar* 110–11; Mao on Lin *MacFarquhar* 119; Lin on repeating things, see *Dittmer* 225; Peng 'I am old' *MacFarquhar* 147; Mao writes to Ochab Labedz in *CQ* 3, 97; Khrushchev 'like an owl' *Talbott I* 418; Mao on equilibrium *SW V* 332–47; speaks to businessmen *Wan Sui I* 36–40; to democrats *Chow* 162–3; Chiang's illness *Witke* 268–71.

Chapter 21: THE HUNDRED FLOWERS (1957)

Passim: *MacFarquhar*, *Wakeman* § 6, Ng in *CQ* 13 and MacFarquhar, *The Hundred Flowers Campaign* (New York 1960). Mao on publishing poems *Chen* 318 and Robert Payne, *Journey to Red China* 87; Wang on poems *Wang* 126; Mao on modern poetry *Unrehearsed* 123; Hunan scholar's opinion Chang Shih-chao in *CQ* 13, 62; Kuo's *PD* 12 May '62 and *CQ* 13, 64; Jerome Chen's *Chen* 314; Fou's in *Daily Express* and *Bangkok Post* 12 Nov '68. Mao on grading *SW V* 350–8 and 364–5; telephones Chou *SW V* 365; Teng on Mao *MacFarquhar* 5; walk-out *CQ* 12, 141; Shanghai businessman *Loh* 219–22; *Correct Handling SR* 433–79 and *NYT* 13 Jun '57; Mao on hostile intellectuals *SW V* 423–33; on tearful cadres *SW V* 436–7; on having no mass base see *MacFarquhar* 200; Mao's 30 Apr directive *MacFarquhar* 212; a student on Heraclitus, Tan Tien-jung, see *CQ* 12, 142; ex-KMT general on Mao, Chen Ming-sha, *NCNA* 14 Jul '57 and *CB* 475; Mao cries *SWB/FE*/5617; on revisionism *SW V* 440; on the Party as the core *SW V* 447; democrat on 'venerable' Mao *MacFarquhar* 218; 'snowflakes' *MacFarquhar* 249; 8 Jun directive *SW V* 448–50; Peng on mistakes *MacFarquhar* 270; 'intelligent friends' *CQ* 62, 151; six criteria *SR* 467–8; Mao on little Hungaries *Wan Sui II* 239; on purpose of 100 Flowers *SW V* 453–4; rightist criticism of Mao *MacFarquhar* 282–3 and 289; Mao talks in Shanghai *SW V* 460–71; 'in Yenan' *Wan Sui I* 74; on population *SW V* 486–8; on pests *SW V* 512.

Chapter 22: THE EAST WIND PREVAILS (1957–8)

Passim: *Talbott II*. Mao at Moscow airport *Thought* 436; rejects new Chinese role *Talbott II* 254; advises Khrushchev on strategy *Talbott I* 470; addresses Supreme Soviet *Fan* 211–19; addresses Chinese students *SWB/FE*/5335; address Moscow Conference *SW V* 515–16, *Thought* 407–9 and *Talbott II* 255; talk with Finn *SW V* 152–3; Novotny's reaction *Talbott II* 255; talk at Nanning *Wan Sui I* 81–2; on permanent revolution *Unrehearsed* 94; *Sixty Points Papers* 57–75; 1st talk at Chengtu *Unrehearsed* 99–103; 2nd *ibid* 105–12; 3rd *ibid* 114–21; 'poor and blank' *Thought* 351–2; 8th Congress speech on Marx *Wan Sui I* 92–107; speech to delegation heads *Wan Sui I* 119–34; talk to military forum *Unrehearsed* 126–8; talk with Khrushchev *Talbott II* 262; Mao on Russian blockade plan *Unrehearsed* 190.

Chapter 23: THE GREAT LEAP FORWARD (1958–9)

Passim: Charles in *CQ* 8, 63–76, *Parris* and *Solomon*. Mao on communes *Thought* 350; on schools *Kuangming Daily* 19 Aug '57 and *CNA* 816; on form to build socialism *Wan Sui I* 140; Khrushchev on steel *Talbott I* 463; Mao on pigs *Papers* 63–4; Mao on Stalin's book *Wan Sui I* 191 and 197; on steel targets *Wan Sui I* 210; talks to co-operative directors *Wan Sui I* 133–9; to CC at Wuchang *NCNA* 10 Sep '77 and *Wan Sui I* 140–5; outflanked, see Hughes in *Sunday Times* 22 Mar '59 and 16 Jan '61; dissatisfied *Unrehearsed* 266; on division of leadership *Unrehearsed* 266 and 270; Feb '59 speech on Leap *Wan Sui I* 151–8; 'battle on paper' *Wan Sui I* 242; Apr defence of Leap *Wan Sui I* 175–6; Liu's wife on Mao *CB* 834; Mao on targets *Wan Sui I* 172; defines Leap *Wan Sui I* 180; at Shaoshan *Chinese Studies in Philosophy vol. v, 3* '74 14–15; appoints Hua *Issues* Sep '77, 30 and *SWB/FE*/5619; Mao's poems reply to 'bastards', see *Solomon* 420; Tao and *PD* on greatness per Zorza in *Guardian* 13 Nov '59; Lo and Peng at Lushan *Issues* Aug '70, 94; voting at Lushan see *CNA* 761, *Mainichi* 9 Feb '67 and *Kau* 419; 'all this fucking' *Unrehearsed* 194; Chiang *Witke* 301–2; Mao on balance *Wan Sui I* 183; on law of value *Wan Sui II* 285; sleeping pills speech *Unrehearsed* 131–46; Peng's confessions *Issues* Aug '70, 91–5; Mao thereon *Wan Sui I* 187–8; speaks to MAC *Unrehearsed* 148–57; on Khrushchev and India *Unrehearsed* 190–1; Khrushchev on submarines *Talbott I* 472.

Chapter 24: A WORN-OUT OLD GALOSH (1960–3)

Passim: *Dittmer* and *Parris*. Mao in south Ravenholt in *American University Field Staff Reports* Apr '67; media praise Mao *PD* 2 Feb '60 and *CQ* 2, 63 and 71; Khrushchev on 'galosh' *PR* 7 Dec '63 and *CQ* 17, 268; Montgomery's first visit *Sunday Times* 18 Jun '60; Mao on Khrushchev *Unrehearsed* 191; Khrushchev attacks Mao at Bucharest E. Crankshaw, *The New Cold War: Moscow v. Peking* (London 1963) 107–9; Mao on fighting Khrushchev *Unrehearsed* 191; Mao on Russian textbooks *Wan Sui II* 259–99; Lin on *SW IV, Fan* 339 and 41; Mao talks with Snow *Unrehearsed* 173–4 and *Time* 20 Sep '76; on restoration of landlords *Wan Sui I* 237–45; 'which emperor?' *Dittmer* 51; reprints old article *Wan Sui II* 246; on own shortcomings *Unrehearsed* 106–7; Chou's quarrel Hughes in *Sunday Times* 16 Jul '61; 'half their fill' *NCNA* 7 Sep '77 and *SWB/FE*/5611; Montgomery again *Sunday Times* 15 Oct '61 and *Unrehearsed* 173–4. 7000 cadres conference: Liu *SCMM* 652; Mao' reply *Unrehearsed* 160–87. Liu's book *Long* 82–3; Liu and Mao by Chang Kuo-tao in Liu *Collected Works I* ix; Liu on middle class and underground factories *SCMP* 4363,

SCMM 653, *SCMP* 402 and *Dittmer* 249–51; Peng's document *Long* 78–80; Mao's defence to CC *Unrehearsed* 189–94; Chiang's recovery *Witke* 303; Mao on tombs *NCNA* 16 Sep '77 and *SWB/FE*/5619; on class struggle *Thought* 367; introduces socialist education movement *Wan Sui II* 314–15; on blacks *Thought* 412 and 382–3; on Buddhists *Fan* 292; on Yugoslavia, *On Khrushchev's Phony Communism* 14 Jul '64; CC to Khrushchev *CQ* 19, 187; Mao on cadre behaviour *Papers* 90–2; *NCNA* 8 Sep '77 and *SWB/FE*/6511.

Chapter 25: ALONE WITH THE MASSES (1964–5)

Mao on Yellow River *NCNA* 7 Sep '77 and *SWB/FE*/5611; on his doctor *Wan Sui II* 325; on Russian territorial expansion *Mao* 120 and *CQ* 25, 28; on third force *L'Humanité* 21 Feb '64 and *CQ* 18, 175; on dealing with French *Wan Sui II* 327; on Pu Yi Paul Kramer (ed.), *The Last Manchu* (London 1967) 285 and *Wan Sui II* 326; on exams *Unrehearsed* 204–5; talks to Wang *Issues* May '73, 93–7 (Wang is usually referred to as Mao's niece, but I prefer to follow *Pye* 148 in identifying her as the granddaughter of Mao's maternal aunt – see family tree); to Yuan-hsin *Unrehearsed* 242–9; see operas *PD* 13 Feb '77; Peng and Teng on opra *CB* 842; Teng on Chiang *CB* 842; Mao on philosophy *Wan Sui II* 384–95; on Sakata *Wan Sui II* 397–402; French visitors, see Behr in *Saturday Evening Post* 14 Nov '64; Mao on Dienbienphu, Behr in *Newsweek* 20 Sep '76; talks to Nehru *Long* 208; on surpassing in technology *Wan Sui II* 445; on the backstage master *Wan Sui II* 408–26; on Fou Ts'ong *Wan Sui II* 432; dines with Snow *Long* 191–222; 'vigilance' about Liu *Unrehearsed* 270; Liu on witchhunt *Long* 17; Mao on bureaucratic class *CB* 891; talks to Palestinians *Wan Sui II* 447–8; to Chingkangshan *NCNA* 2 Jan '77 and *SWB/FE*/5409, *Asahi Shimbum* 19 Jun '67 and *Papers* 144; Western reports on health *NYT* 31 May '65 and *Daily Telegraph* 18 Oct '65; Mao on secretaries *Wan Sui II* 338; on Ministry of Health *Unrehearsed* 232–3; *Quotations, Witke* 360–1; André *Malraux* 373–96; Lin on *People's War, PR* 3 Sep '65; Peng and Teng on Mao *CQ* 31, 16.

Chapter 26: THE CULTURAL REVOLUTION (1965–6)

Passim: *Karnow, Dittmer* and *Papers*. *Hai Jui* see Richard Harris in *The Times* 24 Jan '77; Mao asks Chiang *Wan Sui II* 456; Chiang on sneakers *Issues* May '71, 79; Peng telephone, Fernand Gigon *Vie et Mort de la Révolution Culturelle* (Paris 1969) 37–8; Peng on truth *JPRS* 42349; Mao and 8431 *NCNA* 7 Sep '77; Mao's Hangchow address *Unrehearsed* 235–40; Mao on being outmoded *Wan Sui II* 457; writes out poem *PD* 6 Apr '77; advice to daughter *Scharping* 192; Lin on Chiang *Witke* 318; Chiang as moon *CNA* 872; Lin on Mao's Thought *Kau* 410; Mao on Ministry of Propaganda *Wan Sui II* 382; on despots *Papers* 103; Lin on studying Mao's Thought *Wan Sui II* 380; Japanese

Communists *CQ* 35, 59–60; Mao on 'politics course' *Witke* 305; Chiang on fifty days *SCMPS* 216 and *Witke* 335; Kuo's recantation *PD* 5 May '66; Mao on nestlers *PD* 17 May '66; Lin on coups *Issues* Feb '70, 83–92; moral atom bomb *CQ* 27, 207 and 215; Mao's letter to Chiang *Issues* Jan '73, 94–6; reports on Mao's health *New Life Evening Post* (Hong Kong) 8 May and 9 Sep '66; his swim *NYT* 25 Jul '66 and *NYHT* 27 Jul '66; unhappy *Unrehearsed* 253; telephones Tsinghua *Dittmer* 89; uranium experiments *CQ* 28, 3; Mao on anti-Marxist *Papers* 24 and 32; on leading fire *Unrehearsed* 254; Liu on self-examination *CB* 821; Mao supports rebellion *Unrehearsed* 260–1; speaks to Albanians *Wan Sui II* 457; Russian claims see *Dittmer* 95; Lin's speech *Kau* 348; Mao senses danger *Wan Sui II* 449–50; his poster *PD* Aug '66 and *PR* 11 Aug '66; Liu understands *Dittmer* 93; smash the old world *NCNA* 18 Aug '66; free trains *Papers* 128; Chou on work-teams *Papers* 128; on chaos *Papers* 35; protects Hsu *Witke* 363; Chiang on Lin *Witke* 359; Lin on Mao's genius *Kau* 369–70; Liu's and Teng's confessions, Mao's and Chou's comments *Dittmer* 99–100 and *Mao* 96–7; Mao on brief report of Li *Unrehearsed* 264–8; Teng on contacts with Liu *Issues* Oct '77, '76; Lin on Mao's energy *Kau* 384–5; Mao on time so short *Unrehearsed* 270–74; speaks at rally *Papers* 132; 'You have let me down', in Chang, *Problems of Communism*, Mar '69, 3; Chiang's speeches *Witke* 326 and 328; Lin on memorizing *Fan* 215–17.

Chapter 27: THE BLACK HAND (1966–70)

Passim: *Dittmer* and *Kau*. Mao's health *NYT* 26 Dec '66; Montgomery *Sunday Times* 15 Oct '61; Liu's daughter *CB* 821; Mao on Shanghai takeover *Unrehearsed* 275; Chou on Liu *Mainichi* 11 Jan '76; Mao on Shanghai Commune *Unrehearsed* 277–9 and *Wan Sui II* 451–5; writes to Chou *JPRS* 49826; speaks to Albanians on Red Guard *Issues* Oct '73, 98–100; Chou and Liu *Dittmer* 154–5; Chen Yi *Dittmer* 153–4 and *Kuo IV* 684; Teng on Lin *Issues* Oct '77, 76; February current *Issues* Sep '69, 103–4; Lin on Chu *Mainichi* 9 Feb '67, *Kau* 420; Mao tells army *Fan* 281; on chaos *Scharping* 206–7; on succession *Wan Sui II* 458; Lin on mankind *Kau* 430; in *PD* on revolution *Papers* 142; Red Guards on school *CQ* 30, 10; Mao on tour dismayed *Dittmer* 162 and *PD* 14 Sep '67; on dunce hats and killing *Wan Sui II* 462 and 465; on more GPCR *PD* 13 Aug '67; on China as centre *CQ* 35, 66; Brezhnev *SWB/FE/2564*; hot line *Nixon*, 568; Mao on wages *Dittmer* 193; Chiang as screw *Issues* May '71, 77; daughters *Witke* 368 and 522; Mao's house *Witke* 348; Lin on Mao Thought *Kau* 485; on 'great helmsman' *Fan* 495; on Brezhnev *Fan* 499; Shaoshan statue *CNA* 743; traffic police *Kau* 504; Mao on eyesight *PD* 24 Jan '68 and *Papers* 151; talk with Red Guards *Wan Sui II* 469–97; on universities *Thought* 371; draft constitution *Thought* 327; Mao on GPCR *PD* 9 Jul '68; on arteries *Thought* 326; on going to countryside *PR* Dec '68. 9th Congress: guarantee *Kau* 51–2; Mao on old stuff *Unrehearsed* 282–8; Lin speaks *Fan* 439 and 450; film *CNA* 763. Mao on final victory *Fan* 287; poisoning *Witke* 365; Red Sun *Wan Sui II* 498, *Witke* 325; Lin as interpreter *Chekiang Radio* 20 Oct '70 and *CNA* 821; bust of Mao and calligraphy *Witke* 371.

Chapter 28: A LEAKY UMBRELLA (1970–6)

Passim: *Domes, Kau* and *Witke*. Chen Po-ta *Domes* 82–5; Mao on surprise *Unrehearsed* 292–3; his open letter *Kau* 68; atrocities *Fan* 302; Yahya *IHT* 17 Feb '78; talks with Snow *Long* 167–75. Mao moves house *Witke* 372; the Lin plot *Kau* 80–96; attempt on Chou's plane in *Tanjug* 15 Nov '76, and *SWB/FE*/5365; Mao on tour on Lin's wife *Unrehearsed* 292–9; the bombing attempt see Philip Bridgham; The Fall of Lin Piao, CQ 55 '73 Mao on Lin's thinness *Unrehearsed* 133; Lin as 'dogshit' *Domes* 120; *Nixon* 580; Kissinger in *Sulzberger* p. 7; Chiao on Marcos *CNA* 1036; Tanaka per Nikaido, Tanaka's colleague present at interview, *Tokyo Shimbun* 27 Sep '72; Chiang *Witke passim*; she separates from Mao *Kyodo* 15 Aug '77 and *SWB/FE*/5593; asks for money *Ming Pao* (Hong Kong) 28 Oct '76 and *Issues* Sep '77, 56; Pompidou *La Nouvelle Observateur* (Paris) '76; Mao on better not see *PD* Dec '76 and *Ming Pao* (Hong Kong) 28 Oct '76; on big hats *NCNA* 22 Aug '77 and *Issues* Sep '77, 53; his slippers *SWB/FE*/5614; Wang Hung-wen appeals *Issues* Sep '77, 101; Mao and Chiang exchange letters Nov '66, per Hua Kuo-feng, *NCNA* 22 Aug '77 and *SWB/FE*/5596; Chiang's self-criticism *Issues* Sep '77, 106; Mao at May PB *NCNA* 22 Aug '77; Yuan-hsin *Kyodo* 15 Aug '77 and *SWB/FE*/5593; Chiang's tape recording *NCNA* 12 Aug '77; Chiang as paper tiger *NCNA* 7 Sep '77; Kukrit *IHT* 11 Jul '75; Schmidt *Die Zeit* 7 Nov '75; Eisenhower *Japan Times* 22 Dec '76; Mao on Wang Hung-wen *Ming Pao* 30 Oct '76; appoints Hua, *ibid*; on Teng *Tanjug* 23 Jul '77 and *SWB/FE*/5574; Chiang on Teng *Issues* Oct '77, 92; Khrushchev re Teng *Talbott II* 252; Ching Ming riots *Kyodo* 15 Aug '77 and *SWB/FE*/5593; Teng in the toilet per *Tanjug, SWB/FE*/5574; Mao to Hua after Muldoon *Ming Pao* (Hong Kong) 26 Oct '76; tells comrades about will *SWB/FE*/5335 (some regard this conversation as forged because Hua was out of Peking on the alleged day, but it is possible the date was misrecorded); Chiang powders Mao *Issues* Sep '77, 56; Mao's poem to Chiang *Witke* 478; Chiang rebukes Hua *Ming Pao* (Hong Kong) 26 Oct '76; her wreath *PD* 12 Sep '76.

Acknowledgements

The author is grateful to the many friends and colleagues who helped in this book in all kinds of ways, from translating – or checking translations – from Japanese, German, Russian and Chinese to locating apparently inaccessible materials and correcting details of history. In particular he thanks Adam Baillie, Gwyneth Hughes and Caroline Oakman for their sustained contributions to the book's realization, and Jerome Ch'en, Andrew Nathan and Roxane Witke for their careful criticisms.

INDEX